T0329100

CRUCIAL DECISIONS

CRUCIAL DECISIONS

Leadership in Policymaking and Crisis Management

IRVING L. JANIS

THE FREE PRESS
A Division of Macmillan, Inc.
NEW YORK

Collier Macmillan Publishers
LONDON

The Free Press
A Division of Macmillan, Inc.
866 Third Avenue, New York, N.Y. 10022

Collier Macmillan Canada, Inc.

Printed in the United States of America

printing number

2   3   4   5   6   7   8   9   10

Library of Congress Cataloging-in-Publication Data

Janis, Irving Lester
    Crucial decisions : leadership in policymaking and crisis
management / Irving L. Janis.
        p.   cm.
    Bibliography: p.
    Includes index.
    ISBN 978-1-4767-8023-8
    1. Decision-making.   2. Crisis management.   I. Title.
HD30.23.J37   1989
658.4'03—dc19   88-21292
                                                             CIP

The author and publisher thank the following sources of quoted material which appears in
this volume as noted.

P. 7: From *Decision Making at the Top* (pp. 173–74) by Gordon Donaldson and Jay W.
Lorsch. Copyright © 1983 by Basic Books. Published by Basic Books.

Pp. 115–17: From *The Hidden-Hand Presidency: Eisenhower as Leader* (pp. 20–25) by Fred
I. Greenstein. Copyright © 1982 by Basic Books, Inc. Reprinted by permission of Basic
Books, Inc., Publishers.

Pp. 278, 279–80, 311–12: From *Groupthink: Psychological Studies of Policy Decisions and
Fiascoes* (pp. 43, 282–83, 218–19) by Irving L. Janis. Copyright © 1982 by Houghton Mifflin
Company. Used with permission.

Pp. 282–83: From "Victims of Groupthink: The Kent State University Board of Trustees and
the 1977 Gymnasium Controversy" by T. R. Hensley and G. W. Griffin. *Journal of Conflict
Resolution,* 30, pp. 528–29, 529–30. Copyright 1982 by Journal of Conflict Resolution. Reprinted by permission of Sage Publications, Inc.

TO MARJORIE

Contents

Contents

Preface

This book draws upon my prior case study research and intensive interviews of policymakers in a variety of different kinds of organizational settings. My investigations have included foreign policy decisions by heads of state and their advisors, domestic policy decisions by executives in government agencies, major business decisions by executives in large corporations, and strategic decisions by managers of hospitals, social service agencies, and other public welfare organizations. All of my studies of policymaking have focused on social and psychological factors that give rise to uncorrected misperceptions and miscalculations. One of the main goals of the research—and of this book—is to try to answer the following fundamental questions: *When and why do leaders of large organizations make avoidable errors that result in faulty policy decisions? How can such errors be prevented or at least kept to a minimum?*

While working on my most recent research project, which concentrates on crisis management by U.S. leaders in eight presidential administrations since the end of World War II, I have been struck by a number of common features. Those features began to loom very large in my mind when I realized that I had already encountered them in my prior psychological studies of crucial decisions made by executives in business corporations and in public welfare organizations.

In the first six chapters of this book, I describe and illustrate the outstanding features that appear to characterize policymaking in many different types of organizations. As will be seen, the image that emerges of how leaders make crucial decisions is somewhat different from the accounts given by most social psychologists, manage-

ment specialists, and other social scientists who have written books
or articles on policymaking and crisis management.

In the last four chapters, I develop a new theoretical framework
or model for understanding policymaking processes. It incorporates
all the main descriptive generalizations presented in the earlier chapters. The proposed theoretical model is a comprehensive one, which
takes into account a large number of systematic research findings
and case study observations from many different fields in the social
and behavioral sciences, including management studies, political science, history, and sociology, as well as psychology. In my discussion
of the implications of the model, I indicate how it might ultimately
help to improve the quality of crucial policy decisions, especially
those made by leaders in government, business and public welfare
organizations during crises when vital interests of their nation or organization are at stake.

Acknowledgments

Although I make use of a large body of systematic research and case
studies on policymaking by leaders of business corporations and
public welfare organizations, the research findings and the case examples I cite most frequently are from my own current research project on comparative case studies of decisionmaking by U.S. government leaders during major international crises in the nuclear era.
This project was originally funded by a research grant from the National Science Foundation and subsequently by a research grant from
the Carnegie Corporation of New York. The grant from the Carnegie
Corporation enabled me to spend the last three years working full
time on the research project, and it was during this period that most
of the present book was written. I wish to express my deep appreciation to both foundations for their support. The statements made and
the views expressed are, of course, solely the responsibility of the
author.

I am indebted to a large number of research psychologists, management experts, and other social scientists who have contributed
important empirical findings and explanatory concepts that I have
used and sometimes elaborated or re-interpreted in this book. My
greatest debts are to Professors Alexander George and Herbert Simon, whose pioneering work on policymaking forms the starting
point for my observations and theoretical analyses. Professor

George gave me the benefit of his critical reading of the entire first draft and encouraged me through all phases of preparing this book.

Special thanks are due to Professor Richard Ned Lebow, who prepared a detailed critique of the entire manuscript, directed my attention to pertinent research studies in the social science literature, posed several crucial questions that remained unanswered, and then gave me a final set of critical comments about the answers and revisions that I inserted into the book. I also wish to thank the following social scientists who read most or all of the manuscript and gave me valuable criticisms and suggestions that I have used in one or another of the successive revisions: Professors Amitai Etzioni, Lewis Goldberg, Fred Greenstein, Paul Huth, Robert Kahn, Richard Lazarus, Leon Mann, Christine Maslach, Richard Nelson, Jerome L. Singer, M. Brewster Smith, Philip Tetlock, Victor Vroom, and Daniel Wheeler. Once again, I want to express my gratitude to Marjorie Graham Janis for her detailed, critical comments on successive drafts of each chapter and for her indispensable editing of the manuscript.

PART
I

_____

Introduction

1
Order Out of Theoretical Chaos?

Causes of Successful Versus Unsuccessful Outcomes

Leaders of governments, major business corporations, and other large organizations typically make policy decisions with the expectation that the outcomes will be sufficiently successful to achieve fairly well the objectives they have in mind. But all too often they are bitterly disappointed. Obviously, several different causes contribute to unsuccessful outcomes.

Unforeseeable obstacles to effective implementation and uncontrollable events, such as countermoves by adversaries or competitors, can drastically interfere to such an extent that the policy does not work out as intended. Another contributing cause of unsuccessful policy outcomes consists of the leaders' oversimplified beliefs and ideological stereotypes that give rise to faulty assumptions about the requirements for a good solution or about the consequences of their choice. Even when policymakers are open-minded and conscientious about obtaining factual information pertinent to the policy question they are grappling with, the available evidence may be too ambiguous to indicate that their assumptions are wrong. In other instances, the cause of a policy fiasco can be attributed mainly to misleading information that the policymakers had no way of knowing was erroneous because it came from seemingly dependable intelligence reports or the testimony of experts, with no signs of contradictions or lack of consensus. Then, too, there are unknown and chance factors that can adversely affect the outcome, commonly called "bad luck." Nevertheless, among the major causes of unsuccessful outcomes is one that is very much under the leaders' control: *poor quality of the decisionmaking procedures used either to arrive at a new policy or to reaffirm the existing policy.*

Defective procedures—entailing, for example, inadequate information search, biased appraisal of consequences, and lack of contingency planning—do not guarantee that a policy decision will turn out to be a fiasco. The net influence of the uncontrollable, unknown, and chance factors can occasionally result in "good luck." But the likelihood of failure is substantially less if sound procedures of information search, appraisal, and planning are used. (Evidence bearing on this important point will be presented later, in Chapter 6.)

Some of the causal sequences that lead to defective policymaking procedures in government, business firms, and public welfare organizations are well known to practically all executives. For example, when a chief executive is provoked to anger, or becomes extremely apprehensive or extremely elated in response to a sensational event, he or she might decide impulsively to make a drastic change in policy, while dominated by the mood of the moment, without consulting any advisors who could point out flaws and suggest better alternatives to be considered. Or, after a fair amount of information search and deliberation about fresh alternatives to an old policy that has turned sour, the members of an executive committee might conform to powerful social pressures from the chief executive. Sometimes policy advisors assent to what they regard as an inferior choice rather than facing the damaging personal consequences of arguing against the chief's pet initiative. These and a number of other, less well-known, pathways to failure will be elaborated in detail in this book. The defective pathways will be contrasted with a pathway embodying high-quality procedures that increase the chances of successful outcomes. Much of the inquiry will focus on multiple causes for deviating from the latter pathway. Special attention will be given to the preconditions, precipitating events, and catalysts arising from the current situational context, which play a significant role in determining whether executives will use good or poor procedures to arrive at a major policy decision when vital interests of the nation or organization are at stake.

Avoiding Policy Disasters That Could Be Lethal

In a comprehensive review of research on "leadership and power," Edwin Hollander points out that a president who is popular can carry out the main functions of a policymaker expeditiously, with a minimum of resistance from other powerholders, but the president's policy decisions can turn out to be very poor ones that result in disastrous losses.[1] The same can be said about top-level leaders in any organization. Among the defective pathways that lead to disastrous policy decisions are those that fail to correct *avoidable* errors—rectifiable misperceptions, refutable false assumptions, resolvable ignorance, and remediable lapses in judgment concerning the probability or magnitude of expected costs and benefits. Those pathways can prove to be destructive in several ways: The outcome can turn out to be lethal for the careers of the responsible leaders, for the continued existence of the organization, and sometimes for the very lives of large numbers of people who are affected by a major policy decision.

Conventional wisdom says that there is only one answer to the question, "What needs to be done if the top-level leaders repeatedly make poor policy decisions that turn out to be detrimental to vital interests of their organization?" The well-known answer is that they should be fired before they cause such lethal damage that the organization itself cannot survive. But there is evidence suggesting that this bit of conventional wisdom is seldom heeded. William Starbuck, a specialist in management studies who has investigated the survival rates of governmental agencies and business firms, has this to say about what often happens to top-level leaders and their organizations:

> Many organizations drift along, perceiving that they are succeeding in stable environments, until they suddenly find themselves confronted by existence-threatening crises. Most of the organizations my colleagues and I have studied did not survive their crises, but in every case of survival, the reorientations included wholesale replacements of the top managers, and we infer that survival requires this. . . .
>
> . . . Crises evidently afflict all kinds of organizations, although they may be more likely in bureaucracies that have recently enjoyed great success. Some organizations facing crises . . . replace their top managers, reorient, and survive. More organizations . . . die. Thus, nonadaptiveness turns organizations into temporary systems, nearly all of which have short lives. The 50-year-old corporations represent only 2 percent of those initially created, and 50-year-old Federal agencies only 4 percent (Starbuck & Nystrom, 1981). . . . Approximately 30 percent of the 50-year-old corporations can

be expected to disappear within ten years, as can 26 percent of the 50-year-old Federal agencies. (Starbuck 1983, pp. 100–101)

Starbuck's conclusion is that "because organizations modify their behavior programs mainly in small increments that make sense to top managers, they change too little and inappropriately, and nearly all organizations disappear within a few years."

Even if the extremely low survival rates emphasized by Starbuck are somewhat exaggerated, the general thrust of his conclusion may prove to be well warranted for business firms and nongovernmental welfare organizations, such as hospitals, clinics, schools, legal aid societies, social service, child welfare, charity, and philanthropic institutions. Jeffrey Pfeffer and other leading scholars in the field of management studies concur that a substantial percentage of organizations in the private sector go out of existence every year, most notably among small retail and service firms in highly competitive areas.* Many of those failures probably are the result of defective policymaking by the owners or managers, but at present there are no dependable data on the percentage of such instances. Very large business corporations like Lockheed and Chrysler have been brought to the verge of bankruptcy by poor policymaking at the top, but such organizations are likely to be saved at the last moment by a combination of political and economic actions on the part of the federal government to prevent massive unemployment, disruption of military procurement schedules, or other undesirable consequences that national leaders want to avoid. Nevertheless, "there is clear evidence," according to Pfeffer, that firms of all sizes "do disappear" and, unlike those that reappear under a new name following a merger, their disappearance is permanent; many simply do not survive.

Fred Fiedler starts off his well-known book on *Leadership* with the assertion that "an organization's success or failure, indeed *its very survival,* depends in large part on the leadership it is able to

---

*For every chapter, a number of references that contain evidence and arguments in support of major generalizations, such as this one, are cited at the end of the book in the Sources. In addition to citing cogent references that are not mentioned in the text, the Sources section also includes two types of detailed information about certain of the references that are mentioned: Whenever an author is cited for whom there is more than one book or article listed in the References, the year of publication is given to indicate which one it is; whenever a short quotation is presented in the text, the page number in the book or article from which it is extracted is given.

attract." Commenting on the same phenomenon, Gordon Donaldson and Jay Lorsch attribute the relatively high rate of bankruptcy and death of corporations, large and small, during the initial years of the 1980s to the failure of top managers to respond adequately to the upsurge of foreign competition, the higher costs of basic raw materials, fluctuations in interest rates, and other changes in the business environment. Those corporations that remain healthy, they conclude, have leaders capable of making adaptive policy changes in response to the environmental changes. To do so requires overcoming various constraints that make for a potentially lethal form of inertia:

> The movement of a business organization across the decades, as it seeks to escape one increasingly hostile industry environment and relocate in a more benevolent one, can be likened to the journey of an interplanetary spaceship. . . . At first economic, organizational, and psychological forces tend to resist the move; the parameters . . . are dictated by the existing corporate environment just as the parameters of flight are dominated by the forces exerted by the spaceship's existing planetary environment. But the guidance system of the spaceship is . . . the responsibility of the human beings who operate it. So too for the corporate managers: they must anticipate when the existing environment will become incapable of supporting life as they wish to live it and what new environment holds the prospect of better conditions. . . .
> Like spaceships, corporations can only travel toward their objectives if they have skilled pilots at the controls. By dealing with the objective and psychological constraints they face, these executives are able to create the window for independent action and for the strategic choices that ensure their organization's health and survival. Unless corporate managers understand these constraints and develop the distinctive corporate thrust necessary to overcome the limitations they impose and to set a new course, they cannot hope to assure the passage of the enterprise into the next century. (Donaldson & Lorsch, pp. 173–74)

Over and beyond deleterious effects on the organization's health and survival, defective policymaking can be lethal in the literal sense of the term for an industrial plant's employees and for people in the

8

local community when the company's policymakers decide to ignore serious problems of preventing industrial accidents and pollution. Avoidable fatalities are likely to result from their decisions to continue using relatively cheap but dangerous ways to dispose of toxic chemicals or other wastes that pollute the air, the water supply, or the food chain for local produce, despite experts' impressive warnings about cumulative effects expected to become disastrous in subsequent years. More widespread loss of life results when local and state governments, federal regulative agencies, and public health organizations fail to arrive at sound policies to prevent pollution that causes lead poisoning, asbestos poisoning, silicosis, cancer, severe radiation sickness, or other fatal diseases.

Early in the 1970s it became apparent to large numbers of scientists and policy planners that the continuation of increases in industrialization, exploitation of limited natural resources, and applications of new technologies throughout the world, if unregulated by sensible national and international policies, would sooner or later exact intolerable costs in the form of ecocatastrophes. Experts pointed out how certain of those avoidable disasters could be lethal for tens of millions of people, if not for the entire human race. One of the emerging threats, widely publicized at the time, was depletion of the ozone layer of the atmosphere resulting from the chlorofluorocarbons emitted by jet aircraft, aerosol cans, refrigerators, and air conditioners. The available evidence indicated that if unchecked, the depletion of the ozone layer would result in overexposure of people all over the world to ultraviolet rays, which produce dangerous skin cancers along with other disastrous biological effects. The few minor steps that were then taken, such as banning chlorofluorocarbons in spray cans in the United States, have proved to be grossly insufficient. By the late 1980s the threat once again emerged as a problem for all nations, and much more serious than a decade earlier as a result of the discovery that a vast hole in the ozone layer at its fullest seasonal expansion is growing at an alarming rate.

Leaders of all nations have also continued to neglect the threat of other ecocatastrophes that were among those prominently publicized in the 1970s. These include the dangers posed by deforestation, especially of the tropical rain forests that are being transformed into grazing lands or urbanized, and by the "greenhouse effect," from excessive heat in the atmosphere generated by industrial production all over the earth, which can produce drastic changes in climate resulting in melting of the polar ice caps and ultimately the destruction of the entire life-sustaining global environment.

In *An Inquiry into the Human Prospect,* which includes a summary of the warnings by environmental scientists, Robert Heilbroner referred to "the ultimate fatal pollution of an overheated atmosphere" as "an ecological Armageddon." He forecast a series of local catastrophes from this and other sources of uncontrolled pollution that will become more and more devastating in the foreseeable future "as we breach now this, now that edge of environmental tolerance," which could "overwhelm the slender human capabilities for planned adjustment to the future." In order to work, according to Heilbroner, the planned adjustment will require new policies to bring about a massive slowdown of industrialization and economic growth among all nations, along with strict regulatory measures to protect the environment. But the necessity for drastic policy changes to protect the global physical environment from being destroyed raises a depressing question about whether in the process drastic changes in the global political environment might result in democracy being destroyed: Can the policies necessary for global survival be adopted and implemented, he asks, without "the eventual rise of 'iron governments'" that resort to authoritarian measures to exercise coercive power?

Heilbroner's answer is that the only realistic source of hope is *sound leadership* by policymakers who have sufficient power and influence to counteract the powerful economic forces that maintain the status quo. To use their power effectively, these policymakers must also have the knowledge and foresight to prepare carefully devised plans well in advance for preventing the environmental dangers that lie ahead:

> The preservation of democratic forms can only come about as a result of intellectually farsighted and politically gifted leadership. Paradoxically, it is only through leadership that authoritarian rule can be minimized, if not wholly avoided. (Heilbroner, p. 164)

In 1982, William Bevan's presidential address to the American Psychological Association once again warned that fundamental policy changes are needed to deal with potential dangers that continue to be neglected, including "environmental degradation" and "climatic change" as well as various threats of worldwide economic disasters, nuclear proliferation, and the nuclear arms race, all of which pose issues "of transcendental importance." "A conviction is emerging from all sides," he said, "that we now need a major advance in the quality of our political, economic, and social strategies if we are to have any hope of success."

Obviously no such advance will occur if the leaders of the superpowers and other nations table the issues and sit back waiting for Godot in the form of technological fixes from future scientific breakthroughs. In the meantime, heat pollution and all the other environmental contaminants continue to accumulate and stockpiles of lethal weapons continue to multiply. But, of course, the problems are doubly, triply, and quadruply confounded because, in addition to all the constraints that interfere with working out policy changes that will be acceptable within each national government, there is yet another set of political constraints that interferes with collaborative policy-making by the leaders of rival nations who would have to relinquish some of their sovereignty in international agreements. Here again, the chances of high-quality solutions to the problems are not very great unless extraordinarily inspiring and talented leaders emerge to give direction to collaborative policymaking in the context of one or more international organizations.

Leaders of the countries that have (or soon will have) arsenals of nuclear weapons are confronted with a policy issue that is generally regarded as most urgent of all for the survival of civilization and perhaps of all human beings: How to avoid a lethal nuclear war? Three different policy problems can be differentiated, each of which requires collaborative work to arrive at policy solutions:

— How can the nuclear arms race be curtailed and reversed?
— What can be done to keep clashing interests of the nuclear superpowers from mounting, to prevent confrontations that create dangerous crises?
— Whenever a crisis does occur, how can it be managed from the outset to prevent it from spinning out of control and escalating to nuclear war?

To devise viable policy solutions for the problems of arms control, crisis prevention, and crisis management, policymakers will have to draw upon whatever knowledge can be brought to bear from the scientific and other scholarly communities, as well as from governmental intelligence agencies, specialists in command and control, experienced negotiators, statesmen, and stateswomen.

David Hamburg, president of the Carnegie Corporation of New York, has emphasized that to deal effectively with the problems posed by the threat of nuclear war, it is essential "to mobilize the best possible intellectual, technical, and moral resources over a wide range of knowledge and perspectives." One pertinent area of inquiry has to do with the processes of arriving at crucial policy decisions, including analysis of the conditions under which miscalculations, faulty implementation, inadequate contingency planning, and other such errors are most probable. That is the area dealt with by this book.

Knowledge about when, how, and why avoidable errors in policy-making and crisis management are most likely to occur should prove to be useful for executives in all kinds of organizations, from the smallest family business and medical clinic to the largest corporation and government. It could help them to improve their own decision-making procedures so as to avoid mistakes that might be damaging to their own careers and to vital objectives, including survival of their organization. For top-level leaders responsible for policy decisions concerning pollutants and nuclear weapons, it could also help avoid mistakes that might have widespread lethal outcomes—for human lives in the workplace, in nearby communities, across entire continents, and ultimately everywhere on earth.

Disagreements Among Social Scientists

If we had a valid theory describing linkages between procedures for arriving at policy decisions and good versus poor outcomes, we could extract valuable prescriptions for improving the quality of policy-making in government, business, and public welfare organizations. Do we have anything approaching such a theory at present? Unfortunately not. What we do have are numerous unintegrated hypotheses supported to varying degrees by empirical evidence, much of which is subject to debate and disagreements among social scientists. Nevertheless, there are scattered pieces of research that can be used to evaluate and consolidate hypotheses from the work of psychologists, political scientists, sociologists, economists, historians, management scientists, and scholars in other social science disciplines. So far as the development of theory is concerned, this area is still at a very early stage. There are all too many contending theorists, some of whom clash head-on while others simply ignore or bypass their rivals without bothering to analyze points of divergence or convergence, all of which creates an atmosphere of theoretical chaos.

One of the few generalizations about which there is fairly general agreement is that the making of policy decisions is a very fuzzy business. Practically every social scientist who has studied policymaking in government or in the private sector emphasizes that it is pervaded by uncertainties, doubts, and all sorts of complications stemming from conflicting vested interests. The uncertainties are often augmented by misguided efforts to reduce the fuzziness by relying on simple rules of thumb. When outside experts are consulted by policymakers, they almost invariably disagree.

It is not a very closely guarded secret within the social sciences that much the same can be said about what you find when you consult the writings of experts in management, political science, and other social sciences. Those experts have a great deal to say about how policy decisions are made and why they might be better if they were made differently. But within and across these disciplines, the experts certainly do not agree with each other.[2]

I believe that despite all the fuzziness, disagreements, and chaotic lack of integration that currently characterize the relevant social science disciplines, we already have at hand substantial pieces of established knowledge on which to build. Those pieces provide the essential building blocks, as I shall try to show, for constructing a general theory that specifies the *conditions* under which leaders use sound procedures to arrive at policy decisions that are likely to have successful outcomes rather than severely damaging, if not lethal, ones.

Prospects for Developing an Integrated Theory

Here and there one can discern that some order has already been created out of the widespread chaos in the "policy sciences" and it does not seem to me premature to start developing an integrated theory. Perhaps it is unrealistic to aim for a valid theory that will enable us to predict which particular course of action any individual or group of policymakers will choose for each policy decision. But many of the diverse strands of existing theory and research might be brought together in the not-very-distant future to develop an integrated set of propositions concerning social and psychological factors that play a significant causal role in determining whether policymakers will use effective or ineffective procedures to arrive at a policy decision. Although too limited to explain all important aspects of policymaking, such propositions could have considerable diagnostic and prognostic value by specifying the conditions under which individual executives and policy-planning groups are most likely to make avoidable errors that greatly reduce the chances that a new policy will be successful. Those propositions about causal factors, if verified, could also be expected to have considerable practical value by indicating what executives can do to reduce the likelihood of avoidable errors when making vital policy decisions.

Political scientists have been particularly vocal in bemoaning the lack of a comprehensive theory about psychological processes that might account for the frequent failures of the leaders of national governments to arrive at sound policy decisions. For example, Richard Ned Lebow, in a pioneering analysis of international crises containing many insights about errors in policymaking, asserts that research on foreign policy decisions is impeded because "there is as yet no integrated statement of psychological principles and processes that could be considered to represent a paradigm of decisionmaking. There are instead several different schools of thought, each of which attempts to explain nonrational processes in terms of different causation."

The traditional theory of decisionmaking, Lebow points out, is no longer tenable. That theory describes the process of arriving at a policy decision as essentially rational: Policymakers are rational actors who generally deal with policy problems by trying to find the best alternative, the one that emerges from thorough information search and careful deliberation as most likely to succeed in attaining the goals or values they want to maximize. Lebow calls attention to research from several different disciplines indicating that the rational actor model does not stand up very well as a descriptive theory. What has replaced the traditional model is a "variety of models and approaches," which makes us aware of the multiplicity of personal, social, and political factors that shape the process of decisionmaking. But "no one perspective provides a satisfactory explanation of decisionmaking." Each theoretical approach, Lebow concludes, "offers its own particular insights and is more or less useful depending upon the analytical concerns of the investigator and the nature of the decision involved."[3]

Despite all the fragmentation and lack of agreement to be found in the research literature, it seems to me that many bits of theorizing and pieces of sound empirical evidence can be fitted together to form a fairly coherent view of decisionmaking processes. In my opinion, the time to start integrating the seemingly divergent theoretical perspectives is already at hand. Perhaps the pessimists are right when they tell us that we shall never have a comprehensive theory that encompasses fully all the complicated psychological, sociological, political, and economic factors that influence the making of consequential policy decisions. But I see no reason for being inhibited about taking steps in the direction of bringing more order out of the chaos of clashing concepts by sketching a rough outline of an integrative theoretical framework that describes the social and psychological sources of error in policymaking. In any case, that is what I attempt to do in this book.

Main Components of a Theoretical Framework

Most of the components for the type of theoretical framework I have in mind have long been common knowledge among astute political observers. Here are typical comments by two such observers—one an Italian journalist, Luigi Barzini, a member of parliament in the Italian government after World War II who became well known as a newspaper correspondent and author in America; the other, an eminent, late nineteenth-century English historian, Lord Acton, who served as a member of parliament in the British government and is quoted approvingly by Barzini:

> There is, at all times and in all countries, a behind-the-scenes brutal truth which shocks the uninitiated when they discover it; great decisions are never entirely noble; great leaders in all fields are by no means as witty, handsome, magnanimous and farsighted as their official biographies make them out. As Lord Acton (who saw such things clearly, as he was born in Naples, the grandson of a Neapolitan prime minister) put it in a letter to Gladstone's youngest daughter Mary: "Most assuredly, now as heretofore, the men of the time are in most cases unprincipled and act from motives of interest, or passion, or prejudice cherished and unchecked, of selfish hope and unworthy fear." (Barzini, p. 177)

Contemporary psychologists, political scientists, and sociologists have expanded in considerable detail on the reasons why policymakers so often deviate from moral, humanitarian, and rational principles. A great many studies over the past half century have informed us about the causes and consequences of *self-interest* and of *unprincipled actions* in the struggle against rivals within a governmental or corporate bureaucracy for status and power; the role of *passions* that hamper sound judgment, especially when decisionmakers facing a stressful crisis are dominated by *fear;* and, above all, the way ideology, group loyalties, and organizational norms give rise to ignoble *prejudices* that remain "cherished and unchecked." Most recently, psychological research on the overuse of judgmental rules of thumb or heuristics that partially compensate for cognitive limitations of the human mind has helped to explain why policymakers, even at times when they are striving to be rational problem solvers, so often fail to be as *farsighted* as they would like to be.

Most of the ignoble and short-sighted considerations that Barzini and Acton talk about—the self-interests, the passions, and the prejudices—are, in effect, powerful psychological constraints that interfere with effective problem solving on the part of executives who have the responsibility to deal with the threats or opportunities confronting their organization. Top-level policymakers, including chief executives, sometimes make policy decisions with an eye toward one-upmanship in current power struggles or toward purely personal goals, such as enhancing their own income and prestige, rather than looking ahead to the effects on the organization. In addition to their own emotional needs and personal motives, which operate as internal constraints, executives are also subject to the influence of powerful external constraints, such as threats of social disapproval from colleagues and limitations of time or of other organizational resources. These and other such restrictions are emphasized by experts on management as major obstacles to sound and innovative policymaking.

Considerable evidence has accumulated indicating that limited informational resources, group pressures, prior commitments, bureaucratic politics, and a variety of other organizational constraints often lead to defective policymaking. Without engaging in careful search and appraisal, executives sometimes make their choices primarily on the basis of "acceptability" within the organization. Stagner points out that corporate decisions are not always made by seeking for a solution that will be in the best interests of the organization. A chief executive sometimes settles for a "second-best" decision because of the threat of opposition and even sabotage on the part of those employees who have to be counted upon to implement any new course of action. Of course, acceptability within the organization is one of the essential requirements for a sound policy decision because without it the decision would not be implemented in the way intended. But the inappropriate, dominating intrusion of bureaucratic pressures and other organizational constraints constitutes a major reason why top-level policymakers often avoid instituting major changes in policy, no matter how badly needed.

In his insightful analysis of presidential decisionmaking, Alexander George calls attention to the "ever-present constraints" that often require the chief executive to consider "trade-offs" in "the search for high-quality decisions in foreign policy, as in domestic policy." He discusses many different kinds of constraints, almost all of which can be classified into one or another of the three main types in Figure 1-1. In order to take into consideration the requirements posed by any of the constraints represented in the figure, policymakers generally have to make a trade-off in the form of sacrificing

FIGURE 1-1 Constraints Creating Trade-Off Dilemmas in Policymaking

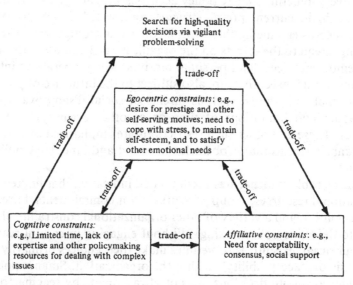

Note: This figure is based on George (1980), with a category added for egocentric constraints.

Adapted from *Presidential Decisionmaking in Foreign Policy: The Effective Use of Information and Advice* (p. 2) by A. L. George, 1980, Boulder, CO: Westview Press.

something that reduces at least slightly the quality of the decision-making process—for example, in order to take account of a deadline that imposes a time limit, the search for relevant information is likely to be much less extensive than desired; in order to take account of the need for acceptability among powerful factions within the organization, a very good alternative might have to be eliminated even though it looks like the best solution to the policy problem.

Cognitive constraints, represented in the box in the lower left of the figure, include all the salient external factors that restrict cognitive inputs (such as limited organizational resources for intelligence gathering and analysis) as well as internal factors (such as the executive's own limited knowledge about the ramifications of the technological issues involved in a problem such as nuclear arms control) that restrict the amount and quality of cognitive activity that executives can devote to working on a given policy question. George asserts that the president cannot allow "the search for a higher-quality decision on one policy question . . . to consume a disproportionate share of the manpower, and the analytical and intelligence resources that must be available to attend to other urgent policy questions." Internal constraints on problem solving become salient when a chief executive realizes that he or she or anyone else might be wasting time and other resources trying to find a good solution because of being handicapped by the enormous complexity of the policy issues and by uncertainties about the expected consequences of alternative courses of action.

Affiliative constraints, represented in the box in the lower right of the figure, include all the various kinds of needs arising from the policymaker's affiliation with the organization as a whole, with a particular division or section of the organization, or with whatever face-to-face committees or informal work groups he or she belongs to. Some of those needs become strong enough to influence the way an executive deals with a policy issue because they are spontaneously mobilized as a result of powerful internal motives, such as the need for approval or anticipatory shame from failing to live up to prior commitments. Others are elicited by external social pressures, and role demands.

One of the ubiquitous role demands that imposes an affiliative constraint on any top-level policymaker is to avoid disrupting the organization by initiating or approving a policy change that will meet with widespread opposition from department heads or lower-level executives whose acceptance is necessary for effective implementation. The affiliative constraints imposed by the need for acceptability are usually accompanied by other common affiliative constraints, such as those stemming from the need for policy legitimacy involving constitutional-legal considerations and the need for social support from fellow members of a policymaking group, even when the policy decision is being made by the chief executive.

A number of other considerations that George discusses pertain to the president's emotional needs and personal motives that can also play an influential role in the policymaking process, although they are "extraneous to the values associated with even a very broad conception of the national interest." This category, which I refer to as "egocentric constraints," is represented in the central box in Figure 1-1. It includes essential personal needs that chief executives share with other people—to realize personal ambitions, to counteract frustrations, to avoid damage to self-esteem, and "to cope with the anxiety, fear, or guilt that they experience from time to time" when dealing with decisional dilemmas.

George's account of the potentially detrimental effect of emotive and other personal constraints on the quality of U.S. presidential decisionmaking, despite all the organizational safeguards designed to curtail the misuse of power for personal ends, probably applies equally to all levels of executive decisionmaking in all types of organizations, inside or outside of the government.

[Personal motives and interests] may lead the president in the same direction as his objective conception of where the national interest lies. But it must be recognized that they also are capable of diluting, if not distorting, his search for a high-quality decision based on the criterion of national interest. At the same time, however, various safeguards against such possibilities do exist. In the first place, the president must justify his foreign-policy decisions with reference to the criterion of the national interest in a manner that is credible to his associates, to Congress, and to public opinion. His awareness of this necessity can serve as an important brake on the tendency to allow personal needs or political interests to dilute his search for quality decisions. Then, too, much of presidential decisionmaking is institutionalized in ways that reduce or contain such tendencies. The operation of organizational, procedural, and staff arrangements in support of presidential decisionmaking serves to structure and discipline a president's choices; thereby, they reduce—though certainly they do not eliminate—the possibility that personal motives and interests will intrude into and distort his judgment. (George 1980, p. 4)

All of the factors included in the three categories of constraints shown in Figure 1-1 influence the way policy decisions actually are made. Therefore, all of them need to be taken into account in any theory about how policy decisions are made that purports to be descriptively valid. In this book, I attempt to do so by integrating many disparate segments of theory and empirical evidence in a preliminary theoretical framework that is intended to be useful for guiding research, for analyzing the sources of error when policy failures occur, and for deducing prescriptions for improving the quality of policymaking. Like most other analyses of organizational behavior, this framework can be directly applied when the focus is upon the individual executive as the unit of analysis. But, as will be seen in Chapters 7 and 8, it is also applicable when the unit of analysis is an executive committee or any other group of powerholders who work or fight together in striving to arrive at a policy decision.

The preliminary framework could be said to span different levels of analysis in that it takes account of various contextual variables, such as structural features of the organization as a collectivity, as well as smaller units. It draws upon the work of cognitive and clinical psychologists who investigate the decisionmaking processes of individuals, social psychologists who study small face-to-face groups of decisionmakers, sociologists and management scientists whose research focuses on large nongovernmental organizations, and political scientists, macroeconomists, and historians who examine national governments and international systems. In effect, the proposed theoretical framework represents an initial attempt to bridge the different levels of analysis by taking account of a broad range of diverse determinants that have emerged from the different approaches to research on policymaking, including the individual psychological context, the group dynamics context, and the organizational and political context, which are typically treated by most scholars as separate and unconnected.

Plan of the Book

My exposition of the main assumptions that enter into the preliminary theoretical framework includes cogent evidence and illustrative examples gleaned from studies of how top-level policymakers in many different types of organizations have attempted to manage major challenges requiring policy decisions. The first assumption, which was mentioned at the beginning of this chapter, is that the quality of the procedures used to arrive at a fundamental policy decision is one of the major determinants of a successful outcome. Until recently there has been practically no dependable evidence bearing directly on this assumption and social scientists have debated its plausibility because some have expressed doubts as to whether any substantial relationship will be found between the quality of the decisionmaking process and its outcome (see Chapter 6).

A second assumption is that most top-level leaders in government, big business corporations, and public welfare organizations are capable of carrying out the procedures that are essential for high-quality policymaking. (Those essential procedures, which I refer to as "vigilant problem solving," are described in Chapter 5.)

A third assumption, which is quite familiar to social scientists and widely accepted, is that policymakers generally make no effort to use high-quality procedures for arriving at a policy decision if they regard the issue as relatively unimportant in terms of what is at stake for the organization or for themselves personally. For issues perceived as unimportant—irrespective of whether or not that judgment is objectively correct—policymakers typically resort to what is sometimes called "quick-and-easy" decisionmaking, also commonly referred to as a "seat-of-the-pants" approach.

The fourth key assumption, unlike the first three, is a new one that has not yet been debated in the social science literature. It has emerged from my own current comparative case-study research on American presidential policymaking during international crises, which bears out suggestive surmises by other social scientists. The new assumption pertains to the constraints represented in Figure 1-1: Even when policymakers are dealing with an issue that they regard as extremely important because vital interests are at stake, one or another of the constraints, under certain specifiable circumstances, can dominate the policymakers' thinking to such an extent that they rely upon simple decision rules to deal with it. In such instances, which seem to occur fairly frequently, what the policymakers do is tantamount to giving the constraint top priority; they do not engage in adequate information search or appraisal of alternatives and fail to carry out other essential steps of effective problem solving.

In the next three chapters, I shall describe the typical quick-and-easy approaches that top-level policymakers commonly use and the various simple decision rules they rely upon to deal with each of the three types of constraints shown in Figure 1-1. Most of the cognitive and affiliative decision rules discussed in Chapters 2 and 3 involve well-known phenomena that I reformulate in terms of coping with constraints—such as the popular C.Y.A. (cover-your-ass) rule, which makes for conformity in response to the affiliative constraint imposed by threatening social pressures. Other decision rules to be described deal with less familiar phenomena—such as what I call the elated choice ("Wow! Grab it!") rule, which accompanies an emotional state of reactive elation following a period of intense frustration (discussed in Chapter 4 along with other egocentric rules).

Chapter 5 gives a detailed account of vigilant problem solving, the high-quality procedural strategy for arriving at policy decisions, which top-level executives seldom use even though most of them may be quite capable of carrying out all the essential steps competently. (This is the high-quality approach represented in the top box in Figure 1-1.) When the policymakers adopt a vigilant problem-solving approach, they do not ignore the various constraints (represented in the other three boxes in Figure 1-1). On the contrary, vigilant policymakers are likely to take full account of all the apparent constraints and even go out of their way to obtain more information about them. But, instead of dealing with one or another of the constraints by giving it top priority and resorting to one or two simple decision rules to cope with it, the policymakers using a vigilant problem-solving approach treat whichever constraints they are aware of as additional requirements to be met in their search for a sound solution to the policy problem they are grappling with.

Evidence is presented in Chapter 6 indicating that the high-quality approach to policymaking is an endangered species and that special efforts should be made to nurture and preserve it if we wish to preserve our global habitat. More specifically, the chapter is mainly devoted to describing the findings from a systematic correlational study that two collaborators and I have recently completed in which we carefully examined the available reports about United States foreign policymaking during the major international crises since the end of World War II. In that study, we used a standardized content-analysis procedure to make blind ratings of the quality of the policymaking process and we obtained blind ratings from outside experts of the outcome of each crisis, so as to investigate the relationship between process and outcome. The findings, as will be seen, strongly support the first of the four key theoretical assumptions. They indicate that the poorer the quality of the decisionmaking process, as manifested by failures to carry out essential steps of vigilant problem solving, the poorer the outcome of the policy decision. In this study a poor outcome was defined in terms of two separate dimensions: failure to attain U.S. objectives pertaining to vital national interests and failure to attain any degree of resolution of the international conflict (that is, escalation or persisting conflict rather than de-escalation).

Chapter 7, which is the heart of the book, presents a preliminary theoretical model embodying the four key assumptions and several ancillary assumptions that are discussed in detail. I propose the preliminary model as a first approximation of an overarching theory of policymaking. This theory, when more fully developed along lines that I shall indicate, might synthesize and integrate many seemingly diverse concepts and research findings from different fields in the social sciences.

A theoretical framework of the type to be presented can be expected to generate at least a few new hypotheses about when, how, and why good versus poor policy decisions are made. Even though incomplete as a theoretical structure, it might also be able to meet other important needs of present-day research on policymaking. For example, it could perhaps start serving as a conceptual model for diagnosing and explaining what has gone wrong whenever a particularly damaging policy failure is investigated, and for suggesting prescriptions about what can be done to prevent repetitions of the same errors. By providing a set of interrelated concepts and general explanatory propositions constituting a core that can be built upon to develop a more complete theory, it could ultimately become a "genuine new paradigm," replete with an extensive research agenda for the future, including many new puzzles to be solved.

Chapter 8 highlights the research implications of the theoretical model for subsequent basic studies of policy successes and failures and for practical investigations intended to lead to improvements in policymaking procedures so as to avoid miscalculations. In that chapter, I examine values and limitations of the theoretical model and specify what can and cannot be predicted when the model is used to analyze the policymaking behavior of an individual executive or group of executives. I indicate how the model enables predictions to be made pertaining to (1) whether the policymakers' procedural strategy will be a vigilant problem-solving or a seat-of-the-pants approach and (2) whether the policy decision they arrive at is likely to have a satisfactory outcome from the standpoint of meeting the organization's or nation's objectives. Included is an account of how the model can be used in two different types of studies: (1) practically oriented investigations by troubleshooters seeking to find the probable causes of an organization's policy failures and (2) basic research by social scientists seeking for generalizations that help to explain the probable causes of ill-conceived policies in all kinds of organizations. For both types of investigation, as will be seen, the model is applicable not only to top-level policymakers but also to lower-level executives who actually help to shape the organization's policies (even when they are officially given no leeway to do so in the policy directives from the top-level echelon) by the way they implement the directives. The chapter also calls attention to what may be a new type of research inquiry that is needed to make the model more complete, which could enable predictions to be made about the particular decision rules policymakers are most likely to rely upon in different circumstances.

The last two chapters explore the implications of the model for the research agendas of social scientists. Thirty-seven testable hypotheses are derived from the model, all of which suggest prescriptive guidelines for improving the effectiveness of policymaking in governmental, business, and public welfare organizations. One set of implications—the 17 hypotheses discussed in Chapter 9—pertains to a central question about *individual differences* among executives in personality and other dispositions. The hypotheses are pertinent to the selection of personnel for policymaking positions: Who is most likely and who is least likely to be an effective policymaker? The second set of implications—the 20 hypotheses discussed in Chapter 10—pertains to a fundamental question about leadership practices: What does it take, according to the theoretical model, to function as an effective executive who practices and promotes high-quality decisionmaking on policy issues that affect the vital interests and survival of the organization or nation? These hypotheses warrant high priority on the research agendas of social scientists. If confirmed, they will point the way for executives who want to improve their policymaking by cutting down on common sources of error.

The research that I draw upon in all the chapters that follow encompasses a broad spectrum of causal factors, including those that influence information processing, probability estimates, scenarios about outcomes, ideological preferences, emotional biases, affiliative loyalties, and conformity to organizational norms and operational codes. Focusing mainly upon what is known about sources of avoidable errors, I try to construct an assemblage of major determinants of effective and ineffective policymaking. Included in the interdisciplinary assemblage are concepts and generalizations from the work of sociologists, economists, management scientists, political scientists, historians, and three types of research specialists in the field of psychology—cognitive, clinical, and social psychologists.

As in the assemblages by Pablo Picasso, Kurt Schwitters, Robert Rauschenberg, and other masters of modern art, the diverse components brought together in a successful work must be organized into a coherent and satisfying pattern in which all the bits and pieces are integrated into a unified whole. This is not an easy requirement to meet when one is trying to develop theory in the social sciences. Even more difficult are the other requirements for any "good" theory of complex human behavior, notably that it should provide valid explanatory insights, account for prior empirical findings more adequately than any rival theory, make novel, nontrivial predictions that are testable, and suggest new prescriptions that are worth investigating. I hope that I am not pushing my optimism beyond reasonable limits when I allow myself to expect that within a few years we shall have a dependable answer as to whether the theoretical framework presented in this book can be developed to meet all these essential requirements.

PART II

Common Simplistic
Strategies Evoked
by Constraints

2

Cognitive Decision Rules

If you ask policymakers how they make decisions, they are likely to tell you that long ago they learned to disregard much of what the textbooks say about the desirability of a systematic rational approach and instead they do it mostly by "the seat of the pants." This is what I have been told over and over again in my interviews during the past 30 years of several hundred executives in government agencies, large corporations, and public welfare institutions in five countries—the United States, England, Australia, Norway, and the Netherlands. When they are being candid, many executives make disillusioning comments similar to those quoted in the last chapter from Barzini and Lord Acton. Their accounts generally are in agreement with the results of numerous research investigations of policy decisionmaking among executives in many different types of organizations—in government, the armed services, business, and public welfare—showing that often the policymakers do indeed deviate considerably from the normative models for problem solving advocated in most management science textbooks.

What do policymakers mean when they say that in their circumstances you have to make most decisions by "the seat of your pants?" As far as I can tell they mean that instead of approaching a crisis or any other challenge as a problem to be worked on by engaging in a careful information search, deliberation about alternatives, and contingency planning, they resort to a *simplistic* strategy for arriving at a decision—relying on a few *simple decision rules,* which enable them very quickly to arrive at a solution that seems to be satisfactory. This appears to be one of the main ways that policymakers cope with time limitations, lack of knowledge, social pressures that threaten loss of power and status, emotional stress, and other constraints that interfere with high-quality decisionmaking.

Doing it by "the seat of your pants" was originally an expression used by old-time flyers to describe approvingly how they piloted their small planes in the good old days when they had to fly intuitively, by feel, rather than by instruments. But even the proudest old-timers would consider it foolish to pilot a huge jet airliner that way. Applying the metaphor to decisionmaking, one could expect a seat-of-the-pants approach to work quite well for minor decisions of small scope, but not for major policy decisions involving the complex issues faced by those who pilot large organizations.

In this chapter I shall survey and give examples of simple decision rules commonly used by top-level executives to deal with two interrelated types of cognitive constraints that are obstacles to effective problem solving: (1) limited cognitive resources of the organization to supply essential intelligence (pertinent information and analysis) and (2) limited cognitive capabilities of the person or persons who make the policy decision.[1] But first we must examine a question that forms the background context for this survey: What are the characteristics of the high-quality policymaking procedures that executives *fail* to use when they adopt a simplistic strategy?

How Good Executives Make Consequential Decisions

In his highly influential book *Administrative Behavior,* Herbert A. Simon makes the assumption that human beings sometimes approach decisionmaking in a "rational way" and sometimes not. His descriptive account of how good executives make their decisions calls attention to several major steps in effective problem solving that they carry out. One involves listing alternative courses of action or choices; another is to examine the major consequences that can be expected to follow from each of the choices; yet another is to carry out a comparative evaluation of the various consequences. Simon adds, however, that an objectively rational approach cannot be carried out fully because of the limited knowledge and capabilities of all human beings:

> Actual behavior [of policymakers] falls short, in at least three ways, of objective rationality . . .

(1) Rationality requires a complete knowledge and anticipation of the consequences that will follow on each choice. In fact, knowledge of consequences is always fragmentary.

(2) Since these consequences lie in the future, imagination must supply the lack of experienced feeling in attaching value to them. But values can be only imperfectly anticipated.

(3) Rationality requires a choice among all possible alternative behaviors. In actual behavior, only a very few of all these possible alternatives ever come to mind. (Simon 1976, p. 81)

There are other cognitive limitations as well. For example, the nature of the threat or opportunity that poses the policy problem may not be well understood because the available information is too ambiguous or incomplete. And even if the essential information about every viable option and its expected consequences were available, there is no valid way to combine all the various organizational, political, economic, ideological, and personal values that might be at stake into a single utility criterion or scale.

In practice, according to Simon's account, good policymakers who are striving for high-quality decisions engage in analytic problem solving, but they do so in a way that only crudely approximates the requirements of a normative rational model. Their procedures, which I refer to as *vigilant problem solving,* involve working to the best of their limited abilities, within the confines of available organizational resources, to exercise all the caution they can to avoid mistakes in the essential tasks of information search, deliberation, and planning.

Carrying out all the essential steps of vigilant problem solving, as described in Chapter 5, enables policymakers to do far better than if they were to use a seat-of-the-pants approach—better in that they are more likely to obtain a comprehensive view of the options, to recognize trade-offs among competing values, to choose a course of action that best meets the essential requirements for a satisfactory course of action, and to develop alternative fallback options in case the chosen option unexpectedly proves to be unworkable or ineffective.

Like many other experts in the administrative sciences, Simon refers to analytic problem solving as a "rational" approach to decisionmaking. But it seems best not to use that label because of its ambiguities. The term "not rational" is especially misleading because it connotes "irrational," "wildly unrealistic," "crazy," and other extreme epithets, which are not appropriate for conceptualizing seat-of-the-pants approaches.

The philosopher of science Max Black reports that when he gave a questionnaire to well-educated people, he found a considerable amount of disagreement about the correct application of the terms "rational" and "irrational" to concrete examples of decisionmaking. Because of this high degree of ambiguity, he proposes replacing these ill-defined terms by less ambiguous ones, such as "reasonable," and "sensible," versus "hasty," and "shortsighted." In agreement with the spirit of his suggestion, I avoid using the terms "rational" or "nonrational," except when quoting other writers. Instead, I use terms like "high-quality" versus "low-quality" when evaluating the procedures used by decisionmakers to arrive at their choices.

Evaluating the Quality of Policy Decisionmaking

When observations are available concerning how a single policymaker or a group of policymakers arrived at a vital policy decision, what criteria can be used to determine whether the process of policymaking is of high quality? The following seven procedural criteria have been extracted by Janis and Mann from the extensive research literature on effective decisionmaking by individual executives and by members of policymaking groups in government, business corporations, and public welfare organizations.[2] To the best of his or her ability, the decisionmaker:

1. Surveys a wide range of objectives to be fulfilled, taking account of the multiplicity of values that are at stake;
2. Canvasses a wide range of alternative courses of action;
3. Intensively searches for new information relevant to evaluating the alternatives;
4. Correctly assimilates and takes account of new information or expert judgments to which he or she is exposed, even when the information or judgment does not support the course of action initially preferred;
5. Reconsiders the positive and negative consequences of alternatives originally regarded as unacceptable, before making a final choice;
6. Carefully examines the costs and risks of negative conse-

quences, as well as positive consequences, that could flow from the alternative that is preferred;

7. Makes detailed provisions for implementing and monitoring the chosen course of action, with special attention to contingency plans that might be required if various known risks were to materialize.

For purposes of investigating the quality of policy decisionmaking, each of the seven criteria should be conceptualized as a continuum such that the individual or group responsible for making a policy decision could be given a low, medium, or high rating. At the lower end of each continuum are instances of executives having implemented a new policy decision without having done hardly anything at all to meet the criterion—for example (1) practically no surveying of objectives, or (2) practically no canvassing of alternatives, or (3) practically no search for new relevant information, and so on. Any gross failure to meet one of the criteria can be regarded as a *symptom of defective policymaking.*

At the upper end of each continuum are instances of policymakers fulfilling the criterion in the most thorough manner that could be expected under the circumstances. But judgments concerning the upper end of the continuum (such as, whether the rating should be very high or not quite so high or maybe even in the medium range) are extremely difficult because of all sorts of ambiguities about what could be expected within the confines of the limited time and organizational resources available and about such considerations as whether the point of diminishing returns had been reached. For example, the amount of information that could be potentially relevant concerning possible consequences of whatever options are being considered is far greater than anyone would ever be able or willing to spend the time, effort, and money collecting. (Some philosophically inclined commentators tell us that the amount is infinite because everything that happens in the world is ultimately connected to everything else.) And, of course, there are no reliable indicators for judging when the point is reached where it is no longer worth the costs of procuring and processing more information even though what has already been acquired still leaves some uncertainties and gaps. Then, too, a very high rating can itself be ambiguous because sometimes policymakers do too much in the way of meeting one or another of the criteria, achieving a very high rating that objective observers see as unwarranted for the policy problem at hand and as excessively costly for the organization.

There are fewer ambiguities to contend with when one is judging whether policymakers have done so little that they have failed to meet one or another of the criteria. Accordingly, both for basic research and for practical purposes, it seems preferable to assess the quality of the procedures used by policymakers in arriving at any given policy choice by examining the available evidence about their decisionmaking behavior in terms of the lower end of the continuum for each of the seven criteria—that is, to see whether or not any of the gross symptoms of defective policymaking can be detected and, if so, how many.

In order to assess the overall quality of the process, then, available observational reports and records can be analyzed to find out whether few or many of the symptoms were manifested at the time the final choice was made—with careful attention to clues that might indicate that memoirs and even documentary records were distorted to make the decisionmaking process look better than it actually was or that meetings were manipulated to give the impression that leaders were using high-quality procedures. For example, to evaluate the quality of decisionmaking by national leaders during a crisis provoked by a destabilizing military action taken by an adversary nation (such as invasion of an allied third country), the investigator could examine—with scholarly skepticism—the records of a policymaking group's discussions, memoranda, and participants' personal accounts to see whether they show manifestations of any gross symptoms. The following rough definitions of the symptoms of defective policymaking indicate what to look for when judging whether the rating for each of the seven criteria should be at the low end of the continuum:[3]

1. *Gross omissions in surveying objectives:* The group never explicitly discusses objectives, or gives them such brief or cursory consideration that the participants fail to specify some of the major requirements for a satisfactory choice that take into account important goals or values implicated by the policy problem.

2. *Gross omissions in surveying alternatives:* The group fails to consider a number of viable alternative policies, confining its discussions to only one alternative. If any of the additional viable alternatives are mentioned at all, they are immediately excluded or dropped without discussion.

3. *Poor information search:* The group fails to obtain available

information necessary for critically evaluating the pros and cons of the preferred course of action and other alternatives. If the group engages in any information search at all, it does so in such a perfunctory and incomplete manner that it fails to obtain a number of important pieces of information that would have been available if requested from experts or other appropriate persons inside or outside their organization.

4. *Selective bias in processing information at hand:* The group shows a definite tendency to accept new information from intelligence reports, the testimony of experts, the mass media, and outside critics only when it supports the preferred alternative. The members generally ignore or refute a number of important pieces of nonsupporting information to which they are exposed.

5. *Failure to reconsider originally rejected alternatives:* The group fails to reexamine the consequences of a number of previously considered alternatives, or reexamines rejected alternatives in a biased manner by discounting favorable information and giving disproportionate weight to information about their negative consequences.

6. *Failure to examine major costs and risks of the preferred choice:* The group fails to consider negative consequences of the preferred alternative, or examines them so incompletely that a number of important ones are overlooked even though information about those consequences is available.

7. *Failure to work out detailed implementation, monitoring, and contingency plans:* The group ignores possible problems in implementation and does not develop monitoring or contingency plans. If the group discusses implementation, monitoring, and contingency plans, they do so in such a vague or incomplete manner that a number of important difficulties or contingencies that are likely to materialize are overlooked.

In my comparative case-study research on foreign policy decisions made by United States presidents and their advisors during major international crises, I have encountered several examples of decision-making of such low quality that all seven symptoms were manifested. Most of the foreign policy decisions, however, were not quite so bad. The policymakers often displayed some of the gross symptoms, but not all (see Table 6–1, p. 125).

Judging from my own observations and that of research col-

leagues, only a very small percentage of policy decisions in large organizations are likely to be rated overall as substantially high-quality
decisions on the basis of receiving no ratings of gross failures, indicating an absence of all seven symptoms.[4] It will become apparent in
Chapter 6, when I discuss the rating data on symptoms of defective
policymaking from a study of major U.S. foreign policy decisions in
five administrations since the end of World War II, that only a minority of such decisions can be expected to warrant being rated overall as *fairly good* quality—manifesting none or only one of the seven
symptoms. Data will also be presented in Figure 6-1 indicating that,
as expected, such policy decisions are less likely to lead to undesirable outcomes than those displaying a large number of symptoms of
defective policymaking.

Rapid-Fire Decisions

Fairly often policymakers in business and public welfare organizations, as well as in government, fail to meet the criteria for high-
quality decisionmaking. Many I have interviewed in all three types
of organizations explain that they are appallingly busy keeping their
offices running, carrying out all sorts of daily routine chores, meeting regular deadlines for budget estimates, and putting out all sorts
of little as well as big fires that are smoldering and raging concur-
rently. So when it comes to making a decision about a policy issue,
they feel that very little of their time and energy can be devoted to
searching for the pertinent information and deliberating about the
pros and cons of alternative courses of action. When Robert
McNamara was Secretary of Defense, Washington bureaucrats
quipped that the reason he looked so good as a policy advisor at
White House meetings, in comparison with the President's other
cabinet members, was that the long drive from the Pentagon gave him
eight extra minutes to do his homework in the back of the limousine.

Policy decisions differ from the routine decisions of everyday executive life in that they are highly consequential for the organization's vital interests and goals. They are in the category of strategic
decisions described by Herbert A. Simon as creating "a new situation which, in turn, influences the decisions that follow them." Simon cites as an example a manufacturer's decision to build a new
factory. It is the existence of these long-term decisions, Simon asserts, "that more than anything else accounts for the relative consis-

tency of both personal and organizational behavior over periods of time. It also accounts for a certain 'inertia' in the adjustment to new situations."

A chief executive facing a policy problem will display many symptoms of defective policymaking if he or she makes a policy decision very quickly. President John F. Kennedy, for example, although sometimes quite cautious and deliberative about deciding whether or not to use military force when confronted by apparent threats to America's security, spent only a few minutes thinking about what to do when a crisis arose in the Dominican Republic in November 1961. He made a very quick decision to order American warships and a contingent of marines to prepare to intervene in order to preserve the endangered coalition government from being taken over in a military coup by members of the Trujillo family, who were threatening to set up a military dictatorship unfriendly to the United States. Obviously, when policy decisions are made so rapidly, most of the criteria for high-quality decisionmaking cannot be met.

Some heads of state may make rapid-fire policy decisions fairly often. Cuban leader Fidel Castro, for example, has been described in this way by a former Cuban government official who defected and was interviewed after being granted asylum in the United States in October 1984. According to this inside observer, Castro typically would seize upon new policy ideas impulsively, making up his mind very quickly to introduce major changes without adequate study or forethought, and without genuine use of his advisors because they would not dare to contradict him even when they realized that the chief was overlooking obstacles that would make his plans unworkable. All the examples cited by the observer to illustrate Castro's impulsive decisionmaking, however, pertain to domestic economic policies; no examples were mentioned of foreign policy decisions with vital national security interests at stake.

President Ronald Reagan, according to many observers, was also inclined to make policy decisions rapidly, with little consultation, analysis, or deliberation. But in his case those "quickie" decisions often pertained to foreign policy issues. (Specific examples will be given later in this chapter.)

Satisficing, Analogizing, and Related Cognitive Rules

Figure 2-1 represents a relatively simple seat-of-the-pants approach that I have inferred from what many executives have told me about

FIGURE 2-1 A Typical Simplistic Approach to Decisionmaking That Incorporates "Satisficing" and Other Cognitive Rules

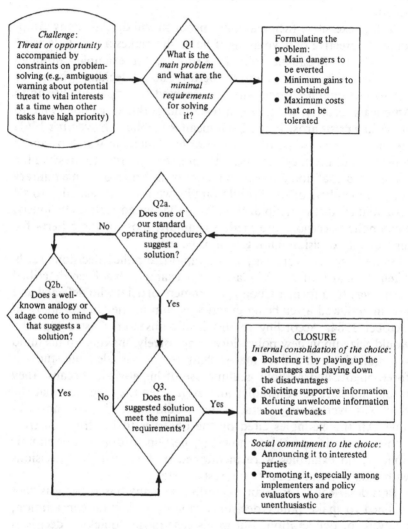

how they arrive at policy decisions. This chart embodies a few well-known decision rules that provide cognitive shortcuts. Using those shortcuts may be a fairly effective way to deal with routine problems of the type that constantly beset busy executives who are caught in an "activity trap." But resorting to simple rules when dealing with vital policy issues can make for avoidable errors that have grave consequences. One such rule is to accept the first alternative that comes to mind that is "good enough" to meet the minimal requirements, without bothering to compare it with other viable alternatives. This simplistic strategy has been described as ubiquitous among administrators by Simon, who refers to it as "satisficing." Simon points out that this approach fits the needs for simplifying complicated decision problems that exceed the information-processing capabilities of human beings, all of whom are creatures of "bounded" or "limited rationality."

Figure 2-1 represents a relatively crude form of satisficing. As the figure shows, the first step is to formulate the minimum requirements (Q1). After that, the policymaker searches his or her memory for a standard operating procedure (SOP) that might be applicable for dealing with the crisis at hand (Q2a in Figure 2-1). Giving priority to an SOP has the advantage of almost guaranteeing that the solution will be seen as legitimate and at least minimally acceptable to practically all interested parties in the organization, including superiors and peers who are expected to review the decision and subordinates who are expected to implement it.

If no relevant SOP comes to mind, the next step is to search one's memory for a well-known analogy or adage that can be applied to the current situation (Q2b in Figure 2-1). Historical analogies are commonly used—as when President Harry Truman viewed North Korea's invasion of South Korea as analogous to Mussolini's and Hitler's invasions and, correspondingly, adopted a belligerent "no appeasement" stance, which he vigorously urged at meetings with his advisors. If Truman and his advisors had considered the possible relevance of other historical analogies as well, they probably would have looked into the pros and cons of other options in addition to military intervention; subsequently they might have been less inclined to make the ill-conceived decision to allow General MacArthur to pursue the North Koreans into their homeland with the new aim of putting all of North Korea under the control of the South Korean government: "A serious look at the apparent analogues," according to Richard Neustadt and Ernest May, "could have helped Truman, Acheson, and others see more distinctly why their initial preference had gone so strongly just to restoring the *status quo ante,*" making it more likely that Truman would "resist enlarging his aim when the war went well." That enlargement occurred when Truman and his advisors ignored warnings from Chinese leaders about the consequences of invading North Korea, which brought

China into the war and soon transformed the American victory into a disastrous defeat.

Commenting on the pervasiveness of metaphorical thinking, which includes seeing a current event as analogous to a similar past event, Cathy J. Wheeler points out that any one analogy gives only a single and very limited perspective on the situation. She asserts that "A switch of metaphor can . . . transform radically one's judgments and evaluations. . . . [Sometimes] a sea-change occurs in which what is judged a serious problem within one metaphor is thought of [entirely differently] . . . within another."

When a decisionmaker searches for a historical analogy, an adage, or an SOP that suggests a solution, he or she usually depends upon what is available to memory. Availability is influenced by whether the analogy, adage, or SOP is coded in a catchy, memorable way, whether it evokes a vivid image, and other factors that determine spontaneous salience.

When the decisionmaker hits upon a suggested solution that seems promising, he or she goes on to the next step, which is to see if it meets the minimal requirements (Q3). If it does not, the decisionmaker goes back to the preceding step (Q2b) to try to find another solution suggested by an analogy or adage that might meet the requirements. After going through this route several times, the decisionmaker might still fail to find a minimally satisfactory course of action, in which case he or she will be inclined to try other decision rules (such as the additional ones discussed later in this chapter).

As soon as the decisionmaker hits upon a course of action that appears to meet the minimal requirements, he or she takes the final steps, as shown in the last box in Figure 2-1: The decisionmaker consolidates the seemingly satisfactory solution by bolstering it in his or her own mind; at the same time or shortly thereafter, the person becomes committed to the decision by announcing it to interested parties and by promoting it, when necessary, to those who do not readily accept it as feasible or worthwhile implementing.

Bolstering the choice involves the well-known psychological tendency toward closure, which may be one of the manifestations of a striving for cognitive consistency. Often bolstering occurs without deliberate intent on the part of the decisionmaker. It can be conceptualized as another decision rule, even though the person may not be fully conscious of using it. If it were verbalized, the bolstering rule would go something like this: "Once you have hit upon a course of action that meets fairly well the requirements you had in mind while making the decision, get your mind off its disadvantages or short-comings; think instead about all the positive features you can." Using this rule provides, in effect, a shortcut that speeds up the time-consuming final steps of decisionmaking. But usually it does so at the cost of reducing the quality of decisionmaking when it comes into play before the policymakers have searched for hidden flaws or completed plans for overcoming implementation difficulties, for monitoring, and for meeting distressing contingencies that might arise if some of the known risks were to materialize. (Of course, any such shortcut that speeds up decisionmaking could have an overall positive effect in unusual circumstances, such as when an unnegotiable deadline is close at hand and the costs of a delay would exceed or nullify its potential benefits.)

Policymakers sometimes end up bitterly regretting decisions about vital policy issues made on the basis of a simplistic strategy. But they rarely discover that they could do better if they used higher-quality procedures. To a detached outside observer it might be apparent that when executives choose highly consequential courses of action by using a quick-and-easy approach that relies entirely on simple decision rules, like those represented in Figure 2–1, they are running an increased risk of undesirable outcomes. The executives themselves tend to be aware only of the advantages of this approach and remain unaware of how the symptoms of defective policymaking lead to avoidable errors. They continue to trust uncritically the answers yielded by their favorite cognitive shortcuts, partly because clear-cut reminders of past failures from using a simplistic approach are seldom present at the time a new decision has to be made.

Then, too, the policymakers' use of the bolstering rule contributes to their resistance to negative feedback. After internally consolidating the chosen course of action, policymakers are likely to persist in believing that they made the right choice even when there are signs that it is not working out successfully. They seize upon whatever ambiguities there are in the negative feedback to interpret unfavorable consequences as very temporary or of minor importance, thereby minimizing the losses. On those rare occasions when they are exposed to negative feedback so unambiguous that it cannot be discounted, they blame the poor outcome on the undermining actions of opponents, the ineptitude or negligence of the implementors, or just plain bad luck.

Although seldom realizing that in the long run they might regret the "quick-and-easy" way they are arriving at their choices, policymakers usually are keenly aware of saving time and impressing fellow executives with their "decisiveness," as well as other immediate rewards they can count upon in the short run. The bolstering rule is especially rewarding to top-level executives in several ways. It enables them to set aside debilitating doubts as to whether their solutions to problems will work out well, to move resolutely to implement their decisions, and to fulfill their leadership role of inspiring colleagues and underlings by the confident way they announce and promote their policies.

The decision rules mentioned so far are certainly not the only ones that policymakers rely upon to deal with their own limited capabilities for comprehending complicated issues, their limited resources for information search and analysis, and other problem-solving constraints. One least-effort rule that is well described in social scientists' accounts of organizational behavior is the "incremental change" rule, which sometimes enables executives to "muddle through" and sometimes does not. It is especially likely to be used in the early stages of a crisis, when warnings of mounting danger are not yet very impressive and policymakers are occupied with other serious problems—as when U.S. officials in the Carter administration received early warnings in the 1970s that the Ayatollah Khomeini's movement, which was strongly hostile to America, might topple the Shah of Iran. If verbalized, the rule runs like this; "Stick closely to the last decision bearing on the issue and make only slight changes to take care of the most urgent aspects of the problem currently at hand."

The "Nutshell Briefing" Rule

There are other cognitive decision rules that can lead to ill-conceived solutions to the problems posed by a crisis, some of which result in drastic rather than slight changes in policy. In my research on United States foreign policymaking, I have encountered one such rule, which I have not seen explicitly mentioned in the social science literature—what I call the "nutshell briefing" rule. It goes like this: "When facing a complicated policy problem, save time and effort by getting someone who has looked into the issues to tell you what it is all about, 'in a nutshell,' and then decide."

Well-documented studies indicate that one reason lobbyists are so successful in swaying members of the U.S. Congress and state legislatures is that they provide nutshell briefings, which call attention to the favorable implications of the policies advocated by the business interest groups they represent in terms of the legislators' own values. As one state legislator explained, "They [lobbyists] can study and present the issues concisely—the average legislator has no time or inclination to do it, and wouldn't understand bills or issues without them."

Top-level executives in government, business, or welfare organizations are likely to turn to one or another of the key members on their staffs to supply a nutshell briefing, and to rely solely on that single channel of information (or misinformation), which is usually biased in favor of one particular course of action. Adhering to the nutshell briefing rule is entirely different from the judicious use of presidential briefings, as occurs when the president raises incisive questions with his national security advisor, or whoever is briefing him, to ascertain the extent to which the recommendation represents a genuine consensus arising from discussions among the relevant policy advisors and to find out the pros and cons of alternative options that were taken into consideration. If, after a single nutshell briefing by an aide, a chief executive accepts the aide's policy recommendation without raising any such critical questions, the chief executive, in effect, is delegating the policy decision. "Let George do it" is not essentially different from "let George tell me what to do and I'll do it."

President Ronald Reagan, noted for his general readiness to delegate decisions, frequently relied upon nutshell briefings even when he was expected not to delegate but to take responsibility himself for making a presidential decision. For example, General Alexander Haig, who served as Secretary of State during Reagan's first term, reports a number of instances when the President made up his mind on consequential foreign policy issues—or changed his mind—immediately after receiving a nutshell briefing. On one occasion in June 1982, Haig learned from William Clark, the White House Chief of Staff, that the President after a briefing had approved, without consulting the Secretary of State, a recommendation made by the White House crisis management team that would entail a marked shift in foreign policy. The recommendation that promptly became a presidential order was to instruct the U.S. representative at the UN to vote in favor of a United Nations resolution condemning Israel for its invasion of Lebanon and threatening sanctions. Haig became highly aroused when he learned of it. He regarded the decision as "an unprecedented step" that "would bring about a major break with Israel." Haig rushed to see the President and gave him a rapid counter-briefing, emphasizing the expected detrimental consequences. As soon as Haig finished the new nutshell briefing, President Reagan agreed to Haig's recommendation that the U.S. should veto the UN resolution, completely reversing his earlier presidential order.

Here we see that whoever gives the latest briefing to a receptive chief executive like Reagan is able to counteract the next-to-last briefing. But it is not always so easy to undo the organizational arrangements made to implement the preceding policy decision. And the reversal can lead to considerable confusion and bureaucratic infighting. That is what happened in this case.

When Haig notified his State Department deputy to arrange for the UN veto, he was told that his orders were being countermanded by the Chief of Staff's deputy (Robert McFarlane), who was operating on the basis of the earlier decision to order the UN representative to vote for the condemnatory resolution. "This new confusion," Haig informs us, "required another meeting with [Chief of Staff] Clark . . . where acquiescence if not agreement was reached after a stormy exchange of words." Afterwards, late at night, Haig was unable to fall asleep because he kept thinking about the implications of the opposition he was encountering; he reports that "my thoughts were deeply disturbed by the dangerous implications of a situation in which a Presidential assistant, especially one of limited experience and limited understanding of the volatile nature of an international conflict, should assume the powers of the Presidency." Secretary of State Haig's night thoughts might well have recurred to his successor and to other government officials four and one-half years later when news media all over the world were headlining the scandals stemming from President Reagan's decision to accept Robert McFarlane's recommendation to sell arms to Iran.

Advantages and Disadvantages of Cognitive Decision Rules

The "nutshell briefing" rule—just like satisficing, incrementalism, the availability heuristic, and other simple decision rules used by decisionmakers in a quick-and-easy approach—can sometimes save time and effort in arriving at adequate judgments. But fairly often reliance on such rules results in judgmental errors, which can create grossly misleading expectations about a chosen course of action.

These conclusions are supported by findings from a large number of psychological experiments as well as organizational case studies.

All cognitive decision rules—or *heuristics* as they are technically labeled by cognitive psychologists—have a number of features in common:

> The heuristics . . . are relatively primitive and simple judgmental strategies. They are not irrational or even nonrational. They probably produce vastly more correct or partially correct inferences than erroneous ones, and they do so with great speed and little effort. Indeed, we suspect that the use of such simple tools may be an inevitable feature of the cognitive apparatus of any organism that must make as many judgments, inferences, and decisions as humans have to do. Each heuristic or, more properly, the misapplication of each heuristic, does lead people astray in some important inferential tasks. . . . Although we characterize the heuristics as "judgmental strategies," the term is misleading in that it implies a conscious and deliberate application of well-defined rules. . . . Instead, the utilization of the heuristics is generally automatic and nonreflective and notably free of any conscious consideration of appropriateness. . . . [T]he heuristics are not applied in a totally indiscriminate fashion. In many contexts in which a given heuristic would promote error, people refrain from using it and probably could articulate why its use would be foolish. On other logically equivalent and equally unpropitious occasions, people readily apply the same heuristic and may even attempt to justify its use. (Nisbett & Ross, p. 18)

By and large, relying on a few simple rules of thumb might generally work out fairly well when an executive is making routine choices or dealing with minor policy issues that are relatively unimportant because they do not entail the threat of any serious losses. (See Chapter 7 for a discussion of factors that influence policymakers' judgments of the importance or consequentiality of a problem.) But as I have already indicated, one of the main themes of this book is that when executives rely upon those rules to make an *important* policy decision, they save time and effort at the cost of risking being stuck with an ill-conceived choice entailing disastrous consequences that could have been avoided.

This theme is consistent with a major point made in Alexander

George's *Presidential Decisionmaking* about simple decision rules that are commonly used by a nation's leaders to cope with problem-solving constraints. In addition to "satisficing," "analogizing," and the "incremental change" rule, several other simple decision rules are described by George. One such rule consists of deciding on the basis of "consensus," which merely requires the leader to find out what most people in the organization will accept. Another simple rule is to scan ideological principles to find one to serve as a guide to action. Yet another rule is to select a rubric from the organization's "operational code," which pertains to the powerholders' shared beliefs about appropriate strategies and tactics for dealing with recurrent problems. An example of such a belief is the assumption made by many American leaders that the nation's best way to deal with any move by an adversary nation that could develop into a threat to vital interests is to deploy military units promptly in order to demonstrate resolve to take military action if necessary. The executive's premature resort to or overreliance on any of these relatively simple ways of dealing with a major threat or opportunity, George concludes, "can be dysfunctional insofar as it interferes with the search and analysis activities that should precede choice of policy."

In this chapter I have summarized the criteria for evaluating the quality of the policymaking process in order to focus on the corresponding symptoms of defective decisionmaking, which help to elucidate dysfunctional ways of arriving at a policy decision. Those symptoms will continue to be the main point of focus of this book as we pursue two main lines of inquiry: What are the *causes* of the symptoms? What are their *consequences?*

The central assumptions that will be elaborated more and more fully in each successive chapter are that (1) symptoms of defective decisionmaking are to be expected whenever policymakers arrive at vital choices primarily by relying upon simple decision rules to deal with the constraints that beset them and (2) those symptoms, in turn, tend to lead to undesirable outcomes. If the assumptions are empirically valid, we can expect that when fundamental interests of the organization or nation are at stake, a chief executive or an executive committee will be more likely to *regret* policy decisions if arrived at by a simplistic approach than if arrived at by high-quality procedures that eliminate symptoms of defective policymaking before implementing policy changes.

3

Affiliative Decision Rules

The decision rules I have talked about so far are the ones used by policymakers to cope with cognitive limitations of the human mind, insufficient time for deliberation, limited organizational resources for information gathering, and related problem-solving constraints. The cognitive rules described in the preceding chapter simplify the intellectual tasks posed by the complicated problems that confront executives who make policy decisions. There are also other types of constraints, as indicated in Figure 1–1 (p. 16), that need to be dealt with. For example, top-level executives usually realize that even a very wise policy decision to accept a settlement that beautifully solves major problems created by conflict with an adversary organization or nation could get them into serious trouble within their own organization if the decision fails to take account of the objections of other powerholders, no matter how mistaken those objections might be.

Whenever a crisis arises, policymakers are likely to seek a solution that will avert threats to important values in a way that will not adversely affect their relationships with any "important people" within the organization, especially those to whom they are accountable, and that will not be opposed by subordinates who are expected to implement the new policy decision. I call requirements of this kind "affiliative" constraints because they pertain to the policymaker's affiliation with others in his or her organization. Most policymakers are highly motivated to take account of affiliative constraints. They want to maintain or enhance their power, compensation, and status within the organization and to continue to obtain social support from their personal network.

In order to cope with the set of demands imposed by affiliative

45

constraints, executives use a corresponding set of affiliative decision rules. Some of the rules are used to preserve the policymaker's relationship with a primary group, such as a small planning committee that meets fairly often to work on major policy recommendations. Other affiliative rules come into play when executives are trying to cope with constraints arising from their membership in a secondary group, most notably the organization that employs them, such as an industrial corporation, a bank, a law firm, a social service agency, a hospital, a city government, or the State Department in the federal government.

The "Avoid Punishment" Rule

Probably the best known and most widely used of all affiliative rules is one known throughout the Pentagon and elsewhere in Washington as the C.Y.A. ("cover-your-ass") rule. In any organization it can be a source of evasive or insincerely compliant advice from top-level executives when they are consulted by the chief executive. The rule is especially popular among middle-level executives who are keen on getting ahead.

Here is a synopsis of what dozens of governmental officials in policy-planning roles have told me about applying that rule when they are asked to participate in policy planning:

> The first thing you do before you open your mouth is to find out what your bosses think should be done. They might secretly favor continuing the present policy unchanged in order to keep a rival faction within the bureaucracy from encroaching on their territory, or they might want a particular modification of the policy in order to enlarge their empire. You had better do enough detective work to find out what it is they really want so that you can keep your ass covered by adopting their position. Arguing for anything else could antagonize them so much that your ass will be carved. If you are quite sure that they have no definite preference and really want innovative proposals, it's OK to try to earn brownie points by suggesting a new policy that you think will be successful, but be careful to do it in a way that does not expose your behind for a whacking later on. Avoid going all-out in advocating any new policy because if it

fails, you will be the fall guy; it will be your ass that will be in a sling.

A central theme of the "cover-your-ass" rule is to make sure you will not be blamed if your advice or decision turns out badly. This is a variant of a more general rule to *avoid punishment*. Its advantages, according to its advocates, is that it keeps you from getting into serious trouble in the short run and increases your chances of survival as an executive in the long run. Nothing is said, however, about the chances of short-run trouble or long-run survival for your organization (or nation).

Even when a chief executive does not overtly convey threats of disapproval or retribution to those who oppose his or her views, the "avoid punishment" rule can prevent advisors from expressing frank judgments on policy issues. On the basis of his observations as an insider in the Reagan administration, David Stockman reports that government officials and other advisors whom President Reagan consulted were often inhibited from giving clear-cut information and arguments that ran counter to the President's domestic policy preferences: "those who differ with Mr. Reagan lack the courage to tell him so." People who disagree violently with Reagan's plans, Stockman asserts, "make their point in a very low-key, sheepish way"; they avoid "head-on collisions or eyeball-to-eyeball confrontations, with the result that choices never get squarely posed."

In the Reagan administration, presidential aides and advisors were also inhibited at times from giving honest evaluations of foreign policy options because of fear of social punishment from persons who were the President's favorite members of his inner circle. A clear-cut example can be found in the testimony of Robert C. McFarlane, who had served as President Reagan's National Security Advisor. In May 1987, he told the joint congressional panel investigating the Iran-Contra scandal that he had felt that the goal of selling arms to Iran was right but the means being chosen were not. "Where I went wrong," he said, "was not having the guts to stand up and tell the President that." When asked to explain further why he had not told the President about his objections, he answered: "To tell you the truth, probably the reason I didn't is because if I'd done that [CIA Director] Bill Casey, [former UN ambassador] Jeane Kirkpatrick and [Defense Secretary] Cap Weinberger would have said I was some kind of Commie, you know."

This type of inhibition from fear of being punished is a well-known problem among managers of business firms. Harold Geneen, speaking about what he has learned from two decades of experience as chief executive officer and board chairman of ITT, gives the following advice to executives in organizations of all sizes:

> People are often reluctant to report unpleasant facts, especially if they contradict the viewpoints of the boss. . . . You have to . . . do your own homework. Then keep in mind that many of the "facts" you read or hear may have been filtered through various people trying to protect themselves, or sometimes, almost unconsciously, telling you what they think you want to hear.
> You have to make it clear in meetings that you're not going to shoot the messenger. (Geneen, p. 1)

Some of its practitioners claim that their motives for using the "avoid punishment" rule are not confined entirely to self-interest. They say that they play it safe not just to preserve or advance their own personal careers within the bureaucratic hierarchy. Allegedly, they also have a praiseworthy motive—to retain their power and status so as to be "effective" in influencing powerful persons, which is essential for doing a good job on behalf of the organization. Whether or not there are such mixed motives underlying the use of the "avoid punishment" rule, it obviously promotes deliberate conformity out of concern about being punished for deviance. Even a chief executive and other top-level leaders are occasionally confronted with threats of retaliations, including extreme forms of punishment such as impeachment or other steps toward removal from office, if they fail to conform to the urgent demands of a powerful coalition or constituency.

Policy planners who regularly rely upon this affiliative rule give a bad name to the ubiquitous game of bureaucratic politics. They contribute their full share to the notorious inertia, lack of initiative, "buck-passing," and "creeping incrementalism" that so often characterize policymaking in the federal government and in other large organizations.

The "avoid punishment" rule presumably has the advantage of enabling executives, including even those at the top who want to avoid retribution from other powerful leaders and constituencies, to continue using a seat-of-the-pants approach without having to worry very much about embarrassment in the future from being caught with their pants down. As is shown in Figure 3-1, it can be combined with simple cognitive rules like the ones represented in Figure 2-1.

Figure 3-1 indicates that when formulating the problem posed by any threat or opportunity that requires a policy decision, an executive who is especially concerned about the possibility of becoming a target for retaliations would apply the rule by devoting his or her initial information search primarily to finding out whether other powerful persons within the organization already favor a particular course of action (Q1a). If the intimidated executive discovers a clearly dominant preference among the powers that be—for example, one of the organization's leaders strongly favors a particular solution and none of the other pertinent powerholders has any objection to it—he or she immediately supports that solution and becomes socially committed to it, without giving any consideration to alternative choices and their consequences.[1] If the executive who is mainly concerned about protecting the seat of his or her pants feels fairly certain that there is no strong preference among the other powerholders, that they are undecided and open to a new solution, he or she will courageously proceed to the next step—formulating the problem posed by the challenge and the minimal requirements for solving it (Q1b). The executive's information search then is concentrated on ascertaining which powerful persons in the organization, if any, are concerned about the problem he or she is working on or are likely to become interested in it later after a solution has been worked out (Q1c).

Once it becomes apparent which persons are the ones it might be dangerous to ignore, the executive who is following the "avoid punishment" rule tries to discover what those powerholders might really want, irrespective of what they say publicly at meetings when they are claiming to be open-minded about the issue. Only if no apparent tilt is favored by anyone who could inflict retaliation will the executive become sufficiently adventuresome to start looking for his or her own solution to the problem by applying a standard operating procedure (Q2a) or a generally accepted analogy or adage (Q2b).

After having found a likely candidate, the wary executive would continue to make use of the same affiliative rule while grappling with the questions concerning whether the suggested solution meets the minimal requirements. The very first minimal requirement he or she thinks about pertains to the likelihood that the proposed solution

FIGURE 3-1 A Simplistic Approach to Decisionmaking Dominated by an Affiliative Rule: The "Avoid Punishment" Rule Combined with the Cognitive Heuristics Included in Figure 2-1

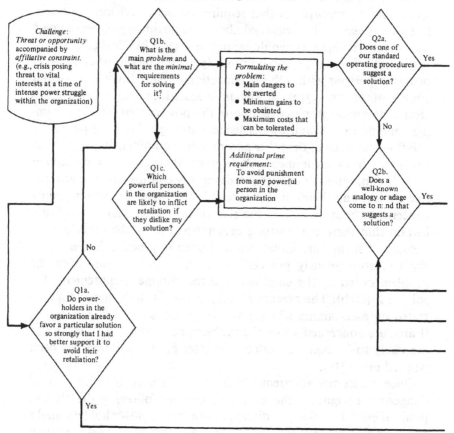

will be acceptable to powerful persons in the organization (Q3a). The executive considers not only whether any powerholders might become opposed to it after the new policy is announced, but also whether he or she is likely to be blamed in the event it turns out to be a failure (Q3b). The executive may take special steps to arrange for the blame to be diffused, rather than directed toward himself, as the one who initiated it. Solutions that appear too risky in this respect are likely to be dropped from further consideration, even though they might meet all the other requirements. This is one of the ways that using the "avoid punishment" rule makes for very

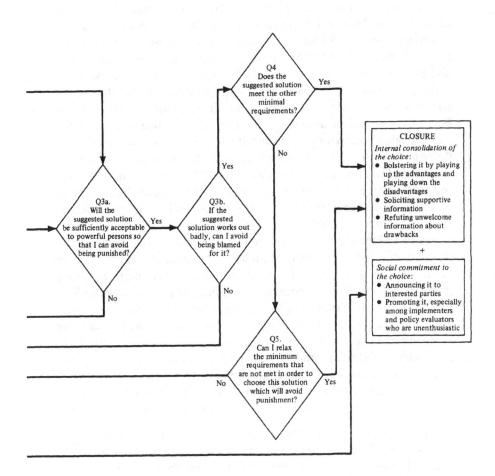

Q4
Does the suggested solution meet the other minimal requirements?

Yes

No

Yes

Q3a.
Will the suggested solution be sufficiently acceptable to powerful persons so that I can avoid being punished?

Yes

No

Q3b.
If the suggested solution works out badly, can I avoid being blamed for it?

No

CLOSURE

Internal consolidation of the choice:
● Bolstering it by playing up the advantages and playing down the disadvantages
● Soliciting supportive information
● Refuting unwelcome information about drawbacks

+

Social commitment to the choice:
● Announcing it to interested parties
● Promoting it, especially among implementers and policy evaluators who are unenthusiastic

Q5.
Can I relax the minimum requirements that are not met in order to choose this solution which will avoid punishment?

No

Yes

conservative policymaking, keeping organizational changes to the bare minimum.

Especially pernicious from the standpoint of making avoidable errors is the tendency to relax essential requirements for a satisfactory solution in order to select a course of action that the executive thinks will be safest for avoiding retaliation, irrespective of its actual consequences for the organization. A vivid example of pernicious reliance on the "avoid punishment" rule is presented in the case study by Auletta of Lehman Brothers Kuhn Loeb. For 60 years this organization had been operating as a highly successful Wall Street

investment firm, but it ended up almost bankrupt as a result of mis-
management and was forced to sell out. The demise of the firm,
according to Auletta's observations, was in large part a result of
cowering overcompliance by the firm's board of directors when the
members were asked by their co-chief executives, Lewis Glucksman
and Peter Peterson, to approve an ill-conceived reorganization plan.

Auletta's account is based on internal documents and also on interviews with leading executives in the firm, including all the members of the board of directors. The proposed change in governance
was initiated and strongly pushed by Lewis Glucksman (as will be
described when I discuss the self-serving rule in the next chapter).
He decided to attempt to take full control of the firm mainly in order
to satisfy his personal need for prestige and he induced Peterson to
agree to leave in exchange for a multimillion-dollar retirement settlement. On July 26, 1983, at a special meeting of the board of the
house of Lehman called by the co-chief executives, the members listened in stunned silence as the two leaders explained the plan. Seven
of the eight acquiesced without raising any serious questions about
possible unfavorable consequences. The only dissenter was Peter Solomon, who argued that the co-chiefs' agreement should be reconsidered. He reminded his passive colleagues that the board had the
power to approve or disapprove of any such momentous change in
governance of the firm and that the millions of dollars offered to get
Peterson to resign belonged to all of them as partners.

After repeated failures to mobilize an open discussion of the issues, Solomon was exasperated by the silence of his fellow directors:

"You guys are nuts to allow this to happen!" shouted Peter
Solomon. "We represent an investment of $40 million, which
dwarfs the investment of Peterson and Glucksman. We are
allowing them to harm our investment." Again, Solomon
looked about for support.
Silence.
"Come on, guys. That's our money!"
Silence. (Auletta 1985a, p. 62)

Subsequently the other board members did discuss the plan, focusing on the fine details of Peterson's severance agreement "like clerks
inspecting the details of a legal document." They also debated the
phrasings to be used in the press release announcing the change. But
they did not voice their misgivings about the self-serving package
deal—concerns about Glucksman's lack of qualifications for being

in full control of the firm's operations, the high financial costs to the partners, and the possible damage to the firm's thriving business. Their unvoiced misgivings, as it soon turned out, were well-warranted: Within a few months, under Glucksman's inept leadership, the firm would be brought to "the verge of bankruptcy." Ten months after the board's meeting, Auletta adds, "Wall Street's oldest continuing investment banking partnership . . . would fail to survive the reign of Lewis L. Glucksman and would be sold to Shearson/American Express."

The important point here is that, as Auletta puts it, "the entire transaction had been rubber-stamped" by the board. Why? From interviews with the board members, Auletta presents numerous indications that their decision to accept the coup was based at least partly on "the fears of Glucksman harbored by some members, not on whether the coup made sense for the firm, not on the violations of the consensual traditions of a partnership, not on whether Glucksman possessed the qualities to lead Lehman or whether it was time for Peterson to move on." Auletta quotes a board member who admitted that "board members were fearful of retribution—'those who rebelled might be remembered.'"

There were several ways that the chief executive could inflict retaliatory punishments, including one very immediate and concrete form of retribution that was feared, according to Auletta's interviews: Glucksman could retaliate by using his prerogative as top manager to cut the annual bonus of any executives who dissented, which would drastically reduce their annual income.[2] This threat of immediate retaliatory punishment by the chief executive appears to have been entirely realistic. Two months after the Board meeting, the bonus Glucksman gave to Peter Solomon, the lone dissenter, was one-hundred thousand dollars less than Solomon expected on the basis of his performance that year. Solomon and other bankers in the firm believed that Glucksman's bonus decision showed that he "was intent on revenge."

Here we have an obvious illustration of a major incentive for adopting the "avoid punishment" rule in response to the affiliative constraint posed by a chief executive's threats of retribution for nonconformity. Failure to adopt that rule runs the risk of arousing anger in the chief executive, which would incline the chief to take action based on the "retaliate" rule (see pp. 72–76). Usually the retaliatory action is much more subtle than in this case, though not necessarily any less damaging.

Although use of the "avoid punishment" rule is generally disadvantageous to the organization, it can sometimes be advantageous by contributing to conformity among personnel at all levels of the hierarchy to vital policies to which the organization is committed. A major incentive for complying with an organizational commitment that affects the actions of every middle- and lower-level executive who is expected to implement directives from top-level policymakers is the threat of being demoted, fired, or punished in some other way if the executive's superiors discover that he or she is making decisions that do not conform with one of the organization's laws, norms, or policies.[3] Widespread reliance on the "avoid punishment" rule can be regarded as having the positive functional value of stabilizing policy implementation insofar as it contributes to each implementer's commitment to major policy decisions—the ones that practically everyone in the organization expects to be monitored.

But, it remains an open question for every organization whether the gains offset the losses when implementers automatically and unreflectively conform to policy directives. Among the most detrimental consequences of widespread use of the "avoid punishment" rule is the withholding of crucial feedback on the part of implementers who become aware of the drawbacks and defects of a new policy. Unanticipated negative consequences of a new policy often become apparent to those who are "on the firing line." It is dysfunctional for the organization if they routinely continue to apply the policy despite their realization that it will eventually result in losses to the organization, instead of holding off temporarily and giving their superiors a chance to make necessary modifications by informing them about what is going wrong. This is probably one of the main types of unpleasant information withheld from top-level executives to which Harold Geneen was referring in commenting on his experiences as chief executive officer of ITT, when he complained about "people trying to protect themselves" by telling you only "what they think you want to hear."

Three Decision Rules Used in Power Struggles: "Follow the Party Line," "Exercise One-Upmanship," "Rig Meetings to Suppress the Opposition"

The "avoid punishment" rule, of course, is not the only affiliative rule that contributes to poor-quality policies in corporate enterprises and in government. A number of other affiliative rules are also frequently used in a simplistic approach, usually again in combination with other cognitive rules, like those shown in Figure 2-1.

Some of the well-known phenomena of intraorganization power struggles (or "bureaucratic politics") have marked effects on the process of policymaking. Most of those effects can be conceptualized as decision rules that executives use to deal with affiliative constraints. One such rule comes into play especially among upwardly mobile people in the middle levels of a hierarchy who find themselves caught in the crossfire of battling forces within the organization. When the leaders of two units or factions within an organization take opposing sides on a policy issue as part of an ongoing power struggle, executives who do not belong to either of the contending parties cannot readily apply the "avoid punishment" rule if they are asked to participate in policy planning, even though they want to avoid antagonizing any of the rival powerholders. For any highly polarized issue, it is obvious that one or another of the powers that be is going to be annoyed and disposed to inflict retaliatory punishments no matter which position the would-be conformist supports. When confronted with this kind of quandary, many executives adopt a decision rule that could be regarded as a modified version of the "avoid punishment" rule: "Find out which party offers most protection and then follow the party line."

A different decision rule is likely to be relied upon by the leaders of the units or factions engaged in a power struggle when they decide what their party line should be. Particularly when the policy issue could affect lines of authority or territorial boundaries of rival units, the constraint to which the factional leaders give priority consists of a felt need to win a victory for their own faction. To deal with this constraint, the leaders adopt a win-lose fighting orientation, relying upon a "one-upmanship" rule: "Choose an option that will enable our faction to gain, or at least retain, power."

Yet another affiliative rule, which I refer to as the "rigging" rule, is used from time to time covertly by a top-level leader who is an uninhibited practitioner of "hardball politics." It involves engineering apparent consensus and legitimacy for a policy decision that may not be acceptable to some of the powerholders on a policy planning or executive committee. It is often used as a supplement to the self-serving rule or to the "one-upmanship" rule.

The "rigging" rule goes like this: "Decide on the policy choice you favor in advance, before consulting the committee; then rig the meetings so as to muffle any opposition.'' Leaders who adopt this rule use various manipulative tactics: They distribute to members of their executive committees only those intelligence reports and experts' appraisals that support their preferred option; they arrange to hold the meetings at times when the strongest dissenters are unable to attend; they chair the meetings with an iron hand to make sure that dissenters who are inclined to give counterarguments have little opportunity to elaborate and are promptly refuted.

When the rigging rule is applied successfully, the leader manages to create an atmosphere of consensus by getting the members of the executive committee to see and hear what the leader wants them to see and hear, also to say and approve what the leader wants them to say and approve. But the preselected policy that the group endorses is the product of a process that is likely to be of much poorer quality than a policy arrived at after unrigged meetings with genuine discussion of the issues and with critical give-and-take to evaluate alternatives before the final choice is made.

The "Groupthink" Tendency: Reliance on the "Preserve Group Harmony" Rule

In an earlier book on fiascos resulting from foreign policy decisions made by governmental advisory committees, I call attention to the subtle effects of a social constraint that is quite different from those just discussed—a "groupthink" tendency among members of top-level groups that are moderately or highly cohesive. The social constraint consists of the members' strong wish to preserve the harmony of the group, which inclines them to avoid creating any discordant arguments or schisms. When this constraint is dominant, the members engage in self-censorship of their doubts about whatever policy position seems to be preferred by the leader or by the majority of the group. They use their collective cognitive resources to develop rationalizations to support expectations of a successful outcome, usually by invoking shared illusions about the invulnerability of their organization or nation, and they display other symptoms of concurrence seeking (referred to as "the groupthink syndrome").

Instead of fear of retaliations, which is the main motivation for conformity when the "avoid punishment" rule is used, the underlying motivation for the "groupthink" tendency appears to be a strong desire to avoid spoiling the harmonious atmosphere of the group upon which each member has become dependent for maintaining self-esteem and for coping with the stresses of policymaking. The members are concerned about preventing any internal disruptions that might deprive them of the benefits of continuous social support from their cohesive primary group of policymakers. They give priority to this affiliative constraint by using a simplistic approach that relies mainly on the following decision rule: "Preserve group harmony by going along uncritically with whatever consensus seems to be emerging." This affiliative rule can come into play without the leader or the members being fully aware of it, as an inner command to set aside one's misgivings about whatever policy seems to be favored by most others in the group so as to be able to concur wholeheartedly.

A number of historic fiascos appear to have been at least partially the result of defective policy planning on the part of misguided government leaders, each of whom obtained social support from an ingroup of advisors intent upon preserving the harmony of the group. My case studies of historic fiascos (Janis 1982a) suggest that groupthink contributed to some extent to the miscalculations made by the following groups of policy advisors:

1. Neville Chamberlain's inner circle, whose members supported the policy of appeasement of Hitler during 1938, despite repeated warnings and events indicating that it would have adverse consequences;

2. Admiral Kimmel's in-group of naval commanders whose members in the fall of 1941 failed to respond to warnings that Pearl Harbor was in danger of being attacked by Japanese planes;

3. President Harry S. Truman's advisory group, whose members supported the decision to escalate the Korean War in 1950 despite firm warnings by the Chinese Communist government that United States' entry into North Korea would be met with armed resistance from the Chinese;

4. President John F. Kennedy's advisory group, whose members supported the decision to launch the Bay of Pigs invasion of Cuba in May 1961 despite the availability of information indicating that it would be an unsuccessful venture and would damage the United States' relations with other countries;

5. President Lyndon B. Johnson's "Tuesday luncheon group," whose members supported the decision to escalate the war in Vietnam during the mid-1960s, despite intelligence reports and

other information indicating that this course of action would not defeat the Vietcong or the North Vietnamese and would entail unfavorable political consequences within the United States.

For each of these groups, there is evidence of a large number of symptoms of defective decisionmaking. One of the contributing causes in each of the five cases appears to have been strong pressures within the group to stick to a harmonious consensus, which inclined the members to avoid raising controversial issues, questioning weak arguments, or calling a halt to softheaded thinking.[4]

Similar symptoms of groupthink have been noted by other social psychologists in the way Nixon and his inner circle handled the Watergate cover-up during the early 1970s. Drawing on their work and my own detailed analyses of the unedited Nixon tapes, I have carried out an intensive case study of the Watergate coverup and have used it to elaborate on the theory of groupthink.

Wheeler and Janis suggest that the groupthink syndrome is likely to occur in top management groups in all kinds of business firms. A likely example we cite, in which groupthink may have played a contributing role, was a policy decision made early in the 1970s by the top-level executives of the Buffalo Mining Company in West Virginia. Their decision was to continue the dangerous practice of heaping slag to dam up Buffalo Creek, despite repeated warnings by engineers and insurance inspectors that their dam could burst at any time and create a major disaster. The experts' warnings proved to be correct: On February 26, 1972, the dam broke; over 125 people in Appalachian communities downstream were killed and thousands were made homeless. Several years later the company was required to pay 26 million dollars to the survivors.

Taking account of prior research findings on group dynamics, I have formulated a set of hypotheses concerning the conditions that foster the groupthink tendency by drawing inferences from my case studies of groupthink-dominated decisions and from comparative case studies of well-thought-out decisions made by similar groups whose members made realistic appraisals of the consequences. One of these counterpoint case studies is of the main decision made by the Kennedy administration during the Cuban missile crisis in October 1962. Another deals with the hardheaded way that planning committees in the Truman administration evolved the Marshall Plan in 1948. These two case studies indicate that policymaking groups do not always suffer the adverse consequences of group processes, and that the quality of the group's decisionmaking depends upon current conditions that influence the group atmosphere, including leadership practices.

My main hypotheses concerning the causes and consequences of groupthink are summarized in Figure 3–2. This chart is a condensed representation of the causal sequence that links defective decision-

FIGURE 3-2 Theoretical Analysis of Groupthink Based on Comparisons of High-Quality with Low-Quality Decisions by Policymaking Groups

From *Groupthink: Psychological Studies of Policy Decisions and Fiascoes* (2d ed.) by I. L. Janis, 1982, Boston: Houghton Mifflin. Copyright © 1982 by Houghton Mifflin Company. Used with permission.

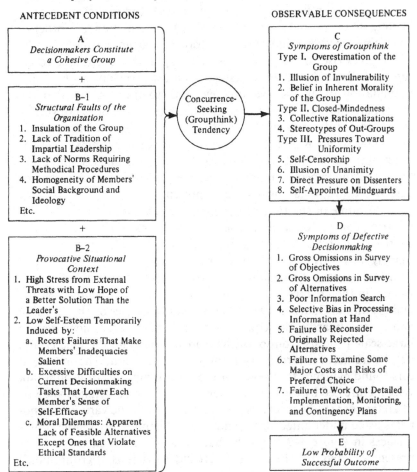

ANTECEDENT CONDITIONS   OBSERVABLE CONSEQUENCES

A
Decisionmakers Constitute a Cohesive Group

+

B-1
Structural Faults of the Organization
1. Insulation of the Group
2. Lack of Tradition of Impartial Leadership
3. Lack of Norms Requiring Methodical Procedures
4. Homogeneity of Members' Social Background and Ideology
Etc.

+

B-2
Provocative Situational Context
1. High Stress from External Threats with Low Hope of a Better Solution Than the Leader's
2. Low Self-Esteem Temporarily Induced by:
   a. Recent Failures That Make Members' Inadequacies Salient
   b. Excessive Difficulties on Current Decisionmaking Tasks That Lower Each Member's Sense of Self-Efficacy
   c. Moral Dilemmas: Apparent Lack of Feasible Alternatives Except Ones that Violate Ethical Standards
Etc.

Concurrence-Seeking (Groupthink) Tendency

C
Symptoms of Groupthink
Type I. Overestimation of the Group
1. Illusion of Invulnerability
2. Belief in Inherent Morality of the Group
Type II. Closed-Mindedness
3. Collective Rationalizations
4. Stereotypes of Out-Groups
Type III. Pressures Toward Uniformity
5. Self-Censorship
6. Illusion of Unanimity
7. Direct Pressure on Dissenters
8. Self-Appointed Mindguards

D
Symptoms of Defective Decisionmaking
1. Gross Omissions in Survey of Objectives
2. Gross Omissions in Survey of Alternatives
3. Poor Information Search
4. Selective Bias in Processing Information at Hand
5. Failure to Reconsider Originally Rejected Alternatives
6. Failure to Examine Some Major Costs and Risks of Preferred Choice
7. Failure to Work Out Detailed Implementation, Monitoring, and Contingency Plans

E
Low Probability of Successful Outcome

making with a set of antecedent conditions (involving a cohesive group of policymakers in an organization characterized by certain types of structural faults when the members are exposed to certain types of provocative situations). When the conditions listed in the left-hand column of the figure are present, there is a relatively high probability that the affiliative constraint arising from the need to preserve group support will become so powerful that it will dominate the entire policymaking process. This can happen even when the executive committee or policy advisory group is made up of leaders who are exceptionally astute and highly competent at analytic problem solving, such as John F. Kennedy, Robert McNamara, Dean Rusk, and others who participated in the Bay of Pigs decision.

Figure 3-2 can be used in subsequent case studies that attempt to investigate the probable causes of policy miscalculations. In order to determine whether reliance on the "preserve group harmony" rule, which gives rise to the symptoms of groupthink, contributed to errors in policymaking, the investigators must carry out a systematic examination of all the available evidence to find out whether the entire pattern represented in Figure 3-2 is present. It does not suffice merely to see if a few of the eight telltale symptoms of groupthink can be detected. Rather, it is necessary to see if practically all the symptoms were manifested and also to see if the antecedent conditions and the expected immediate consequences—the symptoms of defective decisionmaking—are also present.

An example of the type of systematic investigation to which I am referring can be found in a case study by Hensley and Griffin of a controversy at Kent State University during 1977, which was extremely disruptive. The controversy centered on the university's board of trustees' decision to build an addition to the school's gymnasium in the area where students had been shot by members of the Ohio National Guard in 1970. The case study focuses on this decision and on the board's subsequent decisions not to reconsider despite large-scale protests from both the student body and the faculty and despite numerous third-party efforts at conciliation. The investigators found evidence that seven of the eight symptoms of groupthink were manifested by the board. They conclude that a detailed analysis of all the case study observations in relation to all the various components listed under antecedent conditions and under observable consequences in Figure 3-2 "reveals that each major condition . . . was present . . . and that the trustees were indeed victims of groupthink" (p. 497).[5]

One of the most potent conditions making for groupthink, emphasized in Hensley and Griffin's case study as well as in all the prior case studies of groupthink, is *insulation* from direct contact with informative people. The top commanders of the organization may end up concurring on a course of action that many middle-level and lower-level personnel on the firing line could have informed them in advance would not be feasible if only they had been asked about it. Or, as a result of being insulated, the top-level policymakers may fail to take account of a consequential change in the organization's environment that is apparent to others. A clear-cut example of the deleterious effects of insulation of top managers in a business firm is given by Starbuck in a case study of Facit AB. This was a large manufacturing company that produced mechanical calculators and other business machines in factories located in 20 cities in 5 different countries. The company nearly went bankrupt because the top managers did not realize that there would be a switch in demand away from mechanical calculators to electronic ones. They kept relying mainly on information from satisfied customers and did not learn about the new trend in the market from others in their own organization who knew about it. "Although some lower-level managers and engineers within the company were acutely aware of the electronic revolution in the world at large, this awareness did not penetrate upward, and the advent of electronic calculators took Facit's top managers by surprise."

Suppose that a cohesive group of policymaking managers could establish a communication climate that overcomes the tendency of people at the top of a hierarchy to be insulated from others in the rest of the firm: Would there no longer be any danger of the group's vital policy decisions being adversely affected by groupthink? According to my analysis, the likelihood of groupthink would be somewhat reduced, but the danger would still be there if one or more of the antecedent conditions listed in Figure 3–2 were present, including any of the structural faults of the organization other than insulation (listed in box B–1) and/or any of the provocative circumstances (listed in box B–2). The more of those conditions that are present, the higher the probability that reliance on the "preserve group harmony" rule will impair the quality of the group's policymaking and give rise to serious errors that could be avoided.

This view of the dangers of groupthink is somewhat at variance with the position taken by William G. Ouchi in his account of the advantages to be expected if business firms were to foster a "hierar-

chical clan" (or "type Z") form of organization. This type of organization characterizes many of the large industrial corporations in
Japan. According to Ouchi, it has also begun to appear among some
of America's leading companies, such as Hewlett-Packard, IBM,
Kodak, and Procter and Gamble. The clan type of organization, in
his view, is highly efficient because it is a culturally homogeneous
organization in which cohesive working groups are linked together.
In Japan, Ouchi informs us, implementation of decisions is fostered
in the clan type of organization by making use of a special method
(called the Ringi system) for arriving at a consensus on strategic decisions:

> When an important decision needs to be made in a Japanese
> organization, everyone who will feel its impact is involved in
> making it. In the case of a decision where to put a new plant,
> whether to change a production process, or some other major
> event, that will often mean 60 to 80 people directly involved in
> making the decision. A team of three will be assigned the duty
> of talking to all 60 to 80 people and, each time a significant
> modification arises, contacting all the people involved again.
> The team will repeat this process until a true consensus has been
> achieved. Making a decision this way takes a very long time,
> but once a decision is reached, everyone affected by it will be
> likely to support it. (Ouchi 1981, p. 37)

The clan type of organization, according to Ouchi and Price, is
"homogeneous with respect to values and beliefs." Note that this is
one of the structural faults that I have listed in Figure 3-2 as being
conducive to groupthink. Ouchi and Price add that such organizations are characterized by "consensual decisionmaking" and that the
members tend to be "hostile to deviant views, including those that
may be important for future adaptation and survival." Thus, these
authors acknowledge that the clan type of organization could have
some costly drawbacks along with the expected gains.

Other observers of the clan type of Japanese business firm raise
serious questions about its overall effectiveness and its applicability
to firms in America, Europe, and Australia. They claim that there
are additional defects. For example, Lambert asserts that "the fear
of group pressure and reprisal [in Japanese firms] both kills ideas
and allows faults to go unquestioned."

Perhaps Ouchi will prove to be correct about the value of a clan
type of organization for increasing productivity by fostering em-

ployee loyalty, commitment, and implementation of new decisions under routine circumstances. But my analysis summarized in Figure 3-2, based on comparative case studies of U.S. policymaking groups, leads me to expect that the top management group runs a grave risk of making defective strategic decisions, especially when a serious crisis arises, unless special precautions are taken to avoid groupthink. (See Hypothesis 27 in Chapter 10.)

When groupthink occurs in a top management group, it is not always detrimental for the organization. For example, if a group consensus on a vital issue is reached after careful deliberations, the brief appearance of symptoms of groupthink could enable the group to stop discussing the problem they have just finished solving and move on to other pressing matters. Furthermore, when the group is required to make a relatively routine or minor decision, the groupthink syndrome can prove to be more helpful than harmful. It can have the beneficial effect of making for a speedy consensus on an acceptable, or at least harmless, solution, which avoids wasting the precious time of high-level executives. Groupthink also makes for prompt and conscientious implementation, which is generally advantageous for minor decisions that do not require careful search, analysis, or planning.

Consequently, the groupthink syndrome is expected to have detrimental effects for an organization only under special conditions, notably *when it pervades the group's deliberations on a consequential policy choice.* The model of groupthink in Figure 3-2 (p. 59) pertains only to such instances. If those special conditions are present, the ominous final step in the sequence (shown at the bottom of the right-hand column of the figure) can be expected to create consternation and perhaps demoralization among the members of the policymaking group later on, if they are able to see what is happening as a result of their policy decision. The symptoms of defective decision-making arising from the "groupthink" syndrome tend to lead to unsuccessful outcomes, ranging from minor failures from which the organization can rapidly recover to disastrous fiascos that endanger the survival of the policymakers and of the organization itself.

4
Self-Serving and Emotive Rules

In order to prevent individual executives from deciding to make vital policy changes primarily to satisfy their own personal needs, most organizations set up protective shields. The safeguards include official rules governing conflict of interest, role requirements, and institutionalized procedures such as those obliging leaders to obtain the approval of an executive committee or board of directors before issuing any new major policy directive. But despite all the organizational safeguards, leaders from time to time covertly make policy decisions using a seat-of-the-pants strategy that gives priority to satisfying their own personal motives or emotional needs. Often policymakers do not realize that they are doing so. When they are aware of the egocentric basis for a decision, they usually try to conceal it by giving impressive-sounding reasons to justify the new policy in terms of benefits for the organization. Sometimes they end up convincing themselves that the justifications they give to others are the real reasons, in which case their rationalizations enable them to appear to be completely sincere in maintaining that their actions are in the best interests of the organization.

Whether or not policymakers are fully aware of the predominantly egocentric reasons for a policy choice, they can make it appear that they have gone through the required organizational procedures that are supposed to be safeguards against undue personal influences on decisions that could entail a conflict of interest. One way is by conveying subtle threats that motivate powerholders who might object to adopt the "avoid punishment" rule. Another is by making use of the "rigging" rule discussed in the preceding chapter. As a result of the opportunities for concealment, it is sometimes quite difficult to detect instances of policymakers' reliance on egocentric decision rules. Even astute insiders in any large organization have difficulty estimating how often the top-level policymakers give such high priority to constraints arising from their personal needs that they make little effort to find a high-quality solution to the organization's policy problems.

In this chapter I describe two types of egocentric decision rules: *self-serving* rules, directed toward satisfying strong personal motives, and *emotive* rules, directed toward satisfying strong emotional needs.

The Self-Serving Rule

Personal ambitions, greed, or other self-serving motives, as Barzini and Lord Acton assert in the quotations presented in the first chapter, can play a determining role in the making of vital policy decisions, contrary to what is said in public relations releases. When an executive gives priority to one of those personal constraints, he or she looks at the policy problem mainly from the standpoint of "What's in it for me?" The egocentric executive then proceeds to use what could be called the personal aggrandizement or self-serving rule, which goes like this: "Push for an option that will help me get what I want for myself or for my family." What will happen to the organization is considered to be of secondary importance, if not wholly ignored—except for whatever cosmetic considerations the executive deems to be essential to conceal the self-serving purpose and to gain acceptance of his or her choice within the organization.[1]

A prime example of an executive using his influence to inflict a self-serving policy decision on his business organization is to be found in Kenneth Auletta's (1985, 1986) accounts of power, greed, and glory on Wall Street, describing the fall of Lehman Brothers. This is the case study I drew upon in chapter 3 to present an example of unwise conformity among members of a board of directors to a chief executive's new governance proposal. Auletta also includes a detailed account of how Lewis L. Glucksman worked out the plan, in July 1983, to oust his co-chief executive officer, Peter G. Peterson. Glucksman made his crucial decision, Auletta concludes, mainly on the basis of personal motives. Most prominent was his desire for the increased prestige he expected from being the sole chief executive officer. His self-serving motives were reinforced, according to

Auletta, by his feelings of resentment and jealousy toward Peterson, who was more highly esteemed and received more deference from the business community.

As co-chief executive, Peterson agreed to go along with Glucksman's plan, by recommending it to the firm's board of directors and then resigning from the firm, in exchange for Glucksman's offer of a multimillion-dollar severance package, which would come from the firm's funds. In addition to being responsive to the money incentive, Peterson apparently also had another personal motive for acquiescing: He was anxious to avoid the unpleasantness of having to engage in a power struggle with his aggressive co-chief executive officer. Earlier, in chapter 3, I summarized Auletta's account of what happened when Glucksman and Peterson jointly presented the plan they had agreed upon to a meeting of the board of directors. Glucksman was able to manipulate the group to accept immediately the change in governance even though many members had misgivings about the exorbitant severance payment to Peterson, which would come out of their own pockets as partners in the firm, and about Glucksman's lack of qualifications for taking over Peterson's functions. We saw that the "avoid punishment" rule held sway among the members of the board in response to their well-warranted expectations that Glucksman would inflict retribution on anyone who dissented. Giving priority to the constraint imposed by the threat of retaliations, they passively accepted Glucksman's self-serving plan to take control even though some of them correctly anticipated that it would endanger the firm's survival.

In the corporate business world during recent years, reliance on the personal aggrandizement rule appears to be not at all rare among top-level executives faced with the threat of hostile takeovers by outsiders who gain control of a large percentage of the company's stock. Many executives use their power to retain control of the corporation by adopting the policy of buying back large numbers of shares at very high prices, either by paying "greenmail" to the would-be acquirer or engineering a "leveraged buy out" using new loans to buy back stock from public stockholders. This type of action, which usually creates a huge debt requiring large interest payments, prevents the firm from making profitable investments in product development, plant improvements, or personnel recruitment. A substantial proportion of those management decisions, according to Adams and Brock, are attributable to officers of the corporation acting primarily out of self-interest to retain their own executive positions despite the huge losses to the company, because they realize that if the take-over bid were to succeed they would be fired.

In hostile takeover battles, the officers of the target firm are not always the only ones who make decisions mainly in terms of "what's in it for me?" Interviews of heads of large business firms reported by Robert Lamb reveal that many of the chief executives who decide to initiate a hostile takeover do so largely out of self-serving motives. Commenting on a wave of "nonsensical acquisitions" of vulnerable corporations during the 1980s, Nathan R. Owen, chief executive officer of General Signal Corporation, told Lamb that in many instances "it's all ego, building up the ego of the CEO and his desire for excitement, power, and prestige."

Use of the self-serving rule is also to be expected from time to time among other types of policymakers, including government leaders and legislators, despite all the various laws and norms concerning conflict of interest. Paul B. Carpenter, speaking about his experience as a California State Senator during the early 1980s, reports that petty personal considerations frequently influence the voting decisions of legislators, although few ever admit it. Even on important policy issues, he says, legislators often make up their minds on the basis of "personal things that have nothing whatsoever to do with the substance of a specific bill," such as "past slights, real and imagined" by the man or woman who drafted the bill. Many legislators, he adds, are "power players" whose main concern is "What's in it for me?" Their self-centered "pettiness" generates one of the kernels of truth in the quip, "No person's liberty, property, or occupation is safe while the legislature is in session."

Obviously, whenever a group of legislators, government executives, or corporate managers give priority to the personal aggrandizement rule, the entire policymaking process is defective. Little consideration is given to organizational objectives and long-term interests that might be at stake. The survey of alternatives tends to be restricted to those that will be personally satisfying to the decisionmakers. Information search is concentrated on items pertinent to consequences for the decisionmakers' personal goals with little effort to gather information pertinent to consequences for the organization or its constituencies. Costs and risks for the organization that could result from the preferred choice are not in the focus of attention. Implementation and contingency planning tends to be restricted to overcoming possible obstacles to attaining the personal gains expected by the decisionmakers, with little planning to counteract possible setbacks for the organization.

Coping with Personal Emotional Needs by Relying on Emotive Rules

In order to understand the way personal constraints can influence presidential decisionmaking it is instructive to examine President Gerald Ford's decision in September 1974 to grant a pardon to his predecessor, Richard Nixon, who was facing possible criminal prosecution for the Watergate cover-up crimes that had forced him to resign from the presidency. The presidential pardon had extremely detrimental political effects. It immediately evoked a storm of criticism and protest in the nation's press and the Congress. President Ford's approval ratings on public opinion polls plummeted. The persistent negative public reaction may have contributed substantially to Ford's defeat by Jimmy Carter in the subsequent election, an unexpected outcome for an incumbent President running against a relatively unknown contender who could not muster the full support of his own party.

The hostile press reactions included openly expressed suspicions that Ford had made a secret deal with Nixon to give the pardon in exchange for his being enabled to become President by Nixon's resignation. According to those suspicions, Ford's decision to announce the pardon after becoming President must have been a secondary decision based on a prior commitment, perhaps reinforced by the threat of the secret deal being exposed if he failed to live up to it. If so, Ford's main decision must have been made while Nixon was still in office and Ford must have given high priority to his own personal ambition to become President. Thus, if suspicions about the deal were substantiated, it would be a shocking instance of reliance on the personal aggrandizement rule on the part of a man who had devoted his entire career to public service and who had established an excellent reputation as a conscientious and trustworthy statesman.

Historian Robert T. Hartmann in his inside account of the Ford presidency comes to the negative conclusion that there is no substantial evidence that Ford's decision to pardon Nixon was part of a secret deal. Nevertheless, his positive conclusion is that a strong desire for personal satisfaction did play a major determining role in Ford's decision. The personal satisfaction for which he was striving, according to Hartmann, pertained to certain of Ford's emotional needs that gradually developed as powerful sources of distress after he became President—anticipatory feelings of *guilt* from "a recurrent vision of Richard Nixon's blood on his hands" combined with feelings of *frustration* about the Watergate legacy that Ford was impatient to get rid of.

Hartmann asserts that Ford "did fear for Nixon's mental stability and dreaded the prospect of the former President ending his own life." He reports that on one occasion Ford told him, "If anything happened to him, and I hadn't granted the pardon—even though I'd already made up my mind it was the right thing to do but was just waiting around for a better time to announce it—and if anything happened to him, I'd never be able to live with myself." This source of emotional distress, according to Hartmann, occurred against a general background of emotional tension from Ford's feeling "so fed up and frustrated with the legal legacy of the Nixon White House—the mountains of tapes and papers, the subpoenas and endless litigation involving not only the former President but also his associates, the prospect that the press and politicians would continue to harass and hammer away at these unresolved issues as long as he was President—he wanted to sweep it all into the ashcan of ancient history with one bold stroke."

In an emotional state of intense frustration, according to Hartmann, Ford did not display his usual tendency to "confer endlessly" while moving slowly to a decision, but, instead, showed an "impatient streak," which is not conducive to careful search and deliberation. On several other occasions when Ford felt "fed up," just as when he made the decision to pardon Nixon, according to Hartmann, he was quite capable of taking "bold, dramatic action" with little consultation or deliberation. "Every so often," Hartmann says, "out flashed the sword and '*Wham!*' *The hell with the consequences.*" The words I have italicized could be considered as the core of the "Wham! Get-rid-of-distress" rule that is likely to be used when a decisionmaker adopts a seat-of-the-pants approach dominated by strong emotional feelings. As Hartmann points out in drawing "a lesson to be learned" from this case study, when there is little "preliminary game-planning" and little consultation with advisers, "the voice of conscience, or gut feelings, are often inadequate guides" for making presidential decisions.[2]

Emotional needs, such as those arising from anticipatory guilt and intense frustration, can be conceptualized as emotive constraints.

The "Wham!" rule or other emotive rules that dominate the decisionmaking process when any of these internal constraints is given priority are not necessarily used with deliberate intent or verbalized by the decisionmaker. Emotive rules can operate at a preconscious level.

When a policymaker relies mainly upon an emotive decision rule, just as when he or she relies upon the self-serving rule to satisfy personal motives of ambition or greed, the quality of the decisionmaking process tends to be very poor. Right from the outset, the dominating emotional constraint influences the way the decisionmaker formulates the problem and assigns priorities to various requirements (highest priority being given to satisfaction of his or her own emotional needs). The dominating emotive constraint also limits the range of alternatives he or she considers, restricts the search for information, biases the assimilation of pertinent factual evidence, and, above all, precludes careful examination of the costs and risks of the preferred course of action ("the hell with the consequences!").[3]

"Rely-on-Gut-Feelings," "Retaliate!," "Can Do!," and Other Emotive Rules

Whenever a person uses an emotive rule to make a decision, he or she, in effect, is allowing emotional reactions to play a guiding role in deciding what to do. The most extreme example is the "rely-on-gut-feelings" rule, which says you should do whatever your gut feeling dictates at the moment—whether you are in an emotional state of depression, elation, fear, relief, anger, affection, hatred, or whatever. This very crude emotive rule, which usually results in impulsive, ill-conceived decisions, is seldom likely to be a dominant one that is relied upon by men and women who have managed to get to the top as leaders in government or in any other large organization. But a similar emotive rule is probably used quite frequently by top-level executives as a supplement to cognitive rules like satisficing and it may generally be an aid rather than a hindrance to effective policymaking. The supplementary emotive rule goes like this: "When you hit upon a suggested solution that meets the minimal requirements, ask yourself whether you have any negative feelings about committing yourself to carrying out the decision—including any vague feelings of repugnance or apprehensiveness, even if you cannot understand what might be wrong with the choice that is making you feel that way."

If this emotive rule is part of either a vigilant problem-solving strategy or a simplistic approach like the one represented in Figure 2-1 (p. 36), the policymaker regards his or her negative emotional feelings, if any, as equivalent to a failure to meet an added essential requirement. The supplementary emotive rule can help to prevent premature closure and thereby improve the quality of policymaking. In this respect, Freud may be quite right in suggesting that important decisions should not be based solely on conscious goals and related rational considerations because "the unconscious" should also be allowed to have its say. Even vague feelings of uneasiness may be sufficient to induce the policymaker to return to the earlier step of trying to find a more satisfactory solution, one that meets all the essential requirements. For example, by taking account of his or her vague feelings of shame and guilt, a chief executive might be led to reconsider a tentative decision to authorize an unethical hostile intervention or to gamble on a risky initiative that might result in the loss of many lives.

Another example of an emotive rule that can contribute to effective policymaking is the following: "If after completing your information search and deliberations about pros and cons, you have two candidates that look about equally good, consult your gut reaction to see which one you prefer." When an executive adds this emotive rule to a combination of other rules and procedures, he or she might sometimes increase the chances of arriving at a choice that will prove to be satisfactory. It too functions as a valuable addition if it inclines policymakers to be responsive to their own feelings of antipathy or liking, which can introduce important considerations into their deliberations that might otherwise be neglected. Thus, emotive rules can be used in a way that has positive effects on the quality of policymaking, even though they often promote erroneous judgments when used mindlessly.

Most often, the emotive rules that are used in combination with other types of decision rules pertain to negative emotions such as anger or fear. For example, when decisionmakers become angry as a result of being thwarted in a crisis created by an opponent's seemingly unwarranted aggressive action, they feel strongly impelled, without necessarily verbalizing it to themselves or to anyone else, to inflict retaliatory punishment. The dominating emotive rule, which I refer to as the "retaliate!" rule, goes like this: "When you are thwarted, injured, or humiliated, don't let the bastards get away with it; do something to punish them in retaliation." The essential components of this emotive rule are shown in Figure 4–1.

When a policymaker uses this emotive rule, his or her behavior superficially resembles but nevertheless differs in significant ways from what it would be if he or she had thoughtfully arrived at a decision to apply the "tit-for-tat" guiding principle, developed by Anatol Rapoport, as elaborated by Robert Axelrod. (This guiding principle includes making efforts to break a vicious cycle of retaliation by initiating some conciliatory actions.) Like any other guiding principle used in conjunction with the essential steps of vigilant problem solving, the "tit-for-tat" (or "reciprocity") principle is helpful at the outset in suggesting a course of action but is followed by critical scrutiny. As he or she gathers and carefully evaluates all the information about the suggested plan to reciprocate in accordance with the "tit-for-tat" principle, the policymaker in a relatively unexcited state carefully considers whether it is likely to have the intended effect of discouraging any further aggression and encouraging cooperative behavior in the future. As a result, the initial plan is likely to be modified to fit the existing circumstances. In contrast, the emotive rule to retaliate, which is used by a policymaker to deal with the internal constraint imposed by his or her state of aroused anger, is immediately applied as an imperative, with little forethought about its consequences. The action taken in a heated state of emotional arousal is likely to be a much cruder form of aggression, inappropriate to the circumstances, leading to escalation rather than fostering cooperation.

Although statesmen seldom acknowledge that their policy decisions are influenced by passion, they are far from immune. Impressive instances can be cited to illustrate how a national leader's anger can contribute to a shift to an aggressive policy that inflicts retaliatory punishment on another nation whose leaders are suddenly perceived as intolerably frustrating. One such example was a consequence of the series of poor-quality decisions made by President Eisenhower in 1960 authorizing the U-2 flights over the Soviet Union, followed by his publicly denying them until the Soviet leader presented incontrovertible evidence, and then refusing to give an apology. This sequence of provocative actions evoked intense anger in Soviet leaders, according to a number of observers, and led to a shift in foreign policy that has been interpreted by a leading commentator on U.S.–Soviet relations as a tragic loss of an opportunity

FIGURE 4-1 A Simplistic Approach to Decisionmaking Dominated by an Emotive Constraint: The "Retaliate!" Rule Combined with the Cognitive Rules Included in Figure 2-1

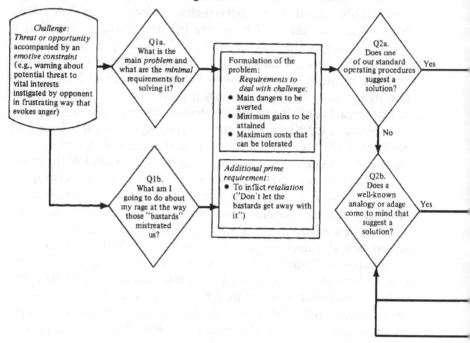

to reverse the nuclear arms race. R. J. Donovan attributes this shift mainly to Nikita Khrushchev's retaliatory action, fueled by his rage in response to the humiliating blows inflicted by America's president:

> The story . . . of Eisenhower's struggle to reach an agreement with the Soviets on disarmament and an end to nuclear testing is little short of tragic. The President tried to enlist the Soviets in the Atoms for Peace and the Open Skies programs, but Nikita Khrushchev balked. . . . Then, just as he had succeeded in arranging a summit meeting to be held in Paris in 1960 to consider a test-ban agreement, the U-2 espionage plane piloted by Francis Gary Powers was shot down over Soviet terri-

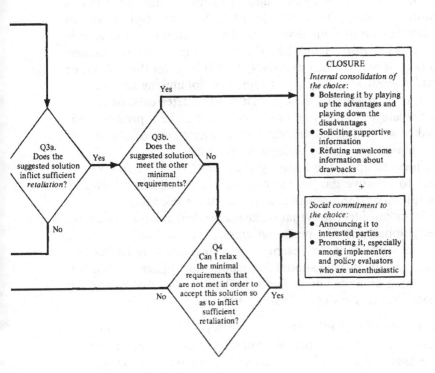

tory. . . . An enraged Khruschchev demolished the meeting in Paris and withdrew an invitation to Eisenhower to visit the Soviet Union. (P. 1)

The intensity of Khrushchev's emotional reaction was apparent when he "complained to [Britain's Prime Minister] Macmillan that 'his *friend* (bitterly repeated again and again) his friend Eisenhower had betrayed him.'"[4]

Eisenhower was noted for his calm handling of major crises but, like Khrushchev, was not always free from the dominating influence of his own aroused emotion. An example will be given later (in Chapter 8) of how President Eisenhower's anger, igniting an urgent need for retaliation, may have played a role during the Suez crisis in two of his ill-considered policy decisions that adversely affected U.S. relations with major European allies.

Another emotive rule appears to be used especially by decisionmakers who pride themselves upon being capable and courageous leaders. It occurs in circumstances that evoke emotional reactions of apprehensiveness about the enormous risks and considerable chances of failure of a desperate course of action that they feel obliged to carry out despite obvious deterrents. This "Can do!" rule, as it is called, goes like this: "Don't be chicken about resorting to a dangerous course of action when necessary, even if it scares the hell out of experts; concentrate all your available decisionmaking resources to find ways of overcoming the deterrents." The deterrents, of course, include whatever dangers or obstacles would make a prudent decisionmaker worried about carrying out a risky course of action that for one reason or another is deemed necessary.

Readiness to apply the audacity ("can do!") rule when deciding whether to approve dangerous missions is a well-known tendency within military establishments, which on some occasions may outweigh other considerations that make for prudent caution. The same tendency apparently can be found among civilian leaders in other types of organizations. For example, it is singled out by Richard C. Cook, an insider at the National Aeronautics and Space Administration, as a major contributing factor in the decisions that resulted in the space shuttle disaster of January 1986.

> The analyst who [had] warned . . . of a possible space shuttle catastrophe said today that a "gung-ho, can-do" ethic at the space agency made it difficult to raise concerns about safety seals on the space shuttle's booster rockets. . . .
> . . . Richard C. Cook, said . . . such concerns got submerged because the "whole culture of the place" calls for "a can-do attitude that NASA can do whatever it tries to do, can solve any problem that comes up" as it "roars ahead toward 24 shuttle flights a year."

In some circumstances the use of the audacity ("can do!") rule can serve the positive functions of galvanizing leaders to take heroic actions and mobilizing—even inspiring—implementers to exert their fullest efforts despite seemingly overwhelming deterrents. But it can also have devastating negative effects, counteracting justifiable apprehensiveness about a dangerous course of action that suffers from serious defects, as Richard C. Cook claims happened at NASA when the decisions were made that led to the shuttle explosion.

A more fully documented instance in which government leaders used the audacity ("can do!") rule, as will be seen (in Chapter 8), was the ill-fated Iranian rescue mission, which was urged by White House Chief of Staff Zbigniew Brzezinski and approved by President Jimmy Carter after meetings with his advisors in 1980. The readiness of some national leaders to adopt the audacity rule, with its emphasis on not being deterred by the obvious dangers, raises serious questions about the validity of the assumption that in confrontational crises between two nations possessing large stockpiles of nuclear weapons, the threat of nuclear retaliation will always be a deterrent to prevent a decision to launch a first strike against a seemingly intractable enemy.

Decision Rules Used to Cope with the Emotional Stress of Decisional Dilemmas

Emotive rules arise not only from the threat that poses the policy problem and from negative feelings evoked by one or another of the choice alternatives but also from the psychological or emotional stress of facing the dilemma created when a vital decision is required. Emotional stress is aroused whenever policymakers realize that whichever course of action they choose could turn out badly, that they are likely to be held responsible and could suffer a loss of self-esteem. These expectations evoke strong anticipatory reactions of anxiety, shame, or guilt, which are among the emotive constraints that can—but need not—interfere drastically with vigilant problem solving.

A considerable body of evidence from psychological experiments, field observations, and case studies of men and women in all walks of life indicate that a high level of emotional stress interferes with judgments and gives rise to ill-considered actions. Arousal of anxiety, which characterizes emotional stress, sometimes enables the person to respond adaptively to urgent needs. This is most likely to occur when the person's level of emotional arousal is low or moderate. But when emotional arousal is extremely intense and persistent, it becomes disruptive and produces nonadaptive behavior.

In a review of the extensive evidence from research on the behavioral effects of psychological stress presented in an earlier book, *Decision Making*, Leon Mann and I analyzed the different ways that people cope with the stress of making highly consequential choices. Our analysis, which we refer to as "conflict theory," describes a number of basic patterns of coping with the stress generated by any realistic challenge (threat or opportunity) requiring a person to make a major decision.[5] Each pattern is associated with a specific set of antecedent conditions and a characteristic level of conflict with a correspondingly low, moderate, or high level of emotional stress.

When decisionmakers display one particular pattern, which we label "vigilance," they tend to go about the tasks of decisionmaking in a careful manner, carrying out to the best of their ability the essential steps of problem solving. They search painstakingly for relevant information, assimilate information in a relatively unbiased manner, appraise alternatives carefully before making a choice, and do everything else required to meet the criteria for high-quality decisionmaking.

As a result of being vigilant, a decisionmaker who is at least moderately competent will tend to display relatively few symptoms of defective decisionmaking (none at all if he or she is highly competent). But if the very same decisionmaker does not adopt the vigilant coping pattern, he or she will fail to carry out the steps of problem solving adequately and will display many symptoms of defective decisionmaking. (See the seven symptoms listed on pp. 32–33, each of which is equivalent to failure to meet one of the seven criteria for sound decisionmaking presented on pp. 30–31.) Of course, those decisionmakers who are extremely incompetent or suffering from severe psychological disorders may practically always do a poor job and make gross errors, irrespective of whether their coping pattern is vigilance or one of the nonvigilant patterns. Such persons, however, are rarely found among national policymakers or in other top-level management positions. If stricken by acute depression or any other emotional disorder, an official usually is promptly removed from office—as in the case of Secretary of Defense Forrestal in President Truman's cabinet.

The vigilance pattern, according to conflict theory, is the dominant approach to decisionmaking only when the decisionmaker's level of emotional stress is in the moderate range, which corresponds to a moderate degree of internal conflict. When his or her level of stress is either very low or very high, corresponding to slight or intense conflict, other coping patterns become dominant. There are four such coping patterns, all of which make for a seat-of-the-pants approach and are labeled as defective when elicited by an *authentic warning*—one that, if interpreted correctly, would require a vital decision to prevent or mitigate threatened losses. The four coping patterns have an important feature in common: The policymaker relies on simple decision rules without carrying out the steps of vigilant problem solving. The four differ markedly, however, in antecedent conditions and in the type and content of the dominating decision rules.

The first two patterns are to be expected when the policymaker experiences so little conflict while deciding what to do that his or her low level of emotional stress makes for low motivation to work on the decisional problem; he or she is inclined to settle the matter quickly by relying on simple *cognitive* rules appropriate for unimportant problems:

1. *Unconflicted inertia* occurs when there is a weak challenge— that is, because of the decisionmaker's ignorance or for some other reason the warning about expected losses is unimpressive. This results in reliance on decision rules that foster recommitment to the existing policy, such as the adage, "if it ain't broke, don't try to fix it."

2. *Unconflicted change* occurs when there is a strong challenge but little prior knowledge of and no impressive warnings about potential losses from changing. This results in reliance on decision rules that enable a rapid choice to be made of an alternative course of action—for example, "Do whatever is recommended by an available advisor who can give you a nutshell briefing."

The two other coping patterns, which differ from the first two in that they involve powerful emotive constraints, are to be expected when the policymaker experiences such intense conflict that he or she is inclined to rely upon simple *emotive* rules to escape psychologically or behaviorally from the situation that is evoking intense emotional stress:

3. *Defensive avoidance* occurs when there are: (a) impressive warnings that evoke expectations of severe losses if the current policy remains unchanged, but also if it is changed, and (b) few signs of available resources that foster hope of finding a satisfactory solution. These conditions result in a defensive

type of emotional state, which can be conceptualized as a strong tendency to rely preconsciously on a dominant emotive rule. If it could be verbalized, the rule would go like this: "Don't beat your head against the wall; avoid thinking about the distressing problem." Along with this general rule, there are supplementary rules concerning ways to avoid thinking about it: "Procrastinate if you can; otherwise pass the buck; or, if necessary, select the least objectionable alternative and bolster it by focusing on supporting arguments and ignoring opposing arguments."

4. *Hypervigilance,* characterized by impulsive action in an attempt to escape from the dilemma as rapidly as possible, occurs when there are: (a) impressive warnings that create conflict by evoking expectations of severe losses if the current policy remains unchanged, but also if it is changed, (b) signs of available resources fostering hope of finding a satisfactory solution, and (c) communications about an imminent deadline or other time pressures that evoke expectations of insufficient time to search and deliberate. These conditions in extreme instances result in a panic-like emotional state with loss of cognitive efficiency and with a strong tendency to rely on a dominant emotive rule that can be regarded as a variant of the "Wham! Get-rid-of-distress" rule. If verbalized, the specific version of the rule would go something like this: "Try anything that looks promising to get the hell out of this agonizing dilemma as fast as you can. Never mind any other consequences."

When policymakers use a sheer seat-of-the-pants approach as a result of adopting any of the above coping patterns, the simple decision rules they rely upon can in certain unusual circumstances be quite good guides to appropriate action. For example, the emotive rule that dominates when decisionmakers are in a panicky state of hypervigilance can occasionally be more adaptive than vigilant deliberation by enabling them to escape an imminent catastrophic blow before it strikes. Nevertheless, as indicated in my discussion of an earlier key theoretical assumption, reliance on decision rules without engaging in adequate information search, critical appraisal, or any of the other essential features of vigilant problem solving increases the likelihood of avoidable errors, which generally will prove to be highly detrimental for major policy decisions that affect vital interests of the organization or nation. Because they generally are expected to reduce the decisionmaker's chances of averting serious losses, the nonvigilant coping patterns are regarded as defective ways of making major policy decisions.

The different conditions that make for vigilance and for each of the four defective coping patterns in response to warnings are summarized in Figure 4-2, which is based on the Janis and Mann conflict model of decisionmaking. In addition to specifying the psychological conditions that mediate the various coping patterns, the figure also indicates the level of emotional stress that accompanies each of them.

The model represented in Figure 4-2 appears to be compatible with Herbert Simon's analysis of the role of motivation and emotion in controlling cognitive behavior. Drawing on concepts formulated by cognitive psychologists, Simon views the human being as "a basically serial information processor endowed with multiple needs [who usually] behaves adaptively and survives in an environment that presents unpredictable threats and opportunities." He postulates that the arousal of anxiety or any other unpleasant emotion interrupts ongoing activity to enable the person to respond adaptively to urgent needs. But he also emphasizes that when emotional arousal is extremely intense and persistent, it becomes disruptive and produces nonadaptive behavior. The conflict-theory analysis attempts to specify the contrasting conditions that determine whether the stress engendered by decisional conflict will facilitate or interfere with effective search for and processing of relevant information that could be essential for averting catastrophic losses.

Figure 4-2 indicates that the coping patterns are determined by the presence or absence of three psychological conditions: (1) awareness of serious risks for whichever alternative is chosen (i.e., arousal of conflict), (2) hope of finding a satisfactory alternative, and (3) belief that there is adequate time in which to search and deliberate before a decision is required. Only when all three conditions are present will the vigilance coping pattern be the dominant one.

Although there may be marked individual differences in preference for one or another of the coping patterns, all five are assumed to be in the repertoire of practically every person when he or she functions as a decisionmaker. In different circumstances the same person will use different coping patterns depending on which of the three crucial conditions are present or absent. (The research findings that provide supporting evidence for this assumption and for other main assumptions of the conflict-theory analysis of coping patterns are reviewed by Janis and Mann.)[6]

FIGURE 4-2 The Conflict-Theory Model of Decisionmaking
Adapted from *Decision Making: A Psychological Analysis of Conflict, Choice, and Commitment* by I. L. Janis and L. Mann, 1977, New York: The Free Press. Copyright © 1977 by The Free Press.

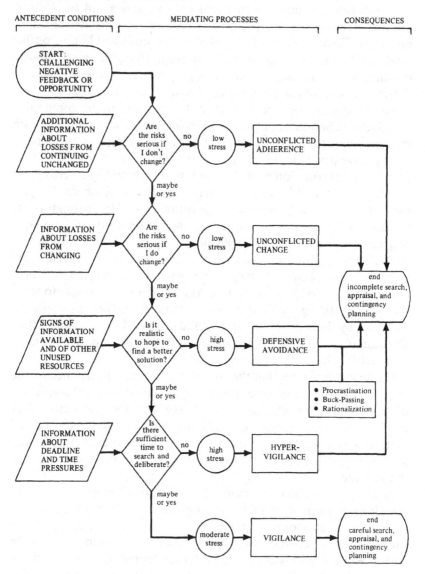

The "Wow! Grab it!" Rule Evoked by Reactive Elation

The use of emotive rules to deal with emotive constraints is not limited to coping with *negative* emotional states, such as those characteristic of high levels of emotional stress. Various emotive rules accompany *positive* emotional reactions, such as elation, and they too can exert a marked influence on decisionmaking. One of these that I have noticed in several case studies of business and governmental decisionmaking is what I call the elated choice or "Wow! Grab it!" rule. It is likely to be invoked when a policymaker frustrated by difficulty in finding a good solution suddenly becomes elated when he or she discovers a choice alternative that beautifully satisfies a few of the most essential requirements, without having any apparently insurmountable defects. The decisionmaker's strong positive emotional state of exuberance is expressed by such phrases as "Wow! This is it!; I'm raring to go!" The emotive rule that dominates the decisionmaker's thinking in this state of reactive elation, if it could be verbalized, would be along these lines: "If you hit upon a promising solution, much better than any you have been considering, grab it; don't take any chance of losing the terrific opportunity by wasting time looking into it further."

When the elated choice rule dominates their thoughts and feelings, policymakers are inclined to move rapidly toward closure even though their information search and deliberations are grossly incomplete. This tendency appears to have been a major contributory factor in the momentous decision made by President Harry Truman and his advisors to approve using America's first A-bombs to destroy Japanese cities in 1945. Later (at the end of Chapter 8), this decision will be examined in detail; it provides an example of what happens to the decisionmaking process when the "Wow! Grab it!" rule becomes dominant in response to a new technological development.

Even if policymakers start off being vigilant in their efforts to find a good solution, they stop being so once they become elated about a new alternative and start using the elated choice rule. They no longer try to ferret out faulty assumptions about benefits to be expected, hidden costs, and as yet undetected ways in which essential requirements might fail to be met, which could lead them to continue searching for a better alternative. Instead, they discount and minimize any signs suggesting that there might be high costs or potential risks. If they encounter unwelcome information indicating that the financial, political, or moral costs of carrying out the attractive course of action will be so excessively high as to exceed what they had regarded from the outset as the upper limit, they are willing to waive the original requirement. They feel that it is entirely justifiable to do so in order to take advantage of the extraordinary "target of opportunity." In an elated state about having found a wonderful solution, they maintain high optimism about overcoming all obstacles, even though information may be available to them indicating that such expectations are not warranted.

A Basic Question About Disadvantages of a Simplistic Approach

In this chapter and the preceding ones I have tried to show that many well-known sources of error in policymaking on vital issues—and some that are not so well-known—can be viewed as stemming from the policymakers' use of a simplistic strategy. When they adopt that type of strategy, the policymakers rely mainly upon simple decision rules—cognitive, affiliative, or egocentric—in order to give priority to dealing with constraints that interfere with vigilant problem solving. From my survey of typical decision rules, a basic question emerges that requires intensive inquiry: When is it wise and when is it foolish for policymakers to use a simplistic approach? Under what conditions do the disadvantages loom so large that they outweigh the advantages? The answer, as we shall see when this question is explored further in later chapters, is that it depends in large part on the type of problem confronting the policymaker. For the present, it will suffice to take note of the major factor I have been emphasizing throughout my discussion of cognitive, affiliative, and egocentric decision rules, which has to do with how *consequential* the decision is likely to be with regard to attaining important objectives.

By and large, when busy executives are dealing with routine decisions or minor crises that are *not* very consequential, the advantages of using a quick-and-easy approach may often exceed the disadvantages. For such decisions, reliance on simple decision rules can make for efficient use of an executive's time and other resources, with little risk of serious penalties. The avoidable errors arising from oversimplified and uncorrected biased thinking, which are bound to become apparent from time to time, do not matter very much if they do not affect any major short-term or long-term goals. But when it comes to making *major* policy decisions, especially when dealing with momentous crises, the errors can be very serious indeed. The more that is at stake, the more dangerous it is to rely exclusively on simple decision rules instead of carrying out the essential steps of vigilant problem solving, as described in the next chapter.[7]

Sound Policymaking Procedures

5

An Uncommon Strategy: Vigilant Problem Solving

Suppose that a chief executive of a national government or a large corporation always used a seat-of-the-pants approach even for the most consequential policy decisions and for the most momentous crises. That chief executive would not be likely to survive in office for very long—or else the government or corporation itself would not be likely to survive. When all vital decisions are made on the basis of a simplistic strategy, the gross misperceptions and miscalculations that remain uncorrected are likely to lead to disaster sooner or later—usually sooner rather than later.[1] Those policymakers who do survive can be expected to have something more in their repertoire than a collection of simple decision rules (like the ones described in Chapters 2, 3, and 4) to draw upon when they are required to make important policy decisions. That "something more" consists of the components essential for vigilant problem solving.

Essential Steps of Vigilant Problem Solving

When executives are asked how they go about making the most consequential decisions, some of them acknowledge that when they believe the stakes are really very high, they do not stick to the seat-of-the-pants approach that they ordinarily use in daily decisionmaking. In fact, their accounts of what they do in such circumstances are not very different from the analytic problem-solving approach recommended in most standard textbooks in management sciences.

Anyone who looks over the numerous textbooks used in university courses that deal with policymaking will notice that the authors do not agree on many important details in their descriptions of how policy decisions usually are made or in their prescriptions for improving the quality of policymaking. For example, in some widely used textbooks, the authors recommend procedures that apply a mathematical or statistical model of rational choices, making use of Bayesian theory; whereas, in other textbooks, the authors belittle those rational quantitative models and recommend, instead, a variety of decision aids to promote creativity in generating alternatives and they encourage a qualitative rather than a quantitative evaluation for arriving at a choice. But despite all the controversies and polemics, there is nevertheless a fair amount of agreement about the desirability of using a problem-solving approach for crucial policy decisions. There is also some agreement about the essential steps required. (These steps form the basis for the seven procedural criteria for high-quality decisionmaking listed in Chapter 2.)

The essential steps of vigilant problem solving are represented in Figure 5-1, which summarizes the main components described by social scientists who have studied policymaking.[2] The figure is not intended as an ideal model for the making of policy decisions but as a realistic *descriptive* model of what most executives demonstrate by their actions that they are *capable* of doing when they try to do the best job of decisionmaking they can under the circumstances. The model describes what executives can do within the confines of incomplete knowledge, unresolvable uncertainties, limited capacity to process information, and all the other usual constraints, which can hamper sound thinking about the generally ill-defined problems that require policy decisions. The sequence of the four steps is not necessarily carried out by vigilant policymakers in exactly the order shown in the figure. In any case, they are likely to go back and forth, especially when a new step changes their understanding of the subtleties and ramifications of the problem or makes them aware of difficulties that prevent an "obvious" solution from being as satisfactory as it initially seemed to be.

The hallmark of high-quality decisionmaking, as I have already indicated, is that by the time the policymakers arrive at their final choice and move toward closure, they have carried out the essential steps of vigilant problem solving (by answering all the key questions listed in Figure 5-1) sufficiently well that they do not display any of the symptoms of defective decisionmaking. Of course, insofar as the available evidence reviewed in the next chapter indicates that the

FIGURE 5-1 Main Steps Characterizing a Vigilant Problem-Solving Approach to Decisionmaking

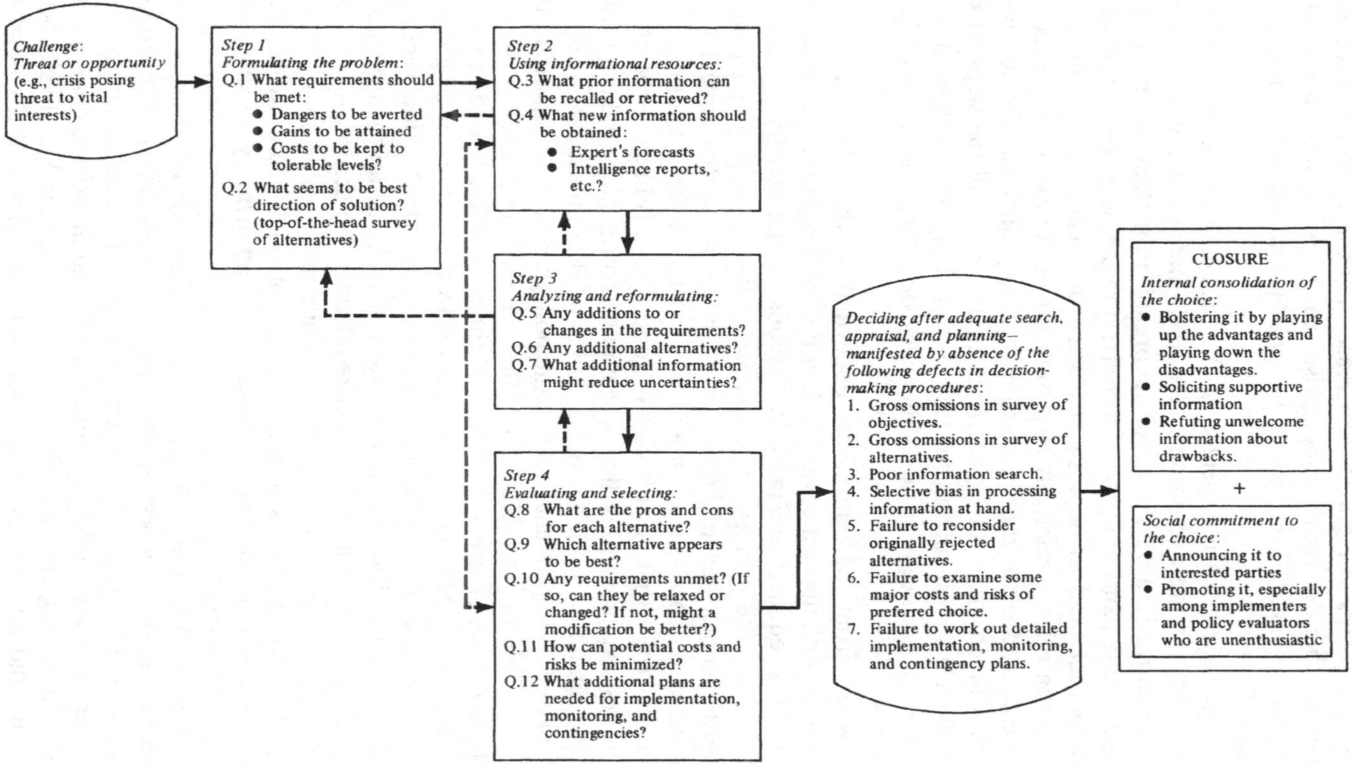

Challenge:
Threat or opportunity
(e.g., crisis posing
threat to vital
interests)

Step 1
Formulating the problem:
Q.1 What requirements should
be met:
- Dangers to be averted
- Gains to be attained
- Costs to be kept to
tolerable levels?

Q.2 What seems to be best
direction of solution?
(top-of-the-head survey
of alternatives)

Step 2
Using informational resources:
Q.3 What prior information can
be recalled or retrieved?
Q.4 What new information should
be obtained:
- Expert's forecasts
- Intelligence reports,
etc.?

Step 3
Analyzing and reformulating:
Q.5 Any additions to or
changes in the requirements?
Q.6 Any additional alternatives?
Q.7 What additional information
might reduce uncertainties?

Step 4
Evaluating and selecting:
Q.8 What are the pros and cons
for each alternative?
Q.9 Which alternative appears
to be best?
Q.10 Any requirements unmet? (If
so, can they be relaxed or
changed? If not, might a
modification be better?)
Q.11 How can potential costs and
risks be minimized?
Q.12 What additional plans are
needed for implementation,
monitoring, and
contingencies?

*Deciding after adequate search,
appraisal, and planning—
manifested by absence of the
following defects in decisionmaking procedures:*
1. Gross omissions in survey of
objectives.
2. Gross omissions in survey of
alternatives.
3. Poor information search.
4. Selective bias in processing
information at hand.
5. Failure to reconsider
originally rejected
alternatives.
6. Failure to examine some
major costs and risks of
preferred choice.
7. Failure to work out detailed
implementation, monitoring,
and contingency plans.

CLOSURE

*Internal consolidation of
the choice:*
- Bolstering it by playing
up the advantages and
playing down the
disadvantages.
- Soliciting supportive
information
- Refuting unwelcome
information about
drawbacks.

+

*Social commitment to
the choice:*
- Announcing it to
interested parties
- Promoting it, especially
among implementers
and policy evaluators
who are unenthusiastic

steps depicted in Figure 5-1 increase the chances of successful outcomes, this descriptive model also can be used, with due caution
about its limitations, as a *prescriptive* model (see Chapters 9
and 10).

The four steps represented in this schematic diagram, it will be
noticed, require a decisionmaker to do much more work and use
more of the resources of his or her organization than does the typical
seat-of-the-pants approach. In contrast to the relatively simple questions that need to be answered when one relies on a small set of
decision rules, a relatively large number of questions need to be answered and often those questions are very difficult. Obviously, it
takes much more time and effort to carry out all the steps of the
vigilant problem-solving strategy shown in Figure 5-1 than to use a
simplistic strategy, such as the ones described in Chapters 2, 3,
and 4.

Right from the outset, the policymaker who adopts a vigilant
problem-solving strategy to deal with a challenging threat or opportunity is required to engage in arduous mental activity in order to
formulate the problem in a comprehensive way. The policymaker
must take account of important goals or values that appear to be
at stake by specifying requirements to be met for a solution to be
satisfactory—that is, sufficiently good that it is likely to be one of
the best available, as well as acceptable to other powerholders within
the organization, including the lower-level administrators who are
expected to implement it. Then the policymaker must answer to the
best of his or her ability the other 11 questions listed in steps 1
through 4 in Figure 5-1.[3] Some of those questions may have to be
answered more than once, as indicated by the dotted arrows going in
the reverse direction. For instance, a policymaker's initial tentative
answer to question 9 may turn out not to be a satisfactory choice
when he or she considers unmet requirements (question 10) and potential costs (question 11), which require more deliberation (returning back to questions 5 and 6) and sometimes more information
gathering (returning back to question 7) and memory searching (returning back to question 3).

It would be overly ambitious and unrealistic for an executive to set
out to find the very best solution, as Herbert Simon has emphasized.
Anyhow, no one can ever know for certain whether or not an even
better alternative might be found if the search were to continue in-
definitely, long after a fairly or very good solution has already been
found and an intensive search seems to have reached the point of

diminishing returns. Nevertheless, an executive would not be likely to take the trouble to carry out all the steps of vigilant problem solving shown in Figure 5-1 unless he or she were quite ambitious about finding a good solution to the particular challenge at hand. The level of motivation would be much higher than at times when the same executive is willing to settle for the first minimally "good enough" course of action that he or she can think of, which characterizes a quick-and-easy approach that relies mainly upon the commonly used heuristic that Simon (1976) refers to as "satisficing" (see Figure 2-1, p. 36).

To go through all the steps depicted in Figure 5-1 to the best of one's ability and to do all the reversing and backtracking required in response to new information that corrects prior misjudgments requires more than simply devoting one's time and energy to the tasks. Executives must also set themselves to do the very best mental work that their minds are capable of.[4] Creative imagination and critical thinking are undoubtedly necessary to find a sound solution to most policy problems, particularly when it comes to generating and modifying viable alternatives (the tasks posed by questions 2, 6, and 10 in Figure 5-1). As Milan Zeleny points out, "the *absence* of a prominent [that is, an acceptable, conflict-free] alternative constitutes the source of most [decisional] conflicts." Such problems, he says, are not resolved by agonizing between pairs of known alternatives but through the *discovery* of one that had not been thought of before: "Making a [policy] decision often means inventing a creative new alternative, not just choosing one among the 'givens.' "

Ingenuity as well as common sense is needed when performing the essential chores of conducting a productive information search (the tasks posed by questions 3, 4, 7 and the information-gathering implications of question 12). An executive cannot do an adequate job simply by putting in requests for computer printouts of all the organization's stored information bearing on a policy issue. It is certainly not true, as Zeleny emphasizes, that the more information one obtains, the better. "More information," he says, "does not necessarily imply better decisions: it is the *quality,* the *relevance,* and the *timing* . . . of information which are much more important aspects of successful decisionmaking." Taking account of the research of Tversky and Kahneman, he argues that:

> *People tend to utilize whatever information is available—even though it might be erroneous or unrelated to the task at hand.*

Consequently, people may actually be hindered from
penetrating to the core of a decision problem when they are
overloaded with extraneous information. Without specific
information, people tend to use whatever knowledge of logical
analysis, statistical laws, and rational evaluation they can
muster. When worthless information is given, they tend to use it
and ignore the laws and rules! It is no wonder that the age of
information explosion is often characterized by incompetent,
sloppy, and sometimes disastrous decisionmaking. (Zeleny,
p. 359)

While carrying out all the burdensome and sometimes demoralizing tasks of critical appraisal, policymakers need to go through the
subjective discomfort of raising skeptical doubts about their own
best ideas for a promising solution, and listening attentively to what
their critics are saying. While doing so, they have to contemplate all
the crucial things that could go wrong, as Stein and Tanter point out.
This has to be done even after they have decided upon the best available choice—at a time when it is especially painful to counteract the
natural tendency to indulge in elated feelings and to move toward
complete closure by bolstering the choice—in order to work out
high-quality implementation, monitoring, and contingency plans (in
answer to question 12 in Figure 5-1).

Successful policies generally are the product of an iterative process
(involving the making of a series of subsequent nested decisions after
the initial policy decision) in order to deal with negative feedback.
For example, the policymakers may be confronted with serious implementation difficulties or specific setbacks indicating that costs or
losses are turning out to be greater than anticipated. Effective executives must continue to be open to unpleasant information if they are
to have the appropriate mental set for iteration of the steps of vigilant problem solving each time it is necessary. (Nested decision will
be discussed in Chapter 8.)

Executives are not likely to have the high level of motivation
needed for doing the very best they can under the circumstances
when they encounter each successive challenge, or to draw extensively upon the organizational resources required for high-quality information gathering and appraisal, unless they judge the threat or
opportunity confronting them to be one that poses a very *important*
problem. They will make that judgment only if they can see that a
great deal could be at stake. Later (in Chapter 7) I shall specify major
determinants of the perceived importance of any challenge. Those

determinants help to explicate various psychological sources of error (such as policymakers' faulty ideological assumptions) that give rise to misjudgments of what might be at stake when executives screen the steady flow of internal memoranda, expert reports, news clippings from the mass media, and other messages about potential challenges that are constantly crossing their desks.

When a policymaker responds to a challenge by carrying out adequately all four steps of vigilant problem solving, he or she will not display any of the symptoms of defective decisionmaking listed in the fourth column of Figure 5-1. The seven symptoms are indicators of failure to meet the elementary criteria of sound decisionmaking (listed in Chapter 2). When none of the steps shown in the figure is carried out adequately by a chief executive or an executive committee, we can expect to observe all seven symptoms.

The presence or absence of these symptoms can be used to judge the quality of decisionmaking not only of top-level policymakers but also of middle-level and lower-level administrators who are pursuing the goals and interests of their own unit—for example, the administrators of a division or subsection of a government agency or the managers in a chain-store firm who are in charge of purchasing, personnel recruitment, or sales in a local branch office. The seven symptoms can also be applied to assess the quality of decisionmaking of an entire set of nested decisions by executives who arrive at a strategic choice by adopting a "logical incrementalism" approach. Those step-by-step decisions will not necessarily prove to be of poor quality, as manifested by a large number of symptoms of defective decisionmaking. As Quinn observed in his study of managers of multibillion-dollar corporations, "In the hands of a skilled manager, such incrementalism was not muddling."

After going through all the steps of vigilant problem solving to deal with a serious problem, policymakers sometimes exert considerable caution about all sorts of residual uncertainties and hedge against unanticipated losses by deliberately planning to take one small move after another in a series of remedial actions. The plan that emerges as a product of vigilant problem solving consists of making an initial commitment only to the very first move and then monitoring carefully to see how it is working out before proceeding to the next one. The successive moves to be made are sometimes well elaborated, with flexible options specified that will depend upon the success or failure of preceding moves in the series. This planned sequential incrementalism is obviously entirely different from reliance upon the simple "incrementalism" rule (described in Chapter 2). It has been described by Alexander George as a "sophisticated variant of incrementalism."

Limitations of Vigilant Problem Solving

The assumption that symptoms of defective decisionmaking are predictive of unsuccessful outcomes pertains to only one major cause of error in policymaking. It does not imply that when policymakers display no symptoms of defective decisionmaking as a result of using a vigilant problem-solving strategy they will make no false assumptions that remain uncorrected, no major miscalculations about the consequences of the course of action they choose, and no faulty implementation plans. Vigilant problem solving is certainly not a cure-all that can eliminate all human errors in policymaking. Other causes of error may persist despite the best efforts of policymakers to use the highest-quality procedures for arriving at a decision. That is to say, even when all the steps represented in Figure 5-1 are carried out by a highly proficient group of policymakers to the best of each member's capabilities, there are likely to be residual sources of error that can sometimes make for crucial misjudgments and poor choices.

Proficient policymakers, like all other human beings, are far from infallible when gathering and processing information for the purpose of deciding what to do, no matter how vigilantly they approach the tasks. Among the sources of error are basic perceptual and judgmental processes that give rise to faulty inferences from intelligence reports, such as those bearing on the probability of various outcomes. For example, on the basis of research findings, Kahneman and Tversky conclude that "people are limited in their ability to comprehend and evaluate extreme probabilities, [thus] highly unlikely events are either ignored or overweighted, and the difference between high probability and certainty is either neglected or [amplified]."[5]

Even more serious conceptual errors may arise right at the outset and persist throughout the entire time when a vital policy decision is being made. Such errors may continue uncorrected beyond the initial decision over a lengthy period when one after another in an iterative series of nested decisions bearing on the same policy problem is being worked on vigilantly in response to negative feedback showing that something is drastically wrong. For example, existing knowledge may be so incomplete that policymakers remain unaware of faulty assumptions about an adversary's threatening moves that result in misperceiving the challenging event or its historic context and consequently diagnosing the problem incorrectly. When a misdiagnosis is made, policymakers draw incorrect inferences about what is at stake and they frame the ill-defined problem in a way that misleads them into looking in the wrong direction for a solution. If that happens they fail to request the most essential kinds of information and they misinterpret whatever cogent information they do receive.

The intelligence reports and expert assessments to which policymakers are exposed may themselves suffer from systematic errors because the analysts who prepare the reports or the aides who edit them share the same misdiagnosis. Misleading conclusions in intelligence reports can occur because of the writers' or editors' idiosyncratic biases and blind spots or because they were deceived by false information from adversaries. Quite aside from the unavailability of valid information on such crucial matters as the hidden intentions of opponents who appear to be threatening vital interests, the fragmentary information and the educated guesses to which the policymakers are exposed may be of very poor quality. This can be a result of misconceptions, biases, or self-protective censorship at lower levels of the organization, which affect what gets transmitted upward. In short, the alleged facts taken into account by top-level policymakers after an intensive information search can be misleading as a result of distortions by the transmitters as well as by the receivers:

> Incentives for biased reporting exist throughout the organization. Incoming information will be filtered through and fitted into existing images, preconceptions, preferences, and plans. . . . Thus, officials will tend to screen out at least some of the data adverse to their own interests and to magnify data that are favorable (Downs 1967, pp. 266, 282). Information moving upward in the organization may also be distorted by the tendency to make it reflect, more closely than reality warrants, what superiors want to hear (Downs 1967, p. 265). Quite aside from deliberate distortions that arise from efforts to protect or enhance parochial interests, each step in transmission also results in some information loss. The taller the hierarchy, the greater the distortion and "uncertainty absorption" as the information moves upward. . . . Finally, bureaucratic emphasis on a single formal channel of communication ("going through channels") reduces the opportunities for independent verification of information. (Holsti & George, p. 294)

The vigilant problem-solving strategy cannot be expected to detect and rectify all those distortions. The best that can be said for it is that it increases the likelihood that some of the worst distortions will be corrected before a final decision is made.

Underlying many of the diagnostic and information-processing errors that tend to persist uncorrected throughout all the steps of problem solving are the relatively stable cognitive schemas that policymakers regularly employ to make sense out of what seems to be happening when they are induced by an impressive challenge to formulate a policy problem (step 1) and to figure out what to do about it (steps 2, 3, and 4). Their schemas include concepts that enter into their presumptions about states of affairs essential for protecting vital interests, stereotypes of opponents and allies, and notions about effective strategies and tactics for dealing with recurrent threats and opportunities, including the most pervasive beliefs that constitute their operational code.

Lindblom describes the ideology of American leaders as a set of beliefs that tie together "ideas about democracy, liberty, pluralism, private enterprise, individualism, and social responsibility in a way that guides . . . [their] thinking about public policy." He points out that certain key beliefs in any such ideology are "out of the gunfire of criticism or at least [each believer] throws up some defense of them." He adds that "ideology offers a trade-off between simplifying ideas that help and simplifications that hurt."

Persistence and Change of Erroneous Assumptions

Ideological assumptions as well as beliefs about other nations, concepts like "the need to demonstrate *resolve* to protect our vital interests," and many related cognitive schemas can be regarded as forming the policymakers' "mind-set," functioning as a filter for processing information. Right at the beginning of their deliberations policymakers usually have recourse to schemas that embody notions about "what will fly"—preconceptions about which actions will and will not be appropriate, legitimate, feasible, and acceptable to others in the organization. They immediately exclude certain alternatives and thereafter are not at all inclined to look into the supposed crippling objections to them, to find out whether the judgments they made at the outset were correct. As a result, the policymakers' initial beliefs and attitudes, unless modified by unexpected information, tend to restrict their search and appraisal activities to a very limited set of alternatives, sometimes precluding ones that would be better solutions to the policy problem than any of the preferred candidates.

Little attention has been paid in social science research to discerning when policymakers' faulty assumptions and other conceptual errors are likely to be corrected and when they are likely to persist unchanged. One variable that appears to be relevant is the degree to which the leaders in a policymaking group share essentially the same views of rivals and allies, the same operational code beliefs, and the same ideological attitudes such as those designated as ultraconservative, middle-of-the-road, or ultraliberal in America. Groups vary from very high ideological consensus about basic attitudes and beliefs through intermediate degrees to highly individualized attitudes and beliefs that are different for each member. The following hypothesis seems plausible: Errors arising from misleading assumptions have the best chance of being corrected when there is a *moderate degree of heterogeneity* in basic attitudes and beliefs among the members of the policymaking group—as when a U.S. presidential advisory committee on foreign policy is bipartisan, including statesmen and stateswomen from both ends and the middle of the dove-hawk continuum—*provided that the members of the group participate in a vigilant problem-solving approach.* By a "moderate degree of heterogeneity" I mean that the divergences in "mind-set" among them are such that the members tend to be dubious about each others' key presumptions, particularly those affecting the way the problem is formulated, the types of alternatives that are excluded at the outset, and the way cogent information about positive and negative consequences is interpreted. But, of course, the divergences cannot be considered moderate if they are so great as to lead to persistent disagreements about major objectives or constant bickering about criteria for assessing the means for attaining the objectives.

In my comparative study of major international crises since the end of World War II, I have rarely found instances of policymakers changing any of their fundamental ideological assumptions in response to new information they had gathered. But I have encountered a number of examples of openness to changes in ancillary beliefs or attitudes, including stereotypes about enemies and allies, which play a role in guiding policy choices.

One such example, involving changes in beliefs about an alliance, occurred during the first week of the Korean War crisis in June of 1950. President Truman was notified of an offer by Chiang Kai-shek, head of the Nationalist Chinese government in Taiwan, to send 33,000 of his ground troops to support the small United Nations force aiding the South Koreans to resist the North Korean invasion. In his memoirs, Truman states that he was quite prepared to accept this offer because it would nicely solve the military problem posed by the immediate need to augment the insufficient forces on hand to fight the North Korean invaders. This was a very worrisome problem because of the enormous amount of time it would take to send troops from the United States or from other parts of the world. Evidently Truman was unaware of the complexities of America's relations with Nationalist China, still embroiled in a struggle with the Communist government of mainland China, which led the President to assume that there was a lot to gain from accepting this offer from a would-be ally close to where the fighting was going on and that there was nothing to lose. But when he discussed the decision with Secretary of State Acheson and other advisors, Paige reports, he learned that there were strong political and military objections to cementing a military alliance with Chiang Kai-shek, especially because of its potential for bringing Chinese Communist troops into the fighting in Korea. Truman came to see that his initial assumption had to be changed after he was informed about the serious drawbacks he either had overlooked or had been entirely unaware of, not the least of which was that key members of his administration were unwilling to accept the closer alliance.

As an example of a marked change in a policymaker's stereotype of the leader of an unfriendly nation, the transformation in Secretary of State Henry Kissinger's assessment of Egypt's President Anwar Sadat can be cited. Kissinger reports in his memoirs that prior to the Arab-Israeli War in 1973 he viewed Sadat as a "weak, ineffectual leader." Privately he had labeled the President of Egypt as "a fool," "a clown," "a buffoon who goes on stage everyday to declare a war," making threats that are nothing but "empty talk." This negative stereotype appears to have played a considerable role in Kissinger's decision to reject an urgent invitation to come to Cairo to discuss a peaceful settlement at the time when Egypt was threatening to go to war to regain the territory lost to Israel in the Six Day War of 1967. When Sadat actually carried out his threat by ordering Egyptian troops to invade Israel, Kissinger felt certain that Egypt would be promptly defeated by Israel's far superior armed forces. Although the Egyptians were much more successful than expected during the first few days of the war, they were, in fact, almost completely defeated (with the help of a U.S. airlift of military supplies to Israel) within two-and-one-half weeks. After having led the Israelis to believe that they could continue to pursue the Egyptian forces a bit longer by postponing their compliance with a cease-fire in place that he had negotiated with the Soviet Union, Kissinger found it necessary to exert great effort to get them to comply. Without that effort, Israeli troops probably could have marched into Cairo to conquer the entire country, which could have evoked massive military intervention by the Soviet leaders to protect their client state.

Sadat's humiliating defeat might well have reinforced Kissinger's negative stereotype of the Egyptian leader. After all, it looked as if Sadat was an even bigger fool than Kissinger had thought because he should have had sense enough to be deterred from starting a war that Egypt would certainly lose. But after Egypt's defeat, Kissinger listened carefully to what he was told about Sadat by the Egyptian Foreign Minister who came to consult with him in Washington. He was also open to other sources of information about Sadat's reasons for starting the war, his capabilities, and his aspirations for settling the Middle East conflict, all of which were completely discrepant with the negative stereotype. Kissinger ended up concluding that Sadat was a sensible and capable statesman with whom it would be well worthwhile to negotiate.[6]

Additional examples of responsiveness to intelligence information occurred among U.S. officials during the Vietnam War. In 1967, Robert McNamara began advocating that the U.S. government should de-escalate the war in Vietnam and should seek a military and political settlement. This was a switch from his earlier wholehearted support of a policy of escalation to defeat the Vietcong and the North Vietnamese, which came about largely as a result of his responsiveness to intelligence data that were discrepant with his original conception of the enemy's capabilities. According to the *Pentagon Papers,* his transformation occurred at a time when others in the government were aware of the same intelligence data but remained unchanged in their view of the enemy's vulnerability to stepped-up air and ground warfare: The Joint Chiefs of Staff strongly urged large-scale escalation; President Johnson continued to favor the escalation policy, as did almost all his main advisors; leading members of Congress continued to give it strong backing.

The new information that led McNamara to revise his assumptions was presented in quantitative reports on trends in enemy losses prepared by the Pentagon's systems-analysis section, headed by Assistant Secretary of Defense Alain C. Enthoven, and in memoranda summarizing other data and analyses prepared by another Assistant Secretary of Defense, John T. McNaughton, who himself had become convinced by new information that his earlier conceptions of the enemy were wrong when he was "an advocate of the 'progressive squeeze' on Hanoi through air power." Strongly influenced by the new information presented to him by his two Assistant Secretaries, McNamara repeatedly tried to get President Johnson and other members of the top-level policymaking group to see the implications of the data that had made him change his own assumptions, but he repeatedly failed. For his pains, he was gradually eased out of his powerful position as the President's leading advisor and ended up being removed from office in a "fast shuffle" by the President, who knew that he "would go quietly and suffer the indignity in silence."

Ironically, McNamara's replacement as the new Secretary of Defense, Clark Clifford, up to that time a "dependable hawk," soon became convinced of the unsoundness of the escalation policy by the factual evidence presented to him in the Pentagon and thereafter became the sole advocate of de-escalation in White House meetings. Subsequently, other members of the policymaking group became convinced, partly by the evidence Clifford presented and partly by other impressive considerations, which led them belatedly to urge President Johnson to make a public announcement in March 1968 that he would de-escalate the war (to which he dejectedly added that he would not run for reelection).

Additional examples of executives correcting their conceptual errors in response to new information are presented by Neustadt and May in a detailed analysis of policymaking in business organizations and in government. These authors make a number of impressive recommendations for preventing common errors in policymaking, such as those arising from immediately charging into action, relying on fuzzy analogies, and failing to check on the correctness of key assumptions in light of available facts and expert judgments. Their recommendations implicitly assume that policymakers are capable of correcting many of their conceptual errors if they use certain procedures.

The procedures recommended by Neustadt and May appear to be ones that would facilitate carrying out the essential steps of vigilant problem solving, as represented in Figure 5–1. For example, they recommend that at the outset of their deliberations policymakers should draw up three separate lists of what is actually *known,* what remains *unclear,* and what is *presumed.* Then, for each of the main presumptions the policymakers should explicitly discuss the question. "What fresh facts, if at hand, would cause us to change this presumption?" Neustadt and May suggest that the answers they agree upon should be put in a tickler system and subsequently should be reviewed to see whether the new information that has come in requires amending any of the main presumptions and, if so, what the implications are for redefining the policy problem, the objectives, and the options.

At a later stage in the decisionmaking process, when the policymakers are discussing the pros and cons of viable options, similar questions and a similar tickler system is recommended by Neustadt and May for checking on presumptions and uncertain expectations concerning the consequences of each course of action under consideration. For example, the leader of a crisis management group might ask: "What things worry us about this plan and what fresh information should we watch for that would make us more worried or less worried?" The new information gathered to answer this set of questions would then be examined to see if the initial assumptions about the feasibility or effectiveness of any of the options needed to be corrected.

The examples given by Neustadt and May, like the ones I have just summarized from my case studies of U.S. crisis management during the Truman, Nixon, and Johnson administrations, indicate that some policymakers are capable of changing their faulty initial assumptions or misleading stereotypes when they are exposed to corrective information in the course of working on a policy decision.[7] How often such changes occur and under what conditions such changes are facilitated remain as important problems that should be added to the research agenda of social scientists who investigate policymaking processes.

In order to increase our knowledge of the facilitating conditions it probably would be worthwhile to attempt to collect and compare positive and negative cases. Positive cases are instances like those in the examples just given: While working on a policy decision, an executive ends up evaluating options somewhat differently than at the outset because of vigilant processing of new corrective information that induces modifications of an initial faulty assumption or misleading stereotype. A substantial number of additional positive cases can probably be found in case studies of policy decisions by leaders in private-sector organizations as well as in federal, state, and local governments.

Negative cases that are comparable to the positive cases could also be sought out. These would be instances of *failure* on the part of similar (if not the very same) policymakers, when working on similar policy issues, to change an erroneous assumption or stereotype, despite being exposed to corrective information. If sufficiently comparable sets of positive and negative cases can be assembled, it should be possible to learn a great deal by examining differences between the two samples with respect to organizational norms and leadership practices (such as those specified in Chapter 10 that are expected to promote vigilant problem solving) and in personality predispositions (such as those specified in Chapter 9 on characteristics that are likely to differentiate between good and poor policymakers).

Although studies of governmental, business, and welfare organizations provide few findings bearing on the conditions under which policymakers do and do not correct their conceptual errors, a great deal of evidence is available from psychological research on the conditions under which ordinary citizens do and do not amend cognitive schemas that have adverse biasing effects on everyday judgments and on hypothetical decisions.

On the basis of evidence from social psychological research, Philip Tetlock concludes that "belief perseverance is not . . . an immutable law of human information processing." He cites several systematic studies that report marked changes in judgments and decisions in response to new information, under conditions where people realized that they would be accountable to others for their choice. A study by Rozelle and Baxter, for example, showed that academic judges were highly responsive to new factual evidence under conditions where they were told that their decisions would influence applicants' admission to graduate school and that they would be asked later on to justify their decisions to a faculty review committee. When these conditions were not present, however, judges were found to display relatively little responsiveness to new factual information about the persons being judged.

Other investigators have also concluded that it is not always the case that people accept uncritically information that supports their initial beliefs or cognitive schemas and reject disconfirmatory evidence. On the basis of a large number of findings from research on social schemas, including stereotypes of out-groups whose intentions and expected reactions to one's own actions affect one's own decisions, Susan Fiske and Shelley Taylor draw two conclusions: On the one hand, schemas often win out over informational inputs; but, on the other hand, the influence of misleading schemas can be countered if corrective information is sufficiently unambiguous and impressive.

> . . . [P]eople tend to make the data fit the schema, rather than vice versa. However, when there is a partial fit, the perceiver may not apply the schema with complete confidence . . . [and], probably will make less stereotyped inferences. . . .
>
> . . . Discrepant information is most likely to cause schema change when the lack of fit is undeniable, that is, considerable, unambiguous, memorable, and stable. (Pp. 177 and 178)

If subsequent research indicates that these conclusions hold not only for ordinary citizens but also for many policymakers as well, the efficacy of the vigilant problem-solving strategy for avoiding errors may prove to be somewhat greater than is implied by my comments earlier in this chapter about cognitive schemas that form the policymakers' "mind-set." After all, potent discrepant information of the type to which Fiske and Taylor are referring is most likely to be encountered by policymakers if they adopt a vigilant problem-solving strategy. Every once in a while—although perhaps not very often—vigilant leaders of large organizations will be exposed to impressive discrepant information that could induce them to change a stereotype of opponents or an attitude or belief about efficacious ways to deal with a threat, as apparently occurred in the examples I cited of changes observed in U.S. crisis managers. Consequently, the harmful effects of applying oversimplified and misleading cognitive schemas to frame complex policy problems might occasionally be mitigated when a policymaking executive or group engages in vigilant information search and appraisal.

My expectation would be that when a chief executive makes faulty judgments about a vital policy issue based on ideological presumptions, stereotypes, or operational-code beliefs, the probability that those misjudgments will be corrected as a result of being exposed to discrepant information will significantly increase if he or she engages in vigilant problem solving. In line with the hypothesis stated earlier, the probability will be further increased if the chief executive discusses the policy issues with an advisory group whose members engage in vigilant problem solving and are moderately heterogeneous in pertinent attitudes and beliefs. The group's heterogeneity would affect both the collection and interpretation of discrepant information because some members would be likely to express skepticism and push for an alternate view at meetings when the advisory group discusses essential questions such as: Which experts should be consulted? What types of intelligence data are pertinent? How should a piece of evidence that is startlingly inconsistent with the chief executive's expectations be interpreted? How much weight should be given to each of the seemingly persuasive facts, analytic conclusions, and educated guesses that support the chief executive's views and how much to each of those that do not?

If a moderately heterogenous group of policy advisors does *not* engage in vigilant problem solving, however, the group's potential for constructive skepticism is less likely to be realized. The chief executive and those advisors who share practically all of his or her basic views and values are less likely to correct their conceptual errors because they are less likely to encounter impressive information that is discrepant with their misleading cognitive schemas.

Once again, however, it must be emphasized that while the vigilant problem-solving strategy may reduce somewhat the likelihood of serious errors arising from faulty preconceptions and from other sources of misjudgment, it certainly cannot be expected to eliminate all of them. The advantages of that strategy are extremely limited when policymakers have insufficient knowledge or cannot obtain crucial information essential for making a sound policy decision. For some policy issues, existing knowledge and information may be so restricted that the problem remains unsolvable even if the best-quality procedures were to be used by the best-qualified decision-makers. Sensing that this is the case, many national leaders may steer clear of extremely complicated policy problems, such as those posed by the threats of nuclear war and other worldwide ecocatastrophes in the not-too-distant future. In order to maintain the requisite level of motivation for devoting time, energy, and organizational resources to working out policy plans that are bound to be error-prone, policymakers and their staffs might perhaps need to adopt a somewhat optimistic outlook about solving the crucial problems. Fiske and Taylor make the following comment after discussing the limited prospects for preventing the conceptual errors that arise from over-simplified schemas: "We will likely muddle through, as we have in the past, with the hope and expectation that nothing too dire will result from the errors and biases to which we are so curiously oblivious." Perhaps by accepting that view, with its faint note of optimism, policymakers can maintain their motivation, especially if they realize that they can minimize errors by using a vigilant problem-solving strategy.

Geniuses? Grand Masters?

Are there geniuses extraordinarily adept at policymaking who can avoid errors and surmount crises to such an extent that, unlike most other policymakers, they practically never need to count merely on muddling through? Can we identify grand masters of policymaking, qualitatively superior to all the others, as in chess—the game that Voltaire said "reflects most honor on human wit"? Are there at least a few people who are extraordinarily talented in the sphere of policymaking, as in the arts, mathematics, science, and various fields of technological invention?

So far in my case studies of four decades of foreign policymaking by heads of states and their high-level advisors, I have spotted a few nominees but no really strong candidates for grandmastership. Among the American nominees were a President and a Secretary of Defense who are regarded by many of their associates and a few political scientists as extremely talented. There was also a Secretary of State who, in effect, has nominated himself in his two huge volumes of memoirs, with the approval of quite a few admirers. But while all three may have been well above average in generating clever courses of action and in critically evaluating the options, they also made avoidable errors, some of which ended up as major foreign policy fiascos. Among leaders of other nations, the President of Egypt who declared war on Israel but later came to confer in Jerusalem and Camp David has enjoyed a great reputation for having initiated highly innovative policies that broke through the confines of traditional ideology and perspective. But again, despite achieving a few dazzling diplomatic successes, his overall track record with regard to avoidable errors is not impressive, especially since it includes starting an avoidable war with a neighboring state that brought his nation to the very brink of total military defeat.

Perhaps there are geniuses somewhere out there who are grand masters of policymaking, but all of them are smart enough to avoid leadership positions requiring them to make foreign policy decisions. The right places to look for grand masters might be in the directorship of major corporations and public welfare organizations; possibly, too, in the judiciary and in positions of responsibility for public policy on *domestic* issues in the legislative and executive branches of local, state, and federal governments.

It seems worthwhile to search for grand masters because by studying their policymaking behavior we may learn something about creative intuition and decisionmaking procedures of the very highest quality that might modify or replace some of the steps of vigilant problem solving shown in Figure 5-1. Even if grand masters cannot be identified, psychologists and other social scientists could pursue the line of inquiry I have in mind for future research agendas by comparing policymakers who are rated by knowledgeable observers as most proficient with those rated as mediocre and poor, to find out what they do differently when confronted with a policy problem. Important leads for such inquiry can be gleaned from research on proficiency and expertise among chess players and people in skilled occupations and also from observations and speculative theories about creative processes among innovative artists and scientists.[8] For example, many of the latter studies suggest that innovators are less hampered in generating imaginative solutions to problems because their thinking is less confined to what common sense says is the reasonable thing to do. Is this characteristic of superior policymakers? George Bernard Shaw thought so when he said in *Man and Superman* that reasonable people adapt themselves to the world, whereas unreasonable ones do not and therefore all progress depends on unreasonable people.

But however creatively unreasonable a policymaker might be, he or she would have to combine the capability of taking off into outer space on flights of imagination, which might be essential for inventing new solutions to difficult policy problems, with the capability of making a reentry back down to earth where the critical work needs to be done to meet mundane requirements that are also essential. Some such combination of capabilities is alluded to in a statement by Thornton Bradshaw, chief executive of one of America's largest business corporations (RCA) in 1984. Commenting about the extraordinary attributes of New York financier Felix Rohatyn, whom he and many others in the business world regard as a master policymaker on business ventures and financial aspects of public policy issues, Bradshaw said that the reason he values Rohatyn's advice on crucial decisions so highly is because it "has always been a combination of real imagination, reaching beyond the immediate situation, and good solid common sense. And he's honest. It's the most marvelous combination, and it's very rare."

The search for rare marvelous combinations might be productive for discovering how the most masterful policymakers differ from those who are merely competent. Such discoveries would be especially impressive if it turns out that when the best policymakers are compared with their less talented but equally experienced colleagues in well-controlled psychological studies, very substantial differences are found in imaginative capabilities, in repertoire of stored knowledge, in effective chunking and retrieving of perceptual patterns, and in other plausible components that might form part of the masterful combination.

Of course, none of the comparative studies I am proposing for the research agendas of social scientists can be carried out if no policymakers can be found who are consistently better than their peers across the broad spectrum of policy decisions that leaders of large organizations typically have responsibility for initiating or approving. Nevertheless, even if there are no master policymakers and the category of "superior policymakers" proves to be a null category, the main line of the proposed research need not die out altogether because there is still at least one branch line that will be worth nurturing to keep alive. Although there may be no single individual who functions as a master policymaker there still could be superior *teams* of policymakers who collectively function as grand masters. To put it more specifically, one hypothesis to be considered is that there are specially talented persons who can perform consistently in a superior way on certain of the tasks that are components of effective policymaking across a wide variety of problem areas, although none of the individuals can do consistently well on the entire set of required tasks. Thus, for example, one person might be extraordinarily gifted at intuitively surmising a good diagnosis of the problem whenever a vital challenge confronts the group; another might be wonderful at generating hunches about the best direction to move toward a solution; still another might be especially good at critiquing the hunches and modifying them constructively with successive approximations that get closer and closer to a good solution; etc.

It is quite conceivable that factor analyses of talent and achievement in policymaking performance will reveal relatively independent distributions of individual differences that correspond roughly to the four main steps of vigilant problem solving represented in Figure 5–1. If so, a "master" team might consist of a number of exceptionally talented specialists: one to formulate the problem; a second to plan and carry out the information search; a third to analyze the incoming information in order to reformulate the problem, to specify additional requirements, and to redirect the information search; a fourth to evaluate the pooled information and to select the best alternative. A fifth specialist might be needed whose expertise is working out implementation and contingency plans.

An alternative possibility is that there are policymaking teams that function as grand masters not because each member is especially proficient in carrying out one particular step of problem solving but because of the way the members interact when working together on all the steps. The members might mutually stimulate each other to perform at their very best. In their discussions they may mutually correct each others' misjudgments when answering each of the twelve key questions listed in Figure 5-1.

If it is possible to identify teams of executives who are consistently proficient in carrying out the steps of vigilant problem solving, their performances could be investigated intensively in research inquiries similar to those that could be pursued if individual grand masters can be identified: Which decision rules, if any, do they regularly use as shortcuts? Do they use any special procedures for carrying out the steps of vigilant problem solving in an inventive and efficient way? For example, do they use some form of narrowing-down process, similar to the logic employed in the Twenty Questions game (such as Tversky's elimination-by-aspects approach, which examines each requirement one at a time and drops from consideration any of the alternatives that fails to meet the requirement)? In what ways, if any, do they use intuition to facilitate their mental activities? When, if ever, do they allow themselves to indulge freely in flights of imagination? When, if ever, do they adopt a critical mental set to scrutinize innovative ideas analytically?

Evidence from subsequent research of the type I am proposing on individual differences could have practical implications not only for suggesting how the less proficient policymakers might improve their performances by emulating those who are more proficient but also for selecting personnel to fill high-level leadership positions. (The topic of individual differences is elaborated further in Chapter 9, in which I present specific hypotheses concerning personality attributes that are expected to characterize the most proficient policymakers.)

Comparative studies of the quality of policymaking in different types of organizations would probably bring to light some crucial environmental background conditions that enable proficient individual leaders or teams to function at their highest levels of capability as policymakers. Such studies might reveal the facilitating role of certain organizational structures and norms that provide the necessary resources for carrying out each of the steps of vigilant problem solving, that permit disagreement among participants without incurring recriminations, and that keep all the other potentially interfering constraints to a minimum. The findings might indicate what changes an organization could make in order to enable its top-level policymakers to carry out vigilant problem solving to the very best of their abilities. Pertinent findings can also be expected to emerge from investigations of hypotheses on effective leadership practices (such as those presented in Chapter 10), which have direct implications for organizational norms that promote high-quality policymaking.

Use of Rules of Thumb to Facilitate Problem Solving

The steps of vigilant problem solving represented in Figure 5-1, which require the policymaker to ask and answer twelve key questions (some of them several times), can be conceptualized as a complex set of decision rules. These rules put heavy emphasis on eliciting and critically evaluating informational feedback.

In addition to the decision rules implied by the sequential steps and the feedback loops represented in Figure 5-1, vigilant problem solvers are likely also to use as auxiliary aids many of the simple decision rules described in Chapters 2, 3, and 4. Going through the essential steps of problem solving in a way that meets the criteria for high-quality decisionmaking does not by any means preclude the use of those cognitive, affiliative, or egocentric rules, as I have indicated earlier. The difference between a simplistic strategy like one that relies primarily on "satisficing" (exemplified in Figure 2-1) and the vigilant problem-solving strategy (depicted in Figure 5-1) is *not* that cognitive decision rules or heuristics are used only in the former and never in the latter. Rather, the difference lies in the *degree* to which decisionmakers *rely* upon the heuristics they use. A seat-of-the-pants approach is *dominated* by the use of simple decision rules, whereas the vigilant problem-solving approach is *not*. In the latter approach, the quick-and-easy solutions or judgments suggested by the decision rules and by various guiding principles[9] are regarded merely as preliminary ideas to be looked into further. When thinking about the key questions shown in Figure 5-1, the vigilant decisionmaker uses such rules and principles to generate *tentative* answers, which he or she then carefully checks out with whatever pertinent factual information or informed opinions can be obtained.

When chief executives or members of an executive committee adopt a vigilant problem-solving strategy, they save considerable time and effort by using simple decision rules, but without displaying any of the symptoms of defective decisionmaking. That happens because they limit the use of those rules to a subsidiary function of generating tentative hypotheses. Any of the simple cognitive, affiliative, and egocentric rules may be used to formulate such hypotheses when the policymakers are answering certain of the questions shown in Figure 5-1, including those concerning requirements that might need to be met, specific alternatives that might be worth looking into, the kinds of information to obtain, possible pros and cons of the outcomes to be expected, the alternative that might be better than any of the others, and possible ways of minimizing potential costs and setbacks that might result from implementing the chosen course of action. In this respect, vigilant problem solving can be facilitated by "intuitive thinking" as described by Kenneth R. Hammond, which is geared to dealing with uncertainties and involves making rough-and-ready guesses. As the vigilant policymakers examine incoming information and deliberate, each of these guesses or hypotheses is subjected to critical scrutiny and is modified if it does not check out well. The policymakers remain open to new information and are ready to change if it does not bear out the expectations based on the simple decision rules they initially employed to guide their problem-solving activities.

In contrast, if the same policymakers were to adopt a quick-and-easy strategy, they would depend almost completely on simple decision rules to arrive at a final choice, without carrying out hardly any information search or critical appraisal. As a result, their decisionmaking would be characterized as *premature closure* and they would display all seven symptoms of defective decisionmaking.

The contrast I have just mentioned can be regarded as referring to extreme ends of a continuum, ranging from very poor-quality decisionmaking, rated as defective with regard to *all seven symptoms,* to extremely good-quality decisionmaking, for which *none of the symptoms* is present. Of course, there are many intermediate cases, including the fairly frequent instances of policy decisions based on what can be called a *quasi* problem-solving approach, when most of the steps of vigilant problem solving are carried out adequately but one or another of them is not. A quasi problem-solving approach, which involves partial reliance on simple decision rules, is often adequate for eliminating most of the symptoms of defective decisionmaking by the time the choice is made, although not all. (For further elaborations of intermediate or mixed strategies, see the discussion of Table 7–2 in Chapter 7.)

Variability in the Way a Policymaker Arrives at a Decision

In contrasting the two extremes, I deliberately referred to instances of the *same* chief executive or executive committee using either a very crude simplistic approach or a highly sophisticated problem-solving approach. One of my assumptions, as indicated in Chapter 1, is that the vigilant problem-solving strategy as well as simplistic strategies, along with various intermediate or mixed strategies, are in the repertoire of almost every policymaker. Consequently, although executives may make most decisions by the seat of the pants, it should not be at all surprising that from time to time they use a vigilant problem-solving approach. Almost all executives who arrive at top-level positions in corporations like those on the *Fortune* 500 list, in government, or in large public welfare organizations are likely to know how to carry out the essential steps of problem solving as a result of having had ample opportunities to learn from all sorts of socialization training in our culture, including on-the-job apprenticeship training as junior executives, even if they have not taken any formal courses in management.

A highly competent policymaker would also know how to screen potential challenges, to determine how much time and effort to invest in dealing with each of them by considering what might be at stake, using various cues to judge how important the problem might be. (See the discussion of determinants of perceived importance in Chapter 7.) A top-level leader would be likely to delegate to subordinates many problems he or she judges to be of minor importance. For the minor ones requiring his or her personal attention, the executive would be inclined to make rapid decisions using a simplistic approach.

Most executives would probably use a mixed strategy for problems they judge to be of moderate importance, either when working on the decisions themselves or when reviewing the recommendations made by subordinates to whom the bulk of the work had been delegated. Only when they encounter a challenge that they judge to be of major importance because it could affect vital interests of the organization, such as a new venture that could result in bankruptcy if it fails, would they be inclined to take the trouble personally to go through all the essential steps of vigilant problem solving and to make use of their power to mobilize their staffs and other personnel to prepare intelligence reports, to carry out detailed analysis, and to participate in deliberative meetings.

After calling attention to the contradictory findings from many different studies in management sciences, James March has concluded that there is no universal way that executives arrive at decisions. (See Note 2 for Chapter 1.) According to March, the available evidence does not consistently support either those theorists who say that executives generally adhere to a "rational" problem-solving model or those who argue that they do not because "satisficing" or some other oversimplified approach is what executives typically resort to. It seems to me that there is nothing puzzling about this lack of agreement among empirical observations. That is exactly what would be expected if the assumption is correct that practically every policymaker shows considerable *variability* in the way he or she arrives at policy decisions—often relying almost entirely upon "satisficing" and other cognitive heuristics, sometimes giving priority to affiliative rules, sometimes to egocentric (self-serving or emotive) rules; at still other times using a mixed approach with partial reliance on simple decision rules; once in a while carrying out all the essential steps of vigilant problem solving. This variability assumption is a basic postulate of my theory of policymaking. According to this assumption, even the most compulsively legalistic bureaucrats who try to make practically every decision on the basis of precedent, and even the most laid-back executives who pride themselves on using their power to make important decisions intuitively or according to their whim of the moment, are capable of using the vigilant problem-solving approach and, in fact, will be found to do so when certain circumstances arise. What are the crucial circumstances? Under what conditions do policymakers fail to use a vigilant problem-solving strategy when it is prudent to do so? What are the major sources of error when policymakers are judging whether or not a policy issue deserves to be given full problem-solving treatment? Under what conditions are those sources of error most likely and least likely to occur when a policymaker confronting a new threat or opportunity is choosing how to decide? These are central questions to which I shall return in Chapter 7; the answers are at the very core of my theory of policymaking processes.

Does a "Nonrational Actor" Model Hold True
for Practically All Policy Decisions?

My variability assumption contradicts an assumption that seems to be fairly widely held among social scientists who write about organizational management. Their assumption is one that I regard as an overgeneralization stemming from valid critiques that have challenged the old "rational actor" model, which used to be accepted by large numbers of economists, political scientists, and management scientists. The current overgeneralization represents an extreme pendulum swing in the opposite direction from the old model. Some of the extreme antirationalists evidently believe that Aristotle was completely wrong, man is *not* a rational animal, certainly not when making policy decisions. Among many social scientists, the old comfortable notion that the policymakers who decide our fate generally behave like rational actors, making full use of their resources to obtain information and to appraise the pros and cons of available alternatives, seems to have been replaced by the extremely uncomfortable assumption that policymakers practically *never* do so. This assumption, in effect, replaces the obsolete "rational actor" model with a "nonrational actor" model that supposedly holds true for almost all policy decisions.

Those who take the "nonrational actor" model seriously as universally valid are likely to be surprised when they discover that a chief executive, not at all noted for pursuing an analytic intellectual approach, demonstrates his capability of obtaining very high ratings on the criteria for sound decisionmaking that go along with a vigilant problem-solving strategy. President Dwight D. Eisenhower, for example, showed considerable variability in the way he arrived at major policy decisions. Often he relied upon a simplistic approach but not always. In *The Hidden-Hand Presidency,* Fred Greenstein's revisionist analysis of Eisenhower as a national leader, we get a picture that is completely at odds with the popular image of Ike as a pleasant but fuzzy-minded chief executive, unwilling to read any memorandum longer than one page and unable to explain his policies, except in terms of vague platitudes worded ungrammatically. Here is Greenstein's summary of the new evidence:

> The Eisenhower library files contain many letters and memoranda he composed, some marked "private and confidential," others classified for security purposes, reflecting

the clean, hard writing, and, by extension, thinking. . . . They
include dispassionate, closely reasoned assessments of contemporary issues and personalities that belie the amicable,
informal, and often vague usages of his press conference
discourse. Startlingly, for a man who seemed, to as acute an
observer as Richard Rovere, to have an "unschematic" mind,
many of his confidential writings display geometric precision in
stating the basic conditions shaping a problem, deducing their
implications, and weighing the costs and benefits of alternative
possible responses.

Eisenhower's reasoning ability and method are best revealed
in one of his confidential analyses of a particularly complex,
controversial issue, a six-page single-spaced letter to his one-
time chief of staff, then NATO Commander Alfred Gruenther,
on the "offshore islands" dispute. This dispute, a legacy of the
Chinese civil war, mainly concerned Quemoy and Matsu, which
are immediately adjacent to the Chinese coast. . . .

. . . His statement to Gruenther of his reasoning is carefully
elaborated and tightly organized; he approaches this emotional
issue with analytic detachment; and his use of language reveals
both experience with political analysis and a jaundiced view of
Chiang Kai-shek and his friends and enemies which, if
publicized, would have undermined the image of simple Ike
Eisenhower, incapable of seeing flaws in his contemporaries.

Eisenhower begins by listing and characterizing the foreign
and domestic actors implicated in any possible action that might
be taken on the offshore islands, in effect positing axioms from
which his analysis follows. (Pp. 20–21)

Eisenhower then turned to the likely consequences of the
solution that Chiang and his American supporters urged—that
the United States "state flatly" that it would defend Quemoy
and Matsu. . . .
[He describes the] . . . delicate balance of pros, cons, and
contingencies. . . .
Anchoring his analysis, Eisenhower stressed, was the root
premise "that nothing could be worse than global war." (P. 23)

The letter to Gruenther reveals more than Eisenhower's
rhetorical and cognitive style; it indicates that he had a capacity
for practical political thought. He assessed the political

motivations of others, anticipating their likely responses to alternative courses of action, and had an explicit decision-making criterion—a decision must be in the long-term public interest *and* must be acceptable domestically so that congressional support can be assured. In short, the Eisenhower who was widely thought of as nonpolitical . . . employed reasoning processes that bespoke political skill and sensitivity. (Greenstein 1982, p. 25)

Other examples can be cited of high-quality decisionmaking by well-known statesmen and executives who engaged in vigilant problem solving. A prime example is the development of the Marshall Plan in 1947 by government leaders in the State Department, which was largely the work of an analytic problem-solving group headed by George Kennan, whose deliberations I have analyzed in a detailed case study. Such examples, however, would be surprising only to those who believe that satisficing, creeping incrementalism, and other "nonrational" processes are so pervasive in organizational decisionmaking that an analytic problem-solving approach is hardly ever used.

6

Are the Main Assumptions About Process and Outcome Warranted?

This chapter is devoted to an examination of research evidence bearing on two central assumptions introduced in the preceding chapters. One assumption is that the vigilant problem-solving strategy (as represented in Figure 5-1) is in the repertoire of most policymakers, along with contrasting quick-and-easy strategies that rely primarily on simple decision rules. When I say that both types are in the repertoire of policymakers, I mean that a chief executive or an executive committee sometimes will use one type of approach for arriving at a policy decision and sometimes the other, without necessarily making a deliberate or self-conscious choice in each instance. The second assumption is that the poorer the quality of the decision-making procedures used in arriving at a policy decision, as manifested by symptoms indicative of failures to engage in vigilant problem solving, the greater the likelihood of unfavorable outcomes of the decision.

Are the two assumptions warranted in light of the existing evidence?

A Jaundiced View of Policymaking

Does it really make any difference whether policymakers show few or many symptoms of defective decisionmaking? There are some social scientists who think that it does not. It seems quite fashionable these days, especially among leading theorists in management studies and political science, to take a very jaundiced view of the prospects of improving policymaking in government, corporations, and other large organizations. For example, William Starbuck argues in favor of three pessimistic generalizations about policymaking on the basis of his own studies of business organizations and his surmises from other research in the fields of public administration and political science, drawing especially upon the critique of analytic problem solving by Charles E. Lindblom:

1. Major policy decisions made by most organizations frequently fail, with the result that an extremely high percentage of all organizations replace their leaders or die because of being unable to surmount the acute crises and disasters brought on by those failures.

2. Top-level policymakers very seldom engage in "reflective" (vigilant) problem solving, even though the executives may pay lip service to the value of this approach and even though they may retrospectively try to make it look as if they had been conforming to it.

3. The "reflective" (vigilant) problem-solving approach would not be effective even if it were often used by policymakers because organizational problems are usually too complicated to solve and, besides, that approach leads to strong rationalizations that make for more inflexibility in response to policy failures than when executives take action without thinking carefully about the consequences of alternatives.

In support of the first generalization, Starbuck presents data on the relatively high percentage of organizations that do not survive, which were summarized in Chapter 1 of this book. It is the second and third of Starbuck's generalizations that are especially relevant for my theoretical assumptions about policymaking processes and their outcomes. Starbuck cites numerous studies of business firms to support these two generalizations, but the evidence is very weak and inconsistent.[1]

Although they do not take as extreme a pessimistic view as Starbuck, a number of other social scientists are skeptical about the effectiveness of vigilant problem solving in attaining better outcomes than relying on satisficing, incrementalism, or other relatively nonanalytic approaches. One of the major considerations frequently mentioned by the skeptics is that even the most sophisticated and skilled policy analysts who use the best available procedures are likely to be seriously mistaken about some of the crucial facts and about some of the main inferences they draw from the apparent facts on the basis of their stereotypes of opponents, operational-code beliefs, and ideological preconceptions. These conceptual errors result in faulty framing of the problem from the very outset and gross miscalculations concerning the expected consequences of alternatives.

I certainly agree that conceptual errors occur frequently at the outset of policymaking and fairly often remain uncorrected. But I do not agree with the skeptics who believe that these errors are practically never corrected in response to the new information the policymakers obtain when they conscientiously go through the successive steps of vigilant problem solving (as described in Figure 5-1 on page 91). In the preceding chapter I gave examples of such corrections in foreign policy decisionmaking by national leaders in the Truman, Nixon, and Johnson administrations. It remains an empirical question as to whether or not residual errors are so pervasive even when policymakers carefully go through the procedures necessary to carry out vigilant problem solving that by and large it makes no essential difference to the outcome whether they use those procedures or not. In contrast to the pessimists and the skeptics, I believe that it does make a highly significant difference. This opposing position concerning the effects of vigilant problem solving on outcomes is in line with the views of a number of sociologists, political scientists, management researchers, and historians who have studied policymaking.

The specific hypothesis that I propose as an alternative to the views of the pessimists and the skeptics is this: *For consequential decisions that implicate vital interests of the organization or nation, deliberate use of a problem-solving approach, with judicious information search and analysis (within the constraints usually imposed by limited organizational resources), will generally result in fewer miscalculations and therefore better outcomes than any other approach.* To put it another way, in terms of the components shown in Figure 5-1: *The fewer the steps of vigilant problem solving that are carried out adequately—as manifested by symptoms of defective policymaking—the higher the probability of undesirable outcomes from the standpoint of the organization's or nation's goals and values.*

It is an important theoretical as well as practical question whether there is no significant relationship between process and outcome, as would be expected from the views of Lindblom, Starbuck, and a number of other social scientists, or whether the above hypothesis is closer to the truth most of the time for most policymaking. In the sections that follow, this crucial question will be carefully examined.

If my hypothesis is valid, it carries the implication that Starbuck's first two generalizations are causally related. Insofar as his second generalization holds true (executives in large organizations rarely use vigilant problem solving), his first generalization would follow (organizational policies often tend to work out so badly that most leaders or their organizations fail to survive). New evidence will be presented that bears directly on whether vigilant problem solving is used often, seldom, or not at all by government policymakers, as well as on the relationship between the use of vigilant problem solving and outcome.

Evidence Bearing on Quality of the Decisionmaking Process

Even among the social scientists who acknowledge that policymakers are capable at times of using a "rational" approach, many are skeptical about whether that capability is used often enough to make any difference. In the absence of dependable evidence, it remains an open question as to how often policymakers use a problem-solving approach that can be characterized as a high-quality process, manifested by the absence of symptoms of defective policymaking. Ultimately, the answer to this question probably will turn out to differ for policymakers in different types of organizations, for different personalities, and for different types of policy problems. At present, however, the main issue is whether vigilant problem solving is used so seldom by policymakers that it is practically a null category. If so, it would be unwarranted to include a vigilant problem-solving approach and deviations from it as central features of a descriptive model of policymaking.

Although the evidence now at hand is too fragmentary to provide any definitive answer for any major groups of policymakers, it is sufficient to counteract the view of the extreme skeptics who believe that simplified strategies of decisionmaking are so widely used in arriving at policies that the steps of vigilant problem solving are practically never carried out.

There is some *indirect* evidence from a number of studies that have found that decisionmakers sometimes choose courses of action that are good solutions in that they take account of the requirements for satisfying their objectives and values, which can be interpreted as implying that the policymakers have gone through at least a few of the essential steps of vigilant problem solving. But the evidence is equivocal because the investigators did not make any observations of the decisionmaking process and the findings could be accounted for in other ways.[2]

More direct evidence of the use of a vigilant problem-solving approach is provided in a systematic study by Herek, Janis, and Huth. The main purpose of our study was to determine the extent to which favorable outcomes in international crises affecting the United States are related to the quality of policymaking by the nation's leaders. In order to investigate the relationship between quality of decisionmaking processes and outcome of policy decisions, we assessed the U.S. government's management of each of 19 international crises by making detailed ratings of the presence or absence of each of the seven symptoms of defective policymaking listed in the fourth column of Figure 5-1. We imported into this research on international relations some of the methodological refinements that have been developed in systematic research in the field of social psychology—including special procedures designed to prevent contaminated judgments and to control for other artifacts that can give rise to spurious results.

The study involved four major steps. First, on the basis of independent ratings by three outside experts on international conflicts, a sample of 19 major crises since World War II was selected. Second, bibliographic sources describing the decisionmaking process in each crisis were collected and the adequacy of these sources was rated by the experts. Third, the source materials judged to be of high quality were used to score the decisionmaking procedures during each crisis in terms of the seven symptoms of defective policymaking. Fourth, independent ratings of the crisis outcomes were obtained from two outside experts who remained "blind" to the decisionmaking process scores and to the hypotheses under investigation.[3]

One of the main methodological problems of comparative case studies of this type has to do with the selection of cases. If investigators were to pick the cases themselves, they could easily rig the selection—consciously or unconsciously—in such a way that the comparative study would yield the results that are expected. In order to avoid any such bias, we deliberately arranged to have the sample of cases selected for investigation by outside experts who were unaware of the purpose of the study. The major crises were selected on the basis of independent ratings of their importance with regard to the threat of war with the Soviet Union or China by three leading social scientists who had studied international crises. The final sample selected from their ratings consisted of 19 major crises that occurred during five administrations since the end of World War II (Truman, Eisenhower, Kennedy, Johnson, and Nixon).[4] (The names and dates of each of the 19 crises are listed in the left-hand column of Table 6–1.)

A preliminary list of bibliographic sources for each crisis was compiled from Richard Dean Burns' guide to the literature on American foreign policy and other guides. Because participants in crises are likely to give biased accounts, memoirs and autobiographies were not included. Instead, analysis of the decisionmaking process was based on scholarly accounts by political scientists and historians (who cited and critically analyzed primary sources in describing crisis events).

The bibliography was submitted to the same three experts who had initially ranked the severity and importance of the crises. They were asked to rate the scholarship of each bibliographic source with which they were familiar as high in quality, adequate, or low in quality. Only sources rated as high or satisfactory in quality (or as written by high-rated scholars) were used in this study. The coding of the decisionmaking process, therefore, was based on published accounts and analyses by leading social science scholars, mainly political scientists and historians, who have studied the major international crises involving the U.S. government since World War II, and whose accounts of these crises are generally regarded as being among the very best. (For a list of all 59 of the sources we used, many of which described more than one of the 19 crises, see Herek, Janis, and Huth, pp. 224–26.)

In order to rate the quality of the policymaking process during each crisis, we developed detailed definitions together with coding instructions for ascertaining whether or not each of the seven symptoms of defective policymaking was to be rated as present or absent, along the lines of the general definitions presented earlier (pp. 32–33). On the basis of careful examination of all the selected bibliographic sources, each of the 19 crises was rated for the presence or absence of each symptom by the third author (Paul Huth), who at that time was "blind" to the research hypotheses. A reliability check on three of the crises with the first author (Greg Herek) indicated complete agreement on all 21 of their independent ratings.

Each crisis was assigned a composite score for defective decisionmaking, consisting of the total number of symptoms present in the policymaking process during the crisis.[5]

Examination of the "Total Symptoms" column in Table 6–1 reveals that contrary to the assertions of Starbuck (1983, 1985), policy-

TABLE 6-1 Process and Outcome Scores for 19 Major International Crises
(From Herek, Janis, and Huth, 1987)

Crisis	Quality of Process — Total Symptoms of Defective Policymaking	Outcome — Internat'l Conflict	Outcome — U.S. Interests
Indochina (1954)	0 ⎫	+1	+1
Quemoy-Matsu II (1958)	0 ⎬ 16%	+1	+1
Laos (1961)	0 ⎭	+1	0
Greek Civil War (1947)	1 ⎫	−1	+1
Quemoy-Matsu I (1954–55)	1 ⎪	+1	+1
Berlin Wall (1961)	1 ⎬ 26%	0	0
Cuban Missile Crisis (1962)	1 ⎪	+1	+1
Yom Kippur War (1973)	1 ⎭	+1	+1
Invasion of South Korea (1950)	2 ⎫	0	+1
Suez War (1956)	2 ⎬ 16%	+1	−1
Jordan Civil War (1970)	2 ⎭	+1	+1
Berlin Blockade (1948–49)	3 —— 5%	−1	+1
Tonkin Gulf Incidents (1964)	4 ⎫ 10%	−1	0
Vietnam Ground War (1965)	4 ⎭	−1	−1
Vietnam Air War (1964–65)	5 ⎫	0	−1
Arab-Israeli War (1967)	5 ⎬ 16%	0	0
Cambodian Incursions (1970)	5 ⎭	0	−1
Korean War Escalation (1950)	6 —— 5%	−1	−1
Indo-Pakistani War (1971)	7 —— 5%	0	0

The cases are ordered according to total number of symptoms of defective decisionmaking displayed by the President and other top-level leaders of the United States government. Outcome scores of −1 indicate both outside experts agreed that the crisis outcome was unfavorable, +1 indicates agreement that the outcome was not unfavorable, and 0 indicates disagreement. Table 3 in Herek, Janis, and Huth (1987) is the source for the outcome ratings shown in this table, but a number of typographical errors in the former table have been corrected in accordance with the corrected table, which was published in the December 1987 issue of the *Journal of Conflict Resolution* (Vol. 31, p. 672) under the heading of *Erratum.*

From "Decisionmaking During International Crises: Is Quality of Process Related to Outcome?" by G. Herek, I. L. Janis, and P. Huth, 1987, *Journal of Conflict Resolution, 30,* p. 517. Copyright 1987 by Journal of Conflict Resolution. Reprinted by permission of SAGE Publications, Inc.

makers use fairly high-quality procedures in making a substantial percentage of their decisions: For eight of the nineteen crises (42%) there were either no symptoms at all or only one symptom, indicating that the policymakers who managed those crises met in a minimal way (or better) at least six of the seven criteria of high-quality decisionmaking described by Janis and Mann (1977). Evidently the vigilant problem-solving strategy was in the repertoire of the crisis managers in the White House who dealt with the eight major crises, which occurred during the administrations of four different presidents.

Considerable variability is apparent in the quality of the policy-making process. In contrast to the eight crises (42%) characterized by relatively high-quality decisionmaking, four crises (21%) were of medium quality (two or three symptoms) and seven crises (37%) were of low quality (four or more symptoms).

The variability in number of symptoms displayed by the crisis managers is consistent with the assumption that policymakers are likely to use a vigilant problem-solving strategy in making crisis decisions under some circumstances but not under other circumstances. (The central question concerning the circumstances that are most likely and least likely to evoke a vigilant problem-solving approach will be discussed in detail in Chapter 7.)

One of the implications of the observed variability is that policymakers who demonstrate that they have the capability for vigilant decisionmaking do not always use it. For example, the decision of the top-level policymakers in the Truman administration in 1947 to send military and economic aid to the anti-Communist government during the Greek Civil War was of high quality, but their later decision in 1950 to ignore warnings from the People's Republic of China and invade North Korea failed to meet most of the seven criteria. Similarly, the policymakers in the Nixon administration displayed all seven symptoms in the Indo-Pakistani War crisis, while they displayed few symptoms in two other crises. Policymakers in the Eisenhower and Kennedy administrations displayed the fewest symptoms. But it is well known from studies of presidential decisions that they did not always engage in vigilant problem solving. For example, their handling of two moderately important crises not included in our sample of major crises—the U-2 incident (Eisenhower) and the Bay of Pigs invasion (Kennedy)—have been characterized as extremely defective. Thus, it appears that while there are variations arising from individual differences in the decisionmaking capabilities of different groups of policymakers (such as those occurring in different presidential administrations), the same President and his group of policymakers, as expected, show considerable variation in the quality of their decisionmaking from one policy decision to another.

Relationship Between Process and Outcome

We turn next to the main hypothesis investigated in the Herek, Janis, and Huth (1987) study, namely that the symptoms of defective decisionmaking, which reflect failures to carry out the essential steps of vigilant problem solving, are predictive of unfavorable outcomes.

Ratings for the outcome of each crisis were obtained from two outside experts who have conducted extensive research on international crises. Taking account of the possibility that outcome ratings might be influenced by personal political ideology, we deliberately chose experts from opposite ends of the conservative-liberal continuum in their personal views about the cold war. As in earlier stages of the research, the experts remained "blind" to the research hypotheses. Neither was informed of the process ratings for any of the 19 crises. The experts provided ratings on the outcome variables for the effectiveness of crisis management by U.S. policymakers for each crisis. First, they rated the crisis outcome's effect on U.S. vital interests: whether they were advanced, hindered, or unaffected during the days and weeks following the crisis. Second, the experts rated the level of international conflict during the days and weeks following the end of the crisis: whether there was an increase, decrease, or no change in tension, stability, hostility, or the likelihood of war between the United States and the Soviet Union or China. The two experts' ratings were combined to yield a score of -1 if both agreed that the crisis outcome was negative, $+1$ if both agreed that it was not negative, and 0 if they disagreed. When we compared the ratings on outcomes obtained from the two experts, we found a fairly high degree of agreement, indicating a satisfactory degree of interanalyst reliability.[6]

The results in Table 6-1 show a strong relationship between quality of decisionmaking as manifested by number of symptoms of defective decisionmaking (rated by the investigators) and unfavorable outcomes (based on the average ratings of the two outside experts). The relationships between the process and outcome scores, which are displayed graphically in Figure 6-1, were sizable and in the predicted direction. Quantitative correlational data show that higher symptom scores are significantly related to more unfavorable outcomes for U.S. vital interests ($r=.64$, $p=.002$), and to more unfavorable outcomes for international conflict ($r=.62$, $p=.002$). These results clearly indicate that crisis outcomes tended to have more adverse effects on U.S. interests and were more likely to increase international conflict when the policymaking process was characterized by a large number of symptoms. The findings are consistent with the expectation that when policymakers use vigilant problem-solving procedures they tend to make decisions that are likely to meet their goals. Con-

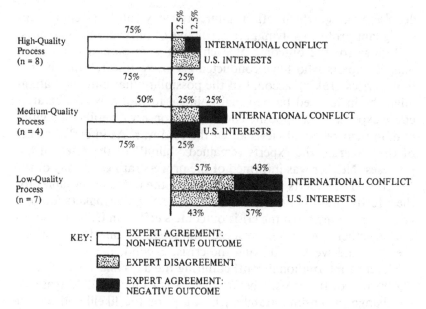

FIGURE 6-1 Relationship Between Decisionmaking Quality and Crisis Outcomes

Note: This figure reproduces Figure 1 in Herek, Janis, and Huth (1987) with one slight change to correct the minor error listed under *Erratum* in the December 1987 issue of the *Journal of Conflict Resolution* (vol. 31, p. 672).

Adapted from "Decisionmaking During International Crises: Is Quality of Process Related to Outcome?" by G. Herek, I. L. Janis, and P. Huth, 1987, *Journal of Conflict Resolution, 30,* p. 517. Copyright 1987 by Journal of Conflict Resolution. Used by permission of SAGE Publications, Inc.

trary to the generalization asserted by pessimists like Starbuck (1983, 1985) and contrary to the expectations of numerous skeptics, the quality of the decisionmaking process *is* related to the policy decision's outcome.

While the correlations between process and outcome support the hypothesis that low-quality decisionmaking leads to unfavorable outcomes, they do not prove this causal relationship. One type of alternative explanation is that the significant correlations result from the influence of a third (unobserved) variable. It is possible, for example, that more serious crises are usually associated with more defective decisionmaking and with less favorable outcomes because more serious crises are more stressful and involve more difficult decisions with higher stakes than do less serious crises. In order to check on this possible type of third-factor explanation, we obtained ratings from two additional experts on seriousness of the crises and difficulty of the decisionmaking. To test the extent to which the correlations between process and outcome were affected by these variables, we constructed stepwise regression equations for each of the two outcome variables (U.S. vital interests and international conflict). This method can be used to control statistically for the effects of any third factor for which ratings are available. The results of this statistical analysis indicated that the substantial correlations we obtained between process and outcome could not be accounted for by a third factor of the type we examined—seriousness or difficulty of the crisis.

Additional alternative explanations for the results also need to be considered. The most obvious such alternative is that the correlations between process and outcome are spurious, the result of faulty methodology. Perhaps, it might be argued, the assessments of the decisionmaking process were not completely independent of outcome ratings. Several precautionary procedures were followed, however, to prevent such contamination. Outside experts who were unaware of the study's hypotheses were enlisted to select the sample of crises, to select the bibliographic sources, and to rate the crisis outcomes. Despite these safeguards, it could be argued that contamination might still occur in subtle ways. For example, the principal rater for the independent (process) variables might have been unconsciously influenced by his prior knowledge of some of the crisis outcomes, even though he was not aware of the hypotheses of the research at the time when he made his ratings. This seems unlikely, however, because interanalyst reliability checks on the process ratings reveal complete agreement between his ratings and the ratings made independently by a second analyst who was unfamiliar with many of the crisis outcomes when he rated their process. Hence, it does not seem probable that the process ratings were biased to any significant degree by the rater's personal judgments about outcomes.

Contamination might also have been introduced unconsciously by the outside experts: their knowledge of how the crisis decisions were reached might conceivably have influenced their outcome ratings. This seems a fairly remote possibility, however, especially because the experts were so completely occupied with discussing outcomes during the rating interviews that they had little chance to think about process; they said nothing at all about the decisionmaking process for any of the 19 crises.

A third possible source of contamination is the bibliographic materials themselves. We avoided crisis participants' memoirs and autobiographies because they might contain self-serving justifications and distortions; we relied entirely on the best available scholarly sources. But perhaps even these scholars' knowledge of crisis outcomes unconsciously influenced their accounts of the decisionmaking process. Our principal safeguard here is our reliance on the standards of sound scholarship. We assume that highly competent historians and political scientists who meet those standards are less likely than others to distort facts to fit their expectations. We also relied on multiple scholarly sources whenever possible, thereby protecting the results from undue influence by any single (potentially biased) source.

Although we were able to rule out seriousness of the crisis and difficulty of decisionmaking as hidden third variables responsible for the results, there is always the possibility that other hidden factors we did not look into could be responsible for the observed correlations. Because our data are correlational, we cannot conclude that the quality of decisionmaking processes, as indicated by the number of symptoms of defective decisionmaking, plays a causal role in producing the policy decision outcomes. It is a plausible interpretation, however, not contradicted or disconfirmed by any of the results.

The findings of the present study thus bear out the surmises of those social scientists who have concluded that poor-quality procedures used in arriving at a policy decision give rise to avoidable errors that increase the likelihood of obtaining an unsatisfactory outcome. Stein and Tanter, for example, assert an equivalent proposition in terms of favorable outcomes in their analysis of policy decisions made during international crises. "Other things being equal," they state, "'good' procedures are more likely to produce 'good' outcomes." Their account of "good" procedures includes the key components of vigilant problem solving: The decisionmakers identify their options, estimate the likely consequences of the options, consider the trade-offs as they examine expected costs and benefits prior to making their selection of "that option which promises the greatest gain or the smallest loss" and then work out detailed implementation and contingency plans. Stein and Tanter add, however, that an *imperfect* positive correlation is to be expected between quality of procedures and outcome: "Those who recommend systematic procedures recognize, of course, that they cannot assure good outcomes in each case."

Why might a large number of symptoms of defective decisionmaking procedures lead to somewhat worse outcomes? To answer this question requires articulating the various determinants of unsuccessful outcomes. It seems likely that when a national government faces international crises, the outcomes result from a combination of the leaders' decisionmaking and implementation and from the actions taken by adversaries together with other uncontrollable events, including chance factors (see pp. 3–4). If the nation's leaders use a nonvigilant approach, they tend to ignore important warnings, facts, and contingencies. A frequent result is avoidable losses and failure to achieve their objectives. A vigilant approach obviously does not guarantee success, since uncontrollable external and chance factors still influence outcomes. The generalization that fewer *avoidable* errors are to be expected from a vigilant problem-solving approach than from any other approach does not overlook the well-known reasons why the best-laid plans can go awry. For example, Richard K. Betts has argued that failures in making estimates from intelligence data are inevitable due to the inherent ambiguity of the available information. And, as I pointed out in the preceding chapter, even when policymakers adopt a vigilant problem-solving strategy and obtain adequate information that is unambiguous and valid, they still might make avoidable miscalculations. For example, their ideological biases may sometimes prevent them from interpreting the implications of discrepant information correctly. As a result, they may fail to realize that the new evidence calls into question a major preconception underlying their strong preference for a particular course of action that is more likely to fail than other viable alternatives.

When policymakers regularly use a vigilant problem-solving strategy, some *unavoidable* errors are bound to occur from time to time as a result of "unresolvable ignorance" as well as unforeseeable accidents and other chance occurrences commonly referred to as "bad luck." Such errors, which can lead to unsuccessful outcomes, are always to be expected; their probability of occurrence will not be affected in any way by the type of decisionmaking strategy used. The absolute level of unavoidable errors depends upon the culture's level of ignorance concerning the consequences of alternative courses of action and other factors, some of which are not yet well understood. But, as general knowledge about consequences increases, some hitherto unavoidable errors will become avoidable.

Because of chronic limitations on the human mind in dealing with the complexities of policy issues, some unsuccessful outcomes resulting from avoidable as well as unavoidable errors in decisionmaking are to be expected no matter how carefully the policymakers carry out all the steps of vigilant problem solving and no matter how creatively and intelligently they make use of decision rules and guiding principles in combination with critical thinking. But vigilant problem solving, which requires the fullest use of available information and judgmental resources, increases the likelihood that the course of action chosen will anticipate the consequences as well as possible and that contingency plans will be ready for counteracting or minimizing setbacks and threats of serious losses when they occur.

Obviously, a vigilant problem-solving approach is not an all-or-none affair. Sometimes the decisionmaker conscientiously carries out some steps, but deals with the tasks required by other steps in a superficial manner or not at all. In such instances, the decisionmaker's procedures are likely to be of intermediate quality, not as good as when all of the steps are taken, but not as poor as when no steps are taken at all. Our results suggest that policy decisions of intermediate quality will tend to have outcomes that are correspondingly intermediate between good and poor.

There are undoubtedly certain types of decisions for which the failure to use a vigilant problem-solving strategy is not related to poor outcomes. For example, James March describes a variety of pseudo-decisions that are made for ceremonial purposes, as social rituals that reinforce "the myth of organizational choice" or fulfill "role-expectations, duties, or earlier commitments." The organization's leaders may act as though they were making a genuine policy decision and talk about various objectives, such as increasing organizational efficiency, eliminating health hazards, or improving relationships with adversaries. But they actually do nothing to implement the decision "after having devoted much time, energy, and enthusiasm to making it." The apparent quality of the decision-making process in such instances would obviously have no effect on the outcome insofar as the alleged objectives are concerned.

There are other pseudo-decisions which differ from the purely ceremonial ones in that they may be partially implemented. Included in this category are policy decisions designed for hidden public relations purposes rather than the objectives that are publicly proclaimed—such as to reduce air pollution or to eliminate discrimination against women or against minority ethnic groups. There is no real intention among the dominant policymakers to implement the new policy except in a token manner to make the organization look good in the eyes of those pressure groups and constituencies that want the policy change. In such instances, the quality of the decisionmaking process would be expected to affect the hidden objective but not the alleged objectives. There would be the same expectation whenever policymakers are deceitful about the purposes of any policy decision that may be fully implemented—as when a government sends a military force to a client state allegedly to protect its citizens but actually with the intention of bringing about political changes at minimal cost, or when a business conglomerate takes over a firm on the verge of bankruptcy allegedly to turn it around and make a profit, but actually with the objective of gaining a tax write-off. (A number of other specific types of decisions that require additional provisos with regard to the expected relationship between quality of process and outcome will be discussed in Chapter 8, when I call attention to limitations of the integrated model of policymaking.)

Further research is required, of course, to test the generality of the positive relationship between process and outcome, which will help to define the limiting conditions under which that relationship can be expected to be observable. Studies similar to the one I have been describing are needed to observe the relationship between process measures and outcome ratings in a variety of decisionmaking contexts—for example, for domestic policy decisions by national, state, and local governments, and for strategic decisions by national committees that influence policies in science, education, medicine, law, or other professions, by business corporations, and by human service organizations—in many different countries.

Earlier I mentioned that a dominant trend in present-day discussions of management science and political science is to take a very dim view of the prospects for changing policymaking processes in government or in other large organizations. This view leads to the expectation that little or no improvement in crisis prevention or crisis management can be expected from introducing systematic methods of problem solving and other aids to effective decisionmaking. The significant relationships between process and outcome in international crises observed in the Herek, Janis, and Huth study support a different view of the policymaking process. The findings reinforce the expectation that international conflict management could be improved by introducing appropriate problem-solving procedures into the policymaking process. Such procedures could make for more successful outcomes, reducing the severity of international conflict while furthering the policymakers' national security objectives and other vital interests.

If subsequent studies in diverse types of organizations confirm the relationship between decisionmaking processes and outcome, the results will also imply that policy decisions can be improved by providing a special type of training for executives in decisionmaking roles— training that focuses on vigilant problem-solving skills and leadership practices that promote vigilance. (For specific hypotheses that indicate how leadership practices might be improved, see Chapter 10). Insofar as the observed relationship holds true, training oriented toward avoiding the seven symptoms of defective decisionmaking can be expected to result in more effective policymaking that will be evidenced by more successful outcomes.

Tentative Conclusions

Although the evidence I have reviewed is not definitive, there appears to be a sufficient empirical basis for regarding as plausible the two major assumptions stated at the beginning of this chapter. The evidence shows that a small but substantial percentage of the policy decisions that have been investigated were of fairly high quality, as manifested by no symptoms or only one symptom of defective decisionmaking. This finding is consistent with the assumption that many, if not all, policymakers are capable of using a vigilant problem-solving approach, even though for the majority of policy decisions they may use it only partially or not at all. The second assumption is that failures to carry out the steps of vigilant problem solving, as manifested by symptoms of defective policymaking, are predictive of unfavorable outcomes. As I have repeatedly emphasized, however, this assumption does not imply that failure to use the high-quality procedures of vigilant problem solving is the only cause of unfavorable outcomes. Use of the vigilant problem-solving strategy must be considered as only one of the major determinants of successful versus unsuccessful consequences of policy decisions—

but one worthy of special emphasis because, unlike almost all the other determinants, it is largely *under the control of the policymakers themselves.*

Since the two key theoretical assumptions appear to be warranted in light of the empirical evidence now at hand, the next step in our inquiry will be to examine the major question posed earlier: *Under what conditions are policymakers most likely to adopt a vigilant problem-solving approach rather than resorting to a simplistic approach (or using a mixed approach) when confronted with the necessity of making a policy decision?* By directing our inquiry toward answering this question, we should learn more about major sources of avoidable errors in policymaking, because it requires us to specify the circumstances least conducive and most conducive to engaging in a decisionmaking process dominated by reliance on simple decision rules, instead of carrying out the essential steps of vigilant problem solving. The preliminary theoretical model presented in the next chapter attempts to answer this key question, taking account of prior research bearing mainly on situational factors that inhibit or promote vigilant problem solving.

A New Theoretical Framework

7

The Constraints Model
of Policymaking Processes

This chapter presents a preliminary theoretical framework that specifies the conditions under which a policymaker will resort to a quick-and-easy strategy that relies primarily on simple cognitive, affiliative, or egocentric decision rules. It also specifies the contrasting conditions under which a policymaker will use a vigilant problem-solving strategy.

At the beginning of this book I pointed out that social science knowledge about the basic processes of policy decisionmaking is in such a fragmentary and chaotic state that many social scientists believe it is utterly unrealistic to expect in the foreseeable future a comprehensive theory that will offer adequate explanations to account for all the decisionmaking of all the people all of the time. Kinder and Weiss, for example, take the pessimistic position that the best we can hope for at present is a "few notions" that are not well integrated to account for "some of the processes for some of the people some of the time." But if the theoretical framework I am attempting to construct is as promising as I think it is, I expect social science theory to attain a much more ambitious objective within the near future—a theoretical model that can account for most decisionmaking processes for most policymakers most of the time.

Key Postulates

My preliminary theoretical model is based on the four main assumptions or postulates stated in the first chapter. One is the key postulate discussed in detail in the preceding chapter—namely, that *the quality of the policymaking procedures is a determinant of the outcome.* The second postulate, which was also discussed in Chapter 6, is that most policymakers are capable of using high-quality procedures, which require carrying out the essential steps of vigilant problem solving. The other two key postulates require additional discussion.

The third postulate is an obvious and widely accepted generalization: *When policymakers are confronted with any threat or opportunity that poses a challenge to continuing business as usual, they will not devote the time or other resources necessary for carrying out the essential steps of vigilant problem solving if they personally judge the problem to be unimportant.* The fourth postulate, which pertains to all the various types of constraints shown in Figure 1-1 (p. 16), is much less obvious and more debatable, so it cannot be expected to be generally accepted by social scientists until it is extensively investigated in studies of many different kinds of policy decisions in a variety of organizations: *Even when policymakers believe that a threat or opportunity poses a problem that is extremely important, they will not adopt a vigilant problem-solving approach unless they perceive or intuitively presume all salient constraints to be sufficiently manageable that none has to be given top priority.* According to this postulate, whenever policymakers consciously or preconsciously evaluate one or another of the cognitive, affiliative, or egocentric constraints as so potent and difficult to manage that dealing with it is more important than finding a high-quality solution to the problem, they will adopt a simplistic strategy. When a policymaker uses that type of procedural strategy (as described in Chapters 2, 3, and 4), he or she relies primarily upon a few simple decision rules to cope with the dominating constraint, instead of carrying out the essential steps of vigilant problem solving.

Perceived Importance of the Issue—A Major Determinant of Vigilant Problem Solving

Most executives realize that vigilant problem solving is very costly in terms of the amount of time, effort, and money they have to spend obtaining relevant information and holding meetings to deliberate about alternative courses of action. They are unlikely to make such high demands on themselves and the resources of their organization unless they are confronted by a policy issue that they perceive to be extremely important because vital interests are at stake. Thus, one major determinant of whether or not a vigilant problem-solving approach will be used is the perceived importance of the challenge requiring a policy decision—the threat to the organization or the opportunity to attain a highly valued goal.

When the powerholders in an organization think that a great deal is at stake, as in a major crisis that threatens the survival of the organization, they are much more likely to initiate and carry out the successive steps of vigilant problem solving than if they judge that very little is at stake. There is, of course, an essential proviso—namely, that the policymakers' emotional stress does not reach such a high level that they misperceive the dangers or resort to using the emotive decision rules of defensive avoidance or hypervigilance, which result in many symptoms of defective decisionmaking. At the opposite extreme, when an executive makes the judgment that a threat is unimportant, he or she, in effect, has surmised that none of the organization's main objectives appears to be jeopardized and that none of his or her own utilitarian or social goals, or moral values appears to be implicated. For such apparently trivial matters, a policymaker can be expected to waste little time or energy by ignoring the alleged problem or delegating it to a subordinate. If asked to decide himself or herself, the executive usually will make a "snap judgment" to initiate an incremental change, relying on one or a few rules of thumb, such as "do what we did the last time this issue arose" or "accept the first suggested solution that any reputable person recommends." A simplistic approach of this kind is relatively "unstressful" because the decisionmaker has no inner conflict about the choice. In extreme instances, it entails practically no critical thinking, which has been characterized by Ellen Langer as "mindless" decisionmaking.

Even the most vigilant executives with enormous organizational resources at their disposal have to limit the vigilant problem-solving strategy to only a small fraction of the potential problems that come to their attention. The most effective policymakers probably have some fairly rapid but efficient selection mechanism to judge the importance of the host of problems described in intraoffice memoranda and mentioned in formal meetings or informal conversations. But, as yet, very little social science research has been devoted to trying to find out about the *problem recognition process* that enables executives to determine which problems will be selected for extended examination, which will be tabled for later consideration, which will be disposed of promptly by delegating them to others or by making an off-the-top-of-the-head decision, and which will be completely ignored. In their comprehensive review of psychological research on decisionmaking, Robert Abelson and Ariel Levi point out that "there is a paucity of research altogether on the problem recognition phase of decisionmaking, perhaps because it is often taken for granted." What cannot be taken for granted, however, is that executives generally will discriminate correctly the degree of importance of the huge number of ambiguous threats and opportunities they have to sort out. When they screen the potential problems their judgments of how much might be at stake may be distorted by political, social, and personal psychological factors that come into play in the face of uncertainties about what might happen in the foreseeable future. The problem-recognition gap must be filled by social science research before a fully comprehensive theory of policymaking can be developed.

Although little dependable knowledge is at hand concerning the ways that top-level policymakers make judgments about how much time and other resources to invest in working on the various problems that confront them, a few leads that point to what may be productive lines of inquiry for filling in the gap can be extracted from studies of policymakers in government and in large business corporations. These leads suggest a number of factors that are likely to influence—often, but not always, adversely—the judgments of policymakers when they answer the recurrent question that comes up each time they screen a potential challenge: Is this so-called problem just another routine item that can be shunted aside or settled off the top of the head; or is it so important that it really requires careful information search and appraisal to arrive at a high-quality decision?

When a leader is deciding how to decide, as Victor Vroom and Arthur Jago emphasize, a primary consideration is how important could it be to the organization to have a high-quality solution to the particular problem—"one that, if implemented, is likely to attain the [major] goals of the organization." Problems judged to be important in this sense, these authors assert, require "a well-reasoned decision, consistent with available information and with organizational objectives and goals." In order to arrive at decisions of this kind it is necessary to invest a considerable amount of personnel time and other organizational resources in carrying out high-quality procedures—those that I designate as comprising the "vigilant problem-solving strategy."[1]

Factors Influencing Policymakers' Judgments
of the Importance of a Potential Problem

One set of factors that affects national policymakers' judgments of the importance of any problematic issue pertains to their beliefs about the vital interests of the nation they are governing. (See the discussion of the role of ideology, operational codes, and other cognitive schemas in problem formulation in Chapter 5.)

The leaders of every nation have an interrelated set of central beliefs about the vital interests of their country and about the characteristics of adversaries who threaten those interests. These and related basic beliefs shape the national policymakers' "definition of the situation" when a potentially threatening event occurs and "influence the search and evaluation aspects of . . . information processing." The policymakers' basic beliefs affect their judgments as to whether or not it is worthwhile or necessary to engage in the time-consuming and costly type of information search and evaluation demanded by a vigilant problem-solving strategy.[2]

A similar set of beliefs influence the judgments of many corporate managers in business firms. This is one of the main conclusions of Donaldson and Lorsch's study of chief executive officers and other top-level policymakers in major industrial companies representing a cross section of America's most successful corporations.[3]

Ideological beliefs probably enter into the comparison baseline that policymakers preconsciously take into account in their intuitive judgments about the desirable gains that could ensue from new opportunities and the undesirable losses that could ensue from new threats. Abelson and Levi suggest that people perceive a problem to be important when they become aware for the first time of a large discrepancy between the *existing* and the *desired* state of affairs, between what *is* and what *should be*. The conception that executives have of the desired state of affairs is likely to be determined partly by their ideology and related beliefs about what would be an ideal future for the organization or nation.

The perception of a sizeable discrepancy between the present and the desired state of affairs may be crucial for judgments about the importance of a potential problem when the challenge is an *opportunity* for the organization to gain certain advantages it does not currently possess. But it seems likely that a somewhat different type of perceived discrepancy would affect judgments about the importance of a potential *threat*. In their study of chief executive officers and other top-level managers in successful industrial corporations, Donaldson and Lorsch noted that when the policymakers were monitoring reports on sales, profits, or share of the market, their judgments of whether or not the corporation was facing a serious threat to its success and possibly to its survival were relative ones, based on comparisons with their competitors' achievements or with the firm's own past performance. Here the discrepancy appears to be between the current situation—or what is expected in the foreseeable future—and what is acceptable as a *tolerable* baseline level of success, even though it may be far from what is regarded as really desirable. An equivalent type of comparison with the tolerable rather than desirable level of success is probably also used by executives in government agencies when judging the importance of potential threats— such as whether they are losing their share of the budget to competing agencies or whether they need to worry about their agency's performance becoming substantially worse than it used to be in the recent past.

Another factor that influences judgements concerning the importance of any new threat has to do with whether it is perceived as linking up with and augmenting a worrisome threat that is already in the focus of attention.[4] Policymakers may be relatively insensitive to any threat that they have not recently heard about, for which they are not "primed." These sensitization and nonsensitization effects would raise or lower the threshold for judging a new threat as important enough to be looked into carefully.

For internal organizational difficulties, such as those arising from employee grievances and jurisdictional disputes between the staffs of two departments, top-level executives are likely to judge whether or not the problem is important enough to warrant using their own time and other resources trying to work out a high-quality decision partly on the basis of their estimates of how many people in the organization might be affected. A related consideration that probably also enters into such judgments is how serious the possible effects might be for adequate functioning of the organization as a whole if nothing at all were done about the problem or if a change were made.

Yet another variable affecting judgments about the importance of any new problem is the total number of important problems already under consideration. The more crowded the agenda of an executive committee or board of directors, the lower the chances that any new problem will be added to the agenda. Any issue that is not put on the agenda for at least a preliminary discussion cannot be expected to receive vigilant problem-solving treatment.

An already overcrowded agenda, according to two of President Carter's advisors, contributed to the unresponsiveness of the Carter White House in 1979 to the dire warnings received from U.S. diplomats and knowledgeable observers about the likelihood that the Moslem supporters of the Ayatollah Khomeini would overthrow the Shah of Iran and that U.S. interests would suffer badly. At that time the President and his national security advisors were devoting their time and energy to the Salt II treaty with the Soviet Union and to a number of other big issues that made the newly developing threat seem comparatively unimportant.

One of the contributing factors that inclined President Carter and his advisors to ignore the warnings about the impending collapse of the Shah's regime was the ambiguity created by conflicting messages from reputable sources, some of which claimed that there was little danger not only because the communist movement in Iran was weak but also because the Shah was still extremely powerful and could count on his military forces to keep the Moslem religious opposition under control. Obviously, warnings sufficiently ambiguous to allow for plausible alternative interpretations that minimize the alleged danger are much less likely than unambiguous warnings to be put on the policymakers' agenda.

The ambiguity factor may at least partially account for a general tendency to ignore threats that develop gradually rather than precipitately. Gradual threats include those detected by monitoring and analyzing trends in data—for instance, ones showing adverse changes in the volume of foreign trade and in other indicators of unhealthy developments affecting an industry or an entire national economy, which reveal a discrepancy between the expected "normal" level of performance and what is now happening. Studies of how public officials and members of a community react to authentic warnings of impending disasters, such as floods, tornadoes, and wartime bombing attacks indicate that threats that build up gradually are much less likely to be taken seriously than those that occur precipitately.

In the sphere of governmental policymaking, a classic example of a precipitate threat is the Cuban missile crisis, which began at the moment that top-level policymakers were informed of the U-2 intelligence photos revealing the sudden, unexpected buildup of Soviet offensive missiles at several sites located only about 50 miles from the

United States. When a threat that is unambiguous arises without any prior warning, it evokes considerable surprise and consternation. This type of threat, as Alexander George says, is immediately perceived by policymakers to be in the category of "non-routine situations that require more than the application of standard operating procedures and decision rules," which includes "wars, interventions, [and termination of] alliances."[5]

Policymakers resist putting any gradually developing threat into the category of nonroutine situations because they realize that introducing any change in policy will require a great deal of work and will entail a political struggle to obtain a new consensus within the organization, which is almost always difficult to achieve. Warner E. Schilling suggests that this resistance makes for continuous adherence to whatever prior policy has been established until an incontrovertible challenge arises, which usually takes the form of a major crisis. The sources of inertia he singles out probably contribute to the tendency to ignore threats that build up slowly and undramatically, in contrast to those occurring precipitately, that create a shocking crisis, arousing formerly apathetic leaders to action—sometimes to extreme overreaction.

> Policies once set in motion tend to go on and on, without much regard, at times, for changes in the circumstances that first occasioned them. In part this is related to the need for agreement; the best way to maintain a consensus is not to disturb it. It also reflects the fact that the time and energy of the policy elites are limited. Most policy problems are very difficult; so, too, is the process of reaching an agreement on what to do about them. The combination of the two difficulties can easily lead the policy elites . . . to adopt an attitude of leaving well enough alone. And so they do until some drastic change occurs in their environment which sharply and dramatically challenges the wisdom and feasibility of the previous course of action. The policy consequence is "outmoded policy," and the stylistic consequence is "crisis-oriented" diplomacy.
>
> The tendency of policy change to wait on crises is reinforced whenever the required consensus necessitates the participation of the general public. (Schilling, pp. 42–43)

The likelihood that an emerging threat will evoke concentrated attention and will be put on the agenda as a problem that needs to be examined carefully, rather than relegated to the category of run-of-the-mill chores to be delegated to an aide or quickly disposed of, depends partly on how familiar the policymakers are with the type of danger to which a valid warning refers. But, even when they have heard or read a great deal about the impending danger, they may promptly dismiss genuine warnings because they do not have an available vivid image of the disastrous events to be expected. That is to say, policymakers may judge whether or not to take warnings seriously partly on the basis of the *availability heuristic,* as described by Amos Tversky and Daniel Kahneman. The rule they use might be something like this: "When a warning refers to a disaster easy to imagine, that disaster will most likely happen, so something had better be done about it; if no vivid image comes to mind, it is not likely to happen, so there is no need to bother about it."

Other factors that might influence policymakers' judgments about the importance of potential problems posed by information about alleged threats to their organization can be inferred from the findings of psychological studies concerning how and when people react to advance warnings about dangers to the community, such as those that occurred during the Three Mile Island radiological disaster, and to warnings about other public health hazards. For example, a number of studies indicate that people's judgments about whether or not to do anything about a warning are influenced by information about recommended protective actions that induce expectations of mastery or control. Richard Lazarus and Susan Folkman assert that when people receive warnings about dangers, "the paramount issues to be appraised include whether it will happen, when it will happen, and what will happen . . . also . . . whether, to what extent, and how the person can *manage* the threat, a secondary appraisal process relevant to the *sense of control.*"[6]

Even among persons who expect to be able to control events in general (the central type of belief that makes for a high level of self-efficacy and confidence), the particular threat at hand may be perceived as unmanageable. In such instances, they will "use coping strategies such as distancing themselves psychologically, avoiding thoughts about the threat, denying its implications." If no protective actions are recommended in the warning communication, and if the decisionmakers do not think of any themselves because of their lack of knowledge about what can be done to avert the predicted dangers, they will have little hope of being able to manage the threat by finding a satisfactory course of protective action, which inclines them to avoid thinking about it. (See the discussion in Chapter 4 of intense emotional stress as an emotive constraint that can interfere with vigilant problem solving by inducing reliance on a defensive avoidance decision rule, which is a simplistic strategy that gives rise to gross symptoms of defective policymaking.)

When decisionmakers are given definite recommendations about what to do to avert serious damage, they will still be inclined to ignore an unfamiliar threat because of having little hope of finding a satisfactory solution if they are given no convincing evidence to build up expectations that the recommended action will be efficacious in eliminating or at least mitigating the predicted danger. New information conveying expectations that some kind of effective solution can be found to manage or control the predicted danger will have the reverse effect and thereby increase the likelihood that the decisionmakers will start thinking about it and adopt a vigilant problem-solving approach.

The controllability and efficacy factors I have mentioned as potential determinants of policymakers' judgments of the importance of a challenge should be regarded as suggestive leads to be put on the research agenda of social scientists who investigate policymaking processes. We do not know as yet to what extent those factors affect the way policymakers in government, business, or public welfare organizations select the policy problems that they will work on. Similarly, empirical investigations are needed to test the conjectures about how policymakers respond to all the various types of constraints, to which we turn next.

Influence of Constraints on Problem Solving

The major constraints that can obstruct vigilant problem solving are listed in Table 7-1, along with typical decision rules used to cope with them. (All three types of constraints and all the cognitive, affiliative, and egocentric decision rules named in this table have been described in Chapters 2, 3, and 4.)

Whenever a decision involving vital interests of the organization is under consideration, a policymaker is likely to be keenly aware of at least a few of the powerful constraints that could be obstacles to a vigilant problem-solving approach, such as the need to avoid overusing the valuable time of top-level personnel within the organization. Any of the constraints listed in Table 7-1 can become so sali-

TABLE 7-1   Major Constraints That Can Obstruct Vigilant Problem Solving and Some Typical Decision Rules Used to Cope with Them.

Cognitive Constraints	*Affiliative Constraints*	*Egocentric (Self-Serving and Emotive) Constraints*
Limited time	Need to maintain:	Strong personal motive:
Perceived limitations of available resources for information search and appraisal	power status compensation social support	e.g., greed, desire for fame
		Arousal of an emotional need: e.g., anger, elation
Multiple tasks	Need for acceptability of new policy within the organization	Emotional stress of decisional conflict
Perplexing complexity of issue		
Perceived lack of dependable knowledge		
Ideological commitments		

Cognitive Decision Rules	*Affiliative Decision Rules*	*Egocentric (Self-Serving and Emotive) Decision Rules*
Availability	Avoid punishment	Personal aggrandizement: "What's in it for me?"
Satisficing	"Rig" acceptance	Angry retaliation
Analogizing	Exercise one-upmanship in the power struggle	Audacity: "Can do!"
Nutshell briefing		Elated choice: "Wow! Grab it"
Operational code	Groupthink: preserve group harmony	Defensive avoidance: procrastinate, pass-the-buck, or bolster
		Hypervigilant escape: "Get the hell out fast"

ent when a policy decision is being made that the policymakers cannot ignore it.

Being keenly aware of one or another of the three types of constraints does not always prevent an executive from carrying out the steps of vigilant problem solving. For example, a department head may cautiously go through all the steps even though she realizes that if she does not select the policy option favored by the chief executive she will become the target of the top leader's retaliation, which could jeopardize her career. She might worry about it and try to protect herself in one way or another but not give in to the powerful conformity pressures from her boss.

From the standpoint of effective problem solving, there certainly is nothing wrong with paying close attention to this type of affiliative constraint or to any of the other constraints. On the contrary, as I have already indicated, the essential first step of vigilant problem solving involves specifying all the various requirements to be met in order to arrive at a good solution to the problem. These requirements include taking account of conformity pressures from dominant powerholders within the organization, one's own emotional feelings, and all sorts of cognitive as well as other affiliative and egocentric constraints that could affect the way the decision is arrived at or the substance of the policy decision. Thus, when a constraint is salient but does not interfere, it nevertheless influences the policymaking process right from the outset, because the requirements essential for dealing with each of the salient constraints are added to the other requirements posed by the threat or opportunity that constitutes the challenge requiring a policy decision. The added requirements may be dealt with, in part, by means of trade-offs.

A policymaker who adopts a vigilant problem-solving strategy concentrates on the primary objective of working out a good solution to satisfy—as well as can be done under the circumstances—the major requirements posed by the threat or opportunity that constitutes the challenge, with due regard for potential risks that could result in disastrously high losses to the organization or nation. The constraints represented in Table 7-1 can be viewed as incorporating this primary objective and three additional objectives that a vigilant powerholder is likely to strive for whenever he or she participates in the making of a major policy decision: (1) to arrive at a policy solution with minimum expenditure of time, cognitive effort, funds for intelligence operations, and other organizational resources available for policymaking; (2) to find a solution that will be accepted by various other powerholders and implementers within the organization, with no substantial recriminations, so as to retain (and possibly expand) power, status, compensation, and social support for the powerholder personally and for his or her primary group of close associates (if any) within the organization; (3) to satisfy his or her own egocentric motives and emotional needs, such as those evoked by the psychological stress of decisional conflict. These objectives are interrelated in that gross failure to meet any one of them is likely to lead to failure to meet one or more of the others.

Of course, every vital policy decision has so many ramifications that no one can expect to meet fully all of the objectives. Compromises and trade-offs are always necessary. But the compromises and trade-offs will be made most judiciously, with minimal risk of overlooking a fatal drawback, when policymakers use a vigilant problem-solving strategy. Once they adopt that strategy, they strive to find a high-quality solution that will take into consideration the entire set of requirements, including those added because they presume that various constraints cannot be ignored. But in the interest of working out a high-quality solution, vigilant executives may find it necessary to make painful trade-offs in which they give relatively little weight to certain of the requirements, including one or another of the constraints. Consider the case of the department head who goes through the steps of vigilant problem solving and announces that she favors a particular policy option as the best one for the organization even though she is worried about threats of retaliation because the chief executive has let it be known in no uncertain terms that he wants a different option to be chosen. In making her decision, she need not ignore completely the social pressure from her boss that constitutes an affiliative constraint. She might include in her implementation plans a concerted effort to line up support from a coalition of fellow executives with the intent of presenting their collective decision along with cogent arguments designed to convince the chief executive to change his mind. An historic example of this way of handling threats of retaliation from the chief executive was mentioned earlier in the example cited concerning the success of Clark Clifford, shortly after he was appointed as Secretary of Defense, in inducing President Lyndon B. Johnson to accept a switch from his seemingly unalterable policy of escalation of the war in Vietnam to a policy of de-escalation (see p. 102).

As stated in the third main postulate, the vigilant problem-solving strategy will be used only if the policymaker expects (consciously or preconsciously) all the salient constraints to be manageable. If he or she apperceives any one of the constraints as so crucial that it must be allowed to play a dominant role in making a choice, the policymaker does not carry out the successive steps of vigilant problem solving.

When the managers in an executive committee believe that the complexities of the issues exceed their capabilities or that the organization lacks adequate resources for working out a high-quality solution to a problem that they judge to be very important, they will make a crucial policy decision by "the seat-of-their-pants," without bothering to examine carefully the pertinent information that is readily available and without even making any phone calls to consult with appropriate outside experts. They will rely almost entirely upon the answer that immediately comes to the focus of their attention when they apply one or two simple cognitive decision rules—such as "analogize" or "satisfice"—instead of using those decision rules as aids to problem solving in a way that does not interfere with careful search, critical thinking, and planning.

Managers react in a similar way when concerned about the threat of retaliations—for example, from the leader of a powerful affiliated constituency (such as a bloc of voters or stockholders) who wants to tell them which policy option to choose. If the managers judge the danger to their careers to be great because they can see no way to protect themselves, they will immediately rely upon the affiliative decision rule to avoid being punished. Each member of the group who expects that this affiliative constraint cannot be managed in such a way as to keep the potential damage to a tolerable level feels that he or she has no choice but to give in to the social or political pressure.

The dominating constraint, as I have repeatedly indicated, need not necessarily be one that the policymaker is consciously aware of. Emotional stress, for example, typically operates as a constraint at the preconscious level. A president might fail to adopt a vigilant problem-solving strategy because of this constraint, despite being very confident that she can effectively manage all the main external and internal constraints she knows about—such as time pressures, the complexities of the issue, limited organizational resources, conformity demands from other officials and from representatives of powerful constituencies, and her own inner desire for personal fame.

Top national leaders may sincerely believe that none of the constraints needs to be given priority over the search for a high-quality solution to the problem posed by an international crisis that could result in an outbreak of war. And yet, their own intense emotional reactions to the distressing dilemma could play such a dominant role that they resort to a simplistic strategy, using either the "hypervigilance" decision rule ("get the hell out of the dilemma fast") or the "defensive avoidance" rule ("don't think about it: procrastinate, pass-the-buck, or bolster whichever alternative seems least objectionable at the moment"). During a major crisis the more constraints a leader is aware of, the more agonizing the decisional dilemma will be and the greater the likelihood that the level of emotional stress will rise above the threshold for becoming a dominating emotive constraint. Examples of poor crisis management by five national leaders, apparently resulting from their hypervigilant or defensive avoidant pattern of coping with severe emotional stress, are presented in Lebow's (1981) series of case studies of international crises during the twentieth century: Germany's Imperial Chancellor Bethmann-Hollweg and Kaiser Wilhelm in 1914, Soviet Premier Stalin in 1941, India's Prime Minister Nehru in 1962, and Egypt's President Nasser in 1967.

The weight given to any constraint depends in large part upon the policymaker's expectations about what is likely to happen if it is ignored. The greater the anticipated losses the higher the probability that it will become dominant. Whenever a constraint does become dominant, the policymaker will arrive at a policy decision by relying almost entirely upon simple decision rules to take care of that constraint, instead of using those decision rules (and other pertinent ones as well) as supplementary aids to problem solving in a way that does not interfere with careful search, critical thinking, and planning.

Main Components of the Constraints Model

Figure 7–1 presents a preliminary descriptive model that embodies the four key postulates (summarized at the beginning of this chapter). It shows the main social and psychological components that are determinants of vigilant problem solving. The model also highlights the determinants of three other procedural strategies, involving reliance on three different types of decision rules, each of which is likely to lead to errors as a result of failing to carry out the essential steps of vigilant problem solving in dealing with serious challenges that affect vital interests.

As in most flow charts, this one starts at the upper left and terminates (in one or another of the four "END" boxes) at the lower right, with mediating processes represented in between. If you look at the box in the upper left, you can see that the psychological processes that enter into the making of a policy decision begin when powerholders become aware of a challenge in the form of a threat or opportunity that poses a problem because the powerholders' organization or nation will suffer losses (or opportunity costs) if it continues business as usual without making any changes. The challenge, as I indicated earlier, may occur precipitately as a result of a single dramatic event or communication (such as an ultimatum threatening war from a rival nation) or it may build up gradually from a series

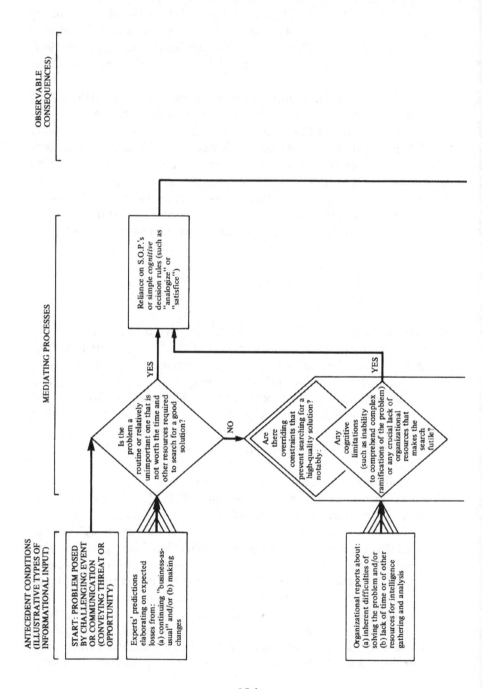

ANTECEDENT CONDITIONS
(ILLUSTRATIVE TYPES OF
INFORMATIONAL INPUT)

MEDIATING PROCESSES

OBSERVABLE
CONSEQUENCES

START: PROBLEM POSED
BY CHALLENGING EVENT
OR COMMUNICATION
(CONVEYING THREAT OR
OPPORTUNITY)

Experts' predictions
elaborating on expected
losses from:
(a) continuing "business-as-
usual" and/or (b) making
changes

Is the
problem a
routine or relatively
unimportant one that is
not worth the time and
other resources required
to search for a good
solution?

YES

NO

Reliance on S.O.P.'s
or simple *cognitive*
decision rules (such as
"analogize" or
"satisfice")

Are
there
overriding
constraints that
prevent searching for a
high-quality solution?
notably:

Any
cognitive
limitations
(such as inability
to comprehend complex
ramifications of the problem)
or any crucial lack of
organizational
resources that
makes the
search
futile?

YES

Organizational reports about:
(a) inherent difficulties of
solving the problem and/or
(b) lack of time or of other
resources for intelligence
gathering and analysis

154

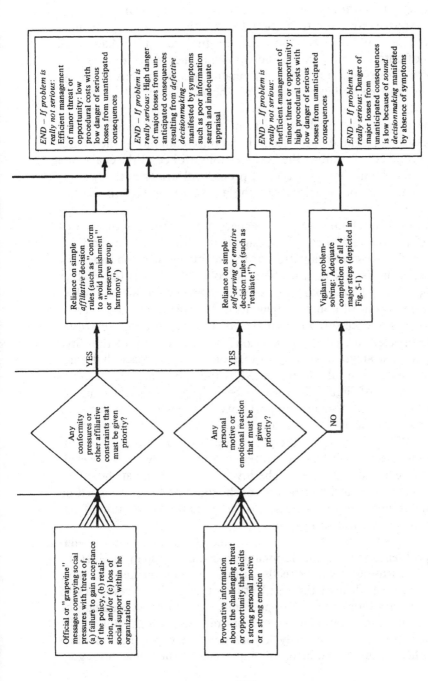

FIGURE 7-1 A Descriptive Model Representing Psychological Effects of Dominant Constraints on Policymaking

of relatively unobtrusive events or communications (such as gradual blocking by a rival nation of access to foreign markets).

Illustrative types of informational inputs that are among the main antecedent conditions are shown in the first column.[7] (Additional types of antecedent conditions not shown in the first column—organizational rules and traditions, personality predispositions of policymakers, and leadership practices—will be discussed in Chapters 8, 9, and 10.)

The core of the model consists of the mediating psychological processes represented in the second and third columns of the figure: The second column shows the key questions evoked by the challenge; the third column shows the type of procedural strategies that policymakers will adopt as a result of the answers they give to the key questions.

The fourth column shows the expected consequences of each of the four procedural strategies designated in the boxes in the third column. The overall evaluation of the adequacy of management of the problem, as indicated in the final column, depends on whether or not the problem actually turns out really to be serious (according to the consensus of honest judgments of knowledgeable observers—which are not necessarily the same as their public pronouncements). If the problem actually is *not* serious, the use of any of the three procedural strategies involving a quick-and-easy approach that relies on simple decision rules (represented by the upper three boxes in the third column of Figure 7-1) would be judged as efficient management of the minor threat or opportunity. There will be low costs for arriving at the decision, with low danger of any serious losses to the organization. If, however, the problem proves to be a really serious one, management of the major threat or opportunity would be evaluated as extremely deficient. The low cost of arriving at the policy decision by using a simplistic approach would be far outweighed by the high danger of serious losses to the organization resulting from the poor procedural strategy used.

The opposite evaluations would be made for instances where vigilant problem solving is the dominant procedural strategy used. If the problem turns out *not* to be really serious, the policymakers will have wasted a great deal of time and other organizational resources to deal with a minor threat or opportunity that poses little danger of any serious organizational losses from miscalculations. But, if the problem proves to be a really serious one, the expenditure of time and other resources will be more than offset by the tremendous gain for the organization from averting potential losses that might otherwise have ensued. In such a case the use of vigilant problem solving, which tends to minimize avoidable errors that could be disastrous for the organization, would be regarded as sound management.

As policymakers go through the process of answering the key questions shown in the second column of the model, they do not necessarily verbalize to themselves either the question or the answer. The process may occur at a preconscious level, which can be detected by observing indirect verbal and nonverbal indicators. (See pp. 190–200.)

The first key question, which embodies one of the main postulates (p. 140), requires the policymaker to judge whether the problem posed by the challenge is a relatively unimportant one, as compared with all the other tasks and potential challenges that are also clamoring for attention. Such judgments are made in the context of vague expectations about the added costs in terms of time, effort, funds for intelligence gathering and analysis, and use of other such resources that may be required to deal with the new problem if it is judged to be important enough to warrant striving for a high-quality decision. These expectations are, in effect, background constraints that tend to inhibit paying attention to and taking seriously the potential problems posed by whatever new apparent threats or opportunities arise. Hence, constraints are already operative from the outset and affect the policymakers' judgments of the importance of the problem.

After the potential problem gets over the first hurdle, there are further obstacles that can prevent the search for a high-quality solution. These are the obstacles posed by the salient cognitive, affiliative, and egocentric constraints that immediately begin to loom large in the foreground as soon as the challenge is judged to be important. According to another basic postulate (p. 190), if any of the salient constraints is judged to require overriding priority, the search for a high-quality solution will be inhibited even if the challenge is judged to be important.

When confronted with a challenging threat or opportunity conveyed by a dramatic event or by a provocative communication, policymakers do not necessarily ask themselves the series of key questions in the order shown in the Figure 7–1. One of the constraints may be dominant right from the outset. For example, an unexpected hostile action by a rival organization or nation in violation of a long-standing treaty, which is perceived by the policymakers as a "stab in the back,'' can evoke such intense anger that it makes the emotive-constraint question immediately salient, simultaneously with the challenge; the policymakers' positive answer to it (''we must retali-ate!'') influences the answer to the key question about the impor-tance of the problem (e.g., ''It's damn important—we have to do something drastic about this outrage''). Nevertheless, the sequence shown in Figure 7-1 may often occur for many major problems that develop relatively slowly in response to a series of events and com-munications that evoke mounting concern as the policymakers grad-ually come to realize more and more about the magnitude and rami-fications of an impending threat or opportunity. In such instances, the answer to the first question may gradually change over a period of weeks or months from yes to maybe, and then to no.

Some of the policymakers' initial search and appraisal of pertinent information may be directed toward the task of giving informed an-swers to the series of questions pertaining to constraints. The an-swers they give to those questions may also change as new informa-tion is obtained, which results in corresponding changes in the procedural strategy they adopt for arriving at a policy decision. (See the section on ''Changes in Procedural Strategy'' in Chapter 8.)

Policymakers' answers to the key questions about the importance of the challenge and to the key questions about constraints may fre-quently be quite unrealistic as a result of gross misunderstandings of warnings, misperceptions, and faulty inferences based on stereotypes or other misleading presumptions. Also they may be misled by incor-rect information and deliberate manipulations by interested parties who have a vested interest in steering the choice toward their own preference. Many studies in the social sciences can be drawn upon, as will be seen in the next chapter, to formulate plausible proposi-tions about the conditions under which policymakers are likely to give unrealistic answers to the key questions.

Pathways to Glory and Ignominy

A number of different pathways are shown in the model, only one of which is likely to end up bringing glory and attributions of great-ness to policymakers who have to grapple with a large number of grave threats to vital interests of the organization or nation during the period when they are the responsible leaders. The one pathway that is likely to lead to success requires policymakers to give negative answers to all the key questions when confronted by each major threat. First, they must believe that an important problem is posed by the challenge, which cannot be delegated or solved immediately off the top of their heads. Second, they must judge, consciously or preconsciously, that all the various constraints can be managed without allowing any of them to be dominating considerations that override all of the other requirements for a good solution. If, and only if, these two conditions are met, the pathway leads to the box at the bottom of the third column, which includes the entire set of four essential steps of vigilant problem solving. Thus, the policymaker is required to answer conscientiously a set of twelve additional questions, as indicated in Figure 5-1 (p. 91).

In answering the twelve questions, vigilant policymakers use various guiding principles. For example, the tit-for-tat reciprocity principle may be taken into account to help specify the requirements for an effective course of action in response to an adversary's aggressive moves; the elimination-by-aspects principle may be used to help narrow down the alternatives to the most promising ones.[8] The answers suggested by such principles are regarded by the policymakers as tentative first approximations, which they re-evaluate during later stages of vigilant problem solving in light of whatever new information has been gathered. Along with the guiding principles, the policymakers also use simple decision rules—including those listed in Table 7-1—as *suggestive leads* that can facilitate the search for a good solution without replacing or interfering with intensive information search and critical thinking. This limited usage contrasts sharply with the high degree of reliance on such rules that characterizes the seat-of-the-pants strategies represented in the other three boxes in the third column of Figure 7-1.

Four of the pathways depicted in Figure 7-1 lead to a simplistic approach. Two of those pathways terminate with many symptoms of defective decisionmaking as a result of reliance on standard operating procedures (SOPs) or simple *cognitive* decision rules.

1. The first pathway is mediated by the policymaker's judgment that the problem is too trivial to bother with. Sometimes this judgment is erroneous, usually because warnings about potential losses are ambiguous and presented in such an unimpressive way that they constitute too weak a challenge to reach the threshold for gaining the attention of busy executives or for competing successfully with many other troubles that appear to be more worthy of time and energy.

If the policymakers' answer to the first key question is yes, they typically dispose of the problem quickly by adopting simple cognitive decision rules, such as those embodied in adages like "let sleeping dogs lie."

2. The second pathway that leads to a quick-and-easy approach involving reliance on simple *cognitive* decision rules is mediated by the policymakers' judgment that there are overriding cognitive constraints that prevent them from seeking a high-quality solution. Among the most common of such constraints are the policymakers' realization that the complex ramifications of the problem exceed their cognitive capabilities and that the organization lacks available resources for intensive information search, appraisal, and planning.

3. A third pathway that leads to a seat-of-the-pants approach is mediated by overriding concern about affiliative constraints, which makes for reliance on simple *affiliative* decision rules. This type of constraint arises when an executive becomes aware of demands for conformity to the wishes of other powerholders in the organization who are in a position to threaten anyone who fails to conform with extreme retributions, such as not being promoted, or being excluded from top-level meetings. Much more often, however, the anticipated social punishments for failing to conform involve more subtle threats of social disapproval. An entirely different but equally powerful affiliative constraint becomes dominant when policymakers who are working together in a cohesive group display the "groupthink" syndrome, which involves reliance on the simple decision rule to "preserve group harmony by going along uncritically with whatever consensus seems to be emerging" (see Chapter 3). Yet another affiliative constraint involves concern about the potentially disruptive effects on the organization of seeking for a high-quality solution to a problem. National leaders who feel responsible for the functioning of the government become keenly aware of this constraint at times when there are unusually intense bureaucratic power struggles among contending factions within the administration. The top-level leaders then tend to curtail the usual steps of problem solving on any new highly controversial issue out of concern that the government will suffer as a result of stirring up even more bitter in-fighting and perhaps alienating one or another faction in the bureau-

cracy. The simple decision rule they are likely to use is to select whichever policy choice will evoke the least opposition from any of the contending factions.

4. The fourth pathway that leads to many symptoms of defective decisionmaking is mediated by the policymaker's self-serving motives or emotional state. Fairly often the questions and answers concerning these *egocentric* constraints are verbalized— for example, when a policymaker thinks about his or her personal desires to become rich and famous. At times, however, the questions and answers are not verbalized even in silent speech. At still other times they are verbalized in modified form, such as "I can't stand this horrible dilemma any longer; I hate to think about it"—which implicitly expresses the decision rule that goes along with *defensive avoidance.*[9] Despite their best conscious efforts, policymakers sometimes cannot avoid being influenced by emotive constraints created by intense arousal of anxiety, guilt, anger, elation, or other strong emotions. They are also subject to the same kind of internal constraints when they have a strong emotional bias in favor of one particular solution to the problem. More commonly, policymakers have strong emotional biases *against* various alternatives that might prove to be viable candidates for a solution and they exclude those alternatives prematurely, without weighing the pros and cons. For example, this type of emotive constraint apparently entered into President Nixon's decision to "tilt" toward Pakistan by using military threats to deter India during the Pakistan-India War crisis of 1971. The alternative of being a peacemaker by encouraging conciliation between Pakistan and India, according to several accounts, was excluded by Nixon from the outset because he had strong feelings of antipathy toward Mrs. Gandhi, India's President. His emotional bias was in part a residue of his disagreeable state visit to India during which he felt that Mrs. Gandhi failed to display proper deference; subsequently, she gave him a hard time by vociferously arguing against some of his cherished policies.

As for all decision rules, those that policymakers rely upon when using a simplistic approach in any of the above four sequences can in certain limited circumstances be quite good guides to appropriate action. For example, the perfunctory way of dealing with alleged threats that are judged to be too unimportant to bother with can be highly functional in the handling of the large number of warning messages that cross the desk of a top-level executive every day—provided that the warnings pertain to trivial, improbable, or nonexistent dangers. Nevertheless, as indicated in the preceding chapter, for major policy decisions that affect vital interests of the organization or nation, reliance on simple decision rules without engaging in essential information search, critical appraisal, or the other essential features of vigilant problem solving increases the likelihood of avoidable errors, which generally prove to be highly dysfunctional.

The model represented in Figure 7-1 is intended to be applicable to a chief executive or to anyone else in a leadership role who is charged with responsibility as a policymaker. It can also be applied to middle- and low-level personnel, including staff who submit policy recommendations to the top level and departmental administrators who modify new organizational policies by putting their own personal stamp on the way the policies formulated by top-level management are implemented. For executives at any level of an organization's hierarchy the model is applicable to whatever policy decisions are delegated to them by senior executives and also to all policy problems that require, as Vroom and Jago put it, some degree of "participation" of "subordinates in managerial decision making," especially those that "fall within [each] manager's area of freedom or discretion . . . on which [he or she] is expected or permitted to act."

The model can be used to analyze sources of error in the decision-making process, whether an executive is making a policy decision entirely on his or her own or is participating in a group decision with fellow members. In the latter case, the investigator would examine the procedures used by the advisory group, committee, or board that collectively participates in making the policy decision.

Mixed, Intermediate Approaches

For purposes of exposition, the theoretical model presented in Figure 7-1 shows the pathways leading to only two end points of a continuum. At one extreme of the "quality-of-procedures" continuum are the simplistic procedural strategies, characterized by a very large number of symptoms of defective decisionmaking. At the other extreme is the vigilant problem-solving approach, characterized by no symptoms at all or only one symptom (from the common-garden variety of human error to be expected whenever someone attempts to carry out conscientiously a series of complicated tasks). But there are intermediate procedural strategies to be considered that result in an intermediate number of symptoms of defective policymaking, which are not represented in the figure. A few additional assumptions pertaining to these intermediate categories need to be introduced in order to enable the basic features of the model to be applied to policymaking approaches that are neither entirely simplistic nor vigilant problem solving, but combine components of both.

The missing intermediate categories not represented in Figure 7-1 are included in Table 7-2, which lists the main consequences of four procedural approaches to policymaking used from time to time by policymakers in national governments, business corporations, public welfare institutions, and other large organizations. The first and the fourth type of approach listed in the table correspond to the two extreme types of approach represented in Figure 7-1.

The second and third type of approach shown in the table pertain to policymaking processes of intermediate quality, characterized by some degree of reliance upon simple decision rules combined with carrying out some but not all of the essential tasks of vigilant problem solving.[10] Even when policymakers display only a perfunctory performance of a few of the essential tasks, according to suggestive evidence presented in the preceding chapter, they are likely to make fewer avoidable errors than when they do not carry out any of the tasks of vigilant problem solving.

Policymakers sometimes adopt a quasi problem-solving approach as a result of their fairly realistic appraisals of the constraints imposed by their own cognitive limitations and the limited resources of

TABLE 7-2 Consequences of the Vigilant Problem-Solving Approach to Policymaking as Compared with Three Other Approaches

Type of Approach in Policymaker's Repertoire	Amount of Time and Effort Required	Quality of Decisionmaking: No. of Defective Symptoms	Probability of Avoidable Errors
1. Vigilant problem solving	Very large	0–1	Low
2. Quasi-vigilant	Moderate to large	2–3	Moderate
3. Quasi-simplistic	Small to moderate	4–6	Fairly high
4. Simplistic	Very small	7	Very high

their organization. They may seek for a good solution to a policy problem within the somewhat narrow confines of what they judge to be feasible. Such judgments about salient constraints may greatly curtail one or more of the major steps of vigilant problem solving. The gathering and analysis of pertinent information is always restricted to some extent because attempts to collect and process everything relevant to the ramifications of all viable options are generally so costly that they would soon exhaust the resources of any organization. Realizing that a fairly high degree of selectivity is essential, policymakers sometimes restrict their information search to such an extent that they overlook important bits of information that would be available to them at a tolerable cost, thereby displaying one of the symptoms of defective decisionmaking. Other symptoms can come about in essentially the same way as a result of misjudging the degree to which the essential tasks of vigilant problem solving need to be curtailed in order to meet the demands imposed by realistic constraints, such as limited time and budget. When policymakers curtail most of the steps of vigilant problem solving, but not all, the procedural strategy is labeled "quasi-simplistic" (the third category in Table 7-2).

Intermediate types of procedural strategy may also arise as a result of initial top-of-the-head judgments by the policymakers concerning constraints that create "crippling objections" to certain policy options that might, if explored, prove to be good candidates for solving the problem (see Etzioni 1986). The initial elimination of an alternative with "crippling objections" probably occurs fairly often as a result of ideological preconceptions linked with strong emotional biases. It is usually followed by closed-mindedness toward any new information indicating that the initially eliminated alternative had been misjudged and ought to be reconsidered. Consequently, in addition to gross omissions in the initial survey of viable alternatives, two other symptoms are also likely to be present—selective bias in processing information concerning the initially rejected alternatives and failure to reconsider originally rejected alternatives in the light of new information. But even when these symptoms occur the policymaker may still carry out most of the steps of vigilant problem solving. This is perhaps one of the most common forms of a quasi problem-solving approach, which, as indicated in Table 7-2, is characterized by: (1) a moderate to a large amount of time and effort working toward finding a good solution to the problem, and (2) two to three symptoms of defective decisionmaking, which makes for a moderate (rather than a low or high) probability of avoidable errors.

The constraints model presented in this chapter is a preliminary theoretical framework for describing alternative procedural strategies that policymakers use to arrive at policy decisions. It is intended to serve the main functions of scientific explanations. Two of the most important of those functions are to help us understand connections among diverse phenomena and to make relevant predictions about future events. In order to fulfill these functions, the model requires further elaboration to indicate when and how it can be applied, which is the subject of the next chapter.

8

Values and Limitations
of the Constraints Model

The Model as a Guide for Inquiry

Although still incomplete in several ways that I shall indicate shortly, the constraints model in its present form can be put to use as a guide for inquiry. In my own comparative case study research on the management of international crises, I have found that in a number of instances this model has enabled me to piece together various bits of partial information to form a coherent pattern. The type of pattern to which I am referring consists of a sequence that starts with some apparently crucial antecedent conditions making one or another constraint highly salient to the policymakers and leads to manifestations of their reliance on one or a few simple decision rules, accompanied by symptoms of defective decisionmaking procedures. Those symptoms, in turn, appear to play a causal role in producing undesirable outcomes from the standpoint of failing to protect vital national interests or failing to decrease international conflict, or both.

It seems to me that the constraints model represented in Figure 7–1 can be especially valuable in investigations that seek to determine the probable causes of any policy fiasco for the purpose of trying to understand what has gone wrong, and with an eye to making recommendations about how to prevent recurrences of such errors in the future. The theoretical model offers a set of alternative explanations to be investigated, which differ markedly from the most popular model currently used implicitly, if not explicitly, by many investigative committees in governments and other large organizations throughout the world. That popular model is based on the notion

167

that the main cause of gross policy errors usually is chronic negligence or incompetence on the part of one or more persons in positions of responsibility within the organization. Those who rely on this model expect their investigation will end up putting the finger on negligent culprits or incompetent bunglers. The main assumption is that if the organization does not get rid of those botchers, they will continue to display again and again the same chronic defects in the future, which will result in more disasters; those disasters would not be produced if the botchers were replaced by others better qualified for their jobs. The latter assumption is clearly implied by the remedy that sincere proponents of this popular model generally recommend, which is to fire or force the resignation of the decisionmakers responsible for the main mistakes as soon as they can be identified. In their view, this prescription could also be good for public relations and for restoring morale within the organization, but those benefits are purely secondary to the main purpose of preventing recurrences of defective policymaking.

Another model, far less popular among investigative committees but occasionally given wide publicity in the mass media when eloquent critics accuse an investigative committee of being guilty of "whitewashing," is the conspiracy theory. According to this theory, the true culprits will turn out to be a number of powerholders in the organization who wanted the bad outcome to happen and actually planned it that way. After the Pearl Harbor disaster, this type of charge was made against President Franklin D. Roosevelt and other top officials in his administration by several influential newspaper columnists and military spokesmen who did not accept the verdict of the official military and congressional investigations. Those investigations had placed the blame on the negligence of Admiral Kimmel, the chief naval commander in Hawaii, and Admiral Stark, the Chief of Naval Operations in Washington, both of whom were court-martialed and removed from their top-level positions by the navy.

In contrast to the two models I have just described, the constraints model does not direct investigators to look primarily for individuals who are chronically negligent, incompetent, or conspiratorial when seeking to explain one or more instances of defective policymaking. Instead, the constraints model offers a number of alternative causal sequences as probable causes of error in policymaking. It incorporates a variety of theoretical concepts, ranging from bureaucratic politics to misleading judgmental heuristics, which have emerged piecemeal from research bearing on policymaking processes in political science, sociology, history, management sciences, psychology, and other social sciences. The constraints model, of course, is much broader in scope than any of the component theoretical concepts that it attempts to integrate into a more comprehensive framework. The model enables investigators to formulate plausible explanatory hypotheses to be examined, which take into account a very broad range of facts and credible surmises from prior empirical research that includes heterogeneous types of observations of policymaking in a variety of organizations.

Whether carrying out applied research for the practical purpose of preventing the recurrence of policy errors in one particular organization or basic research for the scientific purpose of understanding how and why policy errors occur in different kinds of organizational settings, investigators using the constraints model would be prompted to start their inquiry by looking into the five alternative causal sequences (represented in Figure 7-1 [pp. 154–55] and summarized in Figure 9-1 [pp. 212–13]). All five of those pathways are closely linked with existing bodies of theory in one or another of the social science disciplines.

If the investigator of a policy that turned out to have unanticipated bad consequences surmises that the available observations do not fit the pattern for vigilant problem solving but might fit the pattern for one or another of the four defective pathways, he or she would be led to focus the inquiry on finding out which particular constraint was dominant, which particular decision rules were relied upon by the policymakers, and which particular antecedent conditions contributed to inducing this particular procedural strategy. If none of the four patterns for defective policymaking is discerned and the fifth pattern (vigilant problem solving) emerges as the best fit, then the investigator would realize that he or she needs to consider a different type of explanation that lies beyond the scope of the constraints model. (Those other candidates would include the explanations suggested by the chronic incompetence and conspiracy theories, as well as other possible explanations—such as, that the policymakers were striving to satisfy partisan objectives on a hidden agenda; that they persistently misperceived the requirements for a good solution because of uncorrected ideological preconceptions; that they were misled by formerly reliable intelligence sources; or that they were confronted with a policy problem entailing such enormous complexities that even the best qualified and most conscientious policymakers, using the most effective procedural strategy, could not anticipate correctly the consequences of the available policy alternatives.) Obviously, the potential value of the constraints model will be very limited unless a substantial percentage of policy failures do turn out to fall within its scope for fitting one or another of the four causal sequences for defective policymaking.

Because the constraints model is based on the assumption that in different circumstances a policymaker will follow different pathways entailing different sources of error, it puts heavy emphasis on antecedent conditions as instigating causes. This is quite different from most accounts to be found in the social science literature on specific sources of error, such as overuse of "satisficing," "availability," or other simple heuristics to deal with cognitive constraints, in which practically nothing is said about antecedent conditions that determine whether or not the kind of error under discussion is likely to be made. Many of the accounts leave one with the impression that the authors consider the tendency to make that kind of error to be universally strong in everyone at all times.

Various informational inputs that constitute one major type of antecedent condition are listed in the first column of Figure 7-1. (See the discussions of these communication variables in Chapters 7 and 10.) Another major set of antecedent conditions consists of personality deficiencies and other dispositional characteristics that could account for individual differences in responsiveness to the informational inputs. (These are specified in detail in Chapter 9.) The two main categories of antecedent conditions and several additional categories (such as organizational norms, traditions, and doctrines) need to be explored in subsequent studies focusing on the conditions under which each of the four defective pathways is most likely to occur. The constraints model is still quite incomplete in this respect; further specification of antecedent conditions is a major item for future research. New questions for research are posed by the preliminary constraints model, as I shall indicate at the end of this chapter, and one of them is this: What are the main antecedent conditions that foster reliance on *each* of the most commonly used simple decision rules to deal with *each* of the constraints that interferes with vigilant problem solving?

Even though the constraints model in its present form is incomplete, it seems to me that what is already known about the antecedent conditions is sufficient to enable this preliminary theoretical framework to be of some use not only to investigative committees oriented

toward troubleshooting and social scientists engaging in basic research but also to policymakers themselves. It can provide at least a
few prescriptive guidelines, including recommended leadership practices, that might help policymakers avoid some common sources of
error. (In Chapters 9 and 10, I discuss antecedent conditions in detail
and call attention to the implications of the model for prescriptive
guidelines that may prove to be of practical value.)

What Can and Cannot Be Predicted

Insofar as the constraints model is valid, it can be used by social
scientists to make two different kinds of predictions. After examining the way a committee (or any individual) arrives at a policy decision, an analyst can make a diagnosis of the procedural strategy in
terms of the four categories in Table 7-2—simplistic, quasi-simplistic, quasi-vigilant, and vigilant problem solving. The diagnosis can
be made by rating the frequency and severity of symptoms of defective decisionmaking (see pp. 32–33). The seven symptoms, it will
be recalled, correspond to failures to carry out essential steps of vigilant problem solving. One of my fundamental assumptions (supported by the evidence presented in Chapter 6) is that such failures
give rise to avoidable errors that make for lack of success in meeting
the organization's objectives. Insofar as that assumption is warranted, the constraints model can be used to make at least rough
predictions as to whether or not the outcomes of various policy decisions are likely to be successful.

Whenever observations are available for assessing the presence or
absence of the known antecedent conditions specified by the constraints model, predictions can also be made as to whether the policymakers will display a vigilant problem-solving approach, an intermediate approach, or a simplistic approach (and, if it is the latter,
whether it will be a cognitive, affiliative, or egocentric type of decision rule that they will primarily rely upon).[1] Until we learn more
about the antecedent conditions than is known at present, however,
we must expect these predictions at best to be substantially better
than chance when one is making comparisons among a sizeable number of decisions, but not highly accurate for any single case.

The constraints model is *not* intended to predict which particular
alternative a policymaker or group of policymakers will choose from
among those that are being considered. And it certainly cannot be

used to fill the big gap that most policymakers would like to see filled as soon as possible. What they want is a dependable prescriptive theory that will tell them which of the alternatives under consideration is the best one to choose because it will yield a better outcome than any of the others. The best that the constraints model can do, which is a far cry from what is wanted by policymakers, is to predict that if the vigilant problem-solving strategy, rather than any other strategy, is used, the alternative that is chosen will have a better chance of proving to be a *reasonably sound choice*—that is, one of the best of the viable alternatives, even if it is not the very best in terms of the full range of expected benefits and costs.

In order to use the constraints model for the purpose of predicting the likelihood that a policy decision will have a favorable outcome, it is necessary to take account of a number of the model's limitations. Some of the possible limitations are suggested in numerous critiques of analytic problem solving that have appeared in recent years.

Earlier (at the beginning of Chapter 6), we examined the extreme position taken by Starbuck, who claims that differences in the process used to arrive at a policy decision are unrelated to the success or failure of the policy. If his pessimistic assumption were to hold, it would follow that using the constraints model to make a diagnosis of vigilant problem solving rather than a simplistic approach would be of no use whatsoever for predicting anything at all about the outcome of a policy decision. But we have seen in Chapter 6 that Starbuck's claim is strongly challenged by the available evidence on the relationship between process and outcome. There are, however, other arguments by other social scientists who are skeptical about the value of analytic problem solving that need to be taken into account in order to specify how the model can and cannot be expected to be applied in a valid way.

A Critique of Professional Policy Analysis

Charles Edward Lindblom has presented a detailed critique of analytic problem solving. Most of the defects he emphasizes pertain directly to the analytic methods used by professional consultants and applied social scientists who, as specialists in policy analysis, carry out fact-finding, cost-benefit studies, evaluation research, or various formal planning procedures based on systems analysis or a mathematical decision theory. As I have indicated earlier, the systematic procedures advocated by these various practitioners of professional social inquiry may improve the quality of certain limited types of policy decisions, but are not essential for vigilant problem solving. Sometimes attempts to frame problems in the way demanded by the specialists actually interfere with effective problem solving—for example, by inducing the policymaker to ignore the organization's need to maintain its "credibility" or other intangible objectives that do not readily lend themselves to cost-benefit analysis. It is necessary, therefore, to consider—after reviewing Lindblom's critique of the work of professional analysts—in what ways, if at all, each of the shortcomings he has singled out might pertain to the ordinary type of analysis carried out by policymakers who adopt a vigilant problem-solving approach.

Lindblom calls attention to four major shortcomings of available analytic methods. He presents them as cogent reasons why we cannot expect the work of professional policy analysts to eliminate the play of power and the bargaining that goes on among contending interest groups within every organization, which typically enter into the formation of a policy decision and the modifications that are introduced when attempts to implement it are not successful:

1. The professional analysts are fallible and powerholders know it; the analysts can provide only inconclusive, debatable solutions and sometimes they are mistaken about the facts or about the inferences that they draw, especially when the available information is grossly incomplete, as it usually is.

2. The work of professional analysts is very slow and costly; with the resources available, the analysts' reports containing detailed evaluations of policy alternatives can seldom be completed in time to be useful.

3. The professional analysts have no acceptable method for drawing warranted conclusions about which problems to attack; they are limited to the problem definitions that are assigned to them, which are often the product of a political settlement among disputing factions.

4. In the absence of "harmony of interests or values among individuals and groups" within the organization, the professional analysts cannot be expected to find a policy solution that will

be regarded as the best one by all the contending parties; the analysts have no acceptable criteria for resolving conflicts of values and interests.

Lindblom points out that when confronted by the realities of policymaking in government or in other large organizations, professional analysts soon discover that they cannot live up to their ideals of using a purely "scientific" approach to the exclusion of political processes. Sometimes, despite their high ideals, "when scientific problem solvers face a complex problem which they cannot actually master, they fall back on hasty improvisations." Their improvisations can prove to be worse solutions than those worked out by policymakers engaging in ordinary thinking, who accept the necessity for competition among contending parties and proceed "step by step through trial and error rather than by trying to comprehend a problem in its entirety."

Political interaction is a necessary ingredient in policymaking, Lindblom argues, not only because of limited human cognitive capabilities in the face of the complexity of policy issues but also because of the omnipresence of conflicts over goals, values, and criteria for selecting a good policy. "Interactive" policymaking, as he calls it, includes delegating authority, voting, informal bargaining, and formal negotiating, as well as all sorts of "ways in which people exert control, influence, or power over each other," such as "silencing an opponent." But Lindblom acknowledges that "interactive" policymaking does not preclude vigilant problem solving on the part of those who participate in the political struggle: "interactive" policymaking "is always mixed with some elements of analytical problem solving, and the latter can take the form of ordinary analysis by problem solvers or the form of professional social inquiry either by staff attached to some of the participating problem solvers or by practitioners of professional social inquiry at a distance, working on their own."

As will be seen shortly, the constraints model can be applied to most, if not all, of the main forms of "interactive" policymaking. The model specifies some antecedent conditions that can be used to predict the extent to which each of the contending leaders (or factions) will do "ordinary analysis" of the type required for vigilant problem solving and the consequences of doing it to a small versus large extent.

Shortcomings of Vigilant Problem Solving

The constraints model, as I have already indicated, is intended as a descriptive theoretical framework to be applied when analyzing the decisionmaking behavior of any *individual* powerholder or any identifiable *group* of powerholders within an organization, including low-level administrators who can exercise power informally as policymakers by introducing modifications in the way policy directives from top-level management are carried out. The model pertains to the ordinary thinking of the policymakers, which may or may not be supplemented by the work of professional analysts who collect pertinent information and prepare analytic reports containing policy recommendations.

Lindblom's four reasons why politics and bargaining cannot be eliminated, presented in his critique of the analytic problem solving that is carried out by professional analysts, pertain to some extent to shortcomings of vigilant problem solving on the part of anyone who participates in policymaking. If those shortcomings loom very large, they could call into question a central assumption that is essential for using the constraints model to predict outcomes and to extract prescriptive recommendations for improving the quality of policymaking—namely, that failures to carry out the "ordinary analysis" required by the various steps of vigilant problem solving (as represented in Figure 5-1) will make for avoidable errors and thereby reduce the likelihood of successful outcomes. In the discussion that follows, I shall indicate briefly why I think that none of the four major deficiencies of vigilant problem solving undercuts that central assumption, although they require some additional provisos for applying the constraints model.

1. The solutions arrived at by a vigilant problem-solving approach are certainly fallible, as I have indicated in my earlier discussion of unavoidable errors. When the persons who are dominant in the policymaking process use a vigilant problem-solving approach, they will from time to time fail to function perfectly, like all other human beings. Consequently, they will make some avoidable as well as unavoidable errors, with the result that the outcome of their policy decisions will sometimes be unsuccessful. The best that can be expected is that their problem-solving strategy will give rise to relatively fewer avoidable errors than

any of the other approaches. But that is by no means a negligible asset. Avoidable errors can be disastrous.

2. Vigilant problem solving, as indicated in Table 7-2 (p. 163), takes up much more time and is much more costly in terms of organizational resources than a simplistic approach. If an information search were carried out in an extremely thorough manner for every policy decision, the budget of most organizations would soon be exhausted. Furthermore, if policymakers were to wait until they had at hand all the available information that might be pertinent to a major policy decision, as Lindblom has pointed out, it would be too late to be of any use. Nevertheless, within reasonable budgetary limits and within the limited time available, an adequate information search can usually be carried out, along with all the other steps of problem solving. For example, in the Herek, Janis, and Huth (1987) study of 19 major international crises (described in Chapter 6), there were three U.S. policy decisions that showed no symptoms of defective decisionmaking (in the Indochina crisis of 1954, the Quemoy-Matsu crisis of 1958, and the Laos crisis of 1961); each of those decisions was made within a period of a few weeks. (In the other 13 crises, symptoms of defective decisionmaking were observed, but the symptom that occurred least often was failure to collect pertinent information.)

   Even in an extraordinary crisis when only a few hours are available for search and appraisal, most governments and other large organizations have resources to carry out a fairly substantial information search rapidly by obtaining comprehensive briefings from several independent experts who have the appropriate background and have already assimilated much of the pertinent information currently available. Also, multiple briefings can quickly be obtained from leading proponents of diverse policy positions, who can be counted on to highlight the defects of the alternatives they oppose. At a single meeting with appropriate experts and contending advocates, the crisis managers may be able to carry out the four steps of vigilant problem solving adequately enough to avoid gross symptoms of defective policymaking. (See pp. 257–59.)

3. Another shortcoming of vigilant problem solving when carried out by policymakers who rely on ordinary information seeking and ordinary critical thinking—just as when it is carried out by

professional analysts who use systematic "scientific" procedures—is that it cannot be counted upon to pinpoint the crucial
policy problems that require solutions. The problems that are
placed on the agenda of policymaking groups are typically formulated by representatives of powerful interest groups within
the organization in the context of a political struggle. As a result, overall performance gaps and other potentially major
threats to the organization as a whole requiring innovative policy changes may be overlooked until it is too late to avert serious losses. Nevertheless, when policymakers are vigilant and
are not dominated by any of the three types of constraints designated by the model in Figure 7-1, they are more likely to pay
attention to new developments that are potentially dangerous
and to regard them as challenges requiring a policy decision.
The same can be said concerning potential opportunities that
could facilitate advantageous changes in policy, as when the
leaders of a national government take advantage of a temporary lowering of international tensions to work out an agreement with a rival nation to terminate chronically unproductive
forms of cold war competition that could lead to a hot war.
Furthermore, vigilant problem solving is conducive to obtaining new informational inputs, and these can lead to problem
redefinition, as when vigilant members of a wrangling executive
committee receive a startling financial report indicating that the
danger of bankruptcy is looming much larger than they had
thought. A new piece of information of that kind can induce
them to start thinking about relinquishing partisan demands in
order to find an integrative solution that meets hitherto neglected requirements for survival of the organization as a
whole. In general, errors of omission, such as overlooking major threats or opportunities, are more likely to be corrected by
the leading partisans in a power struggle when they are using
the vigilant problem-solving strategy than when they are using
any of the seat-of-the-pants strategies designated in Figure
7-1.

4. Yet another deficiency of vigilant problem solving could interfere with arriving at "good" policy solutions that will satisfy
   the main objectives of all concerned: there is no acceptable procedure for resolving conflicts in goals among contending powerholders, as Lindblom has emphasized. In order to select one

of the best (if not the very best) of the viable policy alternatives, the policymakers need to make their selection on the basis of careful evaluations of the options under consideration. But the representatives of different interest groups and political factions usually do not agree on assigning priorities among different goals, especially when the selection requires troublesome trade-offs, such as tolerating relatively high monetary costs in the immediate future in order to eliminate potential threats that might adversely affect one particular part of the organization or nation in the distant future. In the absence of any available method for ranking goals definitively, disagreements cannot be readily settled in a way that will be satisfactory to all the contending powerholders who need to accept and implement a new policy if it is to be successful.

What happens in practice, as Lindblom points out, is that disagreements usually get settled through interaction among the contending parties, which often includes face-to-face negotiations in formal meetings together with informal bargaining in casual conversations during which they talk about "trading of contingent benefits, payments or favors" that enable them to make "mutual adjustments." Vigilant problem solving can facilitate the bargaining and adjustments required for successful negotiations, as I shall indicate shortly.

At times, of course, powerful participants who are "hardball politics" players engage in internal struggles and fight relentlessly for an extreme version of the policy they prefer by threatening their opponents with retaliatory punishments if they do not accept it. Such threats constitute one of the major affiliative constraints that interfere with effective problem solving, as represented in the constraints model. (See the comments about fear of punishment in Chapter 3.)

Role of Vigilant Problem Solving in the Bargaining Process

When a policy is arrived at via political bargaining within an organization (or between organizations, as in international negotiations on arms control), vigilant problem solving can enter in at two different stages. First, it can play an important role during the pre-negotiation stage. Leading members of a steering committee in each of the rival factions might use a vigilant problem-solving approach to arrive at the policy position that their group will advocate later on when negotiations take place. As Lindblom says, "Various participants in political action use analysis to improve the way they play their interactive roles."

Typically, the persons selected for the role of negotiator actively participate in the "partisan analysis" that goes on during the pre-negotiation stage. If they have engaged in vigilant problem solving, the partisans who attend the crucial negotiation meetings will have done their homework beforehand in a very thorough way and will be well-prepared to engage in *informed advocacy*. That is to say, their preparation from the preliminary work they have done using a vigilant problem-solving approach increases the chances of intelligent and constructive debate. They are likely to be more effective in explaining the reasons for their position, more responsive to sound arguments and pertinent evidence offered by opponents, and less rigid in clinging to initial assumptions that may be questionable. Consequently, they are more likely to react positively to sound compromise proposals that meet the minimal requirements of all the contending parties and more willing to vote in favor of the policy alternative for which the best case has been made during the negotiation sessions. All of these consequences of vigilant problem solving by the partisans in the pre-negotiation stage improve the chances of their arriving at a sensible integrative solution, one that meets the essential needs of the opposing factions and of the organization as a whole.

The second way that the vigilant problem-solving approach can enter in is during the negotiation stage itself. Although it may happen rarely, the participants in the group of negotiators sometimes engage in a mutual effort to go through the steps of vigilant problem solving together, taking account of the rock-bottom requirements of each of the contending parties for a satisfactory settlement. This type of approach is essentially what has been prescribed by a number of leading experts on conflict resolution as the best way to engage in negotiation. For example, Nierenberg speaks about "replacing the outdated win-lose attitude with genuinely creative negotiating," which strives to arrive at "solutions that will satisfy all parties." Nierenberg goes on to say:

> Many negotiations conducted in a highly competitive manner
> have ended in what seemed to be a complete victory for one
> side. The alleged winner was in possession of everything he

wanted and the loser had suffered a humiliating defeat. However, such a "settlement" will rarely stay settled. Unless the terms arrived at had been advantageous in some way to the "loser," he will soon seek means of changing the settlement. Unlike a game, there is no "end" to a life negotiation situation. (Pp. 23–24)

The more steps of vigilant problem solving that are carried out cooperatively by the group of negotiators, the fewer the symptoms of defective decisionmaking, and the higher the probability of a mutually satisfactory outcome—a policy decision that all contending parties can live with, without violating the agreement. The most successful of all negotiated agreements are likely to be those for which vigilant problem solving entered into both stages of the process.

Applying the Model to Interactive Policymaking

The constraints model represented in Figure 7-1 differs in a number of crucial ways from "rational actor" models in economics, political science, and management sciences. This new model does not assume that organizational policy decisions are necessarily made by a unitary actor or a unified set of actors who are "steersmen." Rather, as I have already indicated, it requires an analysis of the policymaking approach used by each of the powerholders in the organization who engages in whatever political and intellectual interactions contribute to the making of a policy decision. For example, the model is applicable to participants at lower levels of an organization who are not usually regarded as policymakers, but who nevertheless help to shape the policies that finally become operative by the way they implement directives from the top. (See the discussion of the feedback loop conception of policymaking power within an organization on pp. 331–34.)

For those policy decisions made by a chief executive or a top-level executive committee that are legally or institutionally binding, the constraints model can readily be applied. In general, the constraints model is most directly pertinent *when an individual decisionmaker or a decisionmaking group has the capacity to mobilize power to implement policy decisions.*[2] But what about the many policy decisions that are the product of a highly interactive process, reflecting deep cleavages among partisans with partial power (such as those manifested by bureaucratic struggles among leaders in rival departments and by the odd provisions in the compromises worked out to settle disputes between the executive branch and the legislative branch of a national government)? The constraints model is also applicable to these decisions but it requires some provisos. Separate diagnoses have to be made of the procedural strategy used by each of the contending leaders and factions within the organization who take part in the bargaining that goes on before a final policy decision is agreed upon. Different factions or partisan groups can be expected to show different procedural strategies, depending partly upon whether for each of the factions the conditions making for vigilant problem solving are present and, if not, whether it is primarily a cognitive, affiliative, or egocentric constraint that is dominant among the members of each of the factions at the time they are developing their policy position.

A plausible variant of my main assumption about the relationship between process and outcome, which needs to be tested in a variety of governmental, business, and public welfare organizations, is the following hypothesis: *The likelihood that the members of a faction will be successful in a political struggle within an organization depends to a substantial degree upon whether they use a vigilant problem-solving approach to arrive at the details of their policy position and to work out their political strategy for attempting to gain support for it among other powerholders (including contingency plans concerning the maximum concessions or accommodations they will be willing to make to their opponents and the minimum concessions or accommodations they expect in return).* Any partisan group, according to this hypothesis, is likely to exert a much greater influence on the final compromise that is arrived at if they use a vigilant problem-solving approach than if they use a seat-of-the-pants approach dominated by simple decision rules.

On essentially the same assumption, predictions can be made about the success of policy innovations introduced via changes in practice by people at middle or low levels of an organization's hierarchy. When there is sufficient evidence to determine who introduced an innovation and what procedural strategy they used, predictions can be made about the likelihood that the innovation will: (1) spread throughout the organization, (2) be tacitly accepted or officially approved by top-level powerholders, and, (3) have a positive outcome from the standpoint of organizational goals.

Policymaking Processes to Which the Model Cannot Be Applied

We have just seen that the constraints model can be applied not only to the policy decisions made by a central policymaker or top-level executive committee but also to various factions that engage in bargaining and to lower-level administrators in the hierarchy to whom authority is delegated or who spontaneously introduce innovations. But there are certain types of policymaking processes to which the model cannot be applied.

Richard Nelson has emphasized that the image of policies being made by a "central steersman controlling a well-working rudder" does not by any means fit all instances. Policy decisions are not always the result of either "the deliberations of a central policymaker and his or her staff" or the "bargaining" among key powerholders and leaders of key constituencies, "who must agree on policy before it can go through." From time to time, "policies bubble up as actions taken or proposals generated from below, only a few of which can be subjected to top executive scrutiny."

The constraints model cannot be applied if the innovators of a policy that "bubbles up" remain anonymous and the policy becomes operative without any identifiable executives having approved it. In such instances, the model cannot be used to make any predictions because it requires identifying the participants in the policy process and obtaining records or interviews bearing on their procedural strategy.

There is another type of policymaking process to which the model cannot be applied—namely, when an unplanned policy emerges from executive actions and political compromises among policymakers without anyone having confronted the policy issue. Lindblom gives a possible example of a policy of this kind:

> We can say that policy in the United States government leaves broad scope for business monopoly, especially in the form of oligopoly, thus restricting prosecution under anti-trust law to no more than a small number of cases. No official or agency so decided. The policy emerges somehow from the policymaking system. (P. 5)

For any unplanned or inadvertently created policy, the constraints model might be applied at least in a limited way to any identifiable participants who contributed to its formation or implementation—

even if they unintentionally initiated or accepted it and contributed to its implementation as an oversight. This often occurs when the first of the procedural strategies shown in Figure 3-1 (relying on SOPs or simple cognitive rules to deal with a problem that is judged to be unimportant) is dominant. But again, if none of the participants can be identified, the model cannot be applied at all. For such instances, where a "hidden hand" appears to be operating in the interactions among large numbers of anonymous participants in a collectivity, a different type of model representing sociological, political, or economic processes would be required.[3]

Supplementary Assumptions Needed to Correct Oversimplifications

In focusing on basic features of the psychological processes involved in arriving at policy decisions, the schematic model presented in Figure 7-1 does not take account of many complexities and complications, which require supplementary elaboration. In the remaining sections of this chapter, I shall call attention to the main oversimplifications and formulate some secondary assumptions for dealing with them. The auxiliary assumptions are compatible with the preliminary model and can be introduced whenever needed to enable analysts to use the model for diagnosing sources of error despite the presence of one or another of the complexities or complications that make the simplified form of the model represented in Figure 7-1 seem inapplicable.

Changes in Procedural Strategy

The constraints model represented in Figure 7-1 is intended to describe the main social and psychological determinants of the procedural strategy used by policymakers. It can be applied to suggest factors that might account for poor, medium, or high-quality decisionmaking displayed by any individual or group. When applied to group decisions it can be used to analyze sources of error that arose in *any particular meeting* when the members discussed a policy or in *any series of meetings* during which the members evolved a new policy decision or reaffirmed an old one in accordance with the thrust of an earlier policy. Some additional assumptions are needed, however, when the model is used to analyze any *change in procedural strategy* that policymakers display during the course of arriving at a policy decision.

The model is directly applicable when policymakers use a vigilant problem-solving strategy or a simplistic strategy from beginning to end of the policymaking process. In such instances, the policymakers' answers to the key questions in Figure 7-1 continue unchanged from the outset when the challenge is first encountered up until closure, when they commit themselves to a new policy decision. Occasionally the final decision is made so rapidly that there simply is no time for any change to occur. This happens, for example, when a powerful emotive constraint becomes dominant at the same time that the challenge is perceived—as when a sudden threat evokes intense fear or an extraordinary opportunity evokes intense feelings of elation. The simple decision rule that policymakers rely upon when their emotions are strongly aroused can make for very rapid, impulsive action (for example, "Get the hell out of this distressing dilemma fast" or "Wow! Grab it!").

Even when the decisionmaking process goes on for many weeks or months, the answers to the key questions sometimes remain unchanged and the procedural strategy correspondingly remains constant. But whenever the policy issue is under consideration for a long period of time, policymakers are likely to be exposed to a great deal of new information (of the type mentioned in the first column [antecedent conditions] in Figure 7-1), some of which is likely to evoke changes in the answers to the key questions, with corresponding shifts in procedural strategy.

The model, with its specification of different pathways influenced by different antecedent conditions, carries the implication that the same person or group will shift from one procedural strategy to another whenever any of the specified conditions change. This point can be well illustrated by the changes in decisionmaking behavior displayed by John Dean, who was one of the major participants in the Watergate cover-up policy evolved by President Nixon and his White House aides. There is considerable evidence, including corroboration from the White House tapes, that Dean shifted from a simplistic approach (with reliance on the simple affiliative rule to conform with whatever his bosses wanted) to a vigilant problem-solving strategy when the conditions affecting him and other members of the policymaking group changed as a result of ongoing criminal investigations and the Senate Watergate hearings.

John Dean's shift to a vigilant problem-solving approach occurred shortly after the threat of being exposed became apparent and he realized that he could end up being convicted, along with Haldeman and others in the White House group, for obstructing justice. After vigilant search and appraisal of a number of alternative courses of action, Dean decided to try to keep his own jail sentence to a minimum by revealing to the Department of Justice and the Senate investigating committee the full details of the cover-up policy. This decision played a major role not only in bringing about the imprisonment of all the White House aides who were co-conspirators but also in initiating impeachment proceedings against Nixon, which led to the President's resignation. As Haldeman later put it, "Dean shifted roles from one of the protectors of the President to the protector of himself—a shift of enormous historical consequence." This particular case happens also to illustrate, therefore, a point made earlier about the potential power of implementers who are not assigned any major policymaking responsibilities. This man was an implementer who, for his own personal reasons, was able to play a major role in counteracting an indefensible policy that could not survive the light of public scrutiny, even though the policy was being promoted by the chief executive and other powerful superiors.[4]

Any policymaker will pursue a vigilant problem-solving approach, according to one of the key assumptions of the constraints model, only so long as he or she continues to presume, consciously or preconsciously, that all of the salient constraints are manageable or surmountable. In terms of the mediating processes represented in Figure 7-1, this means that the policymaker continues to give a negative answer to each of the key questions about constraints.

A chief executive and his advisors may start off with a simplistic approach but later on shift to vigilant problem solving as a consequence of new unsolicited information that makes them much more acutely aware of the importance of the problem or that makes them realize that one or another constraint is by no means as potent as they had originally thought. Or they may display the reverse change, from an initial procedural strategy of vigilant problem solving to a simplistic approach, as a consequence of encountering new information that makes a constraint initially judged to be manageable loom so large that it is given overriding priority.

Once policymakers become so impressed by a cognitive, affiliative, or egocentric constraint that they judge it to require top priority as the most crucial requirement to be met in arriving at a vital deci-

sion, they discontinue the vigilant problem-solving approach and begin to show symptoms of defective decisionmaking. At the moment
a policymaker changes his or her answers to any of the key questions
from no to yes, a switch takes place to one of the quick-and-easy
strategies that relies upon simple decision rules to cope with the new
overriding constraint, derailing the procedural strategy of vigilant
problem solving from its previous course.

If there is any such derailment, the degree to which policymakers
fail to carry out the various steps of vigilant problem solving (and
correspondingly, the number of symptoms of defective decisionmaking) depends on *when* in the sequence of decisionmaking the change
occurs. Suppose that an initially vigilant chief executive changes
from no to yes on any one of the key questions shortly after being
briefed about a highly threatening crisis, but before having completed the first step of formulating the main requirements to be met.
He or she will display a large number of symptoms of defective decisionmaking because from then on his or her procedural strategy will
be a simplistic approach. But now suppose that the same vigilant
chief executive makes no such change until many weeks later, after
having completed almost all the steps of vigilant problem solving. In
such a case, the chief executive's change from no to yes on one of the
key questions would have comparatively little effect on the quality of
the policymaking process. He or she might display only one symptom of defective decisionmaking (e.g., failure to work out complete
contingency plans).

When powerholders work together in an executive committee or
policy planning group, the same kind of change can occur among all
the leading members during one of the meetings as a result of impressive new information about the extremely unfavorable consequences
of failing to give priority to a constraint that up to that time had
been regarded as manageable. Again, the detrimental effect of such
a change on the quality of the policymaking group's deliberations
would be expected to be extreme, moderate, or slight depending
upon how early in the sequence of the group's meetings the change
from a collective vigilant problem-solving approach to a collective
seat-of-the-pants approach occurs.[5]

The point here is that the theoretical model represented in
Figure 7-1 can be used to analyze both persistence and change in the
dominant procedural strategy of an entire group of policymakers
who collectively arrive at a policy decision. Sometimes it is no more
difficult to obtain detailed minutes of meetings and other observa-

tional evidence necessary for using the model to analyze changes in a group's decisionmaking strategy than it is to obtain memoirs, diaries, memoranda, letters, interviews, and other data necessary for using it to analyze changes in an individual leader's decisionmaking.[6]

Multiple Constraints

The model indicates that whenever policymakers do not meet the conditions specified for the pathway that leads to vigilant problem solving, they will adopt a seat-of-the-pants approach that relies on just one type of simple decision rule to deal with one type of dominating constraint. But sometimes more than one type of constraint is given high priority and, as a result, more than one type of decision rule is used in a simplistic approach.

Whenever a policymaker judges that more than one constraint must be given priority, he or she will tend to use a combination of simple decision rules to deal with the multiple constraints. If the dominating constraints lead to incompatible action tendencies, some form of compromise is to be expected. For example, a resentful State Department official who wants to retaliate against the leaders of a foreign nation who have humiliated him may be constrained from deciding to do so openly because the chief executive and other powerholders in the government have settled upon an official policy of conciliation that requires the angry official to engage in negotiations with his opponents. The official might then deal with these contradictory constraints by a compromise form of action whereby he adopts the "avoid punishment" rule by deciding to go through the motions of negotiation but in subtle ways manages to sabotage the proceedings and to inflict retaliatory humiliations on the opponents. This type of compromise, which undermines the policy directives arrived at in the top echelon of the hierarchy, constitutes one of the ways in which implementers sometimes play a determining role in what the actual policy turns out to be.

Applying the Model to a Series of Nested Decisions

Most major policy changes consist of a series of nested decisions that include elaborations or modifications of the original policy decision. Amitai Etzioni has described nested decisions of this kind in his account of "mixed scanning," which he surmises is often used by effective policymakers. It is a combination of two different types of procedural strategies: one involves analytic problem solving to arrive at a fundamental policy decision that provides guidance for the successive decisions that will follow it; the other involves relatively routine decisions in line with the basic policy that make for minor incremental changes. For a fundamental policy decision, according to Etzioni, policymakers typically use "intensive scanning," which refers to intensive searching for and collecting, processing, and evaluating relevant information together with careful deliberation and other components of what I refer to as vigilant problem solving. The routine incremental decisions that are nested in the fundamental policy decision, on the other hand, involve relatively "superficial scanning"—which corresponds to a predominantly seat-of-the-pants approach that relies upon a simple affiliative rule ("select a course of action that conforms nicely with the organization's current policy").

Etzioni cites as an example of "mixed scanning" the Truman Doctrine established immediately after World War II. The fundamental policy decision was to contain the Soviet Union to prevent it from expanding its influence, particularly in Europe, beyond the borders of the countries already within the Soviet bloc, which the United States would not attempt to free from Soviet domination. As new problems involving clashes with the Soviet Union arose in the Balkans and the Near East, incremental decisions were made which were "guided by the fundamental context-setting decision."

A series of nested decisions is especially to be expected whenever the initial policy decision includes contingency plans, which directly influence the next decisions in the series that deal with the new problems that are bound to arise either because the policy is not being implemented in exactly the way intended or because the policy is not always working out successfully even when it is implemented satisfactorily. The nested decisions do not always leave the original policy decision intact, especially when vigilant policymakers deliberately arrange to try out the new fundamental policy on a small scale so as to be able to modify it on a trial-and-error basis. Nested decisions sometimes embody changes that improve the original policy, which can be highly beneficial for the organization.[7] But, of course, they can also embody detrimental changes that undermine the original objectives of the policy, introduced by obstructive powerholders, either inadvertently or deliberately to satisfy their personal hidden agenda.

In general, once policymakers become strongly committed to a new policy, they are motivated to make nested decisions that do not deviate from it despite whatever new difficulties arise. Many people inside and outside the organization become aware of the policymakers' commitment, not only from the policy directives they send to subordinates, but also from the public statements they issue to announce the new policy and to encourage others to accept it, all of which create expectations throughout the organization and its constituencies that the leaders will themselves live up to it. A leader's realization that there are these widespread social expectations gives rise, in effect, to a powerful affiliative constraint that contributes to his or her readiness to use the simple affiliative decision rule to conform with the prior commitment. Thus, in terms of the constraints model in Figure 7-1, the routine nested decisions made by the policymakers themselves after having settled upon a fundamental policy decision can be regarded as the product of the procedural pathway that gives priority to the affiliative constraint imposed by their *commitment* to the earlier policy decision.

A well-known example of the way commitment "freezes" a policy can be seen in President Lyndon B. Johnson's persistent refusal to reverse his Vietnam War policy after he became publicly committed to defeating the communists in Vietnam.

Despite a very high degree of commitment, powerful setbacks and loss of support from other powerholders can have the effect of terminating the series of nested decisions by inducing a policymaker to switch to an entirely different policy. This is illustrated by President Johnson's final decison to abandon his Vietnam War escalation policy and to abstain from running for reelection (see pp. 101-2).

Making the Model More Complete

One of the main deficiencies of the model, which I mentioned earlier, needs to be discussed further in order to call attention to a new set of problems for research that could lead to filling in some gaps to make the model more complete. The deficiency has to do with the incomplete formulations of the antecedent conditions that induce or contribute to each of the three types of constraints that are key components of the model represented in Figure 7-1. If the model in its present form is on the right track, it poses a number of new questions, particularly about antecedent conditions. These questions require basic social science inquiries directed toward increasing our understanding of when, how, and why a simplistic approach is used in making policy decisions rather than vigilant problem solving: What are the conditions that incline policymakers to give positive answers to the questions about being unable to manage the constraints? More specifically, what are the observable antecedent conditions that result in the policymaking process becoming dominated by each of the major cognitive constraints? . . . by each of the major affiliative constraints? . . . by each of the major egocentric constraints? Which decision rule (or set of rules) do policymakers rely upon when each of the major constraints becomes dominant in the policymaking process? Without answers to these questions, the constraints model of policymaking does not enable predictions to be made as to which decision rule (or set of rules) is most likely to be dominant when a policymaker does not use a vigilant problem-solving approach.

To make the model more complete it will be necessary to add further assumptions about the conditions under which policymakers rely upon each of the decision rules that short-circuits the essential steps of problem solving and leads to avoidable errors. Ultimately, studies directed toward answering the new set of research questions posed by the preliminary model should enable us to specify for each of the most commonly used cognitive, affiliative, and egocentric decision rules the prime antecedent conditions that play a causal role in its being used by policymakers and the particular types of avoidable errors that are most likely to result from relying upon it.

In my current comparative case study research on U.S. governmental policymaking during major international crises of the past several decades, I am attempting to give some preliminary answers to this new set of research questions. The methodological approach used in my case study research on international crises is based on the "focused comparison" method elaborated by Alexander George and Richard Smoke and embodies the modus operandi method for determining probable causes of disastrous events described by Michael Scriven.[8]

In order to illustrate the kinds of hypotheses that are starting to emerge from this new line of inquiry oriented toward making the model more complete, Tables 8–1, 8–2, and 8–3 show error-sequence outlines for three fairly commonly used emotive rules. Each outline specifies (a) the antecedent conditions that lead to reliance on a particular decision rule to deal with the emotive constraint, (b) the telltale signs of the first step of the mediating modus operandi indicating that the emotive constraint is exerting a powerful influence on the policymakers during the period they are working on the decision, (c) the telltale signs of the second step of the mediating modus operandi, indicating that the particular decision rule is dominating the decisionmaking process, and (d) the consequences in terms of observable symptoms of defective decisionmaking.

The first outline (Table 8-1) is for the "angry retaliation" rule, which, if verbalized, would be something like this: "When you are thwarted, injured, or humiliated, don't let the bastards get away with it; do something to punish them in retaliation." (See Figure 4-1 on pp. 74-75 and the discussion of it that follows for further details about how this emotive rule operates.)

A historic example that appears to fit the entire pattern shown in this error-sequence outline is the set of nested decisions made by President Dwight D. Eisenhower when he and his advisors unexpectedly were confronted with a major crisis that arose in 1956: Britain, France, and Israel invaded Egypt in response to Egyptian President Nasser's taking control of the Suez Canal and illegally closing it to Israeli ships. Several sources indicate that from the outset and throughout the period of this crisis President Eisenhower displayed strong emotional reactions of anger. The President, who was noted for his calmness in the face of crises, in this instance is described by Herbert Parmet as having been "personally thwarted"; he "reacted with fury and insisted the United States go to the [UN] Security Council immediately and stop [England, France, and Israel from continuing] the invasion." The President was "shocked," according to Sherman Adams, his White House chief of staff, by the dangerously destabilizing military action taken by England and France, without giving him any prior warning, at a time when he was campaigning for reelection, just before election day. "Outside of his illnesses," Adams asserts, "that was the worst week that Eisenhower experienced in all the years that I worked with him in the White House." Adams refers to Eisenhower's "hurt feelings" and describes him as "wrought up . . . over the turn of events." Michael Guhin also characterizes Eisenhower as "irritated by the whole affair" and as having personally taken the initiative in the harsh, punitive actions taken by the U.S. government against its main allies. Guhin quotes Abba Eban, Israel's ambassador to Washington, as having noted that President Eisenhower "was in a mood of someone betrayed."

TABLE 8-1 Error-Sequence Outline for Reliance on the Retaliation Rule to Cope with Anger as an Emotive Constraint

Antecedent Conditions	Telltale Signs of Strong Influence of Anger as an Emotive Constraint	Telltale Signs of Relying on the Retaliation Rule	Consequences for Quality of Decisionmaking
A. *Essential conditions* 1. Crisis provoked by unexpected blow (deprivation, injury, thwarting, or humiliation) inflicted by leaders of another group (or nation). 2. Absence of explanation or evidence indicating that the blow was inadvertent or accidental. B. *Facilitating conditions* 3. Positive evidence indicating that those who inflicted the blow are likely to repeat it. 4. Indications that those who inflicted the blow was intentional. 5. Organizational norms, traditions, or ideological doctrines prescribing prompt retaliation for the type of blow inflicted. 6. Recent policy failures and/or provocative frustrations of policymakers that reduce their threshold of frustration tolerance. 7. Absence of a leader or esteemed advisor who counsels delay and encourages vigilant problem solving.	1. Manifestations of high emotional arousal of anger in response to the blow, with indications of readiness to take immediate action. 2. Verbal expressions of resentment and condemnation of perpetrators of the blow, with high frequency of expletives. 3. Resistance and irritation evoked by anyone's suggestion that anger should be curbed or should not drastically influence the policy decision.	1. Verbal statements of intent to inflict retaliation. 2. Informal conversations or diary entries conveying images of punitive retaliatory actions against perpetrators of the blow. 3. Overt signs of impatience or irritation toward anyone who opposes a retaliatory course of action.	1. Gross omissions in survey of objectives, especially those requiring present or future cooperation with the perpetrators of the blow. 2. Gross omissions in survey of alternatives. 3. Poor information search. 4. Selective bias in processing information at hand. 5. Failure to reconsider originally rejected nonretaliatory alternatives. 6. Failure to examine some major costs and risks of the retaliatory course of action. 7. Failure to work out detailed implementation, monitoring, and contingency plans.

With regard to the behavioral consequences of President Eisenhower's "wrought-up" state, he may have displayed a low degree of cognitive efficiency in dealing with the frustrating crisis, manifested by his overlooking important objectives concerning future relations of America with its main allies. Eisenhower took the lead in putting extreme pressure, accompanied by severe economic threats, on England and France to give up their plan to take over the Suez Canal, forcing them to pull out of Egypt immediately. He gave America's allies no opportunity to save face, thereby inflicting on them a stinging defeat. The governments in London and Paris promptly fell. At the UN, the U.S. voted to censure England and France in a way that was unnecessarily humiliating; during the following weeks, the U.S. government delayed giving urgently needed oil supplies to aid the two countries when they were suffering from a severe oil shortage as a result of the closing of the Suez Canal. This harsh handling under Eisenhower's leadership might have alienated France, contributing to that nation's subsequent decision to withdraw from NATO. It may also have impaired U.S. relations with England.

The second example (Table 8-2) shows the sequence that occurs when policymakers rely primarily upon the audacity ("Can do!") decision rule to counteract or set aside incipient emotional reactions of *apprehensiveness* when they feel it is essential to carry out a risky course of action, even though they realize that the chances of failure are high because of specific obstacles or dangers that will be very difficult to overcome. The audacity ("Can do!") rule, if verbalized, would go like this: "Don't be chicken about carrying out a dangerous course of action even if it scares the hell out of most experts; concentrate your resources on finding ways to overcome the deterrents." (See pp. 76–77.)

I encountered what appears to be a fairly clear-cut example of the audacity ("Can do!") decision rule contributing to faulty planning when I looked into the decision by President Carter and his advisors that led to the ill-fated attempt in April 1980 to use military force to rescue the American hostages in Iran. In the news media it was called a fiasco comparable to the Bay of Pigs. The case study evidence fits the pattern of the error-sequence outline in Table 8-2. In all the available accounts, I noticed that when the rescue mission was discussed and approved it was recognized as being extremely dangerous but was deemed to be essential as a desperate attempt to end the hostage crisis. Deliberations were focused mainly on ways of overcoming the extreme dangers of invading Teheran and then escaping

TABLE 8-2 Error-Sequence Outline for Reliance on the Audacity ("Can do!") Rule (Fostering a Risky Course of Action) to Cope with Inner Conflict as an Emotive Constraint

Antecedent Conditions	Telltale Signs of Inner Conflict About Deterrents as an Emotive Constraint	Telltale Signs of Relying on the Audacity ("Can do!") Rule	Consequences for Quality of Decisionmaking
A. Essential conditions 1. Crisis threatens vital interests with no apparently safe solution; known obstacles or deterrents that pose danger of failure of the least objectionable alternative evoke *apprehensiveness.* 2. Social pressures on policymakers to be "courageous" by agreeing to a risky course of action despite the deterrents, which evoke anticipatory feelings of *shame* for refusing. **B. Facilitating conditions** 3. Personal commitment of policymakers to military or machismo norms requiring willingness to take a risky course of action despite the deterrents, which evokes anticipatory feelings of guilt and low self-esteem for refusing. 4. Organizational norms, traditions, or doctrines foster resorting to a risky course of action even if it appears to be a "mission impossible."	1. Initial manifestations of suppressed *apprehensiveness* about the deterrents and anticipatory *shame* or *guilt* about being deterred. 2. Verbal statements about need to be courageous despite dangers that might scare the chicken-hearted. 3. *Irritation, anger,* and *contempt* expressed toward anyone who is openly apprehensive or unresponsive to talk about the need for audacious action.	1. *Pride* expressed about favoring a risky course of action undeterred by the obvious dangers. 2. *Contempt* expressed toward anyone who questions the "courageous" course of action on grounds of it being too dangerous. 3. *Preoccupation* with the subproblems of surmounting the deterrents in formal planning meetings and in private conversations. 4. Repeated assertions of commitment to risky course of action with *strong emotional bias* expressed in dogmatic supporting arguments—such as "we have no choice"; "it would be cowardly" and "dishonorable" to be deterred.	1. No effect on survey of objectives. 2. Curtailment of survey of alternatives—ignoring those that concede the dangers to be insurmountable deterrents. 3. Restriction of information search primarily to ways of surmounting the deterrents. 4. Selective bias in processing information: discounting information that favors a less risky course of action. 5. Refusal to reconsider any originally rejected course of action that concedes to the deterrents. 6. Failure to examine some of the less obvious costs and risks of the audacious choice—the "unsqueaky wheels" that are not directly linked to the known deterrents. 7. Detailed implementation, monitoring, and contingency plans worked out only for the known deterrents, neglecting the "unsqueaky wheels."

194

without suffering high casualties, which were the obvious deterrents. Questions about the risks of the first phase of the mission (the ill-fated desert rendezvous) apparently were hardly ever raised within the top-level planning group. Pertinent evidence of this defect is inadvertently revealed in the memoirs of Zbigniew Brzezinski, the President's National Security Advisor, who for many months had been urging President Carter to restore America's honor by launching a military attack rather than continuing to try to negotiate. Contrary to the reports of governmental investigative committees, Brzezinski conveys an image of the decision as having been very carefully worked out. But this claim is contradicted to some extent by his own detailed account of how it failed. From what he says it is apparent that the major risks of the first crucial phase of the rescue plan—the rendezvous and refueling of the U.S. aircraft in the Iranian desert—had hardly been examined at all by President Carter and his key advisors. For example, Brzezinski acknowledges that "my concern over the possible failure of the mission did not pertain to something like what finally happened—its early abortion—but rather to . . . its execution in Teheran . . . ."

Brzezinski's memoirs make it clear that the top policymakers in the White House group had not envisaged the possibility that the mission might have to be aborted either because several of the helicopters might malfunction or that the mission might be compromised as a result of being observed by Iranians in passing vehicles on the nearby road. Apparently, certain of the crucial implementation plans were not examined carefully enough by Brzezinski and others in the President's advisory group. A high-level military review group set up by the Joint Chiefs of Staff to investigate what went wrong concluded that the flaws could have been corrected if the small secret circle of planners had asked for their plan to be reviewed by qualified experts within the government. For example, arrangements could have been made to carry out a weather reconnaissance flight in advance of the helicopter flights, and more helicopters could have been added to the mission. The same report also faults the planners for having failed to arrange to have the desert rendezvous "fully rehearsed" in advance and also for having neglected to set up an identifiable on-the-spot command post with adequate communication and control in the event of unanticipated difficulties. If these additional implementation and contingency plans had been worked out, the chances of failures requiring that the mission be aborted, as well as the chances of a disaster, such as the accidental crash of U.S.

aircraft in which eight men were killed, might have been considerably reduced.

From the detailed case studies by Paul Ryan and Gary Sick and from other available accounts, I surmise that a major reason that questions about the risks of the first phase of the mission were not raised by leaders of the top-level planning group is that they were concentrating on overcoming the dangers that were obvious deterrents of a rescue attempt, all of which were in the later phases—the enormous chances of the invading U.S. forces being detected and attacked when they approached Teheran, of the hostages being killed before their would-be rescuers could get to them, and of U.S. aircraft being shot down as they attempted to depart from Teheran. Evidently, as the old saying goes: it is the squeaky wheels that get the oil; any unsqueaky wheel is neglected. When grappling with a complicated multistage plan, while planning to carry out a "mission impossible," policymakers who rely heavily on the audacity ("Can do!") decision rule are likely to focus their implementation and contingency planning on the extremely worrisome steps that are known from the outset to be fraught with danger, the ones that post almost insurmountable deterrents. There appears to be a contrast effect whereby the least risky steps tend to be labeled as relatively easy to handle—"that's not where our main troubles will be." And so the "gung ho" policymakers neglect the unsqueaky wheels; they overlook the less obvious risks and fail to include them in their contingency plans. I refer to this as "the unsqueaky wheel trap" that besets any "can-doers." (Indicators of this form of self-entrapment are included as the last two items listed in the fourth column of Table 8-2, which describes the consequences of reliance on the audacity ["Can do!"] decision rule.)

The third error-sequence outline, shown in Table 8-3, pertains to the elated choice ("Wow! Grab it!") decision rule. This rule is used when the dominating emotive constraint consists of strong feelings of elation with a "raring-to-go" tendency to take advantage of what is seen as a rare opportunity (see Chapter 4). If it could be verbalized, the rule would be something along these lines: "This is better than you could hope for, so grab it; don't take any chance of losing the wonderful opportunity by wasting time looking into it any further."

President Truman's approval of the use of America's first A-bombs to destroy Japanese cities in 1945 was a historic decision that seems to fit the pattern shown in Table 8-3 fairly well, which suggests that reliance on the elated choice rule played a role in the decision-

TABLE 8-3 Error-Sequence Outline for Reliance on the Elated Choice ("Wow! Grab It!") Rule to Cope with Elation as an Emotive Constraint

Antecedent Conditions	Telltale Signs of Positive Excitement as an Emotive Constraint	Telltale Signs of Relying on the Elated Choice Rule	Consequences for Quality of Decisionmaking
A. *Essential conditions* 1. Vital problem: Perceived need for a good solution. 2. *Initially depressed or frustrated* because no satisfactory alternative can be found that meets all major requirements during intensive search. 3. Unexpected discovery of a promising new alternative: Satisfies some hitherto unmet major requirements. B. *Facilitating conditions* 4. Tradition of relaxing some requirements for a target of opportunity. 5. Deadline pressures: Augments sense of "grab it or lose it." 6. Apparent competition: Someone might "grab it away from you."	1. Manifestations of strong feelings of *elation*. 2. Verbal expressions of relief about dilemma, with marked increase in optimism about solving it. 3. Resistance to delaying the choice—concern about losing a unique opportunity.	1. Enthusiasm expressed about the "Wow" choice: global praise with strong emphasis on requirements that are met. 2. Strong desire for closure: Sense of "This is it! No need to search or deliberate any longer." 3. Minimizing of requirements that are not met with optimism about overcoming known obstacles (the high costs and risks). 4. Impatient with skeptics who question the "Wow" choice.	1. Initial canvassing of objectives may be thorough but some objectives are overlooked when the "Wow!" choice is made. 2. Search for good alternatives is curtailed after discovery of the "Wow!" choice. 3. Information search is curtailed after discovery of the "Wow!" choice. 4. Processing of new information is biased in favor of the "Wow!" choice. 5. Originally rejected alternatives are not reconsidered even when unsolicited new information favors them. 6. Potential costs and risks of the "Wow!" choice are ignored or minimized. 7. Little implementation and contingency planning.

making process. The President and several of his close advisors saw the A-bombs as providing a unique opportunity to end the war without the huge losses of American lives required by prior military plans for invading the Japanese home islands. Secretary of State James Byrnes enthusiastically informed President Truman that "the bomb might well put us in a position to dictate our own terms at the end of the war." Henry L. Stimson, Secretary of War in Truman's cabinet, when briefing the President referred glowingly to the new weapon as "a master card in our hand." There are numerous indications that when making plans to use the atomic bomb against Japanese cities, Truman and his advisors regarded it as a master card for the purpose of bringing a rapid end to the war in Japan. Some analysts suggests that they also had in mind the unique opportunity it offered to give a stupendous demonstration of U.S. arms superiority in a way that would help contain the Soviet Union after the war. Whether or not the latter consideration entered in, President Truman and his advisors were so enthusiastic about the attractive technological solution for saving American lives that they were not interested in what the government's intelligence sources had to say about the likelihood that Japanese leaders might already be on the verge of surrendering and that diplomatic maneuvers might succeed without using the A-bombs to kill tens of thousands of Japanese civilians.

Each of the error-sequence outlines specifies the main antecedent conditions that increase the chances of a given constraint being perceived consciously or preconsciously by a policymaker as so overwhelmingly important that he or she will answer yes to the corresponding constraint question in Figure 7-1. Each outline also lists the telltale signs or symptoms that can be used to determine whether or not the policymaking process is dominated by the constraint and the potentially detrimental effects on the quality of decisionmaking processes. The specifications of the antecedent conditions can be regarded, in effect, as additional hypotheses about the circumstances that tend to make the constraint dominant. The outline also designates the consequences of giving it top priority at the expense of ignoring other major requirements for a good solution to the policy problem at hand.

The error-sequence outlines should be regarded as supplements to the constraints model, filling in some of the gaps in the category of antecedent conditions that make for a positive answer to one of the key questions about constraints. Further amplifications of the antecedent conditions can be expected from comparative case study investigations (including my own ongoing research and that of other social scientists), which will provide an empirical basis for constructing error-sequence outlines that will take account of prior suggestive findings from psychological experiments and other types of inquiries. Research projects using a variety of methodological approaches are obviously needed to explicate and verify error-sequence outlines (like those in Tables 8-1, 8-2, and 8-3) for other emotive decision rules and also for each of the most commonly used self-serving, cognitive, and affiliative decision rules. (An example of an error-sequence outline for one particular affiliative rule was presented in Figure 3-2 [p. 59]—namely, the rule to preserve group harmony, inferred from my earlier research on "groupthink.")[9]

Subsequent research will undoubtedly indicate that some corrections are needed in the error-sequence outlines that have been formulated so far and may lead to the discovery of error sequences that have not yet been described in the social science literature. The findings could flesh out the bare bones of the theoretical analysis of the role of constraints represented in Figure 7-1 by providing the missing specifications essential for improving predictions about when an individual executive or a group engaging in policymaking will rely primarily on simple cognitive, affiliative, or egocentric decision rules. And, of course, the new findings are needed to enable one to predict *which particular rule* policymakers will use in various circumstances. Error-sequence outlines (like those illustrated in Tables 8-1, 8-2, and 8-3) should be considered as an essential part of the "assemblage" that I am proposing as a general theoretical framework for describing and analyzing sources of error in policymaking. The entire pattern shown in each error-sequence outline must be observed, with independent evidence bearing on each of the four sets of variables, in order to be at all confident about drawing a conclusion that a given constraint was exerting a strong influence and that heavy reliance on a simple decision rule to deal with that constraint was one of the probable causes of a poor-quality decision.

When there is evidence that a simple decision rule was being used by a policymaker but no independent evidence indicating that the plausible constraint was present and exerting a strong influence during the time when the policy decision was being made, it would be unwarranted to make a circular inference that the policymaker must have given a positive answer to the key question concerning the hypothesized constraint. There are always alternative causal sequences that could account for the use of a particular decision rule, some of which might have as much apparent plausibility as the one that implicates the hypothesized constraint. In general, when the constraints model is used as an aid to investigations of the probable causes of a defective policy decision, evidence of indicators bearing on the policymaker's judgment of the importance of the problem and responsiveness to the various types of constraints is always required in order to make reliable and valid inferences about how the policymaker answered the key questions listed in the second column of Figure 7-1.[10]

Once the various error-sequence outlines are worked out for the simple decision rules most frequently used by policymakers to cope with constraints that inhibit vigilant problem solving, they can be integrated with the other essential components of the assemblage embodied in Figure 7-1. As the theoretical framework becomes more fully elaborated on the basis of empirical findings it should become increasingly helpful to social science investigators and to organization troubleshooters, enabling them to extract more valid "lessons of history" than can be inferred on the basis of the impressionistic analyses now being used. Ultimately, those lessons could lead to improvements in the way crucial policy decisions are made so as to reduce the likelihood of lethal outcomes.

Implications

9

Who Will Be
Good Policymakers
and Who Will Not?
Hypotheses About Personality
Differences Derived from the
Constraints Model

In this chapter and the next one, I shall highlight some major implications of the constraints model in order to illustrate its potential value as a preliminary theoretical framework for generating new hypotheses that appear to be worth pursuing. The hypotheses presented in this chapter pertain mainly to personality differences; the ones presented in Chapter 10 deal with effective leadership practices. The two sets of hypotheses provide tentative answers to a major question about which we know relatively little at present: What does it take to function as an effective leader who promotes high-quality policymaking?

All the various hypotheses formulated with the aid of the constraints model will require careful investigation. They are intended to be added to the research agendas of psychologists, political scientists, sociologists, management experts, and other scholars in the social sciences who are interested in discovering the conditions for effective policymaking with an eye to improving the quality of policymaking in our society. Such improvements are urgently needed in the coming decades, as I pointed out at the beginning of this book, to prevent worldwide disasters from economic collapse, ecocatastrophes, and nuclear holocaust. At a more local and less cataclysmic level, the question of whether a government agency, a business enterprise, or a public service organization will survive depends in the long run upon the quality of the leaders' policymaking. Sometimes even a single gross error in the making of a crucial policy decision can lead to bankruptcy or its equivalent.

The constraints model has a number of specific implications for personality and other dispositional differences among top-level policymakers. It enables us to see in what ways individual differences might play a role in determining whether particular leaders are good or poor as policymakers. Some of the personality variables to be considered have long been familiar in the field of political psychology, particularly from the pioneering work of Harold D. Lasswell and Fred I. Greenstein. Many of the other variables have also become familiar from studies of emotional disorders and from other areas of personality research. A few of the variables, however, have only recently come into prominence or are new ones awaiting systematic exploration. The entire set of hypotheses, which emphasizes the *interaction* between informational inputs and dispositions, may provide a fresh perspective for research on the role of personality in effective crisis management and policy planning.

The hypotheses about personality differences have their counterparts as prescriptive hypotheses that specify what can be done within an organization to improve the quality of policymaking. Each of them, if verified in subsequent research, would have something to say about the types of persons who should be recruited and promoted as promising candidates for high-level positions as policymakers.

A Central Question for Personality Research: What Types of Persons Gravitate Toward a Defective Simplistic Approach?

The implications of the constraints model (represented in Figure 7-1 on p. 155) for individual differences in personality dispositions pertain to both the capabilities and the motivation of executives for carrying out vigilant problem solving. The model can be used as a guide for selecting dispositional variables from existing psychological knowledge about individual differences, so as to generate plausible hypotheses about personality deficiencies of men and women who are not likely to respond appropriately to relevant information, which makes them incompetent as policymakers.

As for all other kinds of defective performance, there are two main types of dispositional characteristics that are likely to be determinants of defective policymaking. One type involves lack of essential skills, which may be purely temporary (as when a novice executive has not yet learned the ropes about how to initiate policy changes within the organization) or chronic (as when a government official lacks the intellectual ability to learn the complicated technological knowledge required to understand the issues posed by arms control proposals concerning new weapon systems). The other type involves some form of personality deficiency, which also may be purely temporary (as when a person has difficulty concentrating on information gathering and evaluation for several weeks as a result of being grief-stricken following the death of a member of his or her family) or chronic (as when a person is constantly inclined to procrastinate as a result of a lifelong obsessive-compulsive neurosis). In the discussion that follows I shall focus mainly on *chronic* personality deficiencies that are expected to be determinants of failures to adopt a vigilant problem-solving approach when dealing with vital policy issues.

In a book on *Personality and Politics,* Alan Elms calls attention to the disappointingly meager contributions to psychological knowledge that have emerged from several decades of extensive research on personality traits, which failed to realize the optimistic hopes of psychologists and other social scientists earlier in the twentieth century. Many studies, Elms points out, were aimed at relating specific personality variables to specific displays of leadership effectiveness, including successful policymaking, with the expectation that specific qualities could be identified that would be characteristic of good leaders. But almost all the hypotheses investigated had to be abandoned because the findings did not support them. Nor did the research provide any impressive new discoveries of unexpected relationships. The findings simply had little to offer in differentiating between effective and ineffective leaders. As a reaction against the disappointments from these leadership studies, Elms states, "personality differences were denounced and ignored; the *situation* was proclaimed the dominant force." But hypotheses emphasizing the influence of purely situational factors soon were seen to have almost as many shortcomings as the original hypotheses about personality traits.

> Almost inevitably from the two extremes a middle view of leadership has emerged, emphasizing the interaction of personality and situation. . . . This revised view includes among other things an appreciation of the diverse roles of leaders and a recognition of how certain leadership traits promote greater . . . effectiveness in some circumstances but not in others. . . . It also allows for the possibility of more than one kind of [effective] leader in any particular group. (Elms, p. 84)

At present, research on the role of personality in leadership still seems to be in the doldrums because few generalizations about the interaction of personality and situational factors have as yet emerged. Nevertheless, despite the unpromising results obtained so far, a number of leading social scientists who study policymaking processes continue to expect that personality variables will be found to be related to good versus poor performances in policymaking in some definable situations. Major personality variables that seem likely candidates as determinants that contribute to the policymaking performances of chief executives and other organizational leaders have been summarized by Alexander George in his book *Presidential Decisionmaking in Foreign Policy:*

> Many individuals—even those who enjoy remarkably successful careers in politics, business, academia, or some other occupation—operate with complex motivational patterns that often include deficits or vulnerabilities in their *self-esteem* for which they attempt to obtain compensation in the pursuit of their careers and in the day-to-day performance of tasks associated with their occupations. . . .
> In addition, it must be recognized that an individual's personality system itself includes more than character-rooted needs and *ego defenses* (such as projection, denial, repression) that are employed to cope with *anxiety, fear* and *guilt.* Thus, an executive's political behavior will be shaped also by a variety of *cognitive beliefs* (ideology, world view, beliefs about correct political strategy and tactics, etc.) that he has acquired during the course of his education, personal development, and socialization into political affairs. . . .

Still another important component of the total personality of a political decisionmaker is the set of *skills* that he has acquired, which, he has come to believe, provide him with relevant tools and resources for effectively meeting the role demands of a political leader and an executive. These skills, and the successful use of them on previous occasions, provide the individual with *a sense of personal efficacy* for addressing at least some of the role tasks associated with executive leadership.

These examples indicate that the task of assessing the impact of an executive's personality on his performance is complex and thereby caution against the common tendency to explain too much of an individual's performance in terms of personality flaws . . . by going for "the jugular of the unconscious" and other forms of psychological reductionism that bypass attention to the situational, institutional, and role contexts in which the executive functions.

Having said this, however, it is still the case that much of value can be learned by studying presidents from the standpoint of the fit or lack of fit between various components of personality and the different role and situational requirements of the enormously complex job of being president. (George 1980, pp. 4–6, italics added)

Do any of the personality variables mentioned in the preceding quotation directly influence policymakers' preferences for one or another of the four types of procedural strategies listed in the third column of Figure 7-1 (pp. 154–55)? We do not yet know. But it seems likely that some of these dispositional variables interact with situational variables, such as exposure to informational inputs of the type shown in the first column of Figure 7-1. If so, we should expect to find consistent individual differences among policymakers in readiness to respond with positive answers to the key questions that lead to one or another of the quick-and-easy approaches that rely on simple decision rules.

In view of the accumulation over several decades of desultory results indicating that many of the most commonly investigated personality traits show little consistency across situations, a substantial number of psychologists in the field of personality research can be expected to be highly skeptical about the value of pursuing the line of empirical inquiry that I am suggesting. They would be inclined to think that the prospects are poor for finding any personality variables that either alone or in interaction with situational variables will account for a substantial proportion of the variance in effectiveness among policymakers. A few personality psychologists, however, take an opposing view; they believe that the field of personality research is emerging from the doldrums it has been in for the past several decades and could begin to illuminate a variety of individual differences in behavior that could prove to be useful knowledge for various practical purposes. McCrae and Costa, for example, argue that as a result of recent advances in the field of personality research, a number of factors have been identified that can be used by clinical practitioners to improve the accuracy of their diagnoses. The authors' arguments might apply equally to personnel managers in large organizations who have responsibility for selecting and promoting promising candidates for higher-level executive positions.

> Clinicians who have turned to the literature in personality psychology in the past 30 years have seen chiefly controversy and skepticism. After a decade of research dominated by the specter of response sets (see Wiggins, 1968), Mischel (1968) undermined the whole enterprise of personality assessment by his influential attack on the cross-situational consistency of behavior. Extraordinary research efforts were needed to reestablish—on a firmer empirical basis—principles that are taken for granted by most clinicians: (a) that there are regularities in behavior (Epstein, 1979); (b) that they endure across time (Block, 1981); (c) that these traits predict behavior (Small, Zeldin, and Savin-Williams, 1983); and (d) that they can be assessed with a reasonable degree of accuracy by both self-reports and ratings.
>   . . . After decades of debate on the number and nature of major dimensions of personality, a consensus is emerging that the five factors proposed by Tupes and Christal (1961) and Norman (1963) are both necessary and reasonably sufficient for describing at a global level the major features of personality. (McCrae & Costa 1986a, p. 1001)

The five factors to which these authors refer are as follows:

1. Conscientiousness—well-organized versus disorganized; careful versus careless; self-disciplined versus lax.
2. Openness—imaginative versus down to earth; independent versus conforming; preference for variety versus preference for routine.

3. Neuroticism—worrying versus calm; insecure versus secure; self-pitying versus self-satisfied.
4. Agreeableness—considerate versus ruthless; trusting versus suspicious; helpful versus uncooperative.
5. Extraversion—sociable versus retiring; fun-loving versus sober; active versus passive.

McCrae and Costa cite evidence from seven systematic research investigations, all carried out during the 1980s, in support of their positive conclusions about the validity and potential applicability of the five personality factors.[1] If their conclusions continue to be supported by subsequent studies of the consistency of the factors across situations and across time they could provide promising leads to personality variables that are among the determinants of effective policymaking.

Later on I shall indicate why the first three of these factors—lack of conscientiousness, lack of openness, and neuroticism—might prove to be dispositional determinants of faulty answers to one or another of the key questions which, according to Figure 7-1, lead to a defective simplistic approach to vital problems requiring high-quality decisionmaking. These same three factors might also prove to be related to chronic motivational deficiencies that could make for relatively poor performances in carrying out the steps of vigilant problem solving, even when the policymakers choose to use a vigilant problem-solving approach. Executives who are diagnosed as low on either the conscientiousness or the openness factor or as high on the neuroticism factor might fail to use their skills fully when they work on the essential tasks required for giving sound answers to the twelve questions shown in Figure 5-1 (p. 91). If that is the case, their solutions to the problems they try to solve would tend to be of relatively poor quality as compared with those of other executives who do not share their personality deficiencies.

The fourth factor—agreeableness—does not seem to be a likely candidate as a personality determinant of the choice of procedural strategy, but it could nevertheless prove to be a determinant of effective leadership with regard to inducing fellow policymakers at the top and implementers at lower levels to adopt a vigilant problem-solving approach on appropriate issues. The last factor—extraversion—could be completely unrelated to any aspect of policymaking strategies, although it might conceivably be related to the type of charismatic leadership that is often needed for setting norms and changing the culture of an organization in the direction that facilitates vigilant problem solving throughout the entire organization.

Who Will Fail to Use a Vigilant Problem–Solving Approach When It Is Needed?

In order to facilitate the discussion of the role of personality deficiencies, Figure 9-1 shows the four main pathways to poor-quality policymaking, which are derived directly from Figure 7-1. Figure 9-1 also includes a new column, not presented in the earlier figure, to designate personality deficiencies. The 17 dispositional variables listed in this column—each of which is expected to affect responsiveness to informational inputs—will be discussed in detail in the remainder of this chapter.

According to the constraints model, the mediating process that leads to one or another of the faulty procedural strategies consists of giving unwarranted positive answers to any one of the four key questions (Questions I, IIA, IIB, or IIC in Figure 9-1). For vital issues that require a fundamental policy decision, the first pathway to poor-quality policymaking involves mistakenly answering yes to the initial question (Question I) as to whether the problem is a relatively unimportant one, when the sensible answer is no. By a "sensible" answer is meant one that would be the consensus among knowledgeable judges in light of whatever information is available about the threat or opportunity at the time the judgment is made. (If there is no such consensus, a diagnosis cannot be made as to whether or not the answer is faulty.)

Three other pathways depicted in Figure 9-1 involve giving faulty answers to one or another of the three key questions concerning whether any cognitive, affiliative, or egocentric constraint must be given top priority (Questions IIA, IIB, and IIC). Answering "yes" in response to any one of the these three questions when grappling with a vital policy issue, according to the constraints model, leads to an approach that relies on simple decision rules rather than using a vigilant problem-solving approach that keeps avoidable errors to a minimum.

Not all executives in top-level policymaking positions in government, business, and other large organizations can be counted upon to deal effectively with most policy issues by giving "sensible" answers to the key questions. At least a small percentage of men and women in policymaking positions manage to get to the top for reasons other than their policymaking capabilities. Such persons might give faulty answers so often that they frequently fail to use a vigilant problem-solving approach when it is needed, with the result that their policy decisions fairly often lead to avoidable losses to the organization. If the gross incompetence of a top-level policymaker is not diagnosed early enough or if, for political or other reasons, the diagnosis does not promptly lead to the removal of the incompetent policymaker from office, the accumulation of errors could prove to be disastrous for the organization and sometimes for its constituencies. Lesser degrees of incompetence, of course, may go undetected for a long time because of ambiguities in the evidence typically available concerning short-term and long-term outcomes.

Often it is difficult for anyone to see the causal connection between the unfavorable outcomes and a policymaker's misjudgments in his or her prior decisions, especially if most of the other power-holders in the organization are motivated to maintain the status quo. Even when an executive has a discernibly poor track record in terms of the outcomes of his or her policy decisions, fellow executives are often inhibited about bringing charges of incompetence because they know that it could disrupt the organization and adversely affect their own careers. Whistle-blowers rarely are rewarded and most often are severely punished. Consequently it is probably much easier to prevent incompetence in the first place by recruiting and promoting executives who are capable of sound policymaking than it is to get rid of incompetent policymakers after they have reached top-level positions. The hypotheses to be presented on personality deficiencies, if confirmed, could be of practical value for such purposes.

One of my main working assumptions is that leaders who differ in dispositional attributes, such as chronic level of conscientiousness, have characteristically different ways of responding to the various types of informational inputs listed in the second column of Figure 9-1, which affect one or another of the answers they typically give to the key questions represented in the fourth and fifth columns of the figure. If we examine the constraints model from the standpoint of differences in the *threshold* of responsiveness to warnings and to the other informational inputs in light of the research literature on personality differences, it is possible to generate a number of plausible hypotheses concerning the role of personality deficiencies.[2] Using this approach, I have arrived at 17 hypotheses that seem sufficiently plausible to warrant systematic investigation. These hypotheses spec-

FIGURE 9-1 Four Pathways to Policy Decisions of Poor Quality in Response to Major Challenges, Contrasted with the Pathway to Vigilant Problem Solving

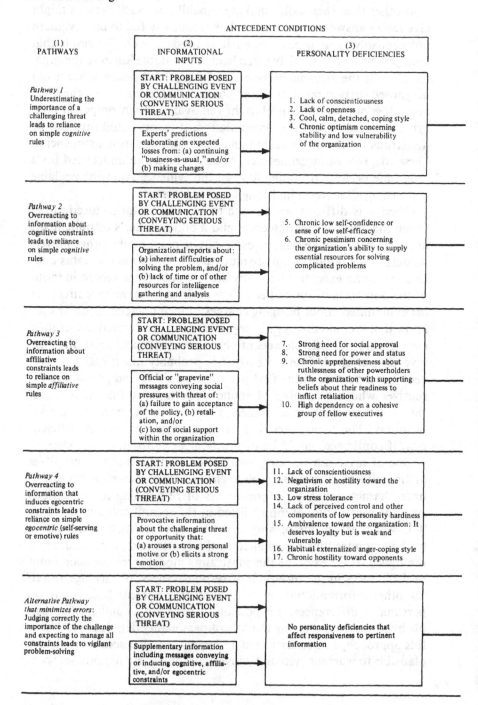

ANTECEDENT CONDITIONS

(1) PATHWAYS	(2) INFORMATIONAL INPUTS	(3) PERSONALITY DEFICIENCIES
Pathway 1 Underestimating the importance of a challenging threat leads to reliance on simple *cognitive* rules	**START: PROBLEM POSED BY CHALLENGING EVENT OR COMMUNICATION (CONVEYING SERIOUS THREAT)** Experts' predictions elaborating on expected losses from: (a) continuing "business-as-usual," and/or (b) making changes	1. Lack of conscientiousness 2. Lack of openness 3. Cool, calm, detached, coping style 4. Chronic optimism concerning stability and low vulnerability of the organization
Pathway 2 Overreacting to information about cognitive constraints leads to reliance on simple *cognitive* rules	**START: PROBLEM POSED BY CHALLENGING EVENT OR COMMUNICATION (CONVEYING SERIOUS THREAT)** Organizational reports about: (a) inherent difficulties of solving the problem, and/or (b) lack of time or of other resources for intelligence gathering and analysis	5. Chronic low self-confidence or sense of low self-efficacy 6. Chronic pessimism concerning the organization's ability to supply essential resources for solving complicated problems
Pathway 3 Overreacting to information about affiliative constraints leads to reliance on simple *affiliative* rules	**START: PROBLEM POSED BY CHALLENGING EVENT OR COMMUNICATION (CONVEYING SERIOUS THREAT)** Official or "grapevine" messages conveying social pressures with threat of: (a) failure to gain acceptance of the policy, (b) retaliation, and/or (c) loss of social support within the organization	7. Strong need for social approval 8. Strong need for power and status 9. Chronic apprehensiveness about ruthlessness of other powerholders in the organization with supporting beliefs about their readiness to inflict retaliation 10. High dependency on a cohesive group of fellow executives
Pathway 4 Overreacting to information that induces egocentric constraints leads to reliance on simple *egocentric* (self-serving or emotive) rules	**START: PROBLEM POSED BY CHALLENGING EVENT OR COMMUNICATION (CONVEYING SERIOUS THREAT)** Provocative information about the challenging threat or opportunity that: (a) arouses a strong personal motive or (b) elicits a strong emotion	11. Lack of conscientiousness 12. Negativism or hostility toward the organization 13. Low stress tolerance 14. Lack of perceived control and other components of low personality hardiness 15. Ambivalence toward the organization: It deserves loyalty but is weak and vulnerable 16. Habitual externalized anger-coping style 17. Chronic hostility toward opponents
Alternative Pathway that minimizes errors: Judging correctly the importance of the challenge and expecting to manage all constraints leads to vigilant problem-solving	**START: PROBLEM POSED BY CHALLENGING EVENT OR COMMUNICATION (CONVEYING SERIOUS THREAT)** Supplementary information including messages conveying or inducing cognitive, affiliative, and/or egocentric constraints	No personality deficiencies that affect responsiveness to pertinent information

212

Note: This figure reproduces the key components of the constraints model represented in Figure 7-1, with another set of antecedent conditions added: personality deficiencies.

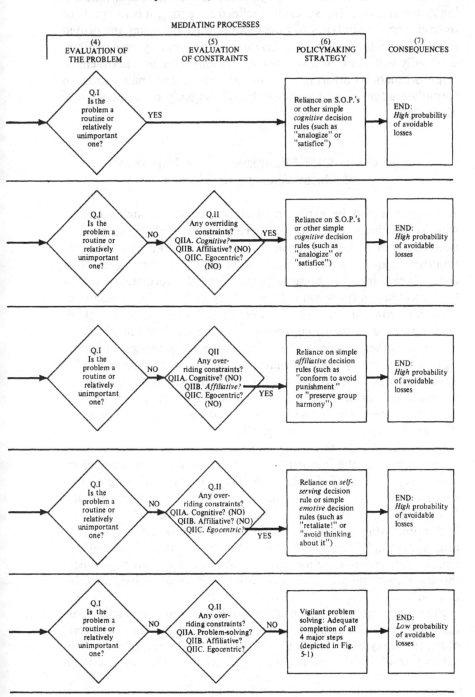

ify *who* is most likely to display symptoms of defective decisionmaking as a result of being generally inclined to ignore, misinterpret, or overreact to certain types of information, thus increasing the probability of avoidable errors. Specialists in personality research undoubtedly will think of additional personality variables pertinent to responsiveness to informational inputs, which will enable them to formulate additional hypotheses that are equally or perhaps more plausible.

Who Goofs Off? Minimizers of the Importance of Major Challenging Threats

Pathway 1 would be expected most frequently among executives who have a high threshold for perceiving and taking account of warnings about potential threats to vital objectives of the organization (which are typically included in the initial challenging event or communication and elaborated by the types of information listed in the second box in the second column of Figure 9–1). These executives are error-prone because they frequently fail to do anything at all despite being exposed to impressive new information that would induce most other people in their circumstances to change an apparently unsatisfactory policy (or lack of policy). Many executives who display such failures probably think of themselves as no less competent and hardworking than their fellow executives; they may not realize that if others were to become aware of their deficient behavior, they would usually label it as "goofing off."

Obviously one set of predispositions that incline some executives to underestimate the importance of challenging threats more often than others is lack of the skills required for discriminating among the flood of warnings that often deluge those responsible for the fate of large, complex organizations. An executive with poor skills in discriminating among the various warnings brought to his or her attention would frequently fail to detect the genuine signals of oncoming danger from the background noise of empty propagandistic threats, unwarranted forecasts of dire trends, and inadvertent false alarms.[3]

Even when executives have adequate skills for making fairly accurate judgments about genuine warnings that should be taken seriously, they may often fail to use those skills to the best of their abilities as a result of chronic personality deficiencies that dispose them to judge many important types of warnings—or perhaps practically all warnings—as unimportant. There are certain personality dispositions that could be expected to contribute to a relatively *high threshold* of responsiveness to serious warnings (which makes for erroneous positive answers to Question I in the fourth column of Figure 9-1). Among them are the following:

HYPOTHESIS 1. Chronic lack of conscientiousness, a personality factor that includes disorganized and careless handling of daily tasks and a low degree of self-discipline: Executives with this predispositional characteristic would tend to be relatively inattentive to cues that function as initial warnings to others. For example, when scientific reports are circulated throughout the chemical industry concerning newly discovered hazards from storing various widely used chemicals, the nonconscientious executives would carelessly toss the reports into the wastebasket. In contrast, the more conscientious executives would contemplate following up on the warnings by taking such steps as asking their plant's most knowledgeable chemical engineers whether the hazardous conditions might be present. Like anyone who for any reason is lethargic, persons lacking in conscientiousness would frequently fail to follow up on early warning signs of potential threats to the organization. (Also, on those relatively rare occasions when such persons do judge a problem to be important, they would be more inclined than others to give priority to their self-serving motives rather than to the vital interests of the organization or nation, as stated below in Hypothesis 11.)

HYPOTHESIS 2. Chronic lack of openness, a personality factor that includes three main components—lack of imagination, failure to think and act independently, and preference for routine. Executives with this disposition would tend to apply existing organizational routines to practically all warnings, including those requiring vigilant initiatives to develop plans for impending danger.

HYPOTHESIS 3. Calm, cool, detached coping style in response to fear-arousing events or communications: Executives in this category include those characterized as relatively "affectless," chronic "deniers," and certain "macho" types who succeed in modeling themselves after movie heroes, going calmly about their business in the face of danger while others around them are upset. These executives would have such a high level of stress tolerance that they would tend to be relatively unresponsive to serious warnings. They would regularly underestimate the probability, magnitude, and imminence of real dangers. Their level of emotional arousal would be so low that the motivational impact of messages about oncoming dangers for the organization would be relatively slight. As a result, these executives with extremely high stress tolerance would make frequent errors of omission, consisting of failures to spot real troubles before they become overwhelmingly obvious as clear and present dangers. When they do focus on serious dangers, they would be more inclined than others to adopt the audacity ("Can do!") rule.

HYPOTHESIS 4. Chronic optimism concerning the organization's stability and invulnerability: Executives with this type of persistent optimism and supporting cognitive schemas concerning their organization's strengths, who are completely sincere in their "upbeat" attitude, would tend to belittle in their own thinking the implications of all sorts of warnings because they expect the organization to have very low vulnerability to whatever dangers might materialize. Their uncritically optimistic disposition would incline them to expect the powerful, stable organization to be impervious to internal disruption from power struggles from within, to threatened attacks by adversaries from without, and to unfavorable environmental changes, such as mounting national deficits and new legal restrictions. As a result, they would tend to disbelieve communications conveying serious threats, such as dire forecasts by recognized experts who inform them that the organization is heading for huge financial losses unless major budget cuts are made.

Who Can't Hack It: Overreactors to Information About Complexity of Policy Issues and Other Cognitive Constraints

Pathway 2 in Figure 9-1 would be expected most frequently among executives who have a low threshold for accepting communications about (1) inherent complexities of problems posed by major threats or opportunities, which make them appear to be extremely difficult to solve, and/or (2) limited organizational resources for finding good solutions to policy problems. These two types of informational inputs make executives aware of cognitive constraints (both of which are represented in the fourth box in the second column [Informational Inputs] of Figure 9-1).

Communications about inherent difficulties include comments

about the complicated ramifications of the problem at hand, making the recipients realize that their knowledge, skills, and other resources needed for solving such problems are very limited. Communications about lack of time or lack of other organizational resources for gathering essential intelligence information, for carrying out detailed analysis of the problem, and for intensive deliberations by qualified experts within the organization typically make the recipients feel that it may be futile to search for a high-quality solution. Any such communication makes cognitive constraints highly salient. Certain enduring personality dispositions can be expected to contribute to a relatively low threshold for accepting these communications about cognitive constraints (which makes for readiness to give a positive answer to Question IIA in the fifth column of Figure 9-1). Among the pertinent dispositions are the following:

HYPOTHESIS 5. Low self-confidence, including chronic sense of low self-efficacy: Executives with this dispositional characteristic would tend to be highly responsive to information that calls attention to the difficulties and complications of any policy problem, with the result that they would feel unable to "hack it." While men and women lacking in self-confidence are seldom promoted or elected to top-level policymaking positions, the few who do occupy such positions would be inclined to overreact to information about the difficulties of solving the policy problems they are required to deal with. They would tend to surmise that their own knowledge and capabilities for grappling with any complicated problem are so deficient that it would be a waste of time and effort for them to strive for a high-quality solution. Their demoralizing self-image would incline them to give high priority to the constraints imposed by their own limited cognitive resources, with the result that they would resort to organizational routines or simple cognitive decision rules without making very much use of whatever problem-solving skills they may actually have.

HYPOTHESIS 6. Chronic pessimism concerning the organization's ability to supply the resources essential for solving complicated policy problems, with supporting beliefs about internal weaknesses that preclude adaptive changes: Executives with this type of pessimism and supporting cognitive schemas would be disposed to accept communications that call attention to lack of expertise, or lack of any other resources within the organization for dealing with policy problems. Although they might feel very confident about their own capabilities, these executives would generally lack confidence in the organization's capability to "hack it." They would be likely to believe unwarranted complaints and rumors that organizational resources are unavailable because of internal power struggles, the pigheadedness of powerholders who control the resources, or the excessive demands already being made on overworked executives and their harried staffs of information gatherers and analysts. A persisting pessimistic image of the organization as internally weak would incline them to overreact to signs of constraints within the organization that imply the futility of seeking for a high-quality solution. This type of disposition might be especially prevalent among executives who have only recently joined the organization and are going through a prolonged period of post-honeymoon disillusionment. With more experience they may gradually correct their derogatory view of organizational resources and also learn how the seemingly unavailable resources can, in fact, be mobilized. In such cases, the executives would gradually modify their pessimistic attitude and display a corresponding decrease in the tendency to overreact to information about apparent cognitive constraints. In other cases, however, the pessimistic lack of confidence in the organization might be much more deep-seated, especially if "burnout" attitudes are repeatedly reinforced by objective signs of debilitating power struggles, rigidity at the top, and excessive demands on executives who participate in policy planning and crisis management.

Who Can't Say No? Overreactors to Social Pressures That Make Affiliative Constraints Salient

Pathway 3 in Figure 9-1 would be most frequent among executives who have a low threshold for accepting communications that convey social pressures from others within the organization, including three types of threats—failure to gain acceptance of the policy, retaliation, and loss of social support. (These three types of social pressures are represented in the sixth box in the second column [Informational Inputs] in Figure 9-1.) Among the enduring personality dispositions that could be expected to contribute to this low threshold (which makes for readiness to give a positive answer to Question IIB in the fifth column of Figure 9-1) are the following:

HYPOTHESIS 7. Chronically strong need for social approval: Executives with this personality disposition would tend to be highly responsive to all forms of social pressure, especially those conveying explicit threats of disapproval. They would be particularly likely to go along uncritically with the policy preferences of others in the organization who have high prestige and status or who are regarded as experts. More than any other executives, they would tend to conform with implicit or explicit demands of other powerholders within the organization on whom they are dependent for reassurance and esteem.

> Evidently the regular and consistent approval-seeking behaviors of individuals with a high need for social approval are the product of attempts to defend and preserve a vulnerable self-esteem. Perhaps individuals with a high need for social approval believe that conformity and submissiveness . . . may involve few risks of the social rejection that would threaten their self-esteem. (Snyder & Ickes, p. 889)

Insofar as executives with a strong need for approval are responsive to all forms of social pressure that evoke affiliative constraints, they would be more likely than others to use simple affiliative rules for dealing with policy problems rather than a vigilant problem-solving approach.

HYPOTHESIS 8. Strong need for power and status: Executives with this personality disposition would tend to be more responsive than others to informational inputs that convey threats of retaliation from others for failing to support their preferred policies. They would be responsive to threats from any individual leader or group in a position to inflict retaliation that could reduce their chances of promotion or curtail their influence within the organization. The relatively low threshold of these executives to such threats would make them more likely than others to deal with major policy problems by using affiliative rules. Those relatively nonaggressive executives who are overly fearful about losing power and status would frequently resort to the most common of the affiliative rules—to conform in order to avoid being punished. Other more aggressively inclined executives who have a strong chronic need to maintain or augment their power and status would tend to operate as "hardball politics players," relying heavily on affiliative rules that involve manipulating fellow executives, such as rigging acceptance and exercising one-upmanship in a power struggle to be "top dog."[4]

HYPOTHESIS 9. Chronic apprehensiveness about the ruthlessness of other powerholders in the organization with supporting beliefs about their readiness to inflict retaliations as "hardball politics players": Executives with this disposition, accompanied by supporting cognitive schemas that create an image of other powerholders within the organization as Machiavellians or authoritarians who are uninhibited about inflicting severe punishment when anyone displeases them, would tend to have a relatively low threshold for informational inputs that convey threats of loss of compensation, power, or status for nonconformity. Like the executives with a strong chronic need for power, they would be inclined to respond to such informational inputs by adopting simple affiliative rules. Among the executives who are chronically apprehensive about the ruthlessness of other powerholders, the relatively nonaggressive ones would tend to rely frequently on the decision rule to conform in order to avoid being punished; the relatively aggressive ones would tend to act like the "hardball players" they fear, resorting to rigging, one-upmanship, and other manipulative types of affiliative decision rules.

HYPOTHESIS 10. High dependency upon a cohesive group of fellow executives for social support: Executives with this disposition would tend to have a relatively low threshold for responding to informational inputs that convey the policy preferences of the group leader or of the majority of the in-group of policymakers, which fosters a "groupthink" type of consensus. Those members who are highly dependent upon the in-group for maintaining a sense of personal worth or for coping with stress would have an exceptionally low threshold of responsiveness to signs of disagreement on a policy issue within the group. They would differ in an important respect from other executives who value their membership in the cohesive group primarily because it enhances their competence rather than because it satisfies strong dependency needs. Highly dependent executives would be much more likely than the others to overreact to any threats to the cozy social atmosphere of apparent unity within the cohesive group by engaging in self-censorship. They would tend to set aside their doubts and to rely upon the simple affiliative rule to preserve group harmony by agreeing with the leader and the other members.

Who Is Self-Serving?: Overreactors to Information That Creates Egocentric Constraints by Arousing Strong Personal Motives

Pathway 4 in Figure 9–1 would occur frequently among executives who have a low threshold for accepting either of two types of informational inputs that make egocentric constraints highly salient: (1) communications that call attention to threats of personal losses or opportunities for personal gains, which arouse strong egocentric motives and (2) communications that elicit anger, fear, elation, or any other strong emotion or emotional bias. (Both types of communications are represented in the eighth box in the second column [Informational Input] of Figure 9–1; both tend to have the effect of inducing the most easily influenced recipients to give a positive answer to Question IIC in the fifth column of the figure.) Executives with personality dispositions that make for high responsiveness to the first type of communication are more prone than others to rely upon the personal aggrandizement rule: "the main thing to consider is 'what's in it for me?'"

Among the dispositions that could be expected to contribute to a relatively low threshold for responding to communications that arouse strong personal motives, such as offers from lobbyists of "baksheesh" (or "payola") or of favorable personal publicity in the mass media, are the following:

HYPOTHESIS 11. Chronic lack of conscientiousness, a personality factor that includes careless execution of assigned duties, and a low degree of self-discipline: Executives with this dispositional characteristic would not only tend to ignore warnings about dangers to their organization (Hypothesis 1) but would also have a low threshold for responsiveness to communications that arouse self-serving motives. When these executives regard a policy problem as important enough to require their time and energy, they would be relatively uninhibited about seizing opportunities for gaining personal satisfaction. Lacking a sense of responsibility in the way that they fulfill their leadership role obligations, they would be inclined to look for and to be delighted by information indicating that they can exploit their power position to indulge in self-aggrandizement. These executives would be much less likely than others to feel anticipatory shame or guilt about using the self-serving rule, which gives priority to their own hidden personal agenda, even though it is at the expense of sacrificing the organization's or nation's best interests.

In some executives, lack of conscientiousness may be a component of a personality syndrome that includes, along with defective superego functioning, lack of empathy, excessive narcissism, feelings of contempt toward social restraints that inhibit self-indulgence in other people, and other antisocial tendencies that comprise, in extreme instances, the disorder referred to as "psychopathic personality." In such persons, egocentric and antisocial tendencies may be difficult to detect because they usually have a pleasant sociable facade, talk a "good game" of social responsibility, and come up with clever, plausible excuses to justify their questionable acts of self-aggrandizement.

HYPOTHESIS 12. Persistent negativism or hostility toward the organization, with supporting beliefs about undesirable features that make it undeserving of loyalty: Executives with this type of disposition and supporting cognitive schemas, which make for lack of identification with the organization, would be more likely than others to be responsive to informational inputs that arouse strong personal motives and to act accordingly. Even among executives who are generally conscientious, negativism or hostility toward the organization would incline them to be less inhibited than others about allowing the organization's goals to be given lower priority than their self-serving goals. This tendency would be most pronounced among executives whose negativism or hostility centers not only on images of the organization as immoral and unworthy of loyalty, which make for feelings of alienation, but also on images of it as so weak and disorganized that self-serving actions will not be detected.

Who Gets Discombobulated?: Overreactors to Information That Creates Egocentric Constraints by Arousing Anxiety or Other Emotional Reactions

Pathway 4 in Figure 9–1 would be displayed frequently not only by executives who have the dispositional characteristics specified by Hypotheses 11 and 12 but also by those who have a low threshold for responding to provocative events and communications that arouse strong emotions. Often the provocative informational inputs with which this defective pathway begins are included in the challenging event or communication itself, especially when it conveys impressive warnings about oncoming dangers for the organization, which typically arouse anxiety. When the initial challenge itself does not evoke a strong emotional reaction, the pathway is sometimes activated by subsequent informational inputs (represented in the eighth box in the second column [Informational Input] of Figure 9-1). For example, a minor challenge posed by a slight decline in a manufacturing firm's monthly sales might be greatly amplified by "grapevine" rumors that some leading customers are waiting for the release of a rival firm's new product, which is expected to be so superior and inexpensive that it will capture the lion's share of the market. Similarly, a minor challenge for U.S. government officials posed by the outbreak of a civil war in a third-world nation could be transformed into a highly threatening major international crisis by a Soviet leader's inflammatory public speech that sounds like the Russians are getting ready to intervene militarily.

Among the personality dispositions that could be expected to contribute to a relatively low threshold for strong arousal of anxiety or other strong emotions in response to provocative informational inputs (which make for a positive answer to Question IIC in the fifth column of Figure 9-1) are the following:

HYPOTHESIS 13. Low stress tolerance—manifested by relatively high level of anxiety with feelings of helplessness and vulnerability, which are among the main components of "neuroticism": Executives with this dispositional characteristic would be more likely than others to adopt a coping strategy of either defensive avoidance or hypervigilance, which is tantamount to giving priority to the emotive constraint imposed by their high level of psychological stress.[5] Of course, few executives who reach the top level of government or of any other large organization are likely to be so severely neurotic that their anxiety and other symptoms constantly interfere with their efficiency in carrying out administrative and leadership tasks. Persons with chronic psychiatric disorders would hardly ever be elected or promoted to top-level positions. If a psychiatric disorder develops after they have attained high office, they would soon be removed from their policymaking role. Nevertheless, fairly extensive individual differences in stress tolerance are to be expected among the powerholders in any organization, with corresponding differences in the degree to which they react emotionally to events and communications that convey threats to the organization.

Executives with low stress tolerance would be especially likely to adopt a defective coping pattern of defensive avoidance if they are also disposed to be chronically pessimistic about finding a satisfactory solution to policy problems, as in the case of persons with chronically low self-esteem who are self-disparaging about their own capabilities. In other words, executives with a combination of the two predispositional characteristics (low stress tolerance and low self-esteem) would be much more likely than others to deal with serious challenges requiring a policy decision by adopting the simple emotive rule that characterizes defensive avoidance: "avoid thinking about the problem by denying or minimizing the potential dangers." As described earlier (pp. 79–80), when an executive adopts this rule, his or her procedural strategy is to procrastinate if possible, otherwise to pass the buck to someone else in the organization or, if that is precluded, to select without much search or deliberation whichever alternative seems least objectionable and then to bolster it with rationalizations that provide false reassurances about the worrisome risks.

Executives with low stress tolerance who are also disposed to be especially responsive to time pressures (as is perhaps the case for some type-A personalities who often feel frustrated and chronically have a sense of time urgency) would be more likely than others to respond to informational inputs about threats to the organization with "catastrophizing" reactions that characterize the panic or near-panic state designated as hypervigilance. That is to say, executives with the combination of persistently low stress tolerance and self-imposed time pressures would be more inclined than others to overreact emotionally to crises and to adopt the emotive decision rule to escape from the dilemma as rapidly as possible. Typically, the use of this emotive decision rule leads to an impulsive choice made with practically no information gathering, analysis, or deliberation.[6]

HYPOTHESIS 14. Lack of perceived control over outcomes (external locus of control), and other components of a low level of personality hardiness: Executives with a low level of personality hardiness are characterized by a chronically pessimistic outlook about being able to control the course of events in the direction they want; they perceive change as something to be feared rather than welcomed; they feel alienated from potentially supportive groups and organizations. Executives with these characteristics would be more likely than others to become hypervigilant when confronted with challenging events or communications indicating that major changes are required in order to avert dangers that lie ahead. They would tend to overreact to warnings and to select a protective course of action in a distraught and inefficient manner because they are lacking in personality resources that operate as a buffer to moderate the disruptive emotional impact of psychological stress. They would also be more likely than other executives to become incapacitated during a serious crisis by becoming physically ill. Like the executives with low stress tolerance who are disposed to react with high anxiety to all sorts of threats, those with a low level of hardiness would have a low threshold for overreacting to events and communications that induce acute anxiety as an emotive constraint, with a correspondingly strong tendency to resort to the simple emotive rule used by decisionmakers when they are in a hypervigilant state.[7]

HYPOTHESIS 15. Persistent ambivalence toward the organization such that it is seen as having positive features that make it deserving of loyalty but is also seen as having negative features that make it weak and vulnerable: Executives with this type of ambivalent attitude would be more likely than others to become emotionally aroused by warnings about remote dangers as well as by dire forecasts about adversities that endanger the survival of the organization, which make for a relatively high level of psychological stress. Consequently, they would be more disposed than others to rely upon the simple emotive decision rules that enter into defensive avoidance or hypervigilance. On the one hand, the positive components of their ambivalent attitude make them feel identified with the organization; they expect their own fate and well-being to be linked with that of the organization. On the other hand, however, the negative components make them exceptionally apprehensive in response to warnings because they regard the organization as vulnerable to all sorts of threats.

HYPOTHESIS 16. Habitual externalized anger-coping style: Executives with this personality disposition would have a relatively low threshold for becoming intensely angry in response to verbal or overt provocations by adversaries; consequently, when challenges occur as a result of hostile or obstructive actions by a rival organization or nation, especially during a confrontation crisis that is moving toward belligerency, these executives would be more likely than others to curtail vigilant problem solving as a result of the powerful emotive constraint imposed by the arousal of their intense anger, which would incline them to rely upon the emotive decision rule to take aggressive action in order to retaliate.

HYPOTHESIS 17. Persistent hostility toward major opponents, with supporting beliefs about their evil and hostile intentions: Executives with this disposition would tend to be more suspicious than others of the opponents' actions; they would have a relatively low threshold for becoming angered by information about potentially threatening or thwarting actions by the "evil" adversary and would have a correspondingly low threshold for relying on the simple emotive rule to retaliate. In these executives, anger would sometimes become a dominant emotive constraint even though the information about what the opponents are doing is ambiguous and most qualified observers do not judge it to be hostile. They would be more inclined than others to accept uncritically any intelligence reports claiming that the opposing organization or nation may be secretly conniving to encroach on their territory or to undermine a major enterprise, which would incline them during a confrontational crisis to become so emotionally aroused that their crisis decisionmaking would be dominated by the emotive constraint imposed by their anger.

Implications for the Unfinished Research Agenda

If subsequent research focuses on dispositional variables like those mentioned in the foregoing 17 hypotheses, there would seem to be a fairly good chance of arriving at dependable generalizations that will account for a substantial proportion of the variance in individual differences among policymakers. Those generalizations would help to specify *who* is most likely to make *what types* of avoidable errors in decisionmaking on vital policy issues. Well-substantiated generalizations would not only be of great practical value for selecting men and women for positions that require effective policymaking capabilities but would also provide an empirical basis for developing basic theory on the role of personality in organizational decisionmaking.

Although it is extremely difficult for research investigators to obtain access to adequate samples of leading policymakers in government, business, and other larger organizations, it may be possible to carry out the essential steps of assessment among management trainees and even middle-level executives, some of whom sooner or later will become top-level policymakers. Perhaps the best available research sites will be graduate schools of management and in-service training workshops for executives.

In order to carry out the necessary research on individual differences, a number of new measures will have to be developed for assessing personality dispositions among executives. Most of the existing personality tests and assessment techniques have been developed either for college students or for disturbed persons of all ages who seek help in psychological clinics. Refinements of some existing personality measures and the development of new assessment techniques are needed to investigate the foregoing hypotheses derived from the constraints model. In attempting to obtain dependable findings on the personality characteristics of those executives who most often fail to use a vigilant problem-solving strategy when making vital policy decisions, it will undoubtedly be most productive to use a pluralistic methodological approach that includes collecting research data obtained by observing how often they act in one way or another when they are asked to work on policy problems; other pertinent measures would be global ratings of personality attributes by observers, self-report measures, and perhaps also performances on various standardized decisionmaking tasks.

The data needed to investigate the research questions posed by the preceding set of hypotheses about *personality deficiencies* will provide evidence for answering the key question on the other side of the coin: *Who are the men and women most likely to be exceptionally good at policymaking on issues of major importance, by virtue of being predisposed to adopt the vigilant problem-solving approach when it is needed?* Research findings from systematic comparisons of executives who are good, medium, and poor as policymakers could inform us about the personality characteristics that make for readiness to adopt the optimal procedural strategy for arriving at sound policy decisions when vital interests of the organization or nation are at stake.

Earlier I suggested that it might be profitable to attempt to identify grand masters of policymaking, as in chess and various arts and sciences (see pp. 107–10). If such grand masters can be identified, it would be relevant to try to find out whether they differ from less talented policymakers on personality variables, particularly with regard to motivations that tend to dampen reactions to informational inputs that induce cognitive, affiliative, or egocentric constraints. In addition to whatever cognitive skills they may have that enable them to get to the heart of a problem quickly and to see the most promis-

ing directions to go in the search for a solution, they may also have
enduring motivational characteristics that enable them to use their
skills more effectively because they have the capability of counteracting or surmounting all three types of constraints.

Even if there is no consensus among experts as to who should be
considered to be grand masters of policymaking, the research question that remains to be answered is whether those executives with the
best track records as policymakers differ from those with medium
or poor track records in that they have identifiable personality dispositions that incline them to adopt the vigilant problem-solving approach when it is needed. The next step in the inquiry would be to
find out whether the personalities of executives who function well in
this respect can be characterized in terms of not having the personality deficiencies specified in the 17 hypotheses concerning who goofs
off, who can't hack it, who can't say no, who is self-serving, and
who gets discombobulated.

For some personality variables, the optimal disposition may not
be at the opposite end of the continuum to that which characterizes
certain of the deficient types of policymakers. For example, the optimal level of stress tolerance for adopting a vigilant problem-solving
approach would be expected to lie in the intermediate range, between
the very high level that makes for an ultracalm ignoring of serious
warnings that should arouse concern (Hypothesis 3) and the very low
level that makes for such strong emotional overreactions that the
executive relies on a simple emotive decision rule (Hypothesis 13).
Similarly, the optimal attitude and supporting beliefs concerning the
strength and stability of the organization would be expected to lie in
the intermediate range. It would probably be between the extreme
optimism that fosters the ignoring of serious warnings because the
organization is regarded as invulnerable (Hypothesis 4) and the extreme pessimism concerning internal weaknesses of the organization,
which makes for readiness to give priority to cognitive constraints
(Hypothesis 6) and to egocentric constraints (Hypothesis 15). It
seems likely that an optimal attitude toward the organization—from
the standpoint of fostering readiness to adopt a vigilant problem-
solving strategy when it is needed—will be found in executives who
have a basically favorable attitude toward the organization as deserving their loyalty but have a highly differentiated view of the organization's weaknesses and vulnerabilities. Their differentiated view
would take account of realistic assessments of the organization's cur-

rent deficiencies and also of its potentialities for changing in a direction that could counteract or eliminate those deficiencies.

In this chapter, I have focused on individual differences in personality dispositions to illustrate the potential value of the constraints model (represented in Figures 7-1 [pp. 154–55] and 9-1 [pp. 212–13]) for generating new hypotheses worth investigating. One of the main reasons for elaborating on this topic is that personality research in the fields of political and organizational psychology seems to be in need of fresh and stimulating ideas. A new theoretical model that provides leads concerning mediating processes and that highlights some neglected variables may enable investigators to pose new research questions. Perhaps research centering on those questions will help to revitalize an area of inquiry that has fallen into the doldrums.

10

Effective Leadership Practices: Additional Hypotheses Derived from the Constraints Model

The constraints model is especially applicable for understanding how and why the same policymaker (or the same group of policymakers) uses different procedural strategies in different circumstances. It provides a theoretical structure that can help to account for changes in the quality of policymaking that occur as a result of changes in leadership practices, as when a chief executive who has been highly authoritarian becomes less directive in the way he or she handles the meetings of policy-planning groups and elicits much less fear of recriminations among the members.

This chapter presents a set of hypotheses about effective leadership practices, all of which are derived from the constraints model. Some of the hypotheses are fairly well-known, having already been suggested by management experts. For these hypotheses, the constraints model provides a more comprehensive theoretical rationale than the piecemeal ad hoc rationales to be found in the management literature. A few hypotheses derived from the constraints model specify leadership practices that are not likely to be familiar to practitioners or to research specialists in the field of management. They provide additional examples of the potential value of the preliminary theoretical framework for generating original hypotheses that appear to be plausible and that warrant systematic investigation.

231

Practical Implications for Improving Policymaking

Among the leadership practices to be considered are several pertinent to setting organizational norms, including those that affect the flow and utilization of essential information from the periphery to the center of the organization. These and several other of the hypotheses have direct sociological implications for new institutionalized procedures and for structural changes to build the type of organizational culture that would facilitate the efforts of well-qualified executives to adopt leadership practices that promote high-quality policymaking.

All of the hypotheses about leadership practices, if verified, will have direct practical implications for improving the quality of policymaking in government, business, and public welfare organizations. They are especially pertinent for training executives who are candidates for top-level policymaking positions. Many of the hypotheses could also prove to be useful for those who have already attained leadership positions. Executives who want to improve their effectiveness in fulfilling leadership functions in the sphere of policymaking might be able to change in the recommended direction once they realize that certain of *their own actions* are imposing detrimental constraints that could be eliminated. Some of the hypotheses may make top-level managers more aware of the constraints imposed by *external circumstances* and point to the steps that can be taken to prevent those constraints from interfering with the quality of their group's decisionmaking processes.

The leadership practices specified in the hypotheses, unfortunately, are *not low-cost means for bringing about improvements.* On the contrary, most of them are probably quite costly, especially because they require additional time and effort from leaders and also in some instances from their support staffs. Furthermore, some of the leadership practices might turn out to have unintentional side effects that create less tangible costs, such as creating animosity and low morale among members of an advisory group, which could result from facilitating open debates about alternative options. In order to ascertain whether any one of the hypotheses is valid, research evidence will be needed to see if the benefits definitely outweigh the obvious costs and whatever losses might result from undesirable side effects. It is my expectation that ultimately many of the hypotheses will prove to be sufficiently valid to warrant recommending the designated leadership practices as prescriptions for leaders who want to improve the quality of their organization's policymaking procedures.

If so, these hypotheses could also form the basis for recommending ways to improve the curriculum of schools of management and in-service training courses designed to groom executives for top-level positions.

A Central Question About Leadership

One of the central questions for behavioral science research on leadership is this: What can an individual leader in a large organization do to eliminate common types of error made by the executives who participate in the formation or modification of major strategic decisions, so as to improve the quality of the organization's policymaking process? Specific answers to this question can be derived from the constraints model represented in Figure 7-1. According to the model, any leadership practice that increases the likelihood that the executives who function as advisors or planners will give negative answers to the four key questions (shown in the second column of Figure 7-1) increases the likelihood that those participants will use a vigilant problem-solving approach, which makes for high-quality policy decisions.

For purposes of explicating the implications of the constraints model, it is helpful to return once again to the diagram of pathways to defective policymaking shown in Figure 9-1 (pp. 212-13), which was introduced in the preceding chapter for the purpose of formulating hypotheses about personality differences. Figure 9-1 is equally helpful for formulating hypotheses about what kind of actions a leader can take when some or all participants in the policymaking process are inclined to give positive answers to one or another of the four key questions when dealing with a *major* threat or opportunity. By inducing those participants to change so as to answer no to all the key questions, according to the model, a leader will prevent them from resorting to a simplistic approach, which results in gross symptoms of defective decisionmaking. Most of the hypotheses to be presented specify what a leader can say or do to *counteract* the influence of various types of informational inputs (listed in the second column of Figure 9-1) that induce members of a policymaking group to give positive answers to the key questions about constraints, which mediate a simplistic approach rather than a vigilant problem-solving strategy.[1]

Although the hypotheses about leadership practices apply most directly to the chief executive or whoever is designated as the chairperson of the policymaking group, they also apply to any influential member who takes the lead in directing the group's activity. That is to say, the leadership practices pertain not only to the actions of the *formal leader* but also to the actions of any member who functions temporarily as an *informal leader* by attempting to insert a new business item on the agenda or to change the group's procedures in conducting its deliberations. It follows directly from the assumptions that enter into the constraints model that the quality of an organization's policymaking process can be expected to become much better than it ordinarily would be if each of the executives who participates in the process accepts a norm specifying that he or she has a dual responsibility when confronted with major policy problems or crises: *to engage in vigilant problem solving to the best of his or her own ability* and also *to function as an informal leader, whenever it seems necessary,* to try to help fellow participants avoid giving priority to one or another of the constraints that may be inhibiting them from carrying out to the best of their abilities all the essential steps of vigilant problem solving.

The hypotheses are formulated in terms that pertain directly to the way a leader conducts formal meetings and informal contacts with members of an executive committee or policy-planning group. Most of the hypotheses, however, are intended to be equally applicable when a leader makes a policy decision largely on his or her own, after consulting briefly with only one or two advisors. In such instances, the group members consist of the one or two subordinates who supply bits of information or advice, perhaps by making a few comments about the choice the leader had in mind from the outset. In extreme instances, the aides who function as members of a minimal group of this kind may not even participate in any face-to-face meetings but simply respond in brief telephone conversations when the boss calls them or in a memorandum when the boss requests one. Nevertheless, whenever subservient aides are asked to give any information, evaluations, or advice that could in any way influence the overall quality of the policymaking process, the hypotheses about leadership practices would be just as applicable as when the final policy choice is made by the vote of an executive committee or board of directors.

In contrast to Hypotheses 1 through 17 presented in Chapter 9, all of which specify variables that *make for defective decisionmaking,* Hypotheses 18 through 37 presented in this chapter specify variables that *prevent defective decisionmaking* and thereby tend to improve the quality of the policymaking process. All 20 of the hypotheses about effective leadership practices appear to be plausible and worth pursuing in subsequent research in light of well-established concepts and findings in social psychology and management sciences.

Each of the hypotheses should be understood as referring to leadership behavior that is *authentic*. None of the leadership practices can be expected to be effective in promoting vigilant problem solving if accompanied by cues indicating that the leader does not genuinely believe in what he or she is saying or doing.

Preventing a Policymaking Group from Inadvertently "Goofing Off"

Low-level warnings about a serious impending threat are often complacently ignored during the early developmental stages of a crisis when the oncoming danger might be mitigated before mounting to a high intensity. Studies of international crises reveal numerous instances of this sort of misjudgment. Prime examples are the outbreak of the Yom Kippur War in 1973 and the fall of the Shah of Iran in 1979, both of which caught most U.S. policymakers completely by surprise even though those crises were forecast by a few alert U.S. intelligence analysts well in advance. Similar failures of business corporations and other large organizations in the private sector to respond to dire warnings are well-known occurrences, which sometimes lead to catastrophic losses and bankruptcy.

One of the reasons for the tendency to ignore low-level warnings is that policymakers are keenly aware of the necessity to be highly selective in deciding which of the numerous threats that are constantly being brought to their attention should be taken seriously. They know that it is extremely costly in terms of time and effort as well as money to set the wheels in motion to gather information, to consult with advisors, and to deliberate about any trouble spot that is labeled as posing a serious danger. In the back of their minds there is also likely to be the inhibiting realization that overestimating a low-intensity danger arising from an adversary's actions can lead to unnecessary protective actions that can be misperceived by the adversary and actually provoke a crisis that might otherwise not occur.

Policymakers and the members of their staffs who have the responsibility for screening warnings are especially likely to ignore

warning signs that remain highly ambiguous as to what might be at
stake. Warnings that are sufficiently ambiguous to allow for plausible alternative interpretations that minimize the alleged danger are
much less likely than unambiguous warnings to be put on the policymakers' agenda. Thomas Schelling has commented on the "*poverty
of expectations*" that prevented U.S. civilian leaders and military
commanders in 1941 from realizing that the warning signals they
were getting from intercepted Japanese government communications, which U.S. cryptographers had discovered how to decode,
might point to an oncoming Japanese attack against Pearl Harbor
and other United States military bases. "Unlike movies," Schelling
points out, "real life provides no musical background to tip us off
to the climax." Some of the hypotheses describe leadership practices
that can supply the missing musical background on occasions when
it is needed.

Perhaps equally if not more important is the need to tone down
the deafening, scary music on those rare occasions when it swells
up so unexpectedly and dramatically that policymakers overreact by
thinking only about worst case scenarios in response to ambiguous
warning signals. Several leadership practices that help to prevent
grossly exaggerated assessments of threats are described in hypotheses about counteracting the adverse effects of the emotive constraint
imposed by high levels of emotional stress.

When crises build up slowly, a group of policymakers with an
overcrowded agenda that includes urgent problems can be expected
to give little attention to the ambiguous signs of newly emerging
threats. Consequently, for these crises, leaders and their advisory
groups will often make *errors of omission*—missing the opportunity
to deal effectively with an incipient crisis before it mounts to a dangerously high level of intensity. In contrast, when crises develop very
rapidly, especially when provoked by an adversary's unexpected
threatening moves, policymakers are likely to drop everything and
react so hastily that they may make *errors of commission*—committing the organization or nation to an unnecessarily risky course of
action when alternative options are available that could have a better
chance of safeguarding organizational or national interests and perhaps also of reducing the intensity of detrimental conflict with the
adversary.

To some degree, errors of omission and commission can be
avoided if a formal or informal leader of the policymaking group
engages in certain practices that encourage the members to adopt a

vigilant approach when confronted with either an ambiguous or a seemingly clear-cut warning of potential danger before deciding either to ignore it or to take drastic action. The first three hypotheses pertain to avoiding errors of omission, which result when policymakers, in effect, inadvertently "goof off" instead of trying hard to "head off" an emerging crisis.

Pathway 1 in Figure 9-1 (pp. 212–13) involves underestimating the importance of a challenging threat and leads to immediate reliance on simple decision rules. It can be expected to occur fairly often when members of a policymaking group receive initial warnings about impending dangers that could be averted before they create a full-scale crisis. At an early stage of a developing crisis, warnings are likely to be unimpressive and ambiguous. As a result, members of the group are likely to give an incorrect positive answer to the initial key question evoked by a major challenging event or communication ("Is the problem a routine or relatively unimportant one?"). If they presume that the answer is yes, the members will "goof off" inadvertently— by delegating, tabling, or giving cursory treatment to an emerging threat that could have ominous consequences for the organization or nation—especially if the group is already burdened with an overcrowded agenda. Certain leadership practices, however, can be expected to counteract this unintentional "goofing off" behavior.

HYPOTHESIS 18. Whenever the discussion of an ambiguous threat in a policymaking or crisis management group reveals lack of consensus as to how important a problem it poses, encourage all the members to adopt a vigilant problem-solving approach: If a leader does this at times when at least a small subgroup regards the threat as important enough to warrant vigilant attention, even though others take the opposite position, he or she will tend to prevent the group from arriving at ill-considered cursory decisions that fail to deal effectively with emerging crises. During group discussion of any such ambiguous threat, before deciding what, if anything, to do about it, the leader can foster a vigilant problem-solving approach if he or she carries out actions such as the following:

a. Recommend that the group should be willing to err on the side of caution by awaiting further evidence and then scrutinizing alternatives carefully rather than accepting any initial proposal (made at the outset of the group discussion before the issues have been adequately explored) to take care of the potential threat by resorting to a simple decision rule, such as "do what we did last time when this type of threat was successfully curbed.''

b. Take a neutral stance with regard to how serious the threat might prove to be by abstaining from making any comments that convey either alarming or reassuring notions about the losses to be expected from continuing business as usual.[2]

c. Arrange for further evidence to be collected and analyzed for the group by the best-qualified staff personnel concerning implications of the ambiguous threat, including the likelihood and magnitude of potential damage to vital interests of the organization or nation.

d. Notify the group that he or she intends to keep the agenda open to enable the group to reconsider the implications of the ambiguous threat if any knowledgeable member of the group or expert on the staff who has the responsibility for screening the flow of warning signals notices new indications that the threat might be a potentially important one requiring protective action. (Of course, if a leader were to keep the agenda open indiscriminately in dealing with a large number of low-level threats, this practice would soon become ineffective as a result of wasting time and other organizational resources on false alarms. The more efficient the personnel to whom the organization assigns the functions of screening potential threats, the fewer will be the errors of both omission and commission, provided that [1] the leader does, in fact, keep the policymaking group's agenda open to discuss the screeners' new information about emerging crises and [2] the members respond by adopting a vigilant problem-solving strategy.)

HYPOTHESIS 19. Whenever the policymaking group has arrived at a consensus to the effect that an emerging threat is of such low importance at present that it can be delegated, tabled, or completely ignored, advise all those who participate in the decision to have relatively low confidence in their judgment and to maintain a vigilant set: If a leader does this, he or she will reduce the chances of failing to deal effectively with emerging crises before they mount to dangerously high levels. The purpose of fostering a vigilant set in such circumstances is to induce the members of the group to be ready to reopen the issue if new evidence indicates that more is at stake than was thought at the time the decision was made. Among the steps that will promote sustained readiness to adopt a vigilant set are the following:

a. Ask the group to continue talking a bit more about each apparently low-level threat, immediately after making a decision to drop it from further consideration, in order to discuss briefly what might happen that could make it become more serious and what indicators could be monitored to see if the threat actually is increasing.

b. Assign one or more members or staff personnel with appropriate expertise the responsibility for continued monitoring of the threat and analysis of pertinent new information.

c. Arrange to have a well-qualified analyst (from inside or outside the group) report to the group if indicators suggest that the threat is growing more serious.

HYPOTHESIS 20. Whenever most members of a policymaking group regard a threat as sufficiently important to require prompt action, but judge the problem it poses as not very serious because they believe that an "obvious" solution is readily available, induce some degree of conflict in the unconflicted members and take steps to create constructive doubts in their minds about adopting a seemingly obvious solution: If a leader does this, he or she will tend to prevent a poor-quality decision by fostering a vigilant problem-solving strategy. More specifically, the likelihood that members of the group will engage in open-minded information search and critical appraisal of alternative courses of action will increase if the leader's actions in such circumstances are along the following lines:

a. Raise critical questions about the ways in which a proposed standard operating procedure [SOP] or a previously worked-out contingency plan might not fit the present case (and encourage others in the organization with appropriate expertise to do so).

b. Ask the group to consider whether the proposed "obvious" solution will meet all the various objectives that need to be attained to deal effectively with the threat.

c. Express skepticism about any "obvious" solution derived from a vivid historic analogy to forestall a premature choice. This can be done by calling attention to the very limited sample of potentially relevant past experiences being taken into account and by asking the group to answer a pair of key questions, as suggested by Richard Neustadt and Ernest May, in order to assess the relevance of any salient analogue from the past: "What are the *likenesses* and what are the *differences* between then and now?"

d. Abstain from making any reassuring comments that minimize the losses to be expected from adopting the "obvious" solution.

e. Call attention to the ways in which the seemingly "obvious" solution might entail negative consequences that are being overlooked (such as tangible and intangible losses to be expected from changing existing policies or from failing to live up to prior commitments.

f. Make salient, if necessary, the most potentially damaging consequences of adopting the "obvious" solution by using visual displays and well-elaborated verbal descriptions to convey vivid images of potential losses that could result.

g. Elicit group discussion about what information is needed to specify the full set of objectives to be met, to compare the pros and cons of the "obvious" solution with those of other options that might be viable alternatives, and to develop realistic implementation and contingency plans before committing the organization or nation to any course of action for dealing with a crisis. (That is, raise appropriate questions that need to be answered realistically to carry out each of the main steps of vigilant problem solving, listed in Figure 5-1 (on p. 91).[3]

The leadership practices designated in the foregoing hypotheses are seldom likely to be put into operation when policymakers are already under severe time pressures, burdened with heavy work loads that allow little time for any additional tasks. Obviously, there can be no fully adequate substitute for a highly competent staff that screens the steady flow of warning signs and subtle indications of incipient threat with sufficient accuracy to enable the top-level policymakers to select the most serious problems on which to concentrate their time and energy. This is one of the reasons why it is cost-effective for an organization to expend the funds required for recruiting and maintaining a well-qualified staff with the requisite expertise for rapidly collecting, processing, and analyzing whatever evidence is readily available for evaluating the importance of each emerging threat that might endanger vital interests (the initial key question in the constraints model represented in Figure 7-1, p. 154). Supplementing the work of such a staff, the leadership practices specified in the hypotheses could prove to be a fairly good second line of defense, serving to correct a relatively small number of the mistakes made by those who engage in the front-line screening operation. Leaders of large organizations might find these practices to be well worth the extra time they require and might willingly bear all the other costs if it becomes apparent that occasionally they prevent catastrophic losses.

Helping a Policymaking Group to "Hack It"

The second pathway to failure depicted in Figure 9-1 involves giving a positive answer to one of the key questions concerning constraints (Question IIA): "Are there any overriding cognitive constraints?" Answering yes to this question, according to the constraints model, leads to a quick-and-easy approach that relies upon simple cognitive rules, such as satisficing or analogizing, which gives priority to coping with the constraints at the cost of abandoning a vigilant problem-solving approach. Acts of leadership are needed to prevent this pathway to defective decisionmaking at times when members of a policymaking group feel unsure of being able to "hack it" as a result of being exposed to impressive communications that convey either of two demoralizing themes: "The problem at hand is so enormously complicated that it will be extremely difficult and perhaps impossible to find a satisfactory solution" or "The amount of time, facilities for information gathering, expertise, or other organizational resources for dealing with the problem at hand are extremely limited."

One of the key assumptions that enters into the constraints model is that policymakers will engage in vigilant problem solving when confronted with a problem that they regard as very important for vital interests of their organization or nation only if they regard all such constraints as manageable. At times when problem-solving constraints loom so large that most members of a policymaking group have grave doubts about being able to "hack it," effective leadership is required to counteract those doubts. A formal or informal leader needs to encourage the members to give priority to the primary objective of working out a good solution that will satisfy—as well as can be done under the circumstances—the major requirements posed by the vital problem at hand, despite the limited resources available.

HYPOTHESIS 21. Whenever an impending threat poses a problem that members of the group believe is a very difficult one requiring an excessive drain on themselves or their organizational resources to carry out a full-scale information search and appraisal, take steps to counteract the members' judgments that there are insurmountable obstacles to finding a high-quality solution: If a leader does this, the likelihood that the group will make a poor-quality decision based on using simple decision rules will be reduced. The counteracting actions of the leader, which are likely to be especially crucial at times when members of the group are expressing negativistic themes (such as that the deadline does not permit careful information gathering and appraisal or that the enormous complexities of the problems posed by the crisis exceed the capabilities of the best and brightest minds to "hack it") could include the following:

a. Persistently demonstrate his or her own resolve, as a role model, to tackle the difficult problem in a conscientious way, by following the complete set of decision rules required for vigilant problem solving and by expressing an "up-beat" stance to promote a group norm that fosters working toward a high-quality solution.

b. Encourage attempts to make temporary arrangements (such as a "cease-fire" agreement with adversaries, or its equivalent) that would enable the policymaking group to "buy time" in order to alleviate time pressures.

c. Call attention to organizational resources that members might not be aware of—for example, personnel with information gathering and analytic skills who can be temporarily shifted from their current assignments without undue loss to the organization.

d. Bring in respected experts to brief the group about low-cost means for carrying out the essential steps of information search, appraisal, and planning.

e. If necessary, in the face of persistent resistance, set up a trial run, within the confines of limited time, limited budget, and other limited organizational resources to see how far the group can get in one or two brief sessions using a vigilant problem-solving approach to appraise alternative courses of action. (If the group makes perceptible initial progress, the members can be expected to become more confident and more willing to devote additional time, effort, and other resources to persist in seeking for a high-quality solution.)

HYPOTHESIS 22. Whenever members of a policymaking group are failing, despite persistent problem-solving efforts, to make progress in their attempts to deal with a very difficult set of issues posed by a major crisis and are beginning to show signs of discouragement, fractionate the complex set of problems into smaller subproblems: If a leader does this, the likelihood that the group will abandon a vigilant approach and resort to a simplistic approach will be reduced. (This fractionating tactic, which breaks down a complicated set of problems into separate ones that are seen as more manageable, was well publicized when Henry Kissinger used it successfully as a peace negotiator in the Middle East following the Arab-Israeli War in 1973.) If a group is able to work out one or more satisfactory partial solutions, each "small win" encourages the members to keep working on the remaining subproblems.[4] As a result of positive changes in their expectations about the manageability of the constraints, the group will subsequently be more likely to work out an integrated solution that satisfactorily combines the partial solutions of the various subproblems into a fairly high-quality policy decision.

It is necessary, of course, to avoid the deleterious effects that are likely to occur when uncoordinated subgroups work on different components. If each of them remains unaware of what the other subgroups are doing or has only a vague idea of how their own work is supposed to fit into the total picture, the piecemeal solutions tend to be either incompatible or inconsistent with the overall policy objectives. These undesirable effects are probably prevented when a leader arranges to have the very same policy-planning group work successively on each component of the problem, if time permits. Otherwise, special arrangements are undoubtedly essential for coordinating the work of the subgroups, such as designating at least one well-rounded executive to function in the role of overall coordinator, in order to use the fractionating tactic successfully.

Enabling Members of a Policymaking Group to Say No to Conformity Pressures

The third pathway to failure shown in Figure 9–1 entails reliance on simple *affiliative* decision rules as a result of giving priority to conformity pressures. Acts of leadership are often required in order to prevent the members of a policymaking group (and also the aides and consultants who supply information or advice to the group) from saying yes to the key question concerning affiliative constraints (Question IIB) in response to explicit or implicit demands for conformity. Such demands usually are accompanied by one or another of three types of threat (listed in the second column of Figure 9–1): (1) threat of failure to gain acceptance of the policy among some major powerholders and implementers within the organization; (2) threat of social punishment from other powerholders who can deprive an executive or consultant of compensation, prestige, status, or power; and, (3) threat of loss of social support from fellow members of a cohesive group.

HYPOTHESIS 23. Whenever members of a policymaking group assert that it will be very difficult or impossible to gain acceptance within the organization for certain options that they regard as strong potential candidates for dealing effectively with the problem, take steps to counteract their tendency to overemphasize this organizational constraint: If a leader does this, the likelihood that the group will abandon a vigilant problem-solving approach essential for working out a high-quality solution will be reduced. Among the steps that tend to counteract excessive emphasis on acceptability are the following:

a. Ask the participants to consider their group's potentialities for persuading others in the organization to accept the best available option on its merits.
b. Correct exaggerated views of the extent and intensity of opposition to be expected by expressing a skeptical attitude about pessimistic estimates. This can be done by adducing facts about current attitudes within the organization and by calling attention to comparable instances in the past when opposition melted following adoption of a high-quality solution.
c. Demonstrate the potentiality for gaining acceptance from seemingly staunch opponents, when time permits, by arranging for the group to hear the testimony of powerholders within the

organization (if any) who have changed their minds after hearing persuasive arguments for a viable alternative they had initially regarded as objectionable.

HYPOTHESIS 24. Whenever the members of a policymaking group show signs of relying upon a simple decision rule to conform in order to avoid being punished, take steps to counteract the strong social pressures: If a leader does this, the likelihood that the group will abandon the search for a high-quality solution will be reduced. Among the steps a leader can take to prevent members from accepting one particular option and rejecting alternatives, irrespective of their merits, are the following:

a. Abstain as much as possible from exerting any social pressure on group members to support or to oppose any given option, so as to avoid giving the impression that nonconformers might be subjected to retaliation from the leader.

b. Call the attention of the members to the full range of powerful groups and constituencies to which they are accountable, so as to decrease the influence of pressures from any one faction within the organization or from any one constituency that has become highly salient.

c. Take on the role of mediator if there are signs of an ongoing power struggle within the policymaking group between members from different departments or between contending factions that favor completely different options, in order to prevent mutual threats of retaliations and other corrosive effects of internecine warfare. In the role of mediator, the leader encourages the members who take opposing positions to engage in constructive negotiations by cooperatively carrying out the essential steps of vigilant problem solving, giving priority to the overall organizational objectives shared by both sides in the dispute, and seeking acceptable trade-offs, so as to arrive at a solution that both sides can live with.[5]

d. Ascertain through informal discussions whether any powerful persons or factions within the organization are subjecting members of the group to demands for conformity that explicitly or implicitly carry threats of retaliations. Then, if any are identified, give persuasive messages to convey the importance of allowing each group member to be free to search for

the best available solution in an effort to induce the perpetra-
tors to withdraw their conformity demands.

e. Give realistic reassurances to the group members to counteract
any threats of retaliations that persist despite efforts to remove them—for example, by calling attention to ways that the
leader together with other powerholders will operate as a coalition in support of high-quality decisionmaking and will use
their power, if necessary, to prevent any attempts at retaliatory punishment for nonconformity to the social pressures.

HYPOTHESIS 25. Take steps to counteract the tendency of subordinates to withhold or distort bad news out of concern for possible
punishment from the top-level managers: If a leader does this, the
information supplied to the policymaking group by key personnel
throughout the organization who function as sources of intelligence
and advice will be of higher quality, which will increase the quality
of the entire decisionmaking process. Among the leadership practices
that tend to have this positive effect on the flow of accurate information are the following:

a. Announce and enforce throughout the organization a policy of
no punishment for transmittal of unwelcome facts or judgments, making it clear by deed as well as word that there will
be no shooting of the messenger.
b. Raise questions about the completeness and accuracy of every
crucial piece of information, on the assumption that this will
increase the supply of essential information because the transmitters will realize that full and accurate information really is
wanted and that it is inexpedient to engage in editing to
dampen bad news.[6]
c. Counsel members of the policymaking group to follow up their
suspicions about possibly incomplete or misleading information by recommending that they contact the information
sources informally, using nonstandard channels if necessary, in
order to reassure them that they will be rewarded, not punished, for helping to provide a more complete and accurate
story.

HYPOTHESIS 26. Whenever there are indications that some members
of the policymaking group are opposed to a course of action the
leader favors, avoid yielding to the temptation to "rig" the meetings: If a leader does this, the group's decisionmaking process gener-

ally will be of higher quality. A leader who gives in to the rigging temptation muffles the opposition to his or her preferred course of action in an effort to create an apparent consensus, which not only interferes with vigilant problem solving but also undermines the norm of gaining legitimacy for crucial policy decisions by honest deliberation about the pros and cons of viable alternatives with fellow policymakers. Among the leadership practices that prevent unintentional as well as intentional rigging are the following:

a. Abstain from using opportunities to hold meetings at times when leading dissenters within the group are unable to attend.[7]

b. Distribute intelligence reports and experts' appraisals in an unbiased way, not limiting the distribution to those materials that support the leader's preferred option.

c. Chair the meetings in an evenhanded manner, making sure that the dissenters who are inclined to give counterarguments against the leader's preferred option have ample opportunity to elaborate and are not promptly squelched.

d. Adopt and convey a genuine attitude of openness to all relevant information and arguments, giving no subtle cues to induce members to say what the leader wants them to say.

e. Encourage all staunch supporters within the group, even if they are emerging as the dominant majority, to adhere to the spirit of the above recommendations and discourage any self-appointed lieutenant within the group who shows an inclination to engage in rigging in an effort to promote the leader's preferred position.

HYPOTHESIS 27. Whenever a policymaking or crisis management group is functioning as a compatible team with a fair or high degree of esprit de corps, take steps to counteract tendencies toward concurrence-seeking or "*groupthink*": If a leader does this, the decision-making process will tend to be of higher quality.[8] Among the leadership practices that tend to discourage members from conforming uncritically with the leader's position or with an emerging group consensus in an effort to close ranks and preserve group harmony are the following:

a. Present the issue to the group at the outset in a neutral manner, without pushing for any preferred option, and continue to chair each meeting impartially to encourage an atmosphere of open, unbiased inquiry so the members will explore with open minds a wide range of alternatives.

b. Assign the role of critical evaluator to each member and encourage the group to air objections and doubts by accepting criticism of his or her own judgments in a manner that shows that members are not expected to soft-pedal their disagreements.

c. Arrange for a sizeable block of time (perhaps an entire session) to be spent surveying any ominous warning signals from an adversary that are regarded by one or more knowledgeable members of the group as potentially significant and constructing alternative scenarios of the adversary's intentions.

d. Ask each member to discuss periodically the group's deliberations with trusted associates in his or her own department or unit in the organization and to report back on their comments, describing accurately all varieties of reactions, not specially singling out those that support his or her own views.

e. Invite one or more outside experts or qualified colleagues within the organization who are not core members of the policymaking group to attend some of the meetings and encourage them to challenge the views of core members.

f. Assign the role of devil's advocate to at least two members (two rather than just one in a sizeable group because they can support each other in resisting the social influence of the majority). In order to avoid domesticating or neutralizing the devil's advocates, give them an unambiguous assignment to present the opposing arguments as cleverly and convincingly as they can at the crucial evaluation meetings, so as to challenge the testimony of those advocating the majority position.

g. Set up, when time permits, two or more independent policy-planning groups to work on the policy issue, each carrying out its deliberations under a separate chairperson. Or, if that arrangement is not feasible, divide the policymaking group from time to time into two or more separate subgroups to discuss the pros and cons of alternative policy options and then bring the subgroups together to hammer out their differences.

h. Hold a "second chance" meeting (after the group has reached a preliminary consensus about what seems to be the best available alternative) at which the members are asked to express as vividly as they can all their residual doubts and to rethink the entire issue before making a definitive choice. Or, in circumstances where some members might be reluctant to assert their misgivings in the presence of those who strongly favor the tentative choice, arrange for the equivalent of a "second-chance" meeting by eliciting written statements and speaking privately with the members.

Curbing Self-Serving Motives

The fourth pathway to failure shown in Figure 9-1 (pp. 212-13) describes schematically the sequence to be expected when policymaking executives give higher priority to satisfying their own personal objectives than to attaining the objectives of their organization or nation. Despite the usual organization safeguards pertaining to conflict of interest, special acts of leadership are generally essential to prevent this sequence when a policymaking group is exposed to provocative communications about a challenging threat or opportunity that arouses strong personal motives. Such communications present one of the major types of informational input listed in the second column of Figure 9-1 as an antecedent condition.

Even executives who do not typically display lack of conscientiousness or any of the other predisposing personality deficiencies listed in column 3 of Figure 9-1 can be expected, from time to time, to be strongly tempted to give a positive answer to the question concerning overriding egocentric constraints (Question IIC) when they encounter threats of dire personal losses (such as being removed from office) or opportunities for extraordinary personal gains (such as obtaining a huge bonus from a business deal). On rare occasions all the members of a policymaking group may be exposed to the same personal threat or opportunity that evokes the same self-serving motive—such as increasing their chances of being reelected by covering up an administration scandal for which they are responsible. All of them may then become inclined to adopt a simplistic approach to a major policy problem, resorting to the personal aggrandizement rule ("the main thing to consider is 'what's in it for me?'"), unless somehow restrained from doing so by a formal or informal leader.

HYPOTHESIS 28. Whenever incentives are present at the outset that might tempt some or all members of a policymaking group to favor a policy option that will satisfy self-serving motives, openly mention the temptation at the initial meeting and call attention to the laws, ethical norms, and role obligations designed to be safeguards against conflict of interest: If the designated leader (or one of the members who emerges as a temporary informal leader) does this, he or she will reduce the likelihood that self-serving motives will interfere with seeking high-quality solutions to vital problems.

HYPOTHESIS 29. Whenever there are indications during a series of meetings of a policymaking group that some members are starting to be unduly influenced by self-serving motives, take steps to counteract any such tendency: If a formal or informal leader does this, the likelihood that self-serving motives will continue to interfere with efforts to arrive at a high-quality policy decision will be reduced. Among the actions that can help to prevent self-serving motives from becoming dominant are the following:

a. Convey a genuine attitude of moral disapproval in response to any comments suggesting that it might be expedient or justifiable to allow a self-serving motive to influence evaluations of policy options.

b. Conduct private discussions with the members in question if there are subtle indications that they are giving priority to a self-serving motive but are not openly admitting it. In the private discussions, describe what the indications are and then convey diplomatically the expectation that, in accordance with the legal and ethical norms and the role obligations pertaining to conflict of interest, any temptation to allow self-serving motives to hold sway will be resisted.

HYPOTHESIS 30. When the members of a policymaking group are moving toward a consensus on a policy option that will give priority to a self-serving motive or an emotional need, defer a final decision and introduce counteracting incentives by making their accountability salient to other powerholders who will object: If a formal or informal leader does this, he or she will tend to prevent an ill-conceived policy choice. For example, a leader can increase the chances that the group will shift to a vigilant problem-solving approach at a time when the members are allowing self-serving motives or emotional needs to be dominant and are rationalizing their egocentric choice by arguing that it is compatible with the vital interests of the organization or nation (as when members of an executive committee are disposed to take dramatic action against an adversary to divert attention away from an administration scandal for which they are responsible, on the grounds that such action will help to restore public confidence in the administration). Among the counteracting actions a leader can take are the following:

a. Arrange for one or more meetings, if time and circumstances permit, with other powerholders in the organization who do not share the same personal motives as the members of the policymaking group and encourage the invited participants to function as critics of the group's evaluations of available options, with the expectation that this will lead to less biased deliberations.

b. Ask the group to examine the pros and cons of alternatives and then to summarize their discussions in a detailed report evaluating all the viable alternatives, based on minutes of the meetings, to be circulated to other powerholders and constituencies to whom the group is accountable.

Minimizing Emotional "Discombobulation"

Probably the most frequent instances of the fourth pathway to failure in Figure 9-1 are those instigated by provocative events or warnings that elicit strong emotional reactions (listed as the second type of informational input for Pathway 4 in column 2 of the figure). When members of a policymaking group are in a temporary state of emotional "discombobulation," the institutionalized safeguards designed to prevent executives from giving more priority to their own personal objectives than to attaining the organization's objectives are likely to be quite ineffective. This is especially so during severe crises that generate high levels of emotional stress. Acts of leadership can reduce the incidence of a policymaking group's ill-considered decisions resulting from relying on a simplistic approach that gives priority to satisfying the members' own emotional needs. A leader can take counteracting measures that either reduce the intensity of the members' emotional reactions or that prevent a buildup of the conditions that are likely to induce them to make choices impulsively in order to alleviate anxiety or to satisfy other emotional needs (see Chapter 4).

HYPOTHESIS 31. Arrange for all members of the policymaking or crisis management group (including the leader) and for all key members of their staffs to be given stress inoculation training via a series of crisis simulation exercises before any anticipated crisis of great magnitude occurs: If a leader does this, there will be substantially less likelihood that the group's performance will be impaired as a result of very high levels of emotional stress when the time comes for them to function as crisis managers. Most valuable for this purpose would be exercises conducted in realistic settings that are as similar as possible to the circumstances of actual crises, with each of them followed by a debriefing session. The main purpose would be to provide the participants with experiential training to improve their capabilities for engaging in high-quality decisionmaking in the face of crisis conditions of great uncertainty, extreme time pressures, and high stress. Plausible scenarios of potential crises could be used. After each simulated crisis, the debriefing sessions give the participants an opportunity to discuss and evaluate what they learned from the experience. The sessions can focus especially on postmortem critiques that call attention to misinterpretations of intelligence messages, miscalculations of the adversary's responses to defensive actions, judgmental biases in estimating the probabilities of outcomes, and other common types of errors, all of which are especially likely to occur under highly stressful conditions. The critiques can form the basis for intensive discussion of how each of the sources of error that showed up during the simulation experience might be avoided or counteracted in the future. It is probably worthwhile for participants to have a second exposure to another crisis simulation with a different scenario to give them an opportunity to apply the lessons learned from the first one.

Prior research indicates that exposing people to simulated crises and then having follow-up debriefing sessions during which they talk about their personal experiences as participants can function as *stress inoculation:* Being exposed to preparatory information and related training experiences make people aware, at the visceral as well as cognitive level, of what anticipated crises will actually be like. It stimulates them to develop personal coping devices. As a result, they are able to control their emotions and perform much more effectively if and when actual crises subsequently materialize. This process of psychological preparation resulting in subsequent stress tolerance is called stress inoculation because it seems to be analogous to what happens when people are inoculated to produce antibodies that prevent disease. Gradual exposure to anxiety-producing situations appears to be especially effective in enabling people to cope better with emotional stress when the threatening events later do occur. It is reasonable to expect, therefore, that participants in crisis simulations designed for the purposes of stress inoculation will be less prone to react to a subsequent dangerous crisis with hypervigilance or defensive avoidance. They will be better able to maintain self-control and self-confidence despite being exposed to extreme anxiety-arousing events that could create a powerful emotive constraint and consequently will be more likely to carry out efficiently the steps of vigilant problem solving.[9]

HYPOTHESIS 32. During a severe crisis, when the members of the policymaking or crisis management group are undergoing considerable stress, raise questions, provide informative briefings, and make statements that are likely to alleviate acute feelings of apprehensiveness: If the formal leader (or else one of the members with sufficient stress tolerance who is capable of functioning as an informal leader) does this, he or she will reduce the chances that the members will adopt a defective coping pattern of defensive avoidance or hypervigilance. Among the counteracting measures that can keep the members' level of emotional stress from mounting so high that it interferes with vigilant information search and appraisal are the following leadership practices:

a. Raise skeptical questions about unfounded rumors or unsubstantiated warnings that play up oncoming dangers and call the group's attention to realistic reasons for discounting dire forecasts as exaggerations.

b. Urge members of the policymaking group and their staffs to be on the alert for new pertinent information, including any that is discrepant with initial alarming reports, which might have been exaggerated or misleading. Also, in line with recommendations by Neustadt and May, ask the members to postpone the natural tendency to discuss immediately "what shall we do?" when an alarming crisis arises until they can define more sharply the emerging crisis situation that seems to call for drastic action by obtaining more dependable answers to the standard questions that journalists are expected to cover when investigating a news story: "When?" "Where?" "What?" "Who?" "How?" "Why?"[10]

c. Arrange to have available for immediate consultation the best-qualified experts on the nature and imminence of each probable source of danger and then call in the appropriate standby experts promptly to brief the group each time a major ominous event occurs that markedly increases the members' level of apprehensiveness. Their statements, especially when endorsed by the leader, can correct exaggerated expectations and present a balanced view of the dangers, which might make the members realize that there are sound reasons for not assuming that the worst case is most probable.

 d. Abstain from elaborating upon dire apprehensions evoked by new information that makes the danger appear to be of greater magnitude than had been expected, and, instead, urge the group to persist in vigilant problem solving—for example, by focusing on evaluations of potentially protective actions that might lessen the danger.

HYPOTHESIS 33. Whenever the danger of severe losses appears to be so imminent that some or all members of the policymaking or crisis management group believe the deadline is too short to allow time to work out a good solution to deal with the harrowing crisis, take steps to counteract the adverse effects of extreme time pressure: If a formal or informal leader does this, he or she will reduce the chances that the quality of decisionmaking will deteriorate as a result of hypervigilant reactions among members of the group. Among the counteracting measures that could have this positive effect are the following:

 a. Initiate efforts to obtain an extension of the short deadline and arrange for other tactical moves that will "buy time" to work on a high-quality solution.
 b. Counsel the members to abstain from drawing any conclusions about what is most likely to happen or about what to do in the face of expected danger until after the group has at least briefly discussed what can realistically be accomplished with regard to information gathering, appraisal, and planning in the very limited time still available.
 c. Strive to function as a positive role model by displaying firm resolve to persist in a vigilant problem-solving approach even though everyone may believe that tomorrow or the next day could bring disaster.

HYPOTHESIS 34. During any long drawn-out crisis, whenever members of a crisis management group are undergoing prolonged emotional stress, provide information and comments that are likely to build up a realistic basis for hope: If a formal or informal leader does this, particularly at times when an attempted course of action has failed to resolve the crisis and some members are starting to express pessimism about finding a satisfactory solution, he or she will tend to prevent the disruptive effects of demoralization and defensive avoidance, which greatly impair the quality of decisionmaking. Among the actions that are likely to be effective preventive measures are the following:

a. Disagree with those who express a hopeless outlook, but abstain from taking an unwarranted upbeat stance by resorting to dubious reassurances that later on, as the crisis continues, are likely to prove false and heighten demoralization.

b. Call attention to whatever reasonable grounds there are for expecting each of the major threats to be manageable and emphasize that the realities of the dire prospects can be faced without losing hope of keeping the potential danger under control and finding a satisfactory way out of the dilemma.

c. Invite appropriate experts to give briefings to the group on the full range of favorable as well as unfavorable forecasts and on the options that could be considered in the event that a worst case scenario seems to be materializing, which could give the members justifiable reasons for maintaining a nonpessimistic outlook, and perhaps also provide fresh perspectives for working out an innovative solution.

HYPOTHESIS 35. On those occasions when some or all members of the group are temporarily displaying intense anger, grief, guilt, elation, or any other strong emotion, intervene to counteract the adverse influence of the members' strong emotional needs that go along with their temporary state of high arousal: If a leader does this, he or she will tend to prevent the quality of decisionmaking from deteriorating. (In some organizations, when the formal leader is unable to function effectively because he or she is personally experiencing the same intense emotion, the group norms may allow one of the members who is capable of doing so to emerge as an informal leader.) Among the ways that a formal or informal leader might intervene for this purpose are the following:

a. Postpone temporarily any definitive decision that would commit the organization to a new course of action until the intense emotional reactions within the group have subsided. (For example, at a time when there is a strong impetus to retaliate for an unexpected "stab in the back" by an adversary, the leader, while allowing the members to ventilate their vitriolic feeling that "the bastards" should pay dearly for their vicious deed, could postpone taking a definitive vote on what action to take until the collective mood of hot rage has cooled down. Similarly, when the dominant mood is elation evoked by a small victory, which may incline the members to become overly optimistic about taking big risks to achieve a greater victory, the leader could use his or her influence to hold off a definitive decision until after their intense emotional mood has subsided.)

b. Direct the attention of the group away from a burning hot issue that is temporarily arousing strong emotional reactions by shifting to an entirely different problem that also requires the group's attention. (This type of shift could restore a vigilant problem-solving set among the members, or at least stem the tide of emotion that would continue to build up from mutual reinforcement if the group were to continue to discuss the emotionally arousing issue.)

c. Dampen the intensity of emotional reactions that are interfering with effective problem solving by calling in experts and senior consultants who will present a dispassionate analysis of a defeat, a victory, a "stab in the back," or any other emotion-provoking event. An insightful analysis could give the group a fresh perspective, enabling the members to view the event in a different light that makes it appear much less provocative and offers less justification for righteous indignation, overconfident elation, or any other emotional impulse.

Deterring Premature Commitment

Despite a leader's best efforts to foster a high-quality decision, some avoidable errors in information search and appraisal, as well as gaps in contingency planning, may remain uncorrected at the time when the policymaking group is ready to commit itself to a course of action. A few of the preceding hypotheses (for example, Hypothesis 20) pertain to deterring premature commitment in certain special circumstances. These hypotheses can be supplemented by taking account of additional implications of the constraints model that bear upon premature commitment.

In terms of the pathways to failure shown in Figure 9-1, residual errors are to be expected via Pathways 2, 3, or 4 if members of a policymaking group continue to give a positive answer to one or another of the key questions about overriding constraints (Questions IIA, IIB, or IIC). Positive answers are especially likely to persist, even if a leader takes appropriate steps to try to induce negative answers, when there are powerful constraints that remain salient throughout the entire period of decisionmaking.

Consider the unrelenting influence of constraints to be expected during severe crises that threaten the survival of the organization or nation. In such circumstances, enormously complicated issues with potentially stupendous consequences that are difficult to comprehend may continue to perplex the members of a policymaking group. They give rise to avoidable errors via Pathway 2, from reliance on simple cognitive decision rules to cope with limited time and other dominating problem-solving constraints. Extraordinarily intense social pressures from deeply concerned factions and constituencies, often accompanied by seemingly insurmountable threats of retaliations or loss of social support in the face of a harassing crisis, may doggedly beset the members. Those affiliative constraints give rise to avoidable errors via Pathway 3, from reliance on simple affiliative decision rules to cope with them. Perhaps most likely of all, the need to alleviate mounting emotional stress evoked by forebodings of seemingly imminent catastrophe gives rise to avoidable errors via Pathway 4, from reliance on simple egocentric rules to cope with the dominating emotive constraints. If any of these salient constraints continues to exert a dominating influence on the members of a crisis management group, the course of action they choose is likely to be defective unless a leader's interventions prevent premature commitment.

In terms of the constraints model represented in Figure 7-1 (pp. 154-55), a leader's interventions are needed to induce the members to change their answers to the key mediating questions about constraints from yes to no. Otherwise they will continue to rely upon simple decision rules and will fail to go through essential steps of vigilant problem solving (shown in Figure 5-1, p. 91).

Even when there is very little time to decide what to do during an escalating crisis, an organization's resources can be mobilized to carry out a substantial information search rapidly, as stated earlier, if the top-level policymakers phone or meet with two types of informants: knowledgeable experts who can supply comprehensive briefings and advocates of one or another option who will forcefully call attention to drawbacks to the options that they regard as objectionable.

Time constraints are especially difficult to surmount during a severe crisis, as I have repeatedly emphasized. (See, for example, p. 176.) Nevertheless, even in only a few hours it may be possible to go through various steps of vigilant problem solving sufficiently to avoid overlooking fatal flaws, thereby preventing gross errors that could readily arise if such steps were not taken. For example, suppose that just a few hours before the decision was made to approve the Bay of Pigs invasion plan, President Kennedy or Secretary of Defense Robert McNamara had taken the trouble to do a last-minute reconsideration of the expected consequences of the CIA's invasion plan by inviting the Joint Chiefs of Staff to spend an hour answering questions about military prospects and then spending another hour hearing about the prospects for uprisings among the people of Cuba by talking with Cuban political experts from the CIA (whose intelligence analysis division was not consulted by the CIA planners or by anyone in President Kennedy's advisory group). The President or the Secretary of Defense might well have come away from those final two hours of consultation with the realization, before it was too late, that the main assumptions of the CIA's Cuban invasion plan were questionable and the entire plan was too flawed to warrant being approved.

Once the crisis managers have reached the stage of selecting what appears to them as the best available option, it can still be advantageous for them to postpone commitment, if the deadline for an ultimatum—or the equivalent—is not yet at hand. One or more sessions of intensive deliberation, with appropriate experts present, may enable them to complete a final overall review of residual problems and a final reconsideration of expected pros and cons, to see if any important consequences are being overlooked or misjudged. The temporary postponement of commitment would also enable the crisis managers to round out plans for implementing the decision, for monitoring, and for handling probable exigencies that might require supplementary actions.

There may also be other advantages whenever the chosen option involves initiating a highly provocative action, such as a military mobilization or alert. The purpose may be to demonstrate resolve to protect endangered national interests and to provide an incentive for a hostile nation to engage in genuine negotiations, but the adversary leaders may see it as a direct threat requiring military countermoves.

The historical record of international conflicts indicates that it is more difficult to work out an agreement after one side has already committed itself to a military course of action. National leaders and the public are generally less resistant to accepting a negotiated settlement requiring them to refrain from sending troops and warships or installing missiles, which maintains the status quo, than to withdraw troops and warships or to remove missiles. After a military commitment is already made, there would be a loss of face from backing down.

Also to be considered are the organizational action programs and relatively inflexible routines. For example, they make it difficult, if not impossible, to reverse a military plan of action after orders have already been transmitted to military commanders in the field and have been set in motion, especially if they have evoked active opposition by the adversary's armed forces. Experts on command and control emphasize the difficulties both sides have in controlling the actions of implementers in local command posts when military forces are alerted. They foresee serious danger of unintended escalation to all-out nuclear war in the event that during a future crisis the leaders of one or another of the superpowers decide to raise the level of alert to the point where military units equipped with nuclear weapons are mobilized for action.

In the private sector, there are comparable provocative decisions made in the heat of a crisis that have enormous and sometimes unstoppable momentum. For example, when a business firm makes an ill-conceived decision to prevent imminent losses by initiating a trade war or a lawsuit against a rival firm, it may not be possible to reverse it because organizational implementation routines have been set in motion and have elicited damaging countermoves by the adversaries, which lead to a spiral of unintended escalation.

When a policymaking group is not confronted with a crisis but has been working for a long time on a fairly important problem, such as how to take advantage of an opportunity to save money or increase revenues by making use of a new advance in computer technology, some avoidable errors and gaps in contingency planning that could be corrected may still remain at the time when the members feel ready to vote for what they regard as unquestionably the best course of action. Such residual errors and gaps are to be expected for a sizeable percentage of decisions made by any policymaking group, even if all the pertinent leadership practices specified in the hypotheses presented so far in this chapter are skillfully applied and even if everyone in the group has the ability and motivation to participate effectively in high-quality decisionmaking.

Earlier I pointed out that some avoidable errors, as well as unavoidable errors, are to be expected even when policymakers have conscientiously carried out the steps of vigilant problem solving. For example, in all of their deliberations up to the point of closure the policymakers may be making an erroneous assumption derived from misleading intelligence reports. Or they may be drawing incorrect inferences from accurate intelligence reports because of their own faulty ideological concepts and oversimplified cognitive schemas, such as stereotypes of their adversaries. But, as I also indicated earlier, residual errors (including even some of those arising from ideological assumptions, stereotypes, and other schemas that enter into the policymakers' "mind set," which makes for distortions of the way they process information) can sometimes be corrected before it is too late. To do so, it is essential for the policymaking group to continue engaging in vigilant information search and appraisal even though the members feel that they have finished and are quite ready to commit themselves to a course of action that they judge to be a satisfactory solution to the problem at hand.

The research evidence cited in Chapter 5, it will be recalled, indicates that when people are exposed to new, clear-cut facts that do not fit certain of their cognitive schemas, they tend to change those schemas to bring them into line with the discrepant information. This may happen only rarely, but when it does the quality of a policy decision can be markedly improved as a result of better comprehension of the problem and of the requirements to be met. Probably much more frequently, the new information obtained after a group of policymakers has reached an initial consensus corrects erroneous expectations by filling in gaps concerning previously unsuspected obstacles to implementation that will be encountered if they adopt what seems to be the best available course of action. This, too, can improve the quality of a policy decision. Sometimes new information about implementation difficulties sends the group back to the drawing board to devise a better plan before making a final commitment.

It appears, then, that when a consensus begins to emerge within a policymaking group about what seems to be the best available option, it is still valuable for the members to persist in maintaining an attitude of skepticism about the soundness of their choice. But it is very difficult for them to do so unless strongly encouraged by the leader. At such a time it is especially burdensome for the members to go through the subjective discomfort of raising doubts about their own best ideas for a promising solution and to listen attentively to what those who are most critical are saying. After the group has finally agreed upon the best available choice, the members are not in a mood to contemplate all the crucial things that could go wrong. But they need to hold in abeyance the natural tendency to indulge in feelings of satisfaction, confidence, and optimism as they move toward complete closure.

Not only may more work be needed to detect and correct residual miscalculations but also to develop high-quality implementation, monitoring, and contingency plans. If the policymakers have not consulted with line personnel who can inform them about implementation difficulties that might arise, their chosen course of action could lead to unanticipated setbacks and losses.[11]

There are several ways, therefore, that a leader can serve a crucial function by inducing members of a policymaking group to remain skeptical about whether the information they have received so far is giving them a correct view of the problem and whether they have as yet explored sufficiently the pros and cons of all the viable options. Inducing this type of skepticism can prove to be highly constructive if it leads the members to use whatever remaining time is available to fill in the gaps and to check further on their main assumptions about the nature of the problem and about what needs to be done to deal effectively with it.

The hypotheses that follow specify leadership practices that tend to prevent a policymaking group from becoming committed prematurely, before having made full use of its capabilities for checking on crucial facts and assumptions, for assessing the full range of viable alternatives, or for working out detailed implementation, monitoring, and contingency plans.

HYPOTHESIS 36. Whenever a policymaking group appears to be reaching the end of its deliberations, after settling upon a consensus as to the best available course of action, make a rapid, rough-and-ready diagnosis of residual symptoms of defective decisionmaking and then take steps to eliminate them: If a formal or informal leader does so, he or she will tend to improve the overall quality of the policy decision. Even without knowing which particular constraint may be responsible for a persisting symptom, the following measures could be sufficient to eliminate it:

a. Call each symptom of defective decisionmaking to the attention of the group and ask the members to correct the defect (for example, by discussing the appropriate key questions that enter into the vigilant problem-solving strategy [shown in Figure 5-1 on p. 91]).

b. When the symptom of defective decisionmaking involves failure to examine adequately the consequences to be expected of viable options, ask the group to discuss what could happen if each of the options is selected by projecting three different scenarios—one for the best case, another for the worst case, and a third for the most likely case.[12]

c. When the persisting symptom is either failure to reconsider originally rejected alternatives or failure to examine some major costs and risks of the preferred choice, arrange for the group to construct a decisional balance sheet, which requires listing all the known pros and cons for each alternative that has been considered.[13]

d. When the persisting symptom is failure to work out implementation, monitoring, and contingency plans, elicit and discuss critical feedback from key implementers: Invite representatives of the main organizational units responsible for implementing the policy decision to participate in the group's deliberations and to give their frank appraisals of the options under consideration; after that, ask the group to examine carefully those critiques along with other available information concerning implementation obstacles or setbacks to be expected and potential pitfalls to be guarded against.[14]

HYPOTHESIS 37. Whenever the leader surmises that the group of policymakers is not functioning at its highest potential level despite his or her repeated corrective efforts (including measures of the type specified in Hypothesis 36), make a careful diagnosis of the constraints that are sources of the resistance and then take steps to counteract their adverse influence: If a leader does this, the likelihood of the decisionmaking process continuing to be of poor quality right up to the point of final closure will be reduced. Among the steps that could be taken are the following:

a. Watch for signs that members of the group are using a simple decision rule—for example, indications that members are relying upon the "nutshell briefing" rule when arriving at a consensus in favor of investing in a new technological system immediately after being briefed about highly technical considerations by an expert who recommends the new system— and then intervene by making the group aware of any such signs and express concern that the group is moving toward a premature commitment without having adequately examined the alternatives.

b. Eliminate the constraint by changing the objective conditions that are producing it—for example, if there are indications that members of the group are being constrained by conformity pressures from one particular faction within the organization, use persuasive capabilities to induce the leaders of that faction to desist for the sake of working out a sound policy that gives priority to vital interests of the organization or nation. Similar eliminating actions can sometimes be taken for cognitive constraints and egocentric constraints.

c. Attempt to persuade the members not to give any persisting constraint undue weight. Advise them to treat it as one of the many requirements to be taken into account when seeking for a satisfactory solution, not as the single most important requirement that cannot be traded off in a compromise, if necessary, to attain other more essential objectives.

Further Implications for the Unfinished Research Agenda

The 20 hypotheses just presented, derived from the constraints model, appear to be plausible in light of existing research findings on leadership. None of them, however, has been sufficiently investigated to warrant being regarded as empirically well supported. They are tentative propositions about potentially effective leadership practices to be added to the unfinished agenda for research on policymaking.[15]

For the present, we must be skeptical about any prescriptive inferences drawn from the 20 hypotheses about what a leader should do to improve the policymaking process in his or her organization. Those inferences have not yet been tried out sufficiently to ascertain whether they actually work well enough to be worth the costs and efforts they may require. And we cannot be sure that they are free from undesirable side effects. The specified leadership practices for improving the quality of policymaking must be validated in subsequent tryouts before they can be applied with any confidence. But they appear to be promising ones, well worth the trouble and expense of being tried out in an open-minded way not only by research investigators but also by qualified members of advisory groups who participate at least peripherally in the policymaking process and who want to improve that process. The prescriptive implications that prove to be ineffective could then be eliminated from further consideration and those in need of modification could be revised. After that, the leadership practices that are working out well might gradually be tried out by higher-level executives.

Any of the leadership practices that continue to stand up well could be incorporated into the standard procedures and operational code of an organization's top-level policymakers. If they are feasible and effective in the judgment of well-qualified observers, including the top-level policymakers themselves, those leadership practices could be consolidated by establishing new institutionalized norms and accountability requirements. The new norms and requirements could bring about a marked improvement in an organization's policymaking procedures by specifying who is expected to do what in order to arrive at sound policy decisions. It seems reasonable to expect that ultimately at least a few of the prescriptive implications of the 20 hypotheses about leadership practices derived from the constraints model will prove to be feasible and effective for improving the quality of policymaking in government, business, and public welfare organizations.

The validated procedures could enable a higher percentage of those organizations to survive. And the chances of survival of their constituencies could also increase. The improvements in policymaking procedures might contribute at least in a small way to help leaders in nations throughout the world arrive at sensible policy decisions to prevent economic collapse, ecological disasters, and nuclear war. Effective leadership in sound policymaking and crisis management is a fundamental requirement to keep the next decades from ushering in an age of irreversible catastrophes.

Notes

CHAPTER 1. ORDER OUT OF THEORETICAL CHAOS?

1. Hollander's analysis of leadership and power includes an elaboration of Tucker's account of the role of leadership in policymaking:

> In his book on *Politics as Leadership,* Tucker (1981) has delineated three phases of the process of engaging people in pursuing a political program: *diagnosing* the problem facing the constituency; *prescribing* a course of action, which is "policy formulation"; and *mobilizing* action, which is "policy implementation." But a president's version of social reality and a needed program can be a shared definition of the situation only as long as the President retains credibility, which often equates with popularity. While that is the case, a president is relatively assured of continued support. This also means that at least for a time a disastrous program could be sustained by the popularity of a president. (Hollander 1985, p. 510)

Other social scientists, whose work is reviewed by Hollander (1978, 1985), view the role of top-level leadership in policymaking in much the same way as Tucker does. James MacGregor Burns (1978, p. 3), for example, emphasizes that the effectiveness of leaders must be judged not by their press clippings but by actual social change measured by " . . . the satisfaction of human needs and expectations." He asserts that "the secret of . . . [effective] leadership is the capacity of leaders to have their goals clearly and firmly in mind, to fashion new institutions relevant to those goals, to stand back from immediate events and day-to-day routines and understand the potential and consequences of change" (1984, p. 103). Selznick (1957) describes a leader's functions in making "critical decisions" in similar terms and adds

265

another important function: reconciling struggles among persons and groups with competing interests within the organization.

In order to define an organization's goals, to reconcile clashing interests, to initiate policy changes, and to see to it that the intended changes are implemented, a leader must have a considerable amount of power. "Quite simply," Hollander (1985) says, "having enough power means you can get your own way." He goes on to describe the complex nature of leadership power and its relationship to persuasive influence by drawing upon French and Raven's classic analysis:

> A well-known formulation (French and Raven, 1959) elaborates several "bases of power," including legitimate power, reward power, coercive power, referent power, and expert power. The first of these is akin to the concept of the leader's legitimacy of authority. . . . Reward and coercive power represent gains or losses for compliance or noncompliance with a person in authority. Referent power represents an extension of reward power through a process of identification with that person. Once such an identification has occurred, it is no longer necessary for the person in authority to monitor the behavior of the less powerful person continuously. As the term suggests, expert power arises from specialized knowledge or distinctive competence that is valued.
>
> . . . Even appointed leaders, "put in charge" within an organization must rely on influence, in the sense of persuasion, as much as or more than on power. The unfettered use of power can be highly dysfunctional in creating numerous points of resistance and lingering negative feelings. Therefore both elected and appointed leaders are called upon to use persuasion in many instances, instead of the full power supposedly at their disposal. (Hollander 1985, p. 489)

Although leaders can exercise a great deal of power and influence, they certainly do not always get their own way. In fact, subordinates fairly often do *not* implement policy decisions in the way the leaders want them to be implemented (see pp. 331–34 and 336–38 [Notes 11 and 14 in Chapter 10]). The high frequency of implementation failures reported by Nakamura and Smallwood and by others in the field of management research attests to the limitations of leadership power and influence. In some instances, however, the implementation failure seems to have come about because the leaders did not take the necessary steps to mobilize their power resources. For example, they may have made little or no attempt to persuade the implementers who objected to their new policy decisions that their objections were not warranted, that the new policy was legitimate, and that it was based on expert judgment. The main point is that two types of implementation failures can be distinguished. One type occurs because the leaders who formulated the policy decision do not have sufficient power and influence to induce subordinates to accept it and implement it properly. The other type arises not because the leaders are lacking in power and influence but because they fail to use it. The latter type should be regarded as *avoidable errors* that usually can be eliminated if policymakers adopt appropriate leadership practices to develop effective plans for implementing each policy decision. Several such practices are described in Chapter 10.

2. For a strong dose of disagreement among experts, just dip into any of the scholarly symposium volumes on policymaking published in recent years. A typical example is *Perspectives on Organization Design and Behavior,* edited by Andrew Van De Ven and William Joyce (1981). Several of the management scientists who contributed to the symposium, including the two editors, give congratulatory applause to new developments that seem to be redirecting mainstream theory in a direction that they believe will soon lead to big improvements in the way strategic decisions are made. But their exuberant cheers are drowned out by the booing section.

One loud and clear voice in the booing section is Jeffrey Pfeffer's. As a final commentator at the conference, he distilled his reactions to the presentations in the form of general laws of organizational research. One is "the law of unresolvable ignorance" and another is "the law of unrequited effort." Cogent reasons for these laws are provided by James March, another leading expert in the booing section. Speaking about the way crucial policy decisions are arrived at, March asserts that "there are no clear universals." Individuals and groups in organizations, according to March, often choose the first barely acceptable alternative that comes along rather than maximizing, but not always. When major policy changes are needed, they frequently stick to obsolete policies by making only small incremental modifications, yet on occasion they make "heroic leaps." Sometimes they take account of a broad spectrum of objectives and long-term considerations when it seems required; sometimes they fail to do so. Certain of their new decisions reflect learning from past mistakes, others do not.

If March's comments about the absence of universals is correct—and from my own observations as well as from my reviews of the literature on organizational decisionmaking, I believe that they certainly are—we must expect to find a variety of different strategies in the repertoire of practically all policymakers. We cannot expect to find any simple law that will prove to be valid, such as the alleged law of creeping incremental change. According to that supposed law, leaders of nations, corporations, and other large organizations generally arrive at new policies via a series of little incremental steps, making one tiny change after another, the first of which differs only very slightly from the current policy. It seems likely that every policymaker is quite capable of manifesting a creeping incremental approach from time to time, but is also capable at other times of using quite a number of different strategies that are in his or her repertoire for making policy changes. The strategies within a policymaker's repertoire may range from mindless inertia to a full-scale problem-solving approach involving an extensive information search and careful deliberation about the pros and cons of a large number of viable alternatives.

Although James March appears to be quite correct about the lack of any universals that could be considered warranted generalizations about the way policymakers typically arrive at their policy decisions, it does not necessarily follow that we cannot expect to find any universals concerning the *conditions* under which policymakers use one or another approach when making such decisions. March, however, expresses an extremely pessimistic view of the prospects for discovering any such universals at all. Existing theories of organizational choice, he points out, are contradictory and none of them tells us very much. Nor are we ever likely, according to March, to have any major breakthrough in this field to enable us to make precise forecasts about how policy decisions will be made. Even in the long run, he says, we cannot expect anything more than a theory that contributes "marginally to ordinary knowledge . . . analogous to the contribution of a good consultant, or possibly a minor poet" (1981, p. 236).

My own view is considerably less pessimistic about the prospects for validating empirical generalizations that can be used to develop an integrative theory. With regard to empirical generalizations, I agree with March that we cannot expect to find any main effects indicating that under practically all circumstances, practically all types of policymakers show a preference for using one particular strategy rather than other strategies that are available to them for grappling with policy problems. But my earlier analyses of the research literature on decisionmaking (Janis and Mann; Janis 1982d, 1985) suggest that we can expect to find many significant interaction effects, particularly between situations and strategies, indicating that most policymakers do, in fact, display a preference for a particular strategy in certain circumstances, but not in other circumstances. (See Chapters 4 and 8.) In the technical language of analysis of variance, there are also likely to be significant triple interaction effects among strategies, situations, and characteristics of the policymakers. The latter category includes such variables as the amount of power policymakers have within the organization, the amount of experience they have had in making similar policy decisions, and personality characteristics such as self-confidence, aggressiveness, and preferred coping style for dealing with psychological stress. (See Chapter 9.)

3. A view similar to Lebow's, emphasizing lack of a comprehensive theory, was presented by Ole Holsti and Alexander George in a paper that provides an initial conceptual framework for studying the effects of stress on policymakers (which I use to elucidate some of the components of the preliminary theoretical model presented in this book):

> Existing empirical materials on foreign policy decisionmaking are fragmentary, uneven in quality and, in general, noncumulative. . . . At this stage priority should be given to the task of conceptualization since available analytical approaches are not wholly adequate. They neither identify all of the different elements of the problem nor deal with them in an integrated comprehensive framework. . . .
>
> * * *
>
> Despite advances in relevant portions of theories of individual psychology, small group dynamics, and organizational behavior, the linkage and synthesis of these . . . theories is still primitive. (Holsti & George, pp. 256–57)

Is the time really ripe for developing an integrated comprehensive framework? A somewhat pessimistic answer is given by Kinder and Weiss in their comments about the present state of theory in a critical review of three books bearing on foreign policy decisions—Jervis' *Perception and Misperception in International Politics,* Axelrod's *Structure of Decision: The Cognitive Maps of Political Elites,* and Janis and Mann's *Decision Making: A Psychological Analysis of Conflict, Choice, and Commitment.* Kinder and Weiss emphasize the divergences in the theoretical approaches presented in the three books, which they treat as representative of the lack of theoretical consensus about the decision process that characterizes current social science. They point out that despite the divergences, all three books—like numerous other recent studies of decisionmaking—converge in that they present cogent evidence as well as theoretical arguments against accepting the rational actor model as a general descriptive or explanatory account of how policymakers actually arrive at decisions. Kinder and Weiss attempt to discern the implications of the convergences and divergences for research and theoretical developments in the immediate future:

> In a general way . . . [the authors of the three books] share the view of the decisionmaker as a limited information processor, but they do not agree on which aspects of the processing are most important to explain. . . .
>
> In the midst of such disarray, it is easy to mourn the loss of the

organizing vision provided by the analytic [rational actor] paradigm. On the criteria of elegance, sweep, and parsimony, the rational model far surpasses a catalogue such as we have outlined.

But elegance ain't everything. . . .

A loosely coupled collection of subtheories may be the most promising way of dealing with the full scope of so complex a phenomenon. . . .

To identify a set of controlling psychological principles of limited scope is of course especially useful when the analyst can go on to specify the various circumstances under which each is likely to be in control. . . . Right at the start, we are tripped up by our frail or nonexistent understanding of situational characteristics themselves—of the circumstances that may influence the processes of decision-making in as complex an arena as foreign policymaking (or, indeed, in any other realm of consequence). . . .

. . . The analytic [rational actor] paradigm is not about to be eclipsed by a well-integrated vision of decisionmaking. (Pp. 731–33)

Although I agree with much of what Kinder and Weiss say about our present low level of knowledge, I do not share their dim view of the prospects for improvement. They are certainly correct in asserting that on the one hand the rational actor model is much more elegant than the emerging "collection of subtheories" and in emphasizing that on the other hand, truth-value must be given precedence over elegance. But I do not agree that a valid "well-integrated vision of decisionmaking" is beyond our reach at present because I see much less "disarray" in the various studies than they do. Like them, I wish we knew much more about the conditions under which diverse psychological processes occur. But I think that Kinder and Weiss are greatly exaggerating when they speak of "our frail or nonexistent understanding of situational characteristics . . . that may influence the processes of decision-making."

CHAPTER 2. COGNITIVE DECISION RULES

1. This chapter does not attempt to present an exhaustive survey of all cognitive decision rules. Rather, it attempts to describe and illustrate ones that are most commonly used when policymakers adopt a seat-of-the-pants approach. A number of decision rules that have been extensively discussed in the social science literature are briefly mentioned; others that are less well known are elaborated in more detail. Additional examples and elaborations of some of the decision rules described in this chapter will be presented in later chapters (see especially Chapter 7).

The cognitive decision rules discussed in Chapter 1—and also the

affiliative and egocentric decision rules discussed in Chapters 3 and 4—
are *not prescriptive* but are purely *descriptive* rules. Each of the decision rules is formulated on the basis of inferences from observations of
the behavioral patterns that policymakers manifest when dealing with
problems requiring policy decisions. (See at the end of Chapter 8 the
comments made about Figures 8–1, 8–2, and 8–3.) Although occasionally policymakers use one or another of the simple decision rules quite
deliberately, often they may not be fully aware of their reliance on simple decision rules, and they may not even be able to put into words
whichever of the rules they are using.

2. Among the main references that summarize studies of decisionmaking
processes, from which the seven criteria were extracted by Janis and
Mann (1977), are the following: Etzioni (1968); Katz & Kahn; Maier;
Miller & Starr; Simon (1976); Taylor; Vroom & Yetton; Wilensky; and
Young. The seven criteria are also consistent with more recent analyses
of the quality of decisionmaking processes, such as the comprehensive
treatment of this area of research by Abelson and Levi in *The Handbook of Social Psychology*. (See also the 22 additional pertinent references, published between 1978 and 1988, listed in Note 2, Chapter 5.)

3. Because more than one person usually participates in making a policy
decision, I have formulated the definitions of the symptoms of defective policymaking in terms of the behavior of a group. Here I am using
"group" in a very broad sense, as the term is often used in social psychology, to refer to two or more persons who work together on a policy
decision—as when a chief executive consults with at least one advisor.
The participants in an executive committee or policy planning group
may meet together in formal conferences or in informal bull sessions
or sometimes they may interact without any face-to-face contact, via
written memoranda or telephone calls. When working on a major decision, of course, the members of a top-level policymaking group in most
large organizations interact in all sorts of ways, both formally and informally. All their various kinds of interactions need to be taken into
account when assessing the presence or absence of the seven symptoms
of defective policymaking.

If a policy decision is made essentially by just one person—which
occurs when a chief executive has the power and uses it to change a
policy entirely on his or her own—the seven symptoms can be used to
assess the quality of the *individual's* policymaking procedures. Obviously, the definitions would need to be worded slightly differently to
pertain to a single individual rather than a group. Those reformulated
definitions could also be used whenever an inquiry focuses on the decisionmaking process of just one member of a policymaking team—for
example, a dissident who opposed the option favored by the majority.

Whenever ratings are made of whether or not an individual executive or a group has displayed any given symptom of defective policymaking, the usefulness of the ratings for research or for any practical purpose depends not only upon the reliability of the rater's judgments but also, of course, upon the quality and completeness of the available observational reports and records. For many policy decisions, the available evidence is too incomplete or too untrustworthy for anyone to make valid ratings. Occasionally even when a considerable amount of trustworthy evidence is at hand, a missing piece of crucial evidence can result in an analyst making an erroneous rating of a symptom as having been present. For example, it could happen that detailed minutes of meetings indicate that objectives were never discussed (symptom no. 1) whereas, in fact, just before the first meeting, the chief executive may have had an intensive discussion of objectives with an advisor in a long telephone conversation, of which no record exists.

When there seem to be ample reports and documentary records, some or all of the material may be misleading because the policymakers deliberately doctored it to give the impression that they had used sound procedures. Minutes that state that a number of viable alternatives were debated may be exaggerating what actually took place. The alleged debate may have been a perfunctory discussion carried out in a ritualistic way, for the sake of the record. Analysts may also be misled when a manipulative chief executive arranges to give a group of advisors the impression that they are looking into alternatives, evaluating them, and choosing the one they most approve of; whereas, in fact, the meetings have been rigged to get the group to express a consensus and to give legitimacy to a policy decision made in advance by the chief executive on the basis of a seat-of-the-pants approach, such as one that relies primarily on the self-interest rule. (See the discussion of rigging in Chapter 3.) A well-trained, highly competent, and vigilant analyst may be able to detect signs of such behind-the-scenes rigging, as well as other distortions.

The ultimate test of the validity of the ratings of symptoms of defective policymaking based on available observational material is whether those ratings are found to be significantly related to independent variables, such as unsuccessful outcomes. In a study of major international crises over a period of about thirty years since the end of World War II, Greg Herek, Paul Huth, and I were able to meet this validity test. We found that the ratings of symptoms of defective policymaking, which had a very high degree of interanalyst reliability (close to 100% agreement on the ratings of all symptoms), were substantially correlated with independent ratings of the outcomes of the decisions. (See Chapter 6 for a summary of this study, including an account of various precautions taken to rule out possible artifacts and to check on hidden third-factor sources of spurious relationships that might impair the validity of the observed correlations.)

When I first began a series of comparative studies of the management of international crises, I rated the quality of the policymakers' decisionmaking processes in terms of the seven criteria of sound decisionmaking listed in the text of Chapter 2. I compared my ratings with those made independently by my colleagues and found fairly high agreement, indicating an adequate degree of inter-analyst reliability. Our disagreements, I noticed, usually had to do with ambiguous circumstances or behaviors that we interpreted differently, which affected our judgments as to whether the group of policymakers who made a given decision during a crisis should be given a moderate rather than a high score on one or another of the criteria. But in most of these ambiguous cases, we found no disagreement in judging whether or not the rating should be low. That is to say, even for the most difficult cases to evaluate with regard to how *high* the rating of quality of policymaking should be, it was usually possible to judge very reliably whether or not the rating should be so *low* as to be regarded as a symptom of defective policymaking. Accordingly, I came to the conclusion that in order to maximize inter-analyst reliability, it is preferable to make ratings that specify whether or not the quality is so low on each of the seven criteria that the policymakers can be described as manifesting a given symptom of defective decisionmaking.

4. In addition to gross failures to meet each of the seven criteria of sound policymaking (corresponding to the seven extreme symptoms listed in the text) there are also failures of a minor character. That is to say, for each of the seven symptoms of defective policymaking, partial failures can sometimes be observed. For example, with regard to the third symptom, a policymaking group may search fairly intensively for relevant information and collect a great deal, but fail to obtain one or two important pieces of information that would have been available if any of the members had requested it from relevant persons in their organization. For some research purposes (particularly when doing comparative studies of organizations whose leaders generally make policy decisions of fairly high quality), it may be worthwhile to obtain ratings of partial failures as well as gross failures, using both obvious and subtle indicators. For example, in rating the policymakers on the seventh symptom (failure to work out detailed implementation, monitoring, and contingency plans) an investigator might first look for obvious indicators by examining available records to see if specific plans were discussed for implementing the decision and for dealing with salient setbacks or contingencies. If no gross omissions are observed, the investigator might look further for more subtle indicators by examining the records to see whether the policymakers actually made *feasible* arrange-

ments to monitor how well the decision was being implemented and how well it was succeeding, so as to find out quickly whether concealed obstacles were being encountered that might require implementing the contingency plans they had worked out.

The partial failures could be included in a total symptom score, giving them less weight than the gross symptoms. Differential weights might also be given to those gross symptoms that are found to give rise to the most serious errors. (See Note 5, Chapter 6.)

CHAPTER 3. AFFILIATIVE DECISION RULES

1. Tetlock (1985) describes the tendency of organizational decision makers to adopt the position that is likely to gain the favor of those powerholders to whom they feel accountable. He refers to this coping strategy as the "acceptability heuristic." His account of how, when, and why this heuristic is used is similar to my account of the "avoid punishment" rule. There is, however, one important difference. Tetlock asserts that the acceptability heuristic is "limited to settings in which one can discern relatively quickly the expectations of the constituencies to whom one is accountable" (p. 314). When it is not obvious what the socially acceptable position is, according to Tetlock, organizational decision makers will tend to use "vigilant information processing . . . to identify the most defensible policy" (p. 310). When this occurs, the decision makers use "more complex judgment and decision strategies" and "consider arguments and evidence on both sides of issues in order to prepare themselves for a wide variety of possible critical reactions to their view" (p. 315). I agree with Tetlock that when there is ambiguity about the most acceptable position, executives concerned about social punishment will engage in somewhat more vigilant information processing. But, as I indicate in my exposition of the implications of Figure 3-1 on pages 46-51, an executive who mainly wants to avoid being blamed and punished for selecting an unacceptable policy choice will direct his or her vigilant information search to finding out about the acceptability of whatever alternatives seem to be viable and will continue to rely on other versions of the "avoid punishment" rule, rather than engaging in vigilant problem solving. My central assumption—which is discussed in detail on pages 157-62—is that executives will use a vigilant problem-solving strategy only when they feel confident about being able to manage (or avoid): (a) possible retaliations from other powerholders who might object to the policy option that is chosen and (b) all the other constraints (described in Chapters 2, 3, and 4).

2. Because of an executive's affiliation with an organization, many of the constraints affecting his or her judgments and decisions pertain to expected personal gains (such as receiving a bonus or being promoted)

for conforming with the organization's norms and expected personal losses (such as being demoted or fired) for failing to conform. It is somewhat arbitrary as to whether these incentives are classified as creating egocentric (self-serving) or affiliative constraints. It is useful, in my opinion, to classify positive and negative incentives that arise from an executive's dependence upon the organization with which he or she is affiliated—such as gaining or losing compensation, power, or status—as affiliative constraints. For example, when an executive is motivated to push for a policy choice in order to avoid the threat of retaliations from a superior, which could result in loss of a financial bonus, the constraint would be classified as affiliative. One reason for classifying it in this category is that this constraint, like others classified as affiliative constraints, could be drastically reduced in potency and perhaps even eliminated entirely when an executive is transferred from one unit to another or when the organization with which the executive is affiliated changes its norms governing relationships among personnel. Such changes, however, would have little or no effect on what I categorize as egocentric (self-serving) constraints, which include all expected personal gains that are not directly under the control of any of the personnel in the organization—as when, for example, an executive is motivated to push for a policy change that will provide an opportunity to make an outside deal from which he or she could make personal financial gains. When the incentive for personal gain is not one that is linked with the executives' affiliation, I classify it as a self-serving constraint. Borderline cases are to be expected, of course, such that a given constraint could be regarded as falling in either or both categories.

3. In addition to the threat of being punished, other negative incentives— along with positive incentives—enter into an executive's commitment to an organizational policy, as described by Janis and Mann (Chapter 11). For example, in some instances, the executive's personal ethical code would be violated by making decisions that deviate from policies that it is his or her duty, according to role prescriptions, to comply with. In such instances, any inclination to deviate would tend to be counteracted by anticipatory guilt and depressive feelings linked with loss of self-esteem, which constitute a strong emotive constraint (see pp. 77–81).

4. For each of the case studies in which I have observed the groupthink syndrome, other causal factors also appear to have been operating. Analyses of these same cases by other social scientists sometimes emphasize one or more of the other factors as the primary ones. For example, in a detailed analysis of the Truman administration's decision to escalate the war in Korea, Neustadt and May (pp. 41–48) emphasize the policymakers' uncritical use of *analogies* that highlighted the failure

of appeasement to deter the Axis powers during the 1930s. These authors state that while the initial decision to enter the Korean war seems to have been wise, the later decision to escalate does not. They argue that if Truman and his advisors had made a "more explicit analysis" of the historical analogs they were using, they could have articulated restoring the *status quo ante* as a primary war aim: "Had he nailed that down as his sole purpose early on, squelching [Ambassador] Austin and others who championed reunification, Truman might more easily have stopped MacArthur's northward march at the first good defense line past the border, hailing UN success where the old League had failed, relishing a victory of principle. Thereby Truman could have spared himself Chinese attack, American retreat, inflationary pressure, allied fears, and two more years of fighting to achieve no further purpose" (pp. 45–46).

It appears to me that the Neustadt and May interpretation of defective decisionmaking by Truman and his advisors is not at odds with the groupthink hypothesis. Failure to examine initial assumptions, whether based on analogies, stereotypes, or ideological notions, is characteristic of groupthink-dominated decisions. Hence Neustadt and May's analysis is compatible with my conclusion that one of the main causal factors was a strong concurrence-seeking tendency in Truman's advisory group as manifested by major symptoms of groupthink—"excessive risk-taking based on a shared illusion of invulnerability, stereotypes of the enemy, collective reliance on ideological rationalizations that supported the belligerent escalation to which the group became committed, and mindguarding to exclude the dissident views of experts who questioned the group's unwarranted assumptions" (Janis, 1982a, p. 71).

A detailed analysis of the Bay of Pigs decision by Etheredge (1985) provides a prime example of an alternative interpretation of what went wrong that downplays the influence of groupthink as compared with "systemic" organizational factors. Etheredge acknowledges that symptoms of groupthink can be found in the evidence concerning the Bay of Pigs decision, but he argues that additional observations indicate that other causes were more important. He states that "Janis's 'groupthink' analysis was originally proposed when, by the data available . . . the invasion decision appeared to have been a mindless aberration. . . . Today we know the plan had a more sophisticated rationale than at first seemed" (pp. 112–13). The only new evidence he cites pertains to Operation MONGOOSE, the arrangement made by the CIA to hire the Mafia to assassinate Castro. This secret operation was supposed to be coordinated with the Bay of Pigs invasion. Etheredge does not cite any clearcut evidence that information about the CIA's assassination plan was given to President Kennedy, Secretary of State Rusk, Secretary of

Defense McNamara, or any other member of the President's inner circle who attended the White House meetings that approved the Bay of Pigs invasion plan. Etheredge explains the lack of any convincing evidence on this point as resulting from a coverup in line with the code of "plausible deniability" (p. 10).

If the members of Kennedy's inner circle did know about the Mafia assassination component of the overall CIA plan, it seems to me that one could hardly up-grade the rating of the quality of the group's decision to approve the Bay of Pigs invasion without knowing to what extent they took account of moral considerations and various pragmatic issues such as the likelihood that the Mafia might sell out to Castro by telling him about the U.S. assassination plan (which they apparently did) and the risk that Castro might retaliate by arranging for an assassination attempt against President Kennedy (which perhaps he did?). It is difficult to see how Etheredge could conclude that "the CIA's plans for the Bay of Pigs and MONGOOSE, although they did not work, under the circumstances and constraints were probably about the best to be devised rationally" (p. 116). At variance with the implications that the quality of President Kennedy's decision-making process might deserve a rating of high quality are other points made by Etheredge about uncorrected errors—"Kennedy's wishful image" of the Cuban invading forces which "could probably have been changed to a more realistic appraisal if he had been told candidly of his error" and Kennedy's failure to realize that if the military operation failed, the invading force would not be able to escape from the Bay of Pigs area to join the guerrilla forces in the Escambray Mountains (p. 107). Even if President Kennedy and members of his inner circle were using a simple satisficing strategy to make a yes or no decision about the plan, they could have been expected to raise critical questions with the CIA and military leaders about these assumptions, in order to see if the plan met the most elementary requirements for acceptance.

Etheredge argues that groupthink played only a minor role in producing whatever shortcomings Kennedy and the members of his inner circle displayed because "several observations can be made to indicate that other causal paths were more significant" (p. 112). But the observations he cites are extremely ambiguous and most of them can be interpreted as being consistent with the hypothesis that groupthink played a major role. For example, Etheredge asserts that critics of the Bay of Pigs plan were invited to say their piece by Kennedy and were heard by the group but "simply lacked ultimate persuasiveness" (p. 113). The main example he gives pertains to Kennedy's invitation to Senator Fulbright to a crucial meeting held in the White House on April 4, 1961, where the Senator was allowed to present his objections. But after Senator Fulbright finished, as I pointed out in my case study, the President did not open the floor for discussion of any of the points that he raised. Instead, the President called for a straw vote.

Thus, wittingly or unwittingly, the President conducted the meeting in such a way that not only was there no time to discuss the potential dangers to United States foreign relations raised by Senator Fulbright, but there was also no time to call upon Schlesinger, the one man present who the President knew strongly shared Senator Fulbright's misgivings.

Of course, one or more members of the group could have prevented this by-passing by suggesting that the group discuss Senator Fulbright's arguments . . . But no one made such a request.

The President's demand that each person, in turn, state his overall judgment, especially having just heard an outsider oppose the group consensus, must have put the members on their mettle. These are exactly the conditions that most strongly foster docile conformity to a group's norms. . . . Open straw votes generally put pressure on each individual to agree with the apparent group consensus, as has been shown by well-known social psychological experiments (Janis, 1982a, p. 43).

Reporting on this same crucial meeting, Secretary of State Rusk told Wyden that he did not speak out about his doubts at that time because he wanted to "close ranks with the president." William Bundy, another participant who was interviewed by Wyden, also said that at that crucial meeting he felt that he and the other members of the executive branch of the Kennedy administration were expected to "stand with the President against Fulbright's arguments to back up the presidential effort at 'rallying the troops' to deal with the lone nay-sayer" (Wyden, p. 149). From all of these observations, it is apparent that although President Kennedy arranged to have the group exposed to an outsider's opposing viewpoint, he did not encourage the members to openly discuss and evaluate the outsider's challenge to their assumptions (see Janis, 1982a, pp. 282–83).

Again at variance with his own conclusion, Etheredge acknowledges that Kennedy and his group displayed closed-mindedness, and he states in a footnote that "Kennedy manipulated the Bay of Pigs decision to keep at arm's length the arguments and considerations he did not want to hear; he cut out Stevenson [who would have expressed objections] and invited Senator Fulbright to only one meeting" (p. 119).

From Etheredge's own account, it is apparent that President Kennedy and members of his inner circle did not discuss or respond to the objections. It should be noted that this type of closed-mindedness is characteristic of groupthink. One of the prime symptoms includes a tendency of the leader and the other members of the group to "discount warnings or other information that might lead the members to reconsider their assumptions" (Janis, 1982a, p. 174). According to the groupthink hypothesis, members of a concurrence-seeking group sometimes engage in mindguarding, which reduces the amount of dissent to which they allow themselves to be exposed. But it does not follow that they never allow themselves to hear or read about dissenting views. Rather, the hypothesis states that when they are exposed to dissenting views they do not take the objections seriously enough to reconsider any of their assumptions or expectations pertaining to the policy option that they collectively favor, even though some members may have strong residual doubts.

Another set of observations adduced by Etheredge as evidence against the pervasive influence of groupthink is that President Kennedy raised some critical questions about the CIA invasion plan and "the more Kennedy thought about the Bay of Pigs plan, the less enthusiastic and the more ambivalent he became" (p. 114). Etheredge claims that the decrease in enthusiasm displayed by Kennedy is the opposite from what the groupthink hypothesis would predict. But this prediction certainly does *not* follow in a case where an intelligent leader sees more and more that is wrong with a deeply flawed plan that he nevertheless is inclined to accept for one or another reason—such as being influenced by the consensus of his advisory group. As to Kennedy's critical questions, his concerns about the plan's weaknesses, and his efforts to improve the plan: various reports about the critical comments and doubts expressed by Kennedy during the meetings at which the CIA plan was discussed indicate that he did not raise questions about the basic plan itself or about most of its main assumptions. His doubts were largely confined to concern about the United States government being blamed for the invasion of Cuba, which was largely a question of public relations effects.

> This limited type of doubting, which led to cosmetic changes of the basic CIA invasion plan, is not inconsistent with Wyden's summary of Kennedy's overall view [which was essentially the same as that of the key members of his inner circle] that the plan entailed "little risk of failure" [Wyden, 1979, p. 308]. . . .
>
> Minimizing the major risks of an ill-conceived plan is a central feature of the *illusion of invulnerability*. When this diagnosis is made, it does not necessarily mean that those who share the illusion are totally oblivious to the risks of a very hazardous venture. Rather, it means that to some extent the major risks are being minimized on the basis of a preconscious assumption that *everything is going to work out all right because we are a special group.* . . . [W]hen states-

men in a cohesive policy-making group share an illusion of invulnerability in the face of a risky venture, their preconscious belief is "if
others try to do it they might fail, *but not us.*" I surmise from all
that has been reported about the exuberant confidence of Kennedy
and his team, as well as their minimization of the major risks, that
the leader, as well as members of the inner circle, shared an illusion
of invulnerability of this kind. (Janis, 1982a, pp. 282–83).

Etheredge's main conclusion is that a "concurrence-seeking, small-
group process may have had a modest psychological effect" but "the
perspective of an additional 20 years . . . suggests that most of the 1961
syndrome correctly observed by Janis is likely caused at a larger, systemic level" (p. 115). He lists seven systemic factors that he believes
were primarily responsible for reducing the effectiveness of Kennedy's
team:

   a. Earlier appointments of men who shared Kennedy's views predeter-
      mined policy outcomes.
   b. Policy meetings were highly ritualized, which prevented partici-
      pants from rethinking their views in the light of arguments and evi-
      dence that could be presented.
   c. Decision procedures were designed to influence choices rather than
      to clarify them, which inhibited learning.
   d. No one in the group accepted complete responsibility.
   e. Distorting the truth within the executive branch and deceptive, po-
      litically "sophisticated" behavior produced a system that moved
      incrementally further from reality.
   f. Bureaucratic assessments were more realistic "upward" than
      "downward"; subordinates were erroneously taken for granted.
   g. Collective learning was inhibited because subordinates were at per-
      sonal risk if they told the truth.

Six of the the seven factors singled out by Etheredge are entirely compatible with the groupthink hypothesis. The first two pertain to conditions that are conducive to groupthink (see Figure 3–2). The next four
factors are defects in the policymaking process that can be produced or
augmented by the symptoms of groupthink. The only factor incompatible with the groupthink hypothesis is the last one, which Etheredge
refers to as "subordinate think." His formulation of this factor makes
it equivalent to conformity out of fear of being punished, which is entirely different from the groupthink type of conformity involving efforts to preserve the harmony of a cherished group whose members
share a high degree of esprit de corps. But what little evidence there is
concerning this factor pertains to peripheral participants in the White
House meetings, not to the core members of President Kennedy's inner

circle, such as McNamara, Rusk, or McGeorge Bundy. Schlesinger (1965) and Wyden (1979) also mention this factor, but again the evidence they cite pertains to peripheral participants; practically all the evidence they present concerning the way the Bay of Pigs decision was arrived at is compatible with the groupthink hypothesis (see Janis, 1982a, pp. 32–34 and 279–81).

The ambiguous and questionable evidence mentioned by Etheredge does not appear to be sufficient to warrant his assertion that groupthink had only a "modest effect" on the decision-making process when Kennedy's inner circle deliberated about the CIA's Bay of Pigs plan. The observations cited are just as compatible with the conclusion that groupthink exerted a very powerful effect and augmented the influence of most of the systemic factors listed by Etheredge as alternatives to an explanation in terms of groupthink. Consequently, I can see no substantial grounds for accepting his conclusion that "other causal paths were more significant" (p. 112). Nevertheless, I fully agree with his methodological comment about determining whether or not groupthink has a powerful effect in this particular case: "Adequate personal data [about how the participants arrived at their collective decision] are lacking to reach a formal conclusion about the weight to be given to such a causal path" (p. 112).

A paper by Barrett (1988) on the Johnson administration's decision in 1965 to escalate the Vietnam War takes an extreme position that groupthink did not enter into the process at all. Barrett asserts that it is a myth that President Johnson was a victim of groupthink because documentation declassified in the 1980s, as well as various secondary sources, show that he willingly received "wide ranging opinions from significant advisors about whether or not to intensify America's military role in Vietnam" (p. 1). His paper, however, does not present any evidence bearing on the question of whether Johnson did anything more than listen respectfully and act deferentially to the politically powerful friends who proffered advice that went counter to the advice he was receiving from his inner circle. In fact, Barrett's paper includes a few indications that the outsiders who disagreed with the inner circle's policy were aware of President Johnson's lack of responsiveness to their dissenting advice. For example, Barrett states that Senator Russell, one of Johnson's "personal intimates" who gave opposing advice, "lamented to friends that McNamara [a central figure in Johnson's inner circle] . . . seemed to 'exercise some hypnotic influence over the President' . . . " (p. 22).

Drawing mainly upon evidence and quotations from the Pentagon Papers, my case study of the Vietnam War escalation decisions concludes that President Johnson and others in his inner circle were exposed to dissenting views but, nevertheless, seriously considered only "a rather narrow range of proposals," made a "superficial assessment of the pros and cons," and made "no effort . . . to reshape their policy" when exposed to a detailed critique "prepared jointly by experts from the three leading intelligence agencies of the government toward the end of 1964" (Janis 1982a, p. 98). As I have already indicated, the groupthink hypothesis does *not* state that when groupthink is operating the reason for defective decisionmaking is that the participants are kept from being exposed to any dissenting advice or information inputs about the defects of their chosen policy and about the advantages of alternative courses of action. The central feature of groupthink (as indicated in Figure 3-2) is "concurrence seeking," manifested by "overestimation of the [inner circle] group," "closed-mindedness," and "pressures toward uniformity" within the group. Although mindguarding is one of the symptoms of groupthink, it certainly cannot be expected to result in very little exposure to conflicting views, especially from important persons within the government outside of the inner circle.

My detailed analysis of the Vietnam War decisions made by President Johnson and the others in his inner circle indicates that mindguarding and other symptoms of groupthink were present, together with most of the antecedent conditions and consequences listed in Figure 3-2. (See Janis 1982a, pp. 108–30.) While the group's miscalculations may well have been the result of a number of different casual factors, the evidence suggests that groupthink was probably one of them.

5. Hensley and Griffin state that one of the purposes of their study is to use the case study observations to identify shortcomings of the groupthink theoretical model presented in Janis (1982a)—which is produced in Figure 3-2 (p. 59)—and to see if it could be condensed so that there would be less lengthy sets of antecedents and consequences. Their final appraisal, however, is that slight expansion is needed rather than condensation:

> When we began our analysis, we entertained the hope that we might find ways to make the theory more parsimonious by eliminating or combining various conditions or symptoms within the theory. After having worked through each element of the theory, we find ourselves in a rather different position. Each specific variable in the theory seems to us important and distinct; further, it appears to us that some additional symptoms of defective decisionmaking need to be incorporated into the theory. One symptom is the *failure to initiate or maintain contact with an opposition group.* Certainly this was true in regard to the lack of trustee interaction with the May 4th Coalition, and it is probably characteristic of several foreign policy fi-

ascoes, given the inherent difficulties of diplomatic negotiations. A second form of defective decisionmaking that may stem directly from groupthink is *a lack of cooperation with third party mediators.* This was a distinctive pattern in the Kent State case, and there is evidence of this in some of the foreign policy cases Janis discusses, for instance, the disregard given by U.S. decisionmakers to Indian efforts to mediate prior to the North Korean invasion. Yet a third symptom missing from Janis's formulation is *the failure to extend the time period for reaching a decision.* On several occasions the trustee majority refused to postpone decisions in order to gain time to discuss matters with various groups or to explore alternative courses of action. The ability of Kennedy and his advisors to do this in the Cuban Missile Crisis is often cited as an important factor in the successful outcome of that situation, and the failure to do so was associated with several foreign policy fiascoes, for example, the Bay of Pigs. (Hensley & Griffin, pp. 528–29)

The authors suggest as one of the implications of their study that the quality of policymaking could be improved by changing the way group members are selected:

The current procedure for selecting members to a university's board of trustees in Ohio and many other states virtually assures that the members will be somewhat cohesive and well-insulated from outside sources of opinion and information, two important antecedent conditions of groupthink. Current procedures give a governor virtually unchecked authority to select trustees, and this has meant that trustees overwhelmingly have been upper-socioeconomic-class white males. A more diverse representation of groups on a trustee board is clearly needed in order that the divergent perspectives of students, faculty, and other groups in society can more faithfully be reflected in discussions and decisions. (Pp. 529–30)

CHAPTER 4. SELF-SERVING AND EMOTIVE RULES

1. Self-serving motives are sometimes linked with ties to an outside organization. For example, a corporate business executive who has taken leave of absence to serve in a governmental regulative agency might be inclined to favor policies that will be advantageous for his corporation. Although conflict-of-interest laws and explicit ethical norms are devised to prevent obvious instances of self-serving policy decisions, there are many loopholes and ill-defined circumstances that allow policymakers from time to time to give priority to self-serving motives linked with outside affiliations. These motives, like those that come into play when a leader indulges in nepotism or seeks personal financial gains, are

difficult to detect because the self-serving decisionmaker usually realizes that the personal consequences will be devastating if he or she fails to cover up the real reasons for the policy choice.

Occasionally, as a result of repression and other defense mechanisms, a leader may be unaware of the main motivation that enters into a self-serving choice. But, as Alexander George (1980, pp. 8–9) emphasizes, unconscious motives are seldom likely to play a predominating role in policymaking because of powerful internal as well as external controls. Included in the latter category are institutionalized rules and practices for relieving from duty any official who shows obvious signs of severe neurotic or psychotic disorder, especially if there are manifestations of uncontrollable aggression, self-punishment, self-aggrandizement, or any other disruptive motive that is interfering with his or her judgments as an executive.

2. One of the reasons Ford was willing to move rapidly to pardon Nixon, Hartmann (p. 269) surmises, was that "he persuaded himself that the flak he would have to take for pardoning Nixon would be no less if he waited and might be worse." Since Ford underestimated the magnitude of public protest, this bit of self-persuasion may have been a rationalization to support the action that he was impatient to take. Hartmann (p. 269) also states that another reason Ford was willing to grant the pardon was that he felt it was the right thing to do for America, because he believed that the country was still "wallowing in Watergate," which interfered with working on essential problems. But Hartmann doubts that Ford's judgment about the country was correct and speculates that "it was a projection of his own personal paralysis." If so, Ford's emotional bias interfered with his judgment when framing the problem of whether or not to pardon Nixon.

3. Taking account of the large body of evidence indicating that emotions influence judgments and actions, Herbert Simon (1967) has explicitly pointed out that emotions can interfere with cognitive processes in decisionmaking. But research findings on psychological effects of emotional arousal and emotional biases are rarely mentioned by most of the other social scientists who analyze how policy decisions are made. Clearly, research on the psychology of emotion has had very little impact on theory and research on policymaking. My own research and case study observations indicate that emotive constraints frequently exert a strong influence on the policymaking process, although policymakers seldom admit it (Janis, 1985, 1986).

Many research findings indicate that marked individual differences are to be expected among executives in intensity of emotional needs as well as in the strength and degree of dominance of personal motives that affect their readiness to use egocentric decision rules when making policy choices on behalf of their organization or nation. Individual differences are discussed in Chapter 9, in the context of elucidating hypotheses about the influence of personality dispositions on policymaking.

4. It is conceivable, of course, that Khrushchev was merely pretending to be enraged by President Eisenhower's provocative actions connected with the U-2 incident in order to exploit the incident, to initiate a deliberate shift in policy that had been arrived at on a nonemotional basis. If so, Khrushchev must have been a remarkably good actor because he succeeded in impressing a number of observers that he was genuinely angry, as indicated in the quotations from Donovan and from Hoopes (1986).

5. The following are among the main references from the research literature on stress and coping that were reviewed by Janis & Mann (1977), from which the basic coping patterns were extracted: Appley & Trumbull; Arnold (1960, 1970); Baker & Chapman; Barton; Coelho, Hamburg, & Adams; Hamilton; Hermann; Holsti; Horowitz; Janis (1951, 1958, 1971); Killian; Lazarus; Leventhal (1968, 1973); McGuire (1969); Radloff & Helmreich; Spielberger & Sarason; Stotland; Withey.

6. According to our conflict analysis, the level or intensity of stress generated by decisional conflict is one of the determinants of the coping pattern that will be adopted: Extremely low stress and extremely intense stress are likely to give rise to defective patterns, whereas intermediate levels are more likely to be associated with vigilant information processing. Whenever a decisionmaker's dominant coping pattern is unconflicted adherence or unconflicted change, the person is so unaroused by the risks to be expected that he or she resorts to "lazy" ways of making judgments because of lack of motivation to engage in careful information search, appraisal of alternatives, and implementation planning before deciding what action to take. It is these unconflicted coping patterns that are likely to be evoked whenever policymakers mistakenly regard a major threat as relatively unimportant or as easily managed by resorting to organizational routines. In contrast, the vigilant coping pattern is linked with a moderate level of stress, which is optimal in that the policymaker is motivated to think carefully about the decision and to search for relevant information. When the policymaker experiences a very high level of stress from decisional conflict, the dominant coping pattern tends to be either defensive avoidance or hypervigilance, which gives rise to gross misperceptions and miscalculations that are avoidable errors.

In our review of pertinent empirical studies, Leon Mann and I have called attention to case studies of organizational as well as individual decisions and to numerous findings from social psychological experiments and correlational field studies that are consistent with the propositions about the determinants and behavioral consequences of vigilant versus nonvigilant coping patterns (Janis & Mann, Chapters 4-12). We have also described a few of our own social psychological experiments that were designed to test prescriptive hypotheses derived from the conflict-theory analysis (Janis & Mann, Chapters 13 and 14). These include studies of the effectiveness of a balance sheet procedure, stress inoculation, and a number of other interventions that counteract the beliefs and perceptions specified in Figure 4–2 as being responsible for defective coping patterns.

Of particular relevance to governmental policymaking are case studies of defensive avoidance and hypervigilance among national leaders facing international crises that pose the threat of war, analyzed and reported by Richard Ned Lebow (1981, 1987). Also pertinent are a few research reports by other social scientists who have investigated the relationship between level of stress and defective coping patterns in the decisional performance of government leaders responsible for foreign policy during major international crises. One such study by Holsti and George (1975) concludes that a high level of crisis-induced stress among top-level policymakers produces cognitive rigidity and reduces their time perspective, leading to overconcentration on immediate goals, restricted search for alternatives, and perfunctory evaluation of alternatives and their consequences. Evidence in support of similar conclusions is reported from studies of international crises by Suedfeld & Tetlock and by Tetlock (1983a, 1983b).

An analysis by Michael Brecher (1980) of Israel's decisionmaking during two major crises also lends support to Holsti and George's main conclusions. Brecher examined 57 decisions made by the Israeli cabinet and kitchen cabinet during the 1967 and 1973 crises. Psychological stress was assessed in terms of perceptions of threat, time pressure, and perceived probability of war. In line with the postulates of the Janis and Mann conflict theory, Brecher found a curvilinear (inverted U) relationship between stress and group performance with regard to the consideration of policy alternatives. None of the five decisions taken under conditions of low stress showed careful evaluation of alternatives. As stress rose to a moderate level, evaluation of alternatives became more careful. Beyond that, as stress became more intense, there was a decline in the care taken to evaluate alternatives and in the overall quality of the deliberations.

7. There is a major exception to the statement that "the more that is at stake, the more dangerous it is to rely exclusively on simple decision rules instead of carrying out the essential steps of vigilant problem solving." That exception is when policymakers have previously carried out a pertinent information search and deliberation, using the high-quality procedures of vigilant problem solving, and have already prepared contingency plans for dealing with a challenge like the one at hand. When the current threat or opportunity has been completely anticipated and

contingency plans have been carefully worked out to deal with it, obviously it is advantageous to use the following simple decision rule in a crisis requiring prompt action: "If you have a well-worked out contingency plan, put it into operation." Nevertheless, an abbreviated form of most steps of vigilant problem solving may be essential to ascertain whether or not the current challenge actually does correspond to the anticipated challenge for which the contingency plan was devised.

CHAPTER 5. AN UNCOMMON STRATEGY: VIGILANT PROBLEM SOLVING

1. The assertion that a simplistic strategy, when used for all vital policy decisions, will result in disastrous outcomes is based on a key general assumption stated in Chapter 1: A poor-quality decisionmaking process (which characterizes simplistic strategies) is more likely than a high-quality process to lead to undesirable outcomes (including disastrous fiascos). For evidence in support of this general assumption, see Chapter 6.

2. Among the social scientists who describe the main steps or components of vigilant ("reflective" or "analytic") problem solving are those listed in the nine references cited in Note 2 for Chapter 2. In addition, the following more recent references were also consulted: Abelson & Levi; Baron; Behn & Vaupel; Donaldson & Lorsch; Einhorn & Hogarth; George (1980); Hammond, McClelland, & Mumpower; Hogarth; Horan; Kahneman & Tversky; Lebow (1981, 1987); Lindblom; Neustadt & May; Pennings; Sanderson; Schön; Simon (1985); Slovik, Fischoff & Lichtenstein (1977); Stein & Tanter; Steiner; Vroom & Jago; Zeleny.

3. A number of supplementary questions are suggested for inclusion in the steps of effective problem solving by quantitative decision theorists who advocate selecting the best choice (in step 4) by using the rule that the best alternative is the one with the greatest utility. The expected-utility model of decisional choice, which was developed in pioneering work by Ward Edwards and elaborated by Luce and Raiffa and others, has been proposed as a *descriptive* theory. As such, the theory assumes that policymakers examine the probable consequences of each viable alternative under consideration and choose the one expected to yield the best outcome with regard to their main objectives. (For a brief summary of evidence bearing on this assumption, see Note 2 in Chapter 6.) When used as a *prescriptive* theory, the model requires using *quantitative* estimates of expected utility values and of the probability of those values materializing as outcomes. Hogarth, who advocates the use of the expected utility rule, explicitly states that the key question for making the choice should be: "Which alternative has the greatest expected utility?"

In order to answer the key question, policymakers would first have to answer the following questions: "What is the numerical value that can be assigned as the overall value of the expected outcome for each alternative under consideration?" "What is the probability that each of those outcomes will occur?" "What is the weighted value for each alternative under consideration when its overall value (utility of the expected outcome) is multiplied by its expected probability of occurrence?"

Hogarth adds several supplementary questions that would need to be answered by a cautious decisionmaker before giving a final answer to the key question about expected utility, once the quantitative estimates have been made: (1) "How wrong are the estimates likely to be?" (2) "What are the costs and benefits of securing additional information (to improve the estimates of expected values and probabilities)?" (3) "Has there been sufficient analysis of outcomes and probabilities, taking account of costs, benefits, and constraints of the situation?" Recognizing that sometimes a decisionmaker might find the expected-utility rule inappropriate to the choice at hand, Hogarth suggests that fairly early in the sequence decisionmakers should answer the following question: (4) "What criterion (i.e., decision rule) will be appropriate for making the final choice?" All four of these supplementary questions might be useful for vigilant policymakers to answer before they reach stage 4. So, too, might another supplementary question suggested by Hogarth: (5) "How should the different dimensions (that is, the objectives and values that are at stake) be weighted when assessing expected outcomes for each alternative?"

The vigilant problem-solving approach (as represented in Figure 5-1), when used as either a descriptive or prescriptive model, does not assume that any quantitative estimates of expected utility are necessary, but it certainly does not preclude them. The effectiveness of a vigilant problem-solving approach for certain limited types of decisions, such as business decisions whose outcomes can be quantified in terms of the amount of profit, sometimes might be enhanced by including the quantitative analytic procedures described by proponents of expected-utility theory. Obviously, vigilant policymakers who use these procedures would do so in a cautious, critical way to make sure that the essential assumptions are met and that their efforts to make quantitative estimates do not entice them to end up ignoring those objectives that cannot be validly expressed in numerical terms.

Generally speaking, policymakers need to take account of multiple goals, some of which cannot be easily quantified with regard to expected values or utilities. Even the most single-minded, quick profit-seeking businessmen are likely to have several goals in addition to wanting to make money quickly. Almost all of them want to reap financial gains without the threat of lawsuits or criminal prosecution for fraud, and without impairing the reputation of the organization or losing other intangible assets to such an extent that profitable deals cannot be made in the future. The trouble with procedures requiring quantitative estimates, as Nakamura and Smallwood put it, "is that many of the things that can be counted do not count with policymakers, and many of the things that count with policymakers cannot be counted" (p. 76).

In short, when making vital policy decisions it is usually very difficult to apply the choice rule recommended by Hogarth and others who are proponents of the expected-utility model because there is no sound way to make the required quantitative estimates. For this and a number of other reasons, the expected-utility principle has been called into question as a descriptive model of how people actually make decisions; see, for example, Kahneman & Tversky; Slovic, Fischoff, & Lichtenstein (1977); Zeleny; see also the review of the research literature by Abelson & Levi, which is summarized in Note 2 for Chapter 6. Nevertheless, some social scientists advocate using the expected-utility principle, to whatever extent is appropriate for the decision at hand, as a *prescriptive* (normative model) specifying how people *should* make sound decisions when they have to make risky choices.

In *A Practical Guide for Making Decisions,* Daniel Wheeler and I point out that even though it may not be possible to make reliable or valid quantitative estimates, the two central ideas of the expected-utility model can still be applied in a way that might improve the quality of the decisionmaking process:

> The first central idea is that in order to make a sound decision it is necessary to make the best estimates of the probability that each of the expected consequences will occur. The second is that a sound decision requires taking into consideration the relative importance of each of the anticipated favorable and unfavorable consequences— their expected utility value from your own standpoint. If you keep in mind these two ideas you are more likely to arrive at a choice that you will not regret even though you do not use any of the mathematics. . . . You will be less likely to overlook serious drawbacks or to give undue weight to vivid considerations that are really not essential to you or that are unlikely to materialize. You will be in a better position to make a choice that meets your main objectives, gives you the best chance of overall gains, and keeps unnecessary costs and risks to a minimum. (Wheeler & Janis, p. 81)

4. Zeleny argues that in order to develop an adequate theory of executive decisionmaking that "aims at overall decision improvement through understanding the decision process itself," it is necessary to replace traditional notions of utility and related axioms of utility maximization "by a single descriptive principle: people do as well as they can under

the circumstances" (p. 327). My assumption is that this is what policy-makers are doing when they use the vigilant problem-solving strategy (as outlined in Figure 5-1) rather than a simplistic strategy to deal with vital policy issues. But I do not agree with Zeleny that they *always*—or in the vast majority of instances—do as well as they are capable of doing. One of my assumptions is that under certain specifiable condi-tions, policymakers use a simplistic strategy to make vital policy deci-sions when they could use a vigilant problem-solving strategy (see Chapter 7). In those instances, which occur fairly often, they make errors that could have been avoided if they had used their capabilities to carry out as well as they could under the circumstances all the essen-tial steps represented in Figure 5-1.

5. In their account of "prospect theory," Kahneman and Tversky also point out that when the time comes to make a choice, decisionmakers are likely to edit the information they have gathered in order to cope with informational overload, uncertainties, and confusion. Because of their lack of understanding of extreme probabilities, they are likely to round off low probability outcomes as having zero probability and thus ignore them completely. They may also simplify the task of evaluation and choice by other editing operations, such as eliminating alternatives that appear to have poorer prospects than others on the basis of super-ficial scanning, which can result in failure to take account of cogent details in information they have gathered.

6. In the heat of the Arab-Israeli War crisis, Kissinger received a great deal of intelligence data about the actions and intentions of the Egyp-tians, the Syrians, and the Israelis, but the new information had little corrective effect on any of Kissinger's preconceptions about the crisis, according to Dowty (p. 305). Nor were Kissinger's views modified by any of the knowledgeable officials in the executive branch of the U.S. government with whom he consulted. Kissinger's lack of openness to new information during the height of the 1973 crisis, Dowty asserts, was in contrast not only to his subsequent behavior but also to his re-sponsiveness to intelligence data in earlier crises: During those less se-vere crises, the intelligence data received by Kissinger and others in the Nixon White House had "corrected prevailing misconceptions" (p. 305).

7. Neustadt and May assert that the initial lists of items in the *known, unclear,* and *presumed* categories can enable policymakers to specify the fresh information needed to obtain a more accurate and complete story about the challenging new threat or opportunity that appears to require a new policy decision, so as to get the facts straight before they start defining their objectives and considering options for dealing with it. They recommend that the items in the *unclear* category as well as

those in the *presumed* category, should be examined to see which questions are the most important ones to try to answer. They say that as new information is obtained and some of the items in the unclear category get shifted to the known category, the policymakers are likely to reconceptualize the policy issue and redefine their concerns, which can turn out to be much more serious or much less so than they had surmised at first. Neustadt and May conclude on the basis of their case studies that the new factual information, together with intelligence reports and analyses that attempt to put the current issues in a historical perspective, can help policymakers correct erroneous presumptions and misleading stereotypes, such as those pertaining to an adversary's probable intentions.

Another of Neustadt and May's recommendations is pertinent for correcting misconceptions that are likely to occur when policymakers frame the problem from the outset in terms of a vivid historical analogy that immediately comes to mind. They suggest that before policymakers start selectively favoring an "obvious" solution for dealing with a new threat or opportunity, derived from a seemingly appropriate analogue from the past, they first should assess carefully its relevance by raising the key questions: "What are the *likenesses* and what are the *differences* between then and now?" Neustadt and May report that their observations of managerial decisionmaking indicate that by discussing these questions, executives can sometimes correct faulty assumptions based on a misleading or inappropriate analogy.

The authors also discuss means of correcting presumptions about implementation, which need to be checked toward the end of the policymakers' deliberations. When the time comes to complete plans for putting into operation whichever course of action is selected, they propose probing into presumptions about the people and organizations upon whom successful execution of the chosen action will depend. This requires collecting and analyzing available information bearing on the implementers' personal outlooks and the institutional proclivities of their organization. For example, rather than relying entirely upon initial stereotypes about an ambassador or military leader who is expected to be a key implementer to carry out a presidential decision during an international crisis, the crisis managers should at least briefly scan the individual's life history to obtain clues about problems to be expected from his or her past performances as well as current attitudes, incentives, blindspots, and coping capabilities.

Something similar can be done, the authors point out, for *organizations*. For example, if a State Department unit is going to be called upon to handle negotiations or if a military service is going to be alerted, useful clues for correcting initial stereotypes can be obtained by scanning highlights of the organization's history, including how its powers, resources, personnel recruitment, and traditions have changed or evolved. From inquiries of this kind, which can sometimes be carried out quite rapidly merely by talking on the phone with a few "old hands," it may be possible to amend initial misimpressions about what the key implementers and their organizations are likely to do and what they are not likely to do, which makes for more realistic implementation and contingency planning. Here again, according to Neustadt and May, information gathering and critical appraisal can enable policymakers to correct conceptual errors.

8. Psychologists and other social scientists might profitably explore the likely possibility that some of the main features noted in prior studies by Dreyfus and Dreyfus and by other investigators of superior performance in chess and in skilled occupations, such as airline piloting, have their counterparts in superior performance in policymaking. Among the counterpart features that investigators might search for in order to elaborate on the mental processes of superior policymakers are those included in the following set of suggestive questions, which use the rather vague terminology that one regularly encounters in the literature in this field of inquiry: Do superior policymakers differ to a substantial degree from the vast majority of others in comparable decision-making roles in their ability to get to the heart of a problem intuitively and to look ahead toward good moves that will put them on the right track toward a superb solution? If so, do they have available in their mental repertoire a relatively large number of meaningful patterns, reflecting a broad knowledge base and a relatively great amount of "chunking" of previously acquired information, as compared with the mediocre performers? Are the superior policymakers better able than others to generate viable alternatives by having available a larger repertoire of analogies to draw upon from past experience and by being able to recognize more rapidly or more completely the similarities and differences between the present situation and seemingly analogous ones? Do the superior policymakers have the capacity to use more categories than others to take account of a multiplicity of objectives and values when making judgments about the pros and cons of alternative courses of action?

   Even vaguer, but nevertheless somewhat suggestive, are the attributes and processes mentioned in accounts of creative mental achievement by great geniuses. Susan P. Gill speaks of creative thinkers in the arts and sciences as being able to see "unfocused patterns that might, through successive approximation, become coherent" (p. 26). They go through a "process of construction," she says, that moves step by step from the general to the specific by means of "inferential leaps [that] are required to specify and fill in the pattern" (p. 41). Using "coherence-seeking" as a key concept (which she does not define), Gill suggests that truly great intellectual achievements are the product of a rare species of problem solving that does not involve setting up goals, objectives, or requirements to be met (as in step 1 of Figure 5-1) but proceeds, instead, by "comparing each present step with a possible next step which is recognized through coherence-seeking" (p. 40). A genius who ends up with a great new invention or a great creative achievement in science or the arts starts off, Gill suggests, with "speculation" and then modifies the original speculation in subsequent "educated guesses" in a series of "successive approximations" using a special heuristic (which, again, she does not define) that sounds quite marvelous—a heuristic entirely different from the ordinary ones described in accounts of chess playing, management decisionmaking, or problem solving of the type investigated by cognitive psychologists:

> It is on the perception of coherence that "educated guesses" are based. Speculation is imagining connections that may not be verifiable, recognizing structure that is only partially suggested, perceiving the pattern implied by partial information and filling in what is missing.
> Michel Foucault refers to the "law of coherence as a heuristic rule": the notion that where contradiction arises in the history of ideas a higher unity [a new frame] is sought to restore coherence. . . . The final frame (fate) or goal of this process is only clear when the final clue is in. When the final move has been made, the form of checkmate is revealed. (Gill, p. 40)

Although research investigators might have great difficulty trying to pin down the observable referents of Gill's key terms, her suggestive comments could inspire social scientists to seek for coherence in studies of superior policymakers. They might try to discover hitherto unrecognized heuristics (perhaps along the lines of Foucault's "coherence-seeking" heuristic), which might conceivably be superior to those in common use. They might also try to elucidate intuitive processes, some of which might prove to be shortcuts that replace or modify one or more of the steps of vigilant problem solving. But maybe you would have to be a genius to make use of their heuristics and other shortcuts!

Many other commentators on the creative processes of literary and scientific geniuses, using language no less vague than Gill's, place heavy emphasis on unfettered flights of imagination. They speak about the geniuses' capacity to project themselves into imaginary or future worlds by introspecting or role playing; to go far beyond the information at hand; to draw upon rich imagery; to engage in "right hemisphere" thinking; to break through the confines of conventional thinking by pushing reasonable ideas to their limits, by focusing on paradoxical or deviant instances of seemingly valid generalizations, or by indulging in free-floating fantasy with temporary "regression in the service of the ego."

Many of these notions are currently being pursued in psychological research on creative thinking among college students, artists, and scientists. The most promising hypotheses that emerge might be further pursued in research on superior policymakers.

9. Two types of guiding principles are likely to be used from time to time when policymakers adopt a vigilant problem-solving approach. One type, which is exemplified by the "tit-for-tat" (or "reciprocity") principle described in Chapter 4, specifies what kind of solution to the problem might be a good one—that is, it suggests the sort of option that might satisfy the essential requirements. The other type, which is exemplified by the elimination-by-aspects principle described by Tversky (1972), specifies procedures that the decisionmaker might profitably follow to find a good solution. For further discussion of the use of guiding principles in vigilant problem solving, see p. 73 in Chapter 4.

CHAPTER 6. ARE THE MAIN ASSUMPTIONS ABOUT PROCESS AND OUTCOME WARRANTED?

1. Many of the studies Starbuck (1985) mentions when discussing his third generalization (namely, that vigilant problem solving is not effective in reducing the chances of unsuccessful outcomes) actually point to the opposite conclusion. He dismisses this contradictory evidence by calling attention to methodological defects, such as the fact that the investigators relied upon self-reports by managers. Starbuck argues that the few studies that report no relationship between systematic planning and successful outcomes are less defective. Nevertheless, the one study he singles out as least defective provides correlational evidence indicating that business firms that engage in systematic planning and extensive information search (which can be interpreted as manifestations of vigilant problem solving) are somewhat more likely than others to have successful outcomes in terms of profits:

> In what is probably the best study of formal planning to date, Grinyer and Norburn (1975) discovered the firms' profitability correlates . . . weakly with the formality of planning ($r = .22$). . . .
> Grinyer and Norburn also found that profitability correlates weakly but significantly with reliance on informal communication ($r = .40$) and moderately with the use of diverse information when evaluating performance ($r = .68$). (Starbuck 1985, p. 371)

The first of the findings cited from Grinyer and Norburn's study ($r = .22$) is not only a weak correlation but it is also weak evidence either for or against any hypothesis about a relationship (positive, negative, or nonexistent) between formal planning and profits. This is especially so because of uncontrolled third factors that could make the correlation spuriously too high or too low. For example, firms that engage in formal planning may differ from firms that do not in that they are also somewhat more likely to invest in plant equipment, new product development, or in other assets for the future that will result in losses in the short-term in order to reap greater profits in the long term; this unobserved third factor would make the observed correlation between formal planning and short-term profits spuriously low. On the other hand, the observed correlation might be spuriously high because of some other unobserved third factor that exerts a strong influence. For example, underfinanced firms cannot afford the costs of formal planning and also may be unable to advertise, to hire good salespersons, and to do other things that might be essential for financial success in the short run as well as in the long run, which would spuriously raise the observed correlation.

The two additional findings cited from Grinyer and Norburn's study ($r = .40$ and $r = .68$) are somewhat more substantial correlations but they too are weak evidence, again because of uncontrolled third factors that could make the correlations spuriously high or spuriously low. If we were to take the findings at face value, however, ignoring the possibilities of third-factor explanations, the findings could readily be interpreted as contradicting Starbuck's third generalization, since policymakers who engage in reflective (vigilant) problem solving would tend to seek and take account of information obtained from informal channels rather than relying solely upon the information right at hand in the organization's formal reports. Commenting on the two correlations, Starbuck asserts:

> Managers in more profitable firms make better use of informal communication channels, whereas managers in less profitable firms communicate primarily through formal reports; and managers in more profitable firms use diverse kinds of information when evaluating their firms' performances, whereas managers in less profitable firms get their information mainly from formal reports. (Starbuck 1985, p. 371)

Starbuck points out that quite a few studies indicate that formal reports prepared by business firms typically contain "misrepresentations and inadvertent biases," which make them highly undependable (p. 368).

Starbuck acknowledges that the evidence bearing on his third generalization is controversial. He relies primarily upon a number of plausible-sounding arguments to support it. One reason he gives to explain why attempts to use reflective problem solving fail badly is that "large organizations' complexity makes it more likely that changes will produce unforeseen consequences" (1985, pp. 343–44). Policymakers rarely have enough "information and understanding" to find satisfactory solutions to the problems confronting their organizations and "attempts to follow unidirectional problem-solving sequences tend to be self-defeating, because such sequences make very weak provisions for correcting ignorance" (1985, p. 347). Furthermore, such attempts, according to Starbuck, encourage policymakers to justify their actions exclusively in accordance with "rational logic," which promotes rigid rationalizations. After using a reflective (vigilant) problem-solving approach, then, policymakers are less sensitive to bad results that should have "the power to instigate changes." Having developed exceptionally strong justifications for their policy decisions, executives will dismiss signs that their policies are not successful by believing that "they would have produced good results if accidents had not happened or enemies had not acted malevolently" and by concluding that "we should strengthen them with more effort and more money and give them enough time to yield good results" (1985, p. 346).

Despite the cogency of Starbuck's arguments, I disagree with his third generalization, although I agree that the limitations and deficiencies of vigilant problem solving that he mentions undoubtedly interfere from time to time with effective policymaking. There are additional limitations emphasized by James March (1981), Charles E. Lindblom (1980), and Richard Nelson (1977) that need to be considered; they will be examined later, in Chapter 8.

2. Much of the indirect evidence (suggesting that policymakers occasionally use at least some components of the vigilant problem-solving strategy) comes from studies that were designed to explore the descriptive validity of expected-utility theory, which postulates that policymakers examine the probable consequences of each viable alternative under consideration and choose the one expected to yield the best outcome with regard to their main objectives and values (see Note 3 for Chapter 5). If policymakers act in accordance with the expected utility model, they would engage in at least some of the information search and critical appraisal that characterizes vigilant problem solving in order to make the two types of estimates that are required: (1) the utility value of the consequences for each alternative under consideration and (2) the probability that the consequences of each alternative will materialize. (Such estimates can be made in terms of categories such as "high," "medium," or "low," without necessarily assigning numerical values.) A number of research studies conclude that although policymakers often deviate from the expected utility model, they sometimes conform to it. (See Abelson & Levi). To put it in more technical terms, the expected-utility model generally has been found to account for a signifi-

cant and substantial proportion of the variance in decisionmaking choices, even though it fails to account for the bulk of the variance. The findings can be interpreted as being consistent with the assumption that at least some components of vigilant problem solving are used by some decisionmakers some of the time. But, as I have already stated, the findings can also be interpreted in other ways.

In their comprehensive review of social psychological studies of decisionmaking in *The Handbook of Social Psychology,* Abelson and Levi state that many different views have emerged from the existing research as to how "rational" or "irrational" decisionmaking is likely to be. They assert that "the human decisionmaker has been variously seen as a corrigible rationalist, a bounded rationalist, an error-prone intuitive scientist, a slave to motivational forces, or as the butt of faulty normative models" (p. 233). In their judgment, no definite conclusion can be drawn as to which of these views is correct. None of these views, they point out, is able to account for all the relevant findings but, on the other hand, none of them seems to be completely wrong.

> Of course, if the accumulated evidence massively disposed toward one or another clear conclusion—that humans are (when tooled up) strict rationalists, or bounded by limited mental resources, or rife with natural misapprehension, or vulnerable to self-defeating motives, or rational in a manner not previously anticipated by theorists—then we would certainly want to endorse that conclusion. It seems to us clear, however, that there is a bit of truth in each position. . . . (Abelson & Levi, p. 235)

The accumulated evidence to which these authors refer does not bear directly on the question of how often a vigilant problem-solving strategy is used by policymakers. Most of the studies, like the ones designed to test the expected-utility model, did not include observations of the decisionmakers' information search or of other steps in the decisionmaking process.

3. Various outside experts in political science, history, and international relations were consulted during the research and generously spent considerable amounts of time giving us the ratings we needed to carry out the study. In all cases they remained blind to the study's hypotheses and overall design. The following seven professors were the experts who assisted us: Alexander George (Stanford University), Richard Ned Lebow (Cornell University), Bruce Russett (Yale University), Paul Seabury (University of California, Berkeley), Gaddis Smith (Yale University), Philip Tetlock (University of California, Berkeley), and Bradford Westerfield (Yale University).

4. Initially, we compiled a master list of international disputes since World War II from the Correlates of War project data on militarized interna-

tional disputes up to 1975, made available through the Intra-University Consortium for Political and Social Research at the University of Michigan. We included in this master list all militarized disputes since World War II that involved the United States or its client states and either the Soviet Union, China, or their client states. The list was supplemented by information from Butterworth. International disputes occurring during the Carter or Reagan administrations were excluded because of the limited availability of published scholarly analyses. The final list, which contained 76 disputes that occurred between 1945 and 1975, was then presented to two outside experts, both of whom had done a considerable amount of research on twentieth-century international crises. They were asked to select the six major crises within each presidential administration and to rank their severity and importance, which were defined "in terms of the overall security of the United States, with special reference to the threat of war with the Soviet Union or China" (Herek, Janis, & Huth, p. 207).

The two experts' rankings disagreed on only a few cases and for those instances a third expert's ratings were used to resolve the disagreements. The final sample (which included crises from the Truman, Eisenhower, Kennedy, Johnson, and Nixon administrations), consisted of the four highest-ranked crises for each of the five administrations, with one omission: Only three crises were included in the sample for the Kennedy administration because insufficient data were available from published sources to permit the ratings of U.S. decisionmaking for either the fourth-ranked crisis (the 1962 Taiwan crisis) or the fifth-ranked crisis (the 1962 Sino-Indian War).

5. In order to assess the quality of a policymaking group's process of arriving at a policy decision, the number of symptoms of defective decisionmaking is used as a rough indicator. When the number of symptoms is fairly large (e.g., four to seven symptoms), the process is rated as poor; when the number is very small (zero or only one symptom), the process is rated as relatively good; when there is an intermediate number, the process is given a correspondingly intermediate rating. This rather crude method of assessing the quality of the policymaking process has proved to have some validity in that the results in Table 6–1 (displayed graphically in Figure 6–1) show that the total number of symptoms is predictive of successful versus unsuccessful outcomes for the vital policy decisions that were investigated.

More refined methods of assessment might be developed in the future that give *differential weights* to various symptoms to take account of the likelihood that certain symptoms might generally involve more detrimental errors than others. But it should be recognized that detrimental errors can result when any one of the seven symptoms occurs. It seems likely that the probability of serious errors is greater, the larger the number of symptoms, as is implied by the substantial correlations between the number of symptoms and "blind" outcome ratings reported on p. 127.

6. As expected, the conservative and liberal experts who rated outcomes were not in complete agreement on whether the crisis decisions led to favorable or unfavorable outcomes (see the zeros in the last two columns of Table 6-1). In general, the conservative expert was inclined to see more of the outcomes as favorable or neutral, while the liberal saw more of them as negative. Nevertheless, they were in agreement for a majority of the outcome ratings. When positive and neutral outcome ratings were combined and compared to negative ratings (i.e., a comparison of "negative outcome" versus "non-negative outcome"), they agreed on 14 of the 19 crises (74%) for U.S. interests, and 13 of the 19 (68%) for international conflict. (See *Journal of Conflict Resolution* [1987], Vol. 31, p. 672).

In the study by Herek, Janis, and Huth, the two outside experts were asked to make the same two types of ratings for the long-term outcomes of the crises, i.e., the consequences in the months and years after each crisis ended. But while they showed fairly high agreement on their ratings of the shorter-term outcomes, they showed a considerable amount of disagreement on the longer-term outcomes. When making their ratings of long-term outcomes, both experts showed considerable hesitation and vacillation. Both also expressed relatively low confidence in those judgments, in contrast to the relatively high confidence they expressed about their ratings of the shorter-term outcomes. Because of the low rates of agreement, the ratings of long-term effects of the decisions were considered unreliable and were omitted from the analysis.

CHAPTER 7. THE CONSTRAINTS MODEL OF POLICYMAKING PROCESSES

1. Vroom and two collaborators (Vroom and Yetton; Vroom and Jago) have developed a theoretical model that specifies when and how leaders of large organizations *should* (and sometimes *actually do*) arrange for the participation of subordinates when dealing with policy problems. According to their model, two initial key questions pertain to the importance of the policy issue: (a) How important is it to arrive at a high-quality decision? and (b) How important is it for subordinates to be committed to the decision? If the leader judges the problem to be important enough when answering either or both of the questions, the model, as formulated by Vroom and Jago (pp. 217-28), requires answers to a series of additional questions that pertain to the following 10 attributes of the problem, all of which are pertinent to making judgments about *who* in the organization should participate in *what ways:*

   a. *Probability of subordinate commitment:* If I make the decision myself is it reasonably certain that my subordinates will become com-

mitted to it? If they don't "buy in" immediately would it be easy
for me to "sell" it to them?

b. *Leader's information and expertise:* Do I have sufficient information to make a high-quality decision or do I need information from
others in the organization? Do I have the necessary expertise or do
I need to draw on the expertise of others?

c. *Leader's perception of the problem as well structured or fuzzy:* Am
I familiar with problems of this kind—that is, do I know how the
current state of affairs differs from the desired state of affairs and
what methods will change the former into the latter? How fuzzy
are the ramifications of the problem, the goals, and the alternatives
for achieving the objectives?

d. *Subordinates' information and expertise:* Do my subordinates have
sufficient information and expertise to deal with the decision
problem?

e. *Shared goals:* Do my subordinates share the organization's goals to
be attained in solving the problem? Can I trust my subordinates to
pursue the best solution to the organization's problem rather than
to pursue their own self-interests?

f. *Conflict among subordinates:* Is there likely to be substantial conflict among my subordinates over which course to pursue? Are they
likely to have widely different views of the problem?

g. *Geographic dispersion:* Are the costs of bringing together geo-
graphically dispersed subordinates prohibitive?

h. *Subordinate skill development:* How desirable is it to maximize the
opportunities for subordinate development of problem-solving and
related skills?

i. *Time constraints affecting subordinates:* Does a critically severe
time constraint limit my ability to involve subordinates? Is this an
emergency that limits the involvement of subordinates because delay to obtain their participation will allow the threat to grow worse
or the opportunity to disappear?

j. *Time expenditures:* How important is it to minimize the amount of
time to be invested in this decision? In doing our jobs, how much
time would I and my subordinates have available to work on this
problem, given our present work loads?

The model developed by Vroom and his collaborators deals with
one particular aspect of the leader's decision about how to decide—the
personnel participation aspect, which overlaps slightly with the aspects
with which I deal. The domain of the theoretical model of policymaking I present in Chapter 7 has to do mainly with the conditions under
which any policymaker at any level of the hierarchy—whether he or
she is making a decision alone or as a participant in a group decision—

will adopt a vigilant problem-solving strategy in an attempt to arrive at a high-quality decision or will resort to a simplistic strategy. The slight overlap between the model developed by Vroom and his collaborators and my model of policymaking strategies occurs because both models take account of a leader's judgment about the importance of the policy problem as a factor that influences how the leader will deal with the problem. In the Vroom and Jago (1988) model, this judgment enters into decisions about making arrangements for the participation of subordinates; in the constraints model, it enters in as one of the determinants of the policymaking strategy that the leader will adopt.

2. Alexander George calls attention to various beliefs that influence the decisionmaking procedures used by policymakers when they are confronted by major challenges, such as the threat of aggressive actions by an adversary:

> [A political] actor's . . . beliefs . . . influence the focus and extent of the search and evaluation aspects of his information processing. Thus, if the actor views the opponent as a "unitary actor" . . . he is likely to engage in less extensive search for information about the adversary's motivations than he would if the opponent were viewed as a pluralistic group of leaders. The latter view raises the likelihood that policy views and preferences on the opposing side are not homogeneous in all respects, a possibility that sensitizes and deepens the search for clues as to the opponent's motivations and calculations.
>
> Search can also be affected by [another] . . . belief: How much control or mastery can one have over historical development? Thus, an actor who believes that he can exert a significant degree of control over events is more likely to undertake extensive search. His informational requirements are greater than those of an actor who feels he can do little to control and shape the course of events. (George 1979, p. 102)

3. Donaldson and Lorsch interviewed the corporate managers of 12 U.S. industrial companies selected from the upper half of the *Fortune* 500 list, which consists of firms controlled by salaried executives rather than owners or bankers. One of the outstanding characteristics of the top-level executives in each firm was a high degree of consensus in their underlying beliefs about the nature of the business world and where their company fitted into it, about "where they wanted their company to go," and "about how to get there" (p. 129). Just as has been observed among government leaders, the shared beliefs among corporate managers have a considerable effect on their judgments when they screen potential problems: "These interrelated beliefs act as a filter

through which management perceives the realities facing its firm. . . . [T]hey . . . translate a world that can be overwhelmingly complex and ambiguous into comprehensible and familiar terms" (pp. 79–80). For example, the corporate managers' beliefs about their organization's potentialities and vulnerabilities influence their judgments about new opportunities for diversification. Most of the executives share a firm belief that the corporation's survival would be threatened if it were limited to only one industry, one product, or one market; and so many of them are constantly on the lookout for opportunities to develop new products and to acquire new businesses. In that perpetual search, some potential opportunities are quickly dismissed as unpromising whereas others are pursued. In the initial screening of opportunities, the executives' judgments about which ones are important enough to be worth looking into can be expected to be strongly influenced by their basic beliefs about the nature of their organization and its future prospects—beliefs about long-term trends in the firm's market, about the expertise, talents, and areas of competence of the firm's personnel, and about the kinds of business activities in which the firm could compete successfully and excel.

Similar types of beliefs about the organization's special strengths undoubtedly influence the judgments of the heads of hospitals, social service agencies, and other public welfare organizations, and also the directors of local, state, and federal agencies when they screen *opportunities* for expanding their organization's activities. When potential *threats* are being screened, however, it would be the executives' beliefs about their organization's special weaknesses or vulnerabilities that would play a dominant role.

What Donaldson and Lorsch say about the beliefs of corporate managers is very similar to descriptions of the beliefs of top-level government leaders who make foreign policy decisions. (See, for example, the quotation from Alexander George in Note 2 above.)

4. There are three fundamental types of threat that beset corporate managers at one time or another, according to Donaldson and Lorsch (pp. 160–72), and each probably has its counterpart in the types of threat encountered by executives in public welfare organizations and in government:

   a. One major type of recurrent threat pertains to the danger that the top-level executives will lose their independence or self-sufficiency to such an extent that they will no longer be able to control their organization's basic policies. The dangers to be averted generally are those of losing control by being taken over by another organization or being unduly influenced by one of the organization's powerful constituencies (it could be the bankers and investors who help finance the firm, the unionized employees who might have the power to shut down the plant's operations, or the firm's leading customers, such as the U.S. government, whose contracts give them leverage as the "product market constituency" [p. 38]).

b. Another major type of threat arises from successful actions of adversaries in the hostile, competitive environment in which the organization functions. The dangers include losing out to competitors in several different spheres—not only losing money, but also losing skilled employees, or losing prestige and status as being one of the leading firms in the industry.

c. Closely related to the most extreme instances of the other two types of danger is the ultimate threat to the survival of the organization— going bankrupt or for some other reason, such as new restrictive legislation, being forced out of existence.

On the basis of extrapolations from extensive research on how people react to warnings about threats to their health, careers, or financial security, it seems fairly likely that when policymakers are currently preoccupied with one of the above three types of threat to their organization, they will be especially sensitive to any new threat of the same type, displaying relatively greater readiness to judge it as important enough to warrant careful search and appraisal. In some instances this heightened sensitivity could have the positive effect of arousing the policymakers' concern about previously neglected threats. But in other instances it could turn out to be detrimental because the policymakers might overreact to minor or false threats, which could result in their wasting their own time and the organization's resources unnecessarily in carrying out the steps of vigilant problem solving. Or, worse yet, their heightened sensitivity to certain types of threat could lead to unwise, panicky decisions, which are made when policymakers are in a hypervigilant state as a result of a very high level of emotional stress (see Chapter 4).

5. Comparable distressing events occur precipitately in the sphere of corporate policymaking, as when a competitive firm unexpectedly launches a superior new product that threatens immediate loss of a large share of the market or when a powerful conglomerate of financiers suddenly threatens a hostile takeover. When these precipitate threats are unambiguous they are immediately perceived as major challenges, irrespective of whatever other problems are in progress, because the policymakers realize that a great deal is at stake, sometimes the very survival of the organization. Such a threat is, as Miller and Starr (p. 151) put it, "so obstreperous that it . . . hits [the policymakers] head-on with the problem."

6. The first part of the quotation from Lazarus and Folkman (p. 147) refers to well-known factors concerning the expected magnitude of the predicted danger, the expected probability that it will occur, and its perceived imminence. All three factors are likely to affect policymakers' judgments as to whether or not an alleged threat poses an important problem. That is to say, a warning is most likely to be effective in inducing decisionmakers to regard the threat as posing a problem that needs to be pursued if it contains apparently trustworthy information indicating that the magnitude of the losses if the danger materializes will be very large, that the probability of the danger materializing is high, and that it is likely to materialize in the near future. In the absence of such information, the decisionmakers may supply it spontaneously from their own prior knowledge; but if they lack the appropriate knowledge they may judge the threat to be so unimportant that they completely ignore the warning or table it for possible consideration at some indefinite time in the future. Their complacent judgment can be reversed, of course, if they are subsequently exposed to new factual information from trusted sources indicating that the imminence, magnitude, and probability of losses will be enormously greater than they had initially expected.

7. One of the assumptions of the model represented in Figure 7-1 is that the likelihood that policymakers will engage in vigilant problem solving is reduced by events or communications that increase the perceived potency of any cognitive, affiliative, or egocentric constraint. The three lower boxes in the first column of the figure designate communications that typically have just such an effect. Included in each of the three boxes are warning communications conveying the message that serious losses are to be expected from ignoring a given constraint.

Sometimes an informational input that affects the answer to the first key question also affects the answer to one or more of the other three key questions. For example, if the chief executive of a nation receives an impressive warning that an opposing government is secretly preparing to invade a strategic outpost, that information will elicit a negative answer to the first key question and is also likely to evoke a very high level of emotional stress with a strong impetus toward egocentric coping by relying upon the emotive decision rule of defensive avoidance or hypervigilant escape. The emotional response to the information, as I stated earlier, can be conceived as a powerful motivational need that constitutes an emotive constraint and in extreme instances it gives rise to an answer of yes to the last key question in Figure 7-1.

Some policymakers tend to be much less responsive than others to informational inputs of the type represented in the first column of Figure 7-1. In certain cases this might be because those individuals have a strong motivational need to make practically every big decision in a particular way, irrespective of the content of the informational inputs. For example, there may be executives who repeatedly display a strong tendency to pass the buck if they can get away with doing so on every important policy decision because they have a low threshold for emotional stress and strive to avoid having to think about decisional dilemmas. Personality predispositions of this kind, which give rise to individual differences in policymaking style, are discussed in Chapter 9.

8. See pages 72–73 for a discussion of the tit-for-tat reciprocity principle formulated by Anatol Rapoport, as described by Axelrod (1984). See page 110 for a brief definition of the elimination-by-aspects principle, as described by Tversky. See also Note 9 for Chapter 5.

9. Defensive avoidance and hypervigilance, as described in Chapter 4 are among the main coping patterns in the conflict model of decisionmaking presented in Janis and Mann. The conflict model is directly applicable and can be "plugged into" the constraints model whenever emotive constraints involving psychological stress play a dominant role.

The constraints model of policymaking processes represented in Figure 7–1 encompasses defensive avoidance and the other defective stress-coping patterns described in the Janis and Mann conflict model. The constraints model, which pertains to the process of arriving at routine as well as vital policy decisions (such as those made during major crises) in governmental, business, public welfare, and other organizations, takes account of many additional defective procedural strategies. It includes those arising not only from psychological stress but also from additional emotive constraints (such as anger and elation), from self-serving motives (such as seeking prestige), and from various cognitive constraints (such as limited resources for information search) and affiliative constraints (such as the need to maintain social support, which makes for "groupthink"), all of which can interfere with vigilant problem solving.

The Janis and Mann conflict model describes two coping patterns that can be regarded as defective when the level of psychological stress is extremely low in response to a trustworthy warning about serious losses to be expected from continuing to act in accordance with existing policies (see pp. 78–79). One of these, labeled "unconflicted adherence" or "inertia," occurs when there is an unimpressive warning about expected losses (or opportunities that will be missed). The other, labeled "unconflicted change," occurs when there is an impressive warning but little prior knowledge of and no impressive warnings about potential losses from changing. It is these unconflicted coping patterns that are likely to be elicited whenever the issue is judged to be relatively unimportant, which makes for resorting to organizational routines or cognitive rules of thumb. These two coping patterns that occur under conditions of very low psychological stress are represented in Figure

7-1 by the initial key question concerning the importance of the problem. An answer of yes to that key question can be regarded as giving rise to unconflicted adherence or unconflicted change, with complete reliance on SOPs or simple cognitive decision rules.

10. Although it is somewhat arbitrary as to where to draw the dividing line between the two intermediate categories, the differentiation between a quasi-simplistic and a quasi-vigilant approach is likely to be useful for predicting whether the outcome will turn out to meet few or many of the organization's policy objectives (see 171–72). The first of these intermediate categories is applicable when policymakers rely mainly upon simple decision rules, but not entirely; they carry out a few but not very many of the essential tasks required to answer adequately the twelve key questions of vigilant problem solving, usually limited to those in the first or second step shown in Figure 5–1 (p. 91). The second intermediate category is applicable when policymakers carry out most of the tasks to answer adequately most of the key questions of vigilant problem solving, but not all. For example, after completing the first three steps shown in Figure 5–1, a policymaker may end up by relying mainly upon a simple decision rule to select a course of action from among alternatives that have been vigilantly explored, with failure to examine some of the major costs of the preferred choice and complete failure to work out any plans for implementation, monitoring, or dealing with contingencies.

CHAPTER 8. VALUES AND LIMITATIONS OF THE CONSTRAINTS MODEL

1. The constraints model is not completely represented in Figure 7–1, as is explained on pages 189–200. Consequently, in order to predict which procedural strategy a policymaker or group of policymakers will be most likely to adopt on the basis of antecedent conditions (only a few of which are specified by the model as represented in Figure 7–1), it is necessary to use supplementary bits of knowledge about antecedent conditions (including special conditions like the ones listed in Tables 8–1, 8–2, and 8–3 and in Figures 3–2 and 9–1).

2. Even when top-level leaders have enormous power, they may miscalculate the degree of stubborn resistance to be expected from other powerholders in the organization who have different values and different interests. Included among the other powerholders are implementers at the lowest level of the hierarchy, who are seemingly powerless but actually can exercise "sabotage power" if they object to a policy decision. Effective policymaking requires taking into consideration the relative distribution of power of all the potential objectors and making accurate judgments about what will and what will not "fly." When leaders overlook the problems of implementation or miscalculate the power of those who oppose their policy choice, they may subsequently find it

necessary to modify their initial decision, sometimes quite drastically, to overcome the unexpected resistance that is interfering with effective implementation. As Etzioni (1968, p. 304) points out, "the more the initial decision took the relevant power into account, the more effective implementation is going to be."

Etzioni elaborates on the crucial role that the distribution of power can play as a determinant of the success of policy decisions, particularly when leaders attempt to implement policies that evoke strong opposition from other powerholders and lack the capacity to mobilize sufficient power to overcome the opposition:

> A decision-maker may choose—because of normative commitments, psychological rigidity, or intra-unit politics—to ignore facts, but—by definition—he [or she] cannot ignore power. An elected government can ignore information about an imminent coup but not the tanks crushing the gates of the Presidential palace. A President might ignore the information that Congress will not pass a bill he favors, but this will not alter the fact that when the vote comes, the bill will not be approved; the decision will be shaped directly by power. . . .
>
> . . . While decisions theoretically can be made without devoting any attention to the question of whether or not the actor has or can marshal the power needed to implement them, the effectiveness of a decision will depend as much on its power-backing as on the validity of the knowledge and the decision-making strategy which were used. . . .
>
> . . . Control is not just a process of information-collection, calculation, and the expression of commitments, but also a process of the mobilization and use of assets. Hence, all other things being equal, the more assets an actor has, the more effective will be his [or her] decisions. (Etzioni 1968, pp. 303–4)

In some instances, leaders who lack sufficient assets may be too weak to be able to implement a policy decision that evokes resistance within the organization. But at least to a limited extent, leaders can mobilize whatever power and influence they possess to keep opposition to a minimum if they engage in vigilant problem solving. (See Note 11 for Chapter 10.) The final step of vigilant problem solving, as shown in Figure 5-1, includes careful planning for implementation. When policymakers carry out such planning they obtain information in advance about which powerholders are likely to pose implementation problems because of their rejection of the policy decision and they make a concerted effort to work out feasible solutions to those implementation problems.

Since the constraints model does not assume that organizational policy decisions are made by a unitary actor, an analysis of the policymaking approaches used by each of the powerholders who participated in an ill-conceived decision may reveal several different causal sequences that help account for various avoidable errors made by different policy-makers. Consider, for example, the case study material presented earlier (pp. 51–53 and pp. 66–67) on the low-quality decision made by the various powerholders in the Lehman Brothers firm to change from having two co-chief executive officers (Glucksman and Peterson) to having only one of them (Glucksman) as the sole chief executive officer. From the account given by Auletta (1985a, 1985b), it appears likely that different decisionmaking strategies were used by Glucksman, Peterson, and the twelve members of the board of directors, all of whom participated in the decisionmaking process. Glucksman arrived at his proposal (to become the sole chief executive officer) by relying heavily on a self-serving decision rule—to gain status and prestige by inducing Peterson to resign from the firm. Peterson might also have relied upon a self-serving decision rule in arriving at his decision to endorse Glucksman's proposal, to take advantage of the millions of dollars in severance pay that he would make on the deal. It is quite possible, however, that he used a vigilant problem-solving approach and that he took account of a number of other considerations, such as the desirability of an attractive career option that was open to him (to become a top executive in a new venture capital firm) and the high personal costs in terms of his own health and emotional state of well-being if he were to try to retain his position by fighting it out with Glucksman in an all-out power struggle. Among the members of the board of directors, who had the power to reject or modify Glucksman's proposal in the interest of preserving the firm and their own investments in it, only one of them showed any signs of using a vigilant problem-solving approach and he failed in his attempts to induce his fellow members of the board to examine the proposal critically. All the other members present at the crucial meeting uncritically accepted Glucksman's plan. The available evidence indicates that they used a simplistic approach dominated entirely by the affiliative decision rule, "avoid punishment."

3. Lindblom asserts that:

> Problem solving through interaction often takes the place of analysis. In contemporary Western societies, for example, market interactions—buying and selling—"solves" the problem of uses to which the nation's resources should be allocated. No one needs to analyze that problem. By contrast, in Soviet-style systems, planners try to analyze it. (P. 27)

For readers who regard the Soviet Union's economic policies as less successful than those of the United States and other capitalist countries, this statement would imply that the unplanned policies that emerge from interactions in a collectivity can turn out to be better than deliberate decisions arrived at by means of analytic (vigilant) problem solving. Lindblom does not discuss explicitly, however, the conditions under which the "hidden hand" type of policymaking process is likely to result in better (or worse) decisions than deliberate ones based on ordinary analysis.

In their book devoted to criticizing the work of professional policy analysts, Lindblom and Cohen make numerous suggestions for avoiding errors, which imply that in some circumstances deliberate analysis may yield better results than the "solutions" that emerge from the "hidden hand" type of interactive processes. Most of their suggestions for improving the work of professional policy analysts would require the analysts to carry out various steps of vigilant problem solving. For example, Lindblom and Cohen suggest that professional social scientists who work on policy problems would do a better job if they deliberately used their skills to do some analysis of costs and benefits before making their decisions about which social problems they will work on. The authors assert that most professional policy analysts decide in a "thoughtless" way to work on whatever social problems seem "important" at the moment or they accept the requests of customers who are willing to pay for their services, which, in effect, allows their professional resources to be allocated by unplanned market interactions: "Confident of the utility of any and all professional social inquiry, its practitioners often choose problems or topics without much thought about—and no extended professional study of—the probable cost or usefulness of the results. The professionalism with which they execute given research projects sharply contrasts with the personal and subjective way in which they choose them" (Lindblom & Cohen, p. 87). These authors add several comments that directly imply that practitioners of professional social inquiry oriented toward solving policy problems would make better decisions about which types of problems to work on and about how to work on them if they were to engage in more analytic problem solving instead of relying almost entirely upon nonanalytic, interactive processes. For example, they state:

> It is not sufficient to defend choice of project simply by reference to a problem's social importance or to considerations of research feasibility. Taking into account, for example, such complications as that professional social inquiry is at best often only supplementary to other inputs into social problem solving or that it rarely achieves authoritative knowledge, *wise choice requires an extremely complex analysis of relevant considerations.* This being so, we suggest that project choice and design may require not a simple weighing of a few relevant issues but the development of complex guidelines for, and new understandings of, the use of professional social inquiry, as well as interactive processes for solving the very problem of what prob-

lems professional social inquiry should attack and in what ways. (P. 97, italics added)

4. John Dean was the least powerful of the four members of the White House group who were responsible for planning and carrying out the Watergate cover-up policy during the early months of 1973. The other three members were President Nixon and his two chief aides, Robert Haldeman and John Erlichman. From June 1972, when the Watergate burglars were arrested, until the middle of March 1973, John Dean consistently functioned as the main implementer of the containment policy, as it was called. He destroyed incriminating evidence, collected and disbursed funds to provide "hush money" to the Watergate burglars and their lawyers, made false statements to the FBI, and coached others to do the same. For many months, Dean was confident that he was acting as a loyal member of the White House team and would be rewarded for doing the President's "dirty work." He relied upon the team to give him social support, especially at times when he felt doubts about whether he was doing the right thing. In his book about Watergate, *Blind Ambition,* Dean reports that "I felt at my toughest and most hopeful after receiving a boost from Haldeman or the President himself" (p. 139). He asserts that for several months he looked forward to the White House meetings with Nixon, Haldeman, and Erlichman because "they offered me confidence" (p. 186). But in March 1973, when publicly accused of criminal obstruction of justice, Dean "began to lose faith" in the power of the White House to protect him.

Dean's participation in the White House meetings prior to the end of March 1973 was characterized by an extremely high degree of agreement with the judgments and plans put forth by his superiors. Far from being vigilant, his procedural strategy appears to have been dominated by the "groupthink" affiliative rule. Instead of functioning in his role as the White House counsel to raise questions about the serious risks of the series of nested decisions involving ill-conceived obstructions of justice, which he was implementing, Dean felt that the right thing to do was to go along with whatever the President and his two chief aides wanted because they were wise, astute, and all-powerful. Together with the others on the White House team, he displayed the characteristic symptoms of groupthink for a period of many months. (See Janis 1982a, pp. 208–38.)

When the Senate's Watergate investigation and adverse press reports began to concentrate on his role in the conspiracy in the early spring of 1973, Dean began to show marked changes in his procedural strategy. First he went through a period of intensely stressful conflict, during which he attempted to maintain a defensive avoidance pattern by resorting to heavy drinking, after realizing that he could be sent to jail.

In late March 1973, he switched to a vigilant problem-solving approach; he examined viable alternatives and conducted an intensive information search, which included consulting a criminal lawyer to determine the full extent of his vulnerability. In early April 1973, after unsuccessfully attempting to induce President Nixon and his chief aides to abandon the cover-up policy, Dean gave up on the alternative of changing the White House group's cover-up policy and made the momentous decision to cooperate with the Watergate prosecutors in the Department of Justice. In June 1973, he told everything he knew about the White House conspiracy at the televised Senate Watergate conspiracy hearings, which played an important role in the Watergate denouement—indictment of numerous co-conspirators and impeachment proceedings in the Congress against President Nixon.

Some of the cogent evidence of John Dean's shift in procedural strategy, which also affected the three other men as their formerly cohesive group began to disintegrate, is summarized in the following excerpts from my detailed study of the Watergate cover-up:

McCarthy (1977) has carried out the most detailed analysis of the unedited White House tapes transcribed from Nixon's secret recordings by the House Judiciary Committee and the Watergate trial prosecutors. As in . . . two [other] studies, he finds numerous signs of groupthink during the period when the White House in-group was carrying out the coverup. . . . In a separate study, . . . McCarthy [1976] carried out a systematic content analysis that provides relevant quantitative data bearing on concurrence in the meetings in the White House of Nixon with his chief aides, Haldeman, Ehrlichman, and Dean. . . .

. . . McCarthy's measure of concurrence consisted of an overall percentage of agreement which can be applied to any single meeting or to any series of meetings. It was used by . . . McCarthy to compare the amount of concurrence in meetings that took place during two successive months during which the major change took place from group solidarity to disintegration. The period from the last week in February 1973 to the beginning of the last week in March 1973 was characterized by concerted cover-up actions by the cohesive White House group to deal with growing threats of exposure. . . . As expected, during the earlier month when the members were functioning as a cohesive group, scores were relatively high on the measure of concurrence, which is presumed to be indicative of groupthink. During the following month, when they were no longer a cohesive group, scores on concurrence fell sharply.

In my own reading of the transcripts of the meetings from June 1972 to March 1973, I find, as . . . McCarthy's content analysis indicates, relatively few instances of disagreement and very little debate about what is the best thing to do. After a suggestion is made by anyone in the group, the others most often accept it immediately and start building on it. . . . [But] indecisiveness increases during the month of March 1973, as more and more revelations in the press pose challenges to the group's defective cover-up policy. By early April 1973, disagreements are being openly voiced and the atmosphere of apparent unanimity can no longer be maintained. (Janis 1982a, pp. 218–19)

5. The differential consequences of early versus late introduction of a new overriding constraint on the quality of the deliberations of a policymaking group that has started off using a vigilant problem-solving approach can be illustrated by considering the typical effects of conformity pressure from the chief executive. The adoption and maintenance of vigilant problem solving in advisory groups generally depends upon whether the chief executive abstains from exerting conformity pressures, encourages open-minded discussion, and adopts related leadership practices—particularly if he or she has considerable power to facilitate or interfere with the status and other organizational rewards of the members (see Chapter 10).

Suppose that a chief executive does not push for or even reveal his or her policy preference during a long series of sessions until the very final meeting, after the executive committee has completed a vigilant information search and analysis. Conformity in response to the new affiliative constraint (threat of retaliations against those who might object to the chief executive's preferred choice) would have a relatively slight effect on the overall quality of the committee's decisionmaking process. It would be characterized as a "quasi problem-solving" approach if the committee members had already engaged in most of the steps of vigilant problem solving. The members' shift to a procedural strategy that relies on the "avoid punishment" rule would interfere only with the last step of choosing and planning for implementation. Even so, the effect on the final choice might be minimal as a result of the information acquired by the members' vigilant search.

After being exposed to the conformity pressure, the members of the executive committee would certainly be very careful to avoid recriminations by not openly expressing all of their objections to the chief's proposal and by not pushing very hard for any alternative they might prefer on the basis of their information search and appraisals already carried out. Nevertheless, having become keenly aware of the pros and cons of viable alternatives, they would be inclined to attempt in a cautiously diplomatic way to persuade the chief executive to modify his or her preferred course of action if they thought it was faulty, at least so as to eliminate its major defects. They might even attempt to persuade the chief executive to change his or her mind in the direction of a better-quality solution. (Their success, of course, would again depend partly on the leader's attributes, particularly his or her open-mindedness and willingness to reconsider.) If they are sufficiently skilled at influencing the chief executive's thinking on the issues at hand, the members of the committee, while continuing to be careful not to do or say anything that would evoke retaliatory actions, might succeed in inducing the chief at least to compromise by accepting some of the main features of an alternative that the group has come to see as a much better policy alternative.

In contrast, if the chief executive were to make the very same threat of retaliations early in the series of meetings, the group's decision-making process would most likely be characterized as a simplistic approach dominated by the "avoid punishment" rule. As a result, the committee members would make practically no effort to appraise the chief executive's proposal critically, to seek for a better one, or to induce the chief executive to modify his or her initial proposal in any way.

This comparison is in line with a point made earlier in the discussion of Table 7–2: A quasi-vigilant approach is likely to result in a better solution to whatever threat or opportunity the policymakers are confronting than either a quasi-simplistic or a completely simplistic approach, both of which entail less information search and less critical thinking about available courses of action.

6. When tape recordings are available, such as President Nixon's White House tapes (and Presidents Kennedy's and Johnson's, which are now available to scholars), we can find out exactly what was said at crucial policymaking meetings. Social science investigators can use those recordings to diagnose policymakers' procedural strategies and symptoms of defective decisionmaking. Such diagnoses of individuals or groups are necessary when the constraints model is applied for the purpose of making predictions about subsequent outcomes (or postdictions about antecedent conditions). But recordings are seldom obtainable even when they exist. Most often it is necessary to rely upon other kinds of records, such as minutes of meetings, memoirs, and interviews of participants. Because these sources are subject to more distortion than tape recordings, diagnoses of the initial procedural strategy and of subsequent shifts on the part of any individual or group are less dependable and, accordingly, applications of the constraints model require greater caution. Whatever conclusions emerge from such records must be regarded with more uncertainty. The same caution applies to any conclu-

sions derived from analyzing the same kinds of records concerning antecedent conditions that contribute to reliance on a simple cognitive, affiliative, or egocentric decision rule rather than going through the steps of vigilant problem solving.

Even when there are tape recordings of the sessions of a policymaking group, analysts must be on the lookout for indications of inauthenticity, as when the participants deliberately make impressive sounding statements for the sake of the record, knowing that what they are saying is being recorded. Analysts must also be alert to the possibility that the sessions were rigged by the leader to give his or her advisors the false impression that they were using high-quality policymaking procedures in order to gain their support and legitimization, as well as to make the record look good. In some instances, the sessions that are recorded may be nothing more than a staged charade that cannot be taken at face value for drawing conclusions about how the policy was actually arrived at.

7. Some components of vigilant problem solving are likely to be introduced from time to time when nested implementation decisions are made. "Mixed scanning," as described by Etzioni (1986), includes planning to monitor how well the fundamental policy decision is working out, watching for difficulties, and examining carefully the options that are compatible with the fundamental policy, all of which entail some degree of information search and evaluation. Consequently the implementation decisions may sometimes involve a quasi-vigilant rather than a predominantly simplistic approach. Quasi-vigilant problem solving is especially likely to occur when monitoring reveals that more and more difficulties are being encountered in attempts to apply the fundamental policy in the way it was originally intended. If incremental changes continue to be disappointing and particularly if gross signs of failure keep recurring despite efforts to adjust the policy to the new sources of trouble (which may include demoralization of the implementers), the top-level policymakers sooner or later realize that they are facing a whole new problem situation, which requires a new fundamental policy change. Thus, the entire mixed scanning process will start all over again "when existing policies are no longer sustainable by modification alone" (Etzioni 1986, p. 9).

In terms of the procedural strategies shown in Table 7–2, we would expect to find that after a fundamental decision is arrived at by using a vigilant problem-solving strategy, a series of nested implementation decisions will follow. The first of these nested decisions usually will be characterized by a predominantly simplistic or a quasi-simplistic approach that relies heavily on the commitment decision rule. Then, if more and more difficulties arise, there will be a shift to the quasi-vigilant strategy. When it becomes clear that the old policy must be changed, work begins on a new fundamental policy decision, using a vigilant problem-solving strategy (provided that in addition to a strong challenge, the other essential antecedent conditions [shown in Figure 7-1] are present).

8. The hypotheses that are emerging as empirically plausible on the basis of my case study findings take account of relevant concepts and prior findings from a number of different research areas in the social sciences. The concepts and empirical generalizations about cognitive decision rules that I draw upon include experimental studies in the fields of cognitive psychology and cognitive social psychology. Those on affiliative decision rules take account of empirical findings from experiments and field studies bearing on group dynamics, sociological studies of organizations, political science research on policymaking in governmental bureaucracies, and research in management and policy sciences. Those on egocentric (self-serving and emotive) decision rules draw upon experimental work in the psychology of personality and emotion as well as case studies in clinical psychology and psychiatry.

9. From the standpoint of the requirements for avoiding any circular inferences discussed on pages 316-19, Figure 3-2 showing the error-sequence for reliance on the "groupthink" decision rule—to preserve group harmony—is somewhat incomplete. It does not list a separate set of indicators for independently assessing whether or not the members of the policymaking group were deeply concerned about preserving their cohesive group and continuing to obtain social support from it— the telltale signs that the affiliative constraint is exerting a strong influence on the policymakers. What needs to be added is a separate column specifying the signs that can be used as indicators of a high degree of responsiveness to the antecedent conditions that create the affiliative constraint, such as the following:

- Verbal statements by members to the effect that they highly value the harmonious social atmosphere of the policymaking group and want to keep it that way.

- Verbal statements by members expressing dependency on the group for coping with uncertainties and stress, such as the kind of statement made by John Dean about gaining confidence from meeting with key members of Nixon's White House in-group. (See page 310.)

- Strong objections expressed to any suggestions that the membership of the group should be changed or that the group should be broken up in some way.

- Overt actions indicating dependence upon the group during periods of high stress,—e.g., more time spent socializing during nonbusiness portions of formal meetings, more frequent informal get-togethers and phone calls among the members.

10. Additional considerations may help explain why error-sequence outlines, like the ones in Tables 8–1, 8–2, and 8–3, are needed to meet certain of the requirements for applying the constraints model represented in Figure 7–1 in a reliable and valid (noncircular) manner when one is investigating the probable causes of a defective policy decision. The outlines include signs that can be used to assess two separable steps in the mediating process: (1) the policymaker's responsiveness to the antecedent conditions that create a powerful constraint and (2) the policymaker's reliance on a simple decision rule to deal with the constraint. These assessments must be made independently of each other and also independently of the antecedent conditions and of the symptoms of defective decisionmaking. The need for doing so in order to avoid unwarranted (circular) inferences can be illustrated by considering what is required to make a sound diagnosis of reliance on a particular type of decision rule to cope with a particular type of constraint.

Suppose that the inquiry is designed to determine whether reliance on the retaliation rule to cope with the emotive constraint of anger (described in Table 8–1) is one of the probable causes of what appears to be a poor policy decision to launch an aggressive course of action against a long-standing adversary who has repeatedly inflicted aggressive blows in the past. Suppose further that at the outset the only observations available show the presence of many of the symptoms of defective decisionmaking (listed in the fourth column of Table 8–1). These observations would confirm the analyst's initial impression that poor procedures were used to arrive at the policy decision. But the constraints model (represented in Figure 7–1) could be used in only a very limited way, namely, to predict that the outcome of the decision will probably be unsuccessful in meeting the policymaker's objectives. Obviously, no inferences would be warranted concerning the probable causes of the policymaker's failure to use sound procedures because there is no evidence available for evaluating the many different causal sequences that could account for this type of failure.

Now suppose that as the case study investigation continues, the analyst turns up clear-cut signs that the policymaker was intent upon retaliation (manifested by the types of indicators listed in the third column of Table 8–1) together with some observations indicating that the adversary had recently inflicted a provocative frustration that was unexpected (corresponding to some of the specifications of antecedent conditions listed in the first column of Table 8–1). At this point in the inquiry, the analyst would certainly be justified in surmising that perhaps anger was operating as a powerful constraint. But this surmise would have to be regarded as a suggestive hypothesis, one of several alternatives that would need to be looked into to see if there were telltale signs that the emotive constraint was operating. The analyst would also want to see whether or not any of the alternative hypotheses are supported. Among the plausible alternative hypotheses to be examined would be the following two, both of which describe probable causes that are entirely different from the one outlined in Table 8–1 for angry retaliation: (1) The recent provocative blow inflicted by the adversary was being used by the policymaker merely as an excuse to implement plans that had secretly been developed long before the adversary struck the recent blow, in accord with a cooly contrived policy decision based mainly on a heuristic derived from the organization's operational code—to use every opportunity to weaken a troublesome adversary. (2) Launching a counteraggressive move in response to the adversary's recent provocative blow was based mainly on the policymaker's commitment to an earlier organizational decision based on a vigilant problem-solving strategy that took into account the "tit-for-tat" rule as a guiding principle; the policymaker's decision in this particular instance was based mainly on the affiliative rule to adhere to the organization's existing policy.

It is apparent from this example that it would be an unwarranted circular inference to conclude that the emotive constraint of anger was a probable cause of defective decisionmaking in the absence of independent evidence indicating that the emotive constraint was actually present when the policy decision was being made (as manifested by signs like the ones listed in the second column of Table 8–1).

In order to draw a dependable conclusion that the angry retaliation sequence shown in Table 8–1 was a probable cause of a defective policy decision, there must be observations of indicators in all four columns of the table. The same holds true for any error-sequence of the type described in the constraints model represented in Figure 7–1. This is what I mean when I say that the entire pattern described by an error-sequence outline (like the ones shown in Tables 8–1, 8–2, and 8–3) must be observed in order to conclude that the sequence was one of the probable causes of a faulty policy.

Of course, finding evidence for the entire pattern for an error-sequence outline does not necessarily preclude the possibility that other sources of error were also contributing to the failure to use sound policymaking procedures. Consequently, each of the alternative hypotheses suggested during the inquiry should be explored fully before being ruled out as a contributory cause. When all the plausible hypotheses have been carefully examined in a detailed case study, it may be possible to make some warranted estimates about the relative weights to be assigned to each contributory causal sequence and to specify which one appears to have been most important.

To summarize, one of the main points I have been emphasizing is that in order to avoid circular reasoning, independent evidence is required showing that the constraint was operating during the period when the policy decision was arrived at. The fact that a case study supplies indications that a given decision rule was being heavily relied upon by a policymaker is insufficient for drawing any dependable conclusion about the type of constraint that gave rise to reliance on that rule. That is why I have repeatedly stated that when using the constraints model represented in Figure 7-1 independent evidence is needed bearing on the policymaker's answers to each of the key questions (listed as mediating variables in the second column of the figure). Evidence that one or another of the three types of decision rules (listed in the third column of the figure) was used does not warrant making any inferences about the policymaker's answers to any of the key questions.

Various verbal and nonverbal indicators can be used to obtain empirical evidence pertinent to the mediating variables concerning a policymaker's answers to the key questions postulated by the constraints model. The following examples suggest the kinds of observations that investigators might search for:

- For the key questions regarding the importance of the problem: Statements by the policymaker about whether or not it is a routine or relatively unimportant problem; policymaker's statements accepting or rejecting experts' forecast about expected losses from ignoring the problem and continuing business as usual; amount of time spent discussing the problem with others outside the organization. (See also my comments about Vroom and Jago's [1988] assessment of the importance of the problem in Note 1 for Chapter 7.)

- For the key questions concerning cognitive constraints (cognitive limitations and lack of organizational resources): Policymaker's statements expressing awareness of his or her lack of the required expertise and about the organization's lack of funds for hiring experts and gathering essential information; policymaker's statements indicating acceptance or rejection of organizational reports about inherent difficulties of solving the problem; overt efforts to obtain an extension of time for working on the problem.

- For the key question concerning affiliative constraints: Policymaker's statements expressing concern about loss of social support, subtle conformity pressures, or overt threats of recriminations; policymaker's statements indicating acceptance or rejection of "grapevine" reports that certain viable solutions will meet with strong opposition within the organization; amount of time spent seeking information about how others would react to viable alternatives.

- For the key questions concerning egocentric constraints: Policymaker's private statements about desire to satisfy a personal motive, such as gaining fame and fortune; policymaker's statements accepting or rejecting private suggestions about taking advantage of the opportunity to select a course of action that would provide personal self-serving gains; displaying emotional reactions and other indications of responsiveness to an emotive constraint of the type listed in the second column of Tables 8-1, 8-2, and 8-3.

We can expect that in subsequent research, additional indicators will be developed.

When investigating predictions derived from the constraints model as to whether vigilant problem solving or a simplistic strategy will be used by the policymakers, it is essential for investigators to confine their observations in such a way that they remain "blind" to the policymakers' procedures bearing on presence or absence of symptoms of defective policymaking. If an investigator already knows that certain steps of vigilant problem solving were or were not taken, this knowledge could color his or her judgments of the answers given to the key mediating questions. To avoid such contaminated judgments, the ideal design of predictive studies would be to complete all judgments about how each policymaker answered the key mediating questions (listed in the second column of Figure 7-1) before being exposed to any information at all about the strategy used by the policymaker to arrive at the decision. By looking only at observations like the ones in the above list of examples, and taking other precautions to remain "blind," investigators should be able to eliminate unconscious bias and other sources of artifact that could give rise to spurious findings when testing predictions derived from the constraints model.

CHAPTER 9. WHO WILL BE GOOD POLICYMAKERS AND WHO WILL NOT? HYPOTHESES ABOUT PERSONALITY DIFFERENCES DERIVED FROM THE CONSTRAINTS MODEL

1. The seven studies cited by McCrae and Costa (1986a) in support of the validity of the five personality factors are as follows: Amelang & Borkenau; Costa & McCrae; Costa, McCrae, & Holland; Digman & Takemoto-Chock; Goldberg (1981); McCrae & Costa (1985, in press); McCrae, Costa, & Busch.

   Waller and Ben-Porath assert that the findings from these studies provide a fair amount of substantial support for the five-factor model but they conclude that the cumulative evidence is not quite as convincing as is suggested by McCrae and Costa. A number of the studies, according to Waller and Ben-Porath, present cogent evidence for the existence of the five factors but should not be regarded as completely independent replications. For example, five of the studies included personality items taken from the same variable set—Raymond Cattell's list of trait clusters. Some of the convergent evidence in support of the five-factor model, these authors argue, should be regarded as demonstrations of the reliability rather than the validity or comprehensiveness of the model. Waller and Ben-Porath recognize, however, "the heuristic value of the five-factor model and its potential contribution to personality assessment" (p. 888).

In 1981, Goldberg critically examined the evidence from studies bearing on personality factors and concluded that the "big five" are fairly robust: "Whether the data come from self reports or from descriptions of other people, whether based on one kind of rating scale or another, no matter what the method for factor extraction or rotation, the results are much the same" (pp. 160–61). He pointed out, however, that there are minor variations from one study to another in the specific personality variables and the factor loadings that enter into each of the "big five." Subsequent studies have continued to support these conclusions (Goldberg 1982; Peabody & Goldberg in press).

It should be recognized that the available evidence comes from studies of college students and older adults in common types of occupations. Validation studies have not yet been carried out for subpopulations of men and women in policymaking roles in government, business, and public welfare organizations.

2. Among the sources on personality (and related predispositions) that I have drawn upon for generating hypotheses about personality deficiencies are the following, which are classified according to the headings used in the text of this chapter:

   a. *Who goofs off?:* Bass; Breznitz; Cattell; Donaldson & Lorsch; Goldberg (1981, 1982); Horowitz; Maccoby; McCrae & Costa (1984, 1986a); Norman; Tupes & Christal.
   b. *Who can't hack it?:* Bandura; Bass; Brown; Singer; Smith (1969).
   c. *Who can't say no?:* Bass; Crowne & Marlowe; Etheredge (1985); Janis (1982a, 1982b); McClelland; Snyder & Ickes.
   d. *Who is self-serving?:* Etheredge (1978); Goldberg (1981, 1982); Horowitz; Maccoby; McCrae & Costa (1984, 1986a); Norman; Singer; Snyder & Ickes; Tupes & Christal.
   e. *Who gets discombobulated?:* Brown; Cattell; Gentry et al.; Gentry & Kobasa; Horowitz; Goldberg (1981, 1982); Janis (1982c); Kobasa & Puccetti; Lazarus & Folkman; McCrae & Costa (1984); Rotter, Seeman, & Liverant.

3. There are probably at least three major types of skills required to maintain a fairly good track record of making sound discriminations between warnings that should be heeded and those that can be safely ignored. One type of skill pertains to making sound appraisals of the credibility of the source of the warning: the ability to judge accurately whether the person or source is in a position to know the truth and is honest. This type of skill includes knowing how to check on the credibility of the communicator if there are serious doubts about the authenticity of the warning. The second type pertains to appraisals of the probability that the threat will materialize. The third type pertains to appraisals of the severity of the threat. The three sets of skills are required to make accurate estimates concerning (a) whether the potential danger to the organization's or nation's vital interests is likely to be of such a magnitude as to be serious, moderate, or slight if and when it materializes, and (b) the likelihood that the danger will materialize so soon that the organization could be caught short if planning for protective action is postponed until there are clear-cut signs that the danger is imminent.

Executives lacking in any of these sets of skills would tend to make many more errors of omission and commission than others who have the requisite skills. In this context, errors of omission consist of ignoring genuine threats to vital interests of the organization that are challenges requiring a high-quality policy decision. Errors of commission consist of taking unwarranted warnings seriously—that is, instituting information searches and holding meetings to deliberate when the threats are so minor or improbable that they should be dismissed as unimportant. The errors of omission on the part of top-level executives could lead to avoidable disasters for the organization. Their errors of commission would usually be less devastating but an accumulation of them could lead to gross inefficiency in the use of organizational resources and other detrimental effects of imposing unnecessary work tasks and informational overloads on busy executives and staff members of the organization. If there are many errors of commission, the organization will not have available the resources needed for intensive search and appraisal when really serious threats are encountered, which can result in catastrophic errors of omission.

Essentially the same types of skills essential for discriminating adequately between warnings that should and should not be responded to as important challenges would also be essential for discriminating adequately between important and unimportant warnings pertaining to *constraints*—such as alarming rumors about possible retaliations from the chief executive officer that might be inflicted on members of an executive committee who argue against the policy choice he or she prefers. Errors of omission in such instances would entail failure to take account of essential requirements for a good-quality solution, which could lead to extremely undesirable consequences for the executives who make the error and sometimes for the entire organization. Errors of commission in appraising warnings about constraints would increase the likelihood of giving undue priority to constraints, which makes for low-quality policy decisions as a result of relying on simple decision rules. Hence, the lack of critical skills for evaluating warnings would be a predisposing factor that contributes to faulty answers to the three key questions about constraints as well as to the initial key question about the importance of the challenge.

These dispositions could, of course, change over a relatively short period of time. For example, as an executive gains experience or undergoes in-service training, he or she might no longer lack the requisite skills for evaluating the various kinds of warnings that need to be judged fairly accurately for sound policymaking.

The same skills, along with a large number of other special skills, are likely to be essential for carrying out successfully the four main steps of vigilant problem solving in order to answer adequately the twelve questions shown in Figure 5-1 (p. 91). Special skills probably are also essential for fulfilling the type of leadership role involved in fostering a vigilant problem-solving approach for dealing with vital policy issues among members of an executive committee and throughout the entire organization (see Chapter 10).

4. Drawing on Kohut's concepts, Etheredge (1985) suggests that "hardball politics players" are excessively ambitious to gain power and status in an effort to overcome feelings of inadequacy and self-doubts. He postulates that inwardly they are insecure and worry about social acceptability, while outwardly they are hyperaggressive, scornful of weakness, manipulative, and hyperactive. They also display weak ethics and little moral restraint as they unrelentingly vie to be "top dog." As yet there is insufficient research evidence to assess Etheredge's personality profile of the "players of hardball politics" and to specify how their personalities differ from the less manipulative executives who are also chronically concerned about maintaining or gaining power and status, including those inclined to cope with their fears in this domain by being passively compliant conformists.

5. Hypothesis 13 refers to low stress tolerance as a general personality characteristic of a subgroup of individual executives, in contrast to those characterized as having moderate or high stress tolerance. Other, quite different subgroups may display low stress tolerance when confronted with certain limited circumstances (such as a prolonged crisis period when there is great uncertainty about whether an adversary is preparing to launch a surprise hostile move) or when dealing with a specific distressing issue (such as control of nuclear weapons). A more

restricted version of Hypothesis 13 might be formulated to apply to any individual who is known to display low stress tolerance when trying to manage a particular kind of crisis situation or when working on a particular type of policy issue.

The other hypotheses presented in this chapter also deal with general personality characteristics that are expected to be manifested in many different kinds of situations and across a wide range of diverse issues. Most, if not all, of them would also have as their counterparts a more restricted version that pertains to personality predispositions that are manifested only in certain limited situations or at times when the executive is dealing with a specific policy issue. On any given policy issue, as Neustadt and May point out, different leaders within the same government agency or business firm are likely to have different blind spots, prejudices, and sensitivities arising from differences in their personal histories.

McCrae and Costa (1986b) describe neuroticism and low stress tolerance as belonging to the category of *general* personality characteristics that are pervasive across a wide variety of situations. They report that on the basis of factor analytic studies, neuroticism is composed of a number of components, including chronic anxiety, self-consciousness, impulsiveness, hostility, depression, and feelings of vulnerability. These authors present empirical evidence indicating that, as expected, measures of neuroticism are significantly correlated with poor coping mechanisms, indicating low stress tolerance. In their research, McCrae and Costa obtained neuroticism ratings from three different sources: self-ratings, spouse-ratings, and peer-ratings based on average responses from a few friends. They observed the same pattern of positive correlations for all three assessments of neuroticism in two separate studies of coping mechanisms. The subjects were several hundred healthy adults, almost all of whom were college graduates in professional, managerial, or white-collar occupations. Each one was asked to give self-reports about how he or she coped with a recent stressful life experience. Both studies showed that the ratings of neuroticism were significantly correlated with the following defective coping mechanisms: escape via fantasy, self-blame, reliance on alcohol or other forms of sedation, social withdrawal, indecisiveness, hostile reactions, and wishful thinking.

Most of the findings suggest that the dominant coping pattern among persons with high neuroticism scores is defensive avoidance. On the basis of their empirical results, McCrae and Costa conclude that "even in a normal population, individuals high in neuroticism are prone to use coping mechanisms [for dealing with stress] generally perceived to be ineffective" (1986b, pp. 396–97). It seems likely that similar correlations would be found among executives in large organizations when assessments of neuroticism are investigated in relation to defensive avoidance and other ineffective coping patterns for dealing with the stresses generated by difficult policy issues.

6. Executives with low stress tolerance may also be inclined to overreact to vague or ambiguous warnings. If so, they would frequently worry about and start working on very minor problems based on speculative forecasts and surmises that should be ignored. When this happens, the executive wastes his or her own time and also the time of staff members who should be concentrating their work on the serious problems posed by genuine warnings. In addition to being grossly inefficient in this regard, executives with low stress tolerance may be easy victims of clever manipulative people inside and outside the organization who use scare propaganda in attempting to sabotage current policies or to induce self-serving changes in policy.

When one examines the constraints model from the standpoint of its implications for individual differences in threshold for responsiveness to various types of informational inputs (listed in the second column of Figure 9-1, p. 212) it becomes apparent that there is more than one way that low stress tolerance can result in poor-quality policy decisions on vital issues. The informational inputs that promote positive answers to the key question pertaining to affiliative constraints (Question IIB in the fifth column of Figure 9-1) frequently are fear-arousing warnings, such as those given by a chief executive that threaten recriminations for failures to agree with his or her policy preferences. Executives with low stress tolerance could therefore be expected to be more prone than others to display defective Pathway 3 as well as defective Pathway 4. Occasionally informational inputs about cognitive constraints might also take the form of warnings that could evoke strong emotional reactions (such as fear of failing to solve a complicated problem, which could reflect badly on one's capabilities as a leader). Persons who are most responsive to such warnings would tend to give a positive answer to the key question concerning cognitive constraints (Question IIA in the fifth column of Figure 9-1). Consequently, executives with low stress tolerance might also become more inclined than others to display defective Pathway 2.

Each of the personality variables specified in Hypotheses 5 through 17 as a determinant of overreactions to information about one type of constraint might also be found to be a determinant of overreactions to information about another type of constraint.

7. Among executives in policymaking positions, personality hardiness may be correlated to some degree with low stress tolerance, but the two variables could nevertheless be sufficiently independent to account for substantial amounts of nonoverlapping variance. The question of how much the two personality variables overlap within the subpopulation of policymaking executives in government, business, or other large or-

ganizations obviously cannot be answered until the cogent personality research data become available for those subpopulations. The same must be said concerning the possibility of overlap among the other personality variables mentioned in the various other hypotheses as potential determinants of a low threshold of responsiveness for informational inputs that can induce overreactions to cognitive, affiliative, or egocentric constraints.

CHAPTER 10. EFFECTIVE LEADERSHIP PRACTICES: ADDITIONAL HYPOTHESES DERIVED FROM THE CONSTRAINTS MODEL

1. The informational inputs listed in the second column of Figure 9-1 on p. 212 are expected to have the strongest effect on policymakers whose personalities are characterized by the deficiencies listed in the third column of the figure, as was indicated in Chapter 9. But it is also to be expected that those same informational inputs will have a similar, though less pronounced effect on policymakers who do not have any such personality deficiencies. That is to say, those who are not predisposed to underestimate threats or to overreact to information about constraints can be expected, from time to time, to give a positive answer to one or another key question and, as a result, fail to adopt a vigilant problem-solving approach to deal with a vital policy issue. The hypotheses on leadership practices presented in Chapter 10 are intended to be applicable to such instances occurring among *non-predisposed* policymakers. In effect, therefore, the third column of Figure 9-1, which lists personality deficiencies of policymakers, is *not* used for formulating the hypotheses about leadership practices. Use is made, however, of all the other columns in Figure 9-1 to specify the expected effects of inputs from a group leader that will counteract the informational inputs that tend to induce a simplistic strategy when a group is dealing with a vital policy problem.

2. When rejecting proposals to table a problem or to handle an ambiguous threat in a routine way, a leader who wants to promote vigilant problem solving (as specified in Hypothesis 18) would need to exercise considerable care to avoid creating the impression that he or she has already concluded that the threat is serious and expects the group to decide to take some drastic form of action. (See Hypotheses 26d and 27a.) In order to maintain a neutral stance, the leader would have to assert repeatedly that he or she is undecided about the best course of action to take but is in favor of further discussion and wants the *potential* dangers to be examined so that everyone in the group will give the issue full attention and will help work out a high-quality decision as to what to do about it, which could be to do nothing at all except wait to see what happens.

3. Leadership practices that counteract premature acceptance of an "ob-

vious" solution by inducing the policymaking group to carry out the four steps of vigilant problem solving represented in Figure 5-1 would include many of the procedures recommended by Neustadt and May. (See p. 253, Note 7 for Chapter 5, and Note 10 below.)

4. What Karl Weick says about solving major social problems in his insightful paper on "Small Wins" probably applies equally to solving major policy problems in government, business, and public welfare organizations:

> Social problems seldom get solved, because people define these problems in ways that overwhelm their ability to do anything about them. Changing the scale of a problem can change the quality of resources that are directed at it. Calling a situation a mere problem that necessitates a small win moderates arousal, improves diagnosis, preserves gains, and encourages innovation. Calling a situation a serious problem that necessitates a larger win may be when the problem starts. (Weick 1984)

5. A hypothesis similar to Hypothesis 24c might be applicable when the policy option that is being pursued requires national leaders, such as the U.S. President and Secretary of State, to enter into negotiations with leaders of an adversary nation—or when similar negotiations are conducted by leaders of two rival organizations. Obviously, in any such negotiations of international or interorganizational disputes it is much more difficult for any leader to function effectively as mediator, especially because the contending parties have much less common ground in ideology, traditions, and objectives than when the factions are from within the same government, corporation, or public welfare institution and have a similar outlook concerning vital interests. Nevertheless, a leader can strive to focus on common objectives of the contending parties—for example, preventing nuclear war or avoiding an ecocatastrophe. This might be a strong incentive for replacing a win-lose orientation with a cooperative, vigilant problem-solving strategy to work out a sound negotiated agreement that takes account of the rock-bottom requirements of the contending parties that each of them can live with. (See Deutsch; see also the references on negotiation cited under *Sources* for Chapter 8, p. 179.)

6. In order to know when and how to raise questions in a productive way, particularly when vital policy decisions have to be made under great time pressure, it is essential for the leader to do a considerable amount of homework prior to meetings with experts and other transmitters of pertinent information, including the policymaking group—and to encourage all the group members to do the same. The participants need to become sufficiently knowledgeable about the facts and the best available estimates to be able to spot inconsistencies and gaps in any new

information that seems to require a drastic reappraisal of a course of action that had been contemplated. But there is little time for homework assignments in the schedules of overworked executives. All the more reason for an organization to maintain a competent staff to screen potential threats and opportunities and to institute effective procedures for evaluating new challenges that might require high-level policy decisions. An adequate screening system can reduce the number of problems the policymakers have to deal with, enabling them to concentrate their time and energy on those of paramount importance. It may also reduce the number of avoidable crises that arise from failing to appraise warning signs correctly before the threats materialize. Thus, if an organization has developed efficient operations for screening potential challenges it should be possible for the top-level policymakers to have time to do the necessary homework on the major problems they are trying to solve.

7. Hypothesis 26a asserts that when a leader indulges in rigging by arranging to hold meetings of a policymaking group when members who disagree with the leader's preferred choice are unable to attend or are not invited, the quality of the decisionmaking process generally turns out to be poorer than when a leader abstains from using this rigging tactic. There are likely to be exceptions, of course, when the dissenters obstruct the exploration of viable alternatives because they always vehemently insist on promoting the one course of action that they regard as the only possible solution, thereby preventing the group from carrying out essential steps of vigilant problem solving. Lebow (1988) reports that newly released records indicate that circumstances of this kind arose during the Cuban missile crisis in 1962: President Kennedy held a crucial meeting that excluded four adamant "hawks" who unrelentingly urged that the U.S. Air Force should destroy the missile sites; because of their absence the others in the policymaking group (known as the Ex Comm) apparently were able to examine other alternatives, which ultimately led to a less risky solution that successfully resolved the crisis. In subsequent research, if such occurrences are found so frequently that they cannot be classified as exceptional instances, Hypothesis 26a obviously will not stand up as an empirically valid generalization.

8. The formulations of Hypothesis 27 (including all the leadership practices designated in 27a through 27h) are taken directly, with minor changes, from Chapter 11 on "Preventing Groupthink" in Janis (1982a), based on an analysis of the conditions that are conducive to groupthink. The suggestion in Hypothesis 27f that it might be more effective if the leader of a cohesive policymaking group assigns the role of devil's advocate to at least *two* members, rather than only one, comes from West. His suggestion takes account of social psychological

research on the conditions under which dissenters within a group are able to resist the social influences of the majority of the members. The research of Charlan Nemeth (1979, 1986) suggests that the persons selected for the role of devil's advocate should be capable of presenting a deviant minority position in a confident and consistent manner, without being rigid. For a general review of research on when and how a small minority of members can influence the majority in group discussions, see Moscovici.

Although the leadership practices listed in Hypothesis 27 are expected to prevent low-quality decisionmaking mainly by counteracting groupthink tendencies, which arise from the members' motivation to preserve group harmony, they might also prove to be effective in counteracting other affiliative constraints that can interfere with vigilant problem solving. For example, some of the practices may dampen concerns about being punished for nonconformity, others may prevent unintentional riggings that preclude critical evaluation of viable options.

Many of the antigroupthink practices listed in Hypothesis 27 probably would be unnecessary if the organization were to adopt the system of "multiple advocacy" recommended by Alexander George (1973, 1980). He proposes that organizations adopt a three-tier structure when making important decisions. First, the chief executive or top-level leader presides over the system, taking the role of a magistrate, and evaluating the relative merits of the competing positions. Second, there is a custodian of the decisionmaking process. This is usually a vice-president or special assistant, whose job as honest broker is to maintain and supervise the adversarial and collegial nature of policymaking within the organization. Finally, there are the advocates who are chosen by the custodian to argue competing positions in policy-planning meetings with the chief executive.

George (1980) points out that multiple advocacy does not guarantee a good decisionmaking process in every instance. The system can malfunction if the advocates do not cover the full range of options, if no advocate can be found for an unpopular option, if advocates for a minority position do not have full access to secret intelligence reports and other essential organizational resources, or if the advocates thrash out their disagreements privately, bringing a unanimous recommendation to the chief executive. That is the reason for the "custodian" role, the person who is responsible for protecting the organization against incomplete or sham multiple advocacy.

In the absence of such a system, the leadership practice specified in Hypothesis 27e—which involves bringing in outsiders from time to time to participate in the group's deliberations—might be especially valuable, provided that the outsiders include proponents of divergent positions within the organization. In order to counteract the tendency to overestimate the group's wisdom, power, and morality, which creates a false sense of complacency about very risky courses of action for dealing with threats when groupthink tendencies are dominant, the outsiders would also have to be trustworthy associates. They would also have to be carefully selected for their capacity to grasp new ideas quickly, perspicacity in spotting hidden catches, sensitivity to moral issues, and verbal skill in transmitting criticism. Such outsiders were deliberately brought into the executive committee's meetings by President Kennedy during the Cuban missile crisis and they were urged to express their objections openly. This leadership practice was quite different from that which President Kennedy adopted throughout the Bay of Pigs planning sessions during which, with rare exceptions, he always had the same men at every meeting and groupthink tendencies were persistently dominant (see Janis 1982a).

An obvious drawback of the leadership practice under discussion is that the invited guests might waste a great deal of the core group's time by raising issues and offering arguments that have already been carefully considered. This drawback might be prevented to a large extent by arranging to supply the guests with detailed reports about the group's prior discussions and asking each of them to do some homework by studying the reports before attending a meeting.

Additional acts of leadership might be needed to ensure that the objective of inviting well-qualified outsiders to attend meetings of the policymaking group is not neutralized or subverted. First, outsiders who are likely to raise debate-worthy objections might need to be invited long before consensus has been reached, not after most of the core members have made up their minds, as was the case when Senator J. William Fulbright was invited to participate in one of the Bay of Pigs meetings. Second, each outsider may need to be asked to speak out freely and to express his or her qualms, not brood silently, as Bowles felt constrained to do when he attended a Bay of Pigs planning session. Third, after the visitor speaks, the chairman might need to call for open discussion of his or her objections, not move on to other business, as President Kennedy did in a final planning session when he called for a straw vote immediately after Senator Fulbright gave his opposing speech about undesirable consequences of the Bay of Pigs invasion plan.

The additional acts of leadership that have just been described as possible requirements for the effectiveness of the leadership practice specified by Hypothesis 27e can be regarded as a set of *provisos* that may prove to be essential. A similar set of provisos may also prove to be essential not only for each of the other antigroupthink measures included under Hypothesis 27, but also for every one of the leadership practices mentioned in Hypotheses 18 through 37. If the hypotheses are investigated systematically, along the lines described in Note 15 below, the provisos that are essential can be expected to emerge from the research studies.

9. Evidence concerning the effectiveness of stress inoculation, and extensive discussions of the background theory and practical implications of the findings can be found in the following three references: Janis (1982d, pp. 259–90); Meichenbaum; Turk & Genest. Crisis managers, their aides, and other support personnel who are given in-service training that includes appropriate crisis simulation exercises can be expected to benefit in other ways, in addition to building up a higher level of tolerance for the hectic pace and emotional stress of actual crises. They could gain a fuller appreciation of the constraints that need to be dealt with and develop a much more knowledgeable approach to crisis management, especially if the training program also includes briefings on organizational resources and action programs, discussions of lessons learned from prior crises, and pre-examination of alternative options for dealing with anticipated future crises.

10. It is difficult to keep a crisis under control when there are alarming verbal warnings about a probable attack by an adversary. A leader's skeptical questions about the initial reports and requests for postponing action until after carrying out a search for more complete information may not be sufficient to alleviate acute apprehensiveness among members of the policymaking group. During a crisis provoked by an adversary's threatening actions, the most difficult question to answer is "Why?" It requires specifying the adversary's intentions, which are generally kept secret and deliberately obscured by disinformation. In the face of all sorts of ambiguities surrounding an adversary's provocative action, crisis managers and their staffs tend to surmise extremely harmful intentions by relying heavily upon their negative stereotypes of the adversary, which often give rise to grossly erroneous expectations that evoke extreme apprehensiveness, which cannot readily be alleviated.

In recommending the use of the journalists' traditional questions, Neustadt and May give special emphasis to the first one: "When?" In order to understand the full story and the ramifications of the issues posed by a current crisis, they propose seeking information about its historical background, beginning with the question, "When did it start?" Then the inquiry would be directed to developing what Neustadt and May call "the time-line," which specifies significant developments, including political struggles and commitments on the part of the major contenders in the conflict. Commenting on several examples of errors in U.S. presidential decisionmaking that might have been avoided, they conclude that "tracing the time-line from the story's start, and asking journalists' questions about trends or change points in the issue's history . . . can [help] to illuminate current concerns" (p. 110).

Neustadt and May suggest that some of the exaggerated inferences by crisis managers in a national government can be corrected if various experts are consulted who can rapidly supply the time-line because they already know a great deal about the cogent political history of the adversary nation and its leading factions. The experts would also need to be familiar with the structures, procedures, values, and traditions of its top-level policymaking body and of the organizations that implement policy decisions (for example, the adversary's military forces). Valuable inputs might also be solicited from experts who are knowledgeable about the life histories of the adversary's current leaders, including their behavior in past crises and significant biographical details concerning their personal, professional, and political development, which could provide clues about what their objectives are likely to be in initiating the present crisis.

When organizations in the private sector are confronted with a crisis as a result of alarming actions on the part of an adversary, such as a hostile takeover attempt, similar inputs can usually be obtained. By consulting appropriate experts, it may be possible to alleviate exaggerated fears of what the adversary wants to do and can do.

If background information about the adversary and its apparently threatening actions is needed in a hurry, staff personnel may be able to obtain it from a series of phone calls to intelligence analysts and "old hands" who have participated in the management of past crises, each of whom is likely to know part of the story. It might be effective for the leader to ask members of the policymaking group to note points of agreement and disagreement among the experts consulted and to take into account any of the impressive points of agreement that are discrepant with the group's initial assumptions. With encouragement from the leader, exposure to newly acquired background information might enable some members to modify the alarming inferences made from their initial negative stereotype. This could lower the level of apprehensiveness and enable the members to make more sophisticated assumptions about the adversary's intentions and probable reactions to alternative courses of action or inaction.

11. Social scientists who study organizations have become increasingly aware of inadequacies of the so-called "classical" hierarchical model of the exercise of power in policymaking. According to that model, policy formulators at the top choose and instruct policy implementers who, as subordinates, proceed to carry out the directives obediently in a "nonpolitical" way. In a detailed critique of the "classical" model, Nakamura and Smallwood cite a large number of research investigations indicating that the process of implementation often does not un-

fold in a sequential "unidirectional" fashion such that policy formulation precedes policy implementation (e.g., Bardach; McLaughlin; Pressman & Wildavsky; Radin; Rein & Rabinovitz; Van Meter & Van Horn).

All the studies they cite emphasize limitations of the power of policymakers at the top who supposedly run things. For example:

> McLaughlin emphasized a reciprocal process of "mutual adaptation" between policy makers and implementors; Bardach classified and analyzed a wide variety of "games" that implementors can play to impede, frustrate, and to subvert policy; and Radin's case study depicted the political intrigue that can surround attempts to implement specific policies . . . . After reviewing this shift in emphasis away from policy makers and toward policy implementors, one might even suspect that the "classical" model had been turned upside-down, which is precisely what M.I.T. political scientist Michael Lipsky suggests. . . . According to Lipsky, "There are many contexts in which . . . policy is effectively 'made' by the people who implement it." Each of these recent studies has produced a more circular view of the policy process. This process appears to be characterized by a fluid and reciprocal series of interrelationships between different groups of actors rather than a straight-line "classical" hierarchy that points directly from the top to the bottom. (Nakamura & Smallwood, pp. 18-19)

The circular rather than linear view of the sequence, as these authors describe it, calls attention to feedback loops between policy formation and implementation. Feedback comes not only from implementers but also from other evaluators, some of whom are likely to be interested parties who are self-appointed monitors. As Lindblom (p. 4) says, "one group's solution becomes another group's problem." He points out, as an example, that if the federal government comes out with a new economic policy that raises the prices of agricultural products, it solves the farmers' problem but evokes protests from consumer groups.

Social scientists who pursue the full implications of the feedback concept find themselves rediscovering the virtues of representative democracy. Of particular interest here are the implications for effective leadership that can be discerned when we consider the change from a linear to a circular conception of policy formation in conjunction with the constraints model.

One obvious implication is that innovative leadership with regard to introducing policy changes is not limited to top-level management. It can sometimes come from the bottom of the organization, from persons who have not been assigned any authority at all to formulate policy. We have seen that the constraints model is applicable to lower-level administrators, provided that their decisionmaking behavior can be observed sufficiently to enable their procedural strategy to be diagnosed.

For any new policy directive that comes down from the top, implementers at all levels of the organization have to choose whether to carry it out as they think it is intended, to ignore it, or to modify it in one way or another. The constraints model, as stated earlier, is directly applicable when lower- or middle-level personnel function as innovative leaders either by implementing an official policy in a way that changes it or by introducing new practices to fill in policy gaps, which enable them to cope with recurrent problems that had been ignored by the official leaders at the top. The constraints model also indicates the conditions under which people at any level in the hierarchy who engage in innovative decisionmaking will use a vigilant problem-solving strategy or one or another of the simplistic strategies, and the consequences of these alternative strategies.

The feedback type of model of organizational power, when combined with the constraints model, also has major implications for the leadership role of the chief executive officer and of other top-level powerholders. Consider, for example, the large number of requirements that top-level policy planners need to take into account in order to promote satisfactory implementation. Rein and Rabinovitz point out that in addition to making sure that a policy will meet legal requirements and will be properly understood and intellectually defensible (in terms of institutional maintenance, protection, and growth), effective policy planners must make sure that it is administratively feasible, that it does not violate any organizational norms, and that it will "attract agreement among contending influential parties who have a stake in the outcome" (p. 315). These implementation requirements always need to be met in addition to whatever other requirements pertain to the problems that the policy planners are trying to solve. The likelihood that all the various requirements will be taken into account sufficiently to yield a high-quality decision, according to the constraints model, depends partly upon whether or not the policy planners adopt a vigilant problem-solving approach.

Effective leadership requires policymakers, especially those functioning as crisis managers, to be responsive to feedback from implementers and others affected by any of their policy decisions. Because no organization is ever a perfect representative democracy, policymaking groups are always unrepresentative in various ways. Most often there is inadequate representation of the lower-level personnel in the organization who are expected to implement the new policy. A chief executive can at least partially overcome this deficiency by deliberately arranging to have representatives of the various groups of implementers in the group that is given the responsibility for policy planning and by paying careful attention to the information they supply about the pitfalls to be expected from attempts to implement various policy alternatives. If representation is still not complete, vigilant information search needs to be carried out by consulting with spokesmen from the various groups that will be called upon to implement the new policy.

After announcing a policy decision, a chief executive and other policymakers need to be vigilantly alert to signs that implementers are not acting in accordance with the policy or signs that the policy is not succeeding when implemented the way intended. The modification stage of policymaking in response to feedback is probably facilitated when new policies are introduced on a small scale and on a trial basis—when time permits—so as to provide ample opportunity to "debug" them before applying them full-scale across the board. Deliberately introducing a planned trial-and-error strategy of this kind would be expected to improve the quality of an organization's policy decisions and thereby increase the incidence of relatively successful outcomes, if the policymakers are able to sustain a vigilant problem-solving approach to deal with whatever setbacks and complications arise throughout the period when attempts are being made to implement each new policy.

12. For purposes of diagnosing defects in the policymaking process and taking steps to correct the defects, as specified in Hypothesis 36, the leader might benefit from having the assistance of a skilled decision process expert who is available as a consultant or as a member of the policymaking group.

    The three scenarios designated in Hypothesis 36b usually can be elicited if the chairperson or a decision process expert asks the group to discuss three questions about each course of action under consideration:

    a. If we choose this option, what is the best outcome that could be expected, on the assumption that everything goes pretty much the way we intend?

    b. If we choose this option, what is the worst outcome that could be expected, on the assumption that things do not work out the way we intend?

    c. If we choose this option, what is the most likely outcome?

    Obtaining the group's answers to these questions could be advantageous not only for exploring nonobvious consequences of the alternatives that might otherwise be overlooked, but also for developing detailed contingency plans for whichever course of action is selected. Generating the various scenarios also might be helpful occasionally in counteracting initial biases among members who are overly optimistic about what appears to be the best available course of action (by assuming the best case and not thinking about possible costs and risks) or who are overly pessimistic about it (by assuming and thinking only about the worst case).

The potentially positive and negative consequences that emerge from the group's discussion of the anticipated scenarios could form the basis for much more detailed analysis of the problems posed by a crisis, which might make the group members more open to pertinent information they had been ignoring and less preoccupied with side issues or tangential arguments. With the help of an aide who has technical skills in decision analysis, a set of decision trees might be constructed. These diagrams could show the crisis managers in schematic form the decision alternatives and their probable consequences with some indications of probability estimates for each of the possible outcomes. As Behn and Vaupel point out in their book on how to construct and use decision trees *(Quick analysis for busy decision makers)*, "decision 'saplings' (simple decision trees with only a few branches) . . . can help even when lead time [for making a decision] is very short. Intuition still plays an important role, as it does in any decision, but it can be aided and focused by using a simple decision sapling to concentrate one's analytical and intuitive energies on the essence of the dilemma" (p. 6).

13. The decisional balance sheet procedure designated by Hypothesis 36c and the research on its effectiveness have been described by Janis and Mann and by Wheeler and Janis. The procedure can be introduced by a leader or by a decision process expert simply by asking one of the members of the group to prepare a first draft of a grid with a separate row for each alternative and with separate columns for expected positive consequences and expected negative consequences—that is, costs and risks. (These columns can be subdivided into high-, moderate-, and low-probability consequences.) The first draft of the grid can be presented to the group on a large blackboard or screen, with plenty of blank spaces left to be filled in. The leader can then ask the group to examine each alternative in detail, filling in additional entries of pros and cons. The entries in the initial balance sheet grid and the new ones to be added by the group could include positive and negative consequences for whatever vital organizational or national interests are at stake and also for broad political, economic, social, moral, and humanitarian objectives. If the leader or any member of the group believes that there are viable alternatives that have not yet been considered, additional ones can be added to the balance sheet. Their pros and cons can then be spelled out and examined in comparison with the entries for the original set of alternatives.

There are several benefits to be expected from spending the time and effort necessary for constructing a balance sheet, which makes it something more than a simple bookkeeping operation for recording what the members of the policymaking group already know. First of all, it often leads decisionmakers to become aware of gaps in their knowledge, especially about drawbacks of the most attractive alternative and the positive features of the others, which make them realize that they need to obtain more information to fill in the gaps. It also helps decisionmakers to carry out a comprehensive evaluation of the alternatives. By looking over the entries in the balance sheet grid, decisionmakers often start using a more complex set of criteria for making the final choice, rather than focusing attention mainly on only one or two criteria. When decisionmakers compare the entries for one alternative with another, it may also help them to notice possible trade-offs that could make one alternative clearly superior to the others. Then, too, the negative entries for whichever alternative is chosen increase the decisionmakers' awareness of the need to work out detailed contingency plans, so as to be prepared for meeting anticipated drawbacks.

After a group has completed constructing a balance sheet, the leader can facilitate its benefits by raising appropriate questions, such as the following:

- What information do we need that is still missing?
- Does your tentative choice based on comparing the balance sheet entries agree with your intuitive or gut feelings? If not, what considerations might we have left out?
- Is the alternative that looks best *good enough?* Does it meet all of our main objectives? If not, can we modify it in some way—maybe by partially combining it with one of the other alternatives—to satisfy the most essential requirements?
- If we feel ready to commit ourselves to the best alternative, what contingency plans would we need to make—taking account of the entries listed in the minus column for that alternative—before starting to implement our decision?

14. Part of the rationale for Hypothesis 36d is presented in Note 11 above. When following up the critiques elicited from key implementers before finalizing a policy decision, the leader might increase the effectiveness of having discussions with the key implementers by asking the policy-making group to consider questions such as these:

- Why might key implementers fail to carry out our decision the way we intend even if they are being conscientious and how could such failures be prevented?
- What objections are to be expected among key implementers when they are asked to carry out the new policy decision? For example, in what ways might they see it as administratively unfeasible, as violating organizational norms, or as failing to meet legal requirements?

- Can we modify the plans in some way to overcome the anticipated objections of key implementers?
- Who among the main implementers are most likely to oppose the policy decision—for political, ideological, or any other reasons?
- Can we create special incentives, trade-off inducements, and compromises on nonessential details for the purpose of gaining the acceptance of those key implementers who are likely to be opposed, without sacrificing the essential policy objectives?
- What indicators can we use to monitor the actions of implementers to see if they are carrying out the decision in the way we intend?

A crisis management group may fail to give careful consideration to these and related questions concerning administrative and internal political obstacles that could jeopardize the success of a new policy decision unless a leader puts such questions on the agenda. It is not likely to be an easy task for a leader to induce the group to continue deliberating about subtle obstacles to successful implementation at a time when the members are all steamed up, raring to go, especially if they are in a state of momentary elation about having ended a long period of frustrating disputation by finally arriving at what they regard as a good policy solution.

Helpful feedback from key implementers can be obtained while new policy plans are being worked out and also again when the plans are being put into operation. But psychological resistances to such feedback among top-level personnel must be overcome in order to make full use of valuable criticisms. A major source of resistance is bias toward operational personnel as being parochial in outlook, uninformed about critical strategic considerations (especially when highly classified details are being kept secret), and unable to comprehend the whole picture. Strong objections and complaints from implementers about unworkable aspects of a new set of plans are likely to be dismissed out of hand as irrelevant. Any operational manager who continues to object that plans for implementing a new policy are unworkable is likely to be told to "get on the ball" by demonstrating a "Can do!" attitude or else he will be replaced by someone who "can do."

There are also other sources of psychological resistance to valuable criticism from implementers. A few top-level policymakers may be concerned about loss of prestige from acknowledging planning errors in response to criticisms from lower-echelon personnel. Some may believe that responsiveness to such criticisms will encourage disrespectful attitudes toward superiors and undermine discipline.

From what has just been said, it is apparent that when a policymaking group is making plans for effective implementation, acts of leadership are needed to attain two subgoals: (a) to arrange to elicit feedback from key implementers; and (b) to overcome resistances within the group of top-level policymakers that inhibit them from using whatever valid criticisms are elicited.

There is also a third subgoal that is likely to be neglected unless a leader takes the appropriate initiative: to arrange to communicate the new policy decision to implementers in messages that will motivate them to carry the plans out in the way intended and to transmit potentially helpful feedback about whatever implementation problems they foresee or encounter. (See Nakamura & Smallwood, pp. 23–25.) More specifically the added tasks include preparing messages to prevent the following typical sources of failure in implementation: (a) giving garbled or ambiguous messages to the implementers that lend themselves to misinterpretations; (b) overloading the implementers with too many communications which produce so much noise that the essential message about the new policy is not grasped; (c) failing to offer incentives to insure that policy directives will be implemented properly; (d) failing to correct false impressions and expectations about how to carry out the policy decision, especially misunderstandings arising from organizational traditions and standard operating procedures; and (e) failing to specify procedures implementers should follow to supply the top-level policymakers with the information they need to find out whether the policy is being carried out as intended.

The communications might be most effective if they contain comments about obstacles to effective implementation that are already known and suggestions for overcoming those obstacles, including suggestions made by the key implementers who were consulted in advance. Instructions might also be included for monitoring the degree of success of implementation actions, along with requests for detailed accounts of new unanticipated difficulties and suggestions for overcoming them.

The leader might also take steps to see to it that the communications to implementers are designed to encourage them to use common sense and to adopt a vigilant problem-solving approach to obstacles and setbacks, rather than approaching the tasks in a routine or "muddling through" manner. Such encouragement can help overcome the implementers' resistance to new plans and increase their motivation to give full support to a policy change.

15. In order to investigate each of the twenty hypotheses concerning leadership practices, the full range of behavioral research methods could be used, including comparative case studies, correlational analyses, experiments in social psychological laboratories, and field experiments in natural settings. (See Aronson, Brewer & Carlsmith; Darley & Gilbert; Ellsworth; Jones; Weick [1985].)

One line of research—in which I am currently engaged—consists of obtaining systematic data from a series of case studies of U.S. government policy decisions, along the lines of the Herek, Janis, and Huth study described in Chapter 6. As in our earlier study, ratings are made of symptoms of defective decisionmaking and are used to subdivide the cases into three main categories—policy decisions arrived at by (1) high-quality procedures (high scores on all seven criteria); (b) medium-quality procedures (mixed scores); and, (c) low-quality procedures (low scores on the seven criteria). These categories are used in correlational analyses to see if they are related, as predicted, to the leadership practices specified by one or another of the hypotheses.

This type of correlational study, of course, suffers from a number of obvious disadvantages with regard to the lack of experimental control over the independent variables under investigation, but has the great advantage of high external validity by dealing with real-life decisions by policymakers. The opposite advantages and disadvantages are to be expected for laboratory experiments where relatively high control over the variables can be achieved but at the expense of obtaining findings that may prove to have little validity outside the laboratory. Controlled field experiments in actual organizational settings might prove to be feasible, in which case we can expect to obtain data on cause-and-effect relationships that will have a high degree of external validity. If field experiments as well as laboratory experiments, correlational studies, and comparative studies of historic decisions all point to the same general conclusion concerning the validity of a hypothesis about leadership practices that foster high-quality policy decisions, we can feel reasonably confident about the generality of the findings.

When I speak of controlled field experiments, I have in mind studies in which the investigator first introduces an experimental intervention under natural conditions with policy planners facing real decisions and, second, determines the effects of the intervention by comparing groups assigned on a random basis to the experimental and control conditions. Few such studies can be carried out because of the enormous expense in time and effort of doing field experiments in large organizations, as well as the difficulties of obtaining the necessary cooperation of policymakers.

A research strategy that may bypass most of these obstacles consists of carrying out small-scale experiments using ad hoc groups of qualified policy planners who agree to cooperate with a research team in exchange for having the opportunity to participate in policy planning on an issue about which they are deeply concerned. Working with advanced graduate students in social psychology, administrative sciences, and related fields when I was at Yale University, I developed a prototype for this type of field research: (a) announcements are made to recruit well-qualified candidates for a policy-planning group with the promise that their policy recommendations will be circulated to people who have the power to change the current unsatisfactory policy; (b) volunteers are selected with an eye to representing appropriate expertise and varying viewpoints, comparable to what is done when a government agency sets up a group to recommend policy changes; (c) the working sessions of the planning group are recorded and are unobtrusively observed by one or more members of the research team; and (d) when the group submits its final report on policy recommendations, the head of the research team carries out his or her promise by circulating it, via informal university social networks, to key persons in the local, state, or federal government who could initiate a change in policy.

If large numbers of qualified volunteers could be recruited, this prototype could be applied to set up ad hoc experimental and control groups. For example, with the help of community organizations, it might be possible to recruit retired executives to participate in making policy recommendations on controversial policies that many people would like to change—such as community policies that affect air and water pollution. Or the cooperation of management training workshops might be obtained: In exchange for the leadership training provided to the participants, workshop administrators would be asked to permit the training to be given in varied sequences so that the performance of groups chaired by a specially trained leader could be compared with those that are chaired by leaders who remain untrained until after the end of the field experiment. A large pool of volunteers or trainees would be needed so that ten or more experimental and control groups could be set up to work on the same policy issue. The seven symptoms of defective decisionmaking (pp. 32–33) could be used as dependent measures. Other measures could also be obtained to ascertain the effectiveness of the leadership practices. These might include blind ratings by well-qualified judges of the quality of the policy recommendations and the arguments for them in the "white papers" produced by each of the policy-planning groups.

If sufficient progress is made from research with ad hoc groups, perhaps ultimately the necessary arrangements could be made to test the most promising hypotheses in field experiments with groups of executives at various levels of the hierarchy in many different types of organizations, in different countries, so as to accumulate evidence on the generality of the conclusions in different organizational and national contexts.

In a comprehensive and critical review of research in the field of applied social psychology, Judith Rodin suggests that the long-standing view of field studies as merely providing opportunities to evaluate existing social psychological theory may prove to be much too narrow. "Field research in real-life settings," she says, "may become a primary domain for the *development* of social psychological theory" (p. 807). Our perspective on psychological laboratory investigations would then be profoundly altered: "We would look to the laboratory to test [and elaborate] the specific hypotheses that were extracted from the network of theory developed in applied settings rather than vice versa" (Rodin, p. 808). Taking account of this view, we can expect field studies designed to investigate systematically the leadership practices specified in the hypotheses presented in this chapter, all of which were derived from the constraints model to lead to fresh discoveries—for example, evidence of hitherto unsuspected limiting conditions and moderating variables that enter into interaction effects. Ultimately such discoveries could lead to a more comprehensive theory to explain when, how, and why leaders are effective in promoting sound policymaking and crisis management.

Sources

CHAPTER 1. ORDER OUT OF THEORETICAL CHAOS?

PAGE

6 "because organizations . . . few years": Starbuck (1983), p. 91.

6 Survival rates of business firms and other nongovernmental organizations: Pfeffer (1985), p. 416. See also Aldrich.

6 "an organization's success . . . attract": Fiedler, p. 1. Italics added.

7 High rate of bankruptcy: Donaldson & Lorsch, pp. 131–32.

9 "an ecological Armageddon": Heilbroner, p. 154.

9 "as we breach . . . future": Heilbroner, pp. 132–33.

9 "the eventual . . . governments": Heilbroner, p. 39.

10 "A conviction . . . success": Bevan, p. 1307.

11 "to mobilize . . . perspectives": Hamburg, D. Quoted in Kalvern & Russell, p. 1.

13 "there is as yet . . . causation"; "no one . . . decisionmaking"; "offers . . . involved": Lebow (1981), p. 102.

13 Accounts of obstacles to innovative policymaking and evidence on organizational constraints: For example, George (1980); Hackman, Lawler, & Porter; Halperin; Janis (1982a); Janis & Mann; Johnson; Pennings; Simon (1976).

15 Choice based primarily on "acceptability": George (1980); Tetlock (1985).

16 "ever-present constraints . . . policy": George (1980), p. 1.

17 "the search . . . questions": George (1980), p. 2.

17 Internal constraints on problem solving: See Simon (1976).

18 "extraneous . . . interest": George (1980), p. 3.

18 "to cope . . . time to time": George (1980), p. 4.

19 Different levels of analysis: See Tetlock (in press).

CHAPTER 2. COGNITIVE DECISION RULES

PAGE

29 Other cognitive limitations: For a detailed analysis see Steinbruner (1974). The lack of a valid way to combine values into a single utility criterion, along with other cognitive limitations, is discussed by March & Simon.

30 "rational" . . . "shortsighted": Black, p. 48.

30 Seven procedural criteria: Janis & Mann, pp. 10–14.

34 McNamara had eight extra minutes to do his homework: Cooper.

34 "a new . . . follow them"; "that more . . . new situations": Simon (1976), p. 66.

35 In November 1961 President Kennedy made a very quick decision to deal with the Dominican Republic crisis: Draper; Martin; Schlesinger, p. 771.

35 Interview with former Cuban government official: Maitland-Werner, L., High Cuban defector speaks out, denouncing Castro as "impulsive." *New York Times,* Nov. 19, 1984, pp. A1 and A60.

36 "activity trap": Odiorne. Commenting on Odiorne's use of the term, Hollander (1978), p. 122, says it can be applied whenever leaders are so busy with daily tasks and routines that they are "kept from looking ahead to foresee the effects of their actions."

37 "bounded" or "limited rationality": Simon (1976), p. xxxiii.

37 For the way historical analogies are commonly used, see Neustadt & May; Tetlock & McGuire.

37 The example of President Truman's analogy: Truman, vol. 2, pp. 332–33.

37 "A serious look . . . well": Neustadt & May, p. 45.

38 "A switch . . . within another": Wheeler (1986), p. 7.

38 Availability: Tversky & Kahneman (1973). See also Nisbett & Ross; S. E. Taylor.

40 "incremental change" and "muddling through": Lindblom & Braybrooke. See also Pfeffer (1985).

40 Lobbyists provide persuasive briefings: Bauer, de Sola Pool, & Dexter; Wahlke, Eulau, Buchanan, & Ferguson.

41 "They . . . without them": Quoted by Lindblom, p. 88, from Wahlke et al., p. 338.

42 "an unprecedented step . . . with Israel": Haig, pp. 338–39.

42 "This new . . . words"; "my thoughts . . . Presidency": Haig, p. 339.

43 Cognitive heuristics: For summaries and critical reviews of the extensive research on this topic, see Abelson & Levi; George (1980); Kahneman, Slovic, & Tversky; Nisbett & Ross; Pennings.

44 Simple decision rules described by George: George (1980), pp. 187ff.

44 "can be . . . policy": George (1980), p. 187.

CHAPTER 3. AFFILIATIVE DECISION RULES

PAGE

45 Policy makers seek solutions that will not adversely affect their relationship with "important" others in the organization and that will not be opposed by implementers: See George (1980); Katz & Kahn; Selznick; Vroom & Jago.

47 "those who differ . . . squarely posed": David Stockman, White House budget director in the Reagan administration, quoted in Higbee, A., American topics. *International Herald Tribune,* Sept. 8, 1986, p. 3.

47 "Where I went . . . Commie, you know": Robert C. McFarlane, quoted in *Newsweek,* May 25, 1987, p. 19.

48 Executives play it safe to be "effective": See Reedy; Thomson.

48 Bureaucratic politics discussed by social scientists: See, for example, Allison & Halperin; Halperin; Johnson; Pressman & Wildavsky.

52 "like clerks . . . document": Auletta (1985a), p. 62.

53 "Wall Street's . . . Express": Auletta (1985a), p. 29.

53 "the fears . . . might be remembered": Auletta (1985a), p. 92.

53 "was intent on revenge": Auletta (1985b), p. 40.

54 "people . . . to hear": Geneen, p. 1.

55 Well-known phenomena of power struggles: See Bacharach & Lawler; Halperin; Pfeffer (1985); Yates.

55 Win-lose fighting orientation: See Argyris; Deutsch; Pressman & Wildavsky.

56 Rigging apparent consensus and legitimacy: See Argyris & Schon; Etheredge (1985); Halperin.

56 Prior research on "groupthink": Janis (1982a, 1982b). See also Tetlock (1979).

58 Symptoms of "groupthink" noted in the Watergate coverup: Green & Conolley; Raven; Raven & Rubin.

58 Detailed analysis of unedited Nixon tapes: Janis (1982a).

58 Comparison of groupthink-dominated decisions with two well-thought-out decisions—Cuban missile crisis and Marshall Plan: Janis (1982a).

61 "Although some . . . by surprise": Starbuck (1983), p. 92.

62 "homogeneous . . . adaptation and survival": Ouchi & Price, p. 574.

62 Other observers of Japanese business firms: For example, Golden; Lambert.

62 "the fear . . . unquestioned": Lambert, p. 41.

CHAPTER 4. SELF-SERVING AND EMOTIVE RULES

PAGE

66 Self-serving motives can play a determining role in policymaking: See Etheredge (1978); Geis & Stotland. See also discussions of conflict of interest in references on role conflict—for example, Katz & Kahn; Merton; Sarbin & Allen; Stryker & Statham.

67 Executives' decisions to engineer a "leveraged buy out" or to pay "greenmail" are often attributable to self-serving motives: Adams, W., & Brock, J. W. An Allegis syndrome: The hidden costs of failed mergers. *New York Times,* June 21, 1987, p. F-3.

68 "in many instances . . . prestige": Lamb, p. 59.

68 "personal things . . . imagined"; "No person's . . . in session": Carpenter, pp. 1218–19.

70 "a recurrent . . . on his hands"; "did fear . . . own life": Hartmann, p. 269.

70 "If anything . . . with myself": Hartmann, p. 268.

70 "so fed up . . . bold stroke": Hartmann, p. 269.

70 "impatient streak"; "fed up"; "bold . . . action"; "Every so often . . . *'Wham!' The hell with the consequences'':* Hartmann, pp. 269–71. Italics added.

70 "a lesson . . . inadequate guides": Hartmann, pp. 270–71.

73 "tit-for-tat" principle: See Axelrod (1984).

75 "complained . . . betrayed him' '': Hoopes (1986), p. 30.

76 The "can do!" rule, which is sometimes used in circumstances evoking emotional reactions of apprehensiveness: Janis (1985).

76 "The analyst . . . flights a year": Boffey, P. M. Analyst who gave shuttle warning faults 'Gung-Ho, Can Do' attitude. *New York Times,* Feb. 14, 1986, p. B4.

77 For the considerable body of evidence on effects of emotional stress, see Janis & Mann; Lazarus & Folkman.

81 "a basically serial . . . opportunities": Simon (1967), p. 39.

CHAPTER 5. AN UNCOMMON STRATEGY: VIGILANT PROBLEM SOLVING

PAGE

93 "the *absence* . . . conflicts": Zeleny, p. 358.

93 "Making . . . the 'givens' '': Zeleny, p. 340.

93 "More information . . . decisionmaking": Zeleny, p. 359. Italics added.

95 "In the hands . . . not muddling": Quinn, p. 17.

96 A "sophisticated . . . incrementalism": George (1980), p. 42.

96 "people . . . neglected or [amplified]": Kahneman & Tversky, p. 283.

98 "ideas . . . public policy"; "out of the gunfire . . . of them"; "ideology . . . that hurt": Lindblom, pp. 38–39.

98 On cognitive schemas forming the policymakers' "mind-set" and functioning as a filter for processing information, see Fiske & Taylor; George (1980); Jervis (1976, 1982); Kelley; McGuire (1985); Markus & Zajonc. Examples of the biasing effects of ideological assumptions, stereotypes, and operational codes of superpower leaders on their assessments of political-military crises, which led to miscalculated escalation, are presented in case studies by Jervis, Lebow & Stein; also by Lebow (1987). For insightful analyses of conceptual errors that enter into the arms race and that may pose the danger of nuclear war, see Deutsch; Lebow (1987); Tetlock (1983b); Tetlock & McGuire; White (1984, 1986).

99 Variations in degree of ideological consensus of a group is likely to affect the way the group functions: See R. I. Hall; Hogarth, Michaud, & Mery; Weick (1979).

100 Sadat was viewed by Kissinger as a "weak, ineffectual leader": Kissinger, p. 215.

100 Kissinger privately labeled Sadat "a fool"; "a clown"; "a buffoon . . . [making] empty talk": Golan, pp. 215–16.

101 The *Pentagon Papers* contrast MacNamara's transformation with the Joint Chiefs, the President, and others who remained unchanged: Sheehan et al., pp. 510–16, 540–41.

102 "an advocate . . . air power": Sheehan et al., p. 531.

102 "fast shuffle"; "would go . . . in silence": Hoopes (1969), p. 91.

102 Clifford, "a dependable hawk," became the sole advocate of de-escalation: Cooper; Hoopes (1969).

104 Evidence from psychological research on conditions under which people modify their cognitive schemas: See Brown; Fiske & Taylor; Jones; Kelley; Kreitler & Kreitler; Markus & Zajonc; Nisbett & Ross.

104 "belief . . . processing": Tetlock (1985), p. 318.

106 "We will . . . oblivious": Fiske & Taylor, p. 283.

108 "has always . . . very rare": Thornton Bradshaw quoted by McClintock, p. 48.

110 The elimination-by-aspects approach: Tversky. For a brief summary of the approach, see Janis & Mann, pp. 31–32.

113 The tendency of executives to delegate to subordinates the problems judged to be of minor importance: See Vroom & Jago.

117 Case study of the development of the Marshall Plan in 1947: Janis (1982a), pp. 159–72.

CHAPTER 6. ARE THE MAIN ASSUMPTIONS ABOUT PROCESS AND OUTCOME WARRANTED?

PAGE

120 The position that vigilant problem solving increases the likelihood of desirable outcomes is in line with the views of a number of social scientists: See, for example, Etzioni (1968); George (1980); Lawrence; Lebow (1981), Neustadt & May.

121 Skepticism among social scientists about whether a "rational" approach is used often enough to make any difference: See the review of decisionmaking theories by Abelson & Levi.

124 Defective handling of the U-2 incident by Eisenhower and the planning of the Bay of Pigs invasion by Kennedy: See Blanchard; Hoopes (1973); Janis (1982a).

130 "other things . . . 'good' outcomes"; "that option . . . loss"; "Those who recommend . . . case": Stein & Tanter, p. 8.

132 "the myth of organizational choice": March, p. 233.

132 "role-expectations . . . commitments"; "after having . . . making it": March & Olson, pp. 10–11.

CHAPTER 7. THE CONSTRAINTS MODEL OF POLICYMAKING PROCESSES

PAGE

139 "few notions . . . some of the time": Kinder & Weiss, p. 717.

141 "unstressful": Janis & Mann.

141 "mindless" decisionmaking: See Langer.

142 "there is a paucity . . . granted": Abelson & Levi, p. 271.

142 "one that . . . organization"; "a well-reasoned . . . goals": Vroom & Jago, p. 20.

143 "definition of the situation"; "influence . . . processing": George (1979), p. 102.

143 Discrepancy between what *is* and what *should be:* Abelson & Levi, p. 270.

144 Discrepancy between what *is* and what is *tolerable:* See Donaldson & Lorsch, p. 162.

144 Judgments of importance of a new problem based on estimates of how many people in the organization might be affected: See Vroom & Jago.

144 Judgments of importance of a new problem influenced by total number

of problems already under consideration: See Abelson & Ɪvi; Mintzberg, Raisinghani, & Thoret.

145 In 1979, President Carter and his advisors were ꞏoccupied with the Salt II treaty and other problems, which made the threat of overthrow of the Shah of Iran seem comparatively unimportant: See Brzezinski; Sick.

145 Studies of community disasters indicate that when threats build up gradually, they are not taken as seriously as when they occur precipitately: See Fritz & Marks; Janis (1962).

146 "non-routine . . . alliances": George (1979), p. 110.

147 The availability heuristic: See Tversky & Kahneman (1973); Slovic & Fischhoff.

147 Psychological studies of how and when people react to advance warnings of community dangers: See Goldberger & Breznitz; Janis (1962); Janis & Mann; Lazarus & Folkman; Slovic & Fischhoff; Slovic, Fischhoff, & Lichtenstein (1985).

147 "the paramount issues . . . *control*"; "use coping strategies . . . implications": Lazarus & Folkman, p. 147.

153 Case studies of effects of severe stress during international crises: Lebow (1981).

160 Bureaucratic politics and power struggles: For references see p. 345, sources for pp. 48 and 55 in Chapter 3.

161 President Nixon's emotional bias against Mrs. Gandhi resulting from her disagreeable behavior toward him: See D. K. Hall, pp. 179–80.

162 "participation . . . decision making"; "fall within . . . to act": Vroom & Jago, p. 31.

164 Elimination of options with "crippling objections": See Etzioni (1986).

165 The main functions of scientific explanations: See Braithwaite; Kaplan.

CHAPTER 8. VALUES AND LIMITATIONS OF THE CONSTRAINTS MODEL

PAGE

172 Social scientists' critiques of analytic problem solving: E.g., Lindblom; March; Nakamura & Smallwood; Nelson; Starbuck (1983, 1985).

173 Four shortcomings of analytic methods; Lindblom, pp. 19ff.

174 "when scientific . . . improvisations"; "step by step . . . entirety": Lindblom, p. 35.

174 "ways . . . opponent": Lindblom, p. 26.

174 "interactive . . . on their own": Lindblom & Cohen, p. 26.

178 "trading . . . adjustments": Lindblom, pp. 54–55.

178 "hardball politics" players: See Etheredge (1985).

179 "Various participants . . . roles": Lindblom, p. 28.

179 Prescriptions for effective negotiations by leading experts on conflict resolution: E.g., Bazerman & Lewicki; Fisher & Ury; Neale & Bazerman; Nierenberg; Pruitt & Rubin.

179 "replacing . . . negotiating": Nierenberg, p. xii.

181 Policymaking hampered by power struggles: For references see p. 345, sources for pp. 48 and 55 in Chapter 3.

182 "central steersman . . . rudder"; "the deliberations . . . go through"; "policies bubble up . . . scrutiny": Nelson, pp. 33–34.

184 Evidence that John Dean shifted from a simplistic to a vigilant problem-solving strategy: See Janis (1982a), pp. 214–41.

185 "Dean shifted . . . consequence": Haldeman, p. 317.

188 "guided . . . decision": Etzioni (1986), p. 8.

189 "Commitment" as a constraint: See Abelson & Levi; Festinger; Janis & Mann; Jervis; Kiesler; McGuire (1985).

189 President Johnson's "frozen" commitment to defeat Communists in Vietnam: See Halberstam; Hoopes (1969); Janis (1982a); Reedy; Thomson.

191 "personally thwarted"; "reacted with fury . . . invasion": Parmet, p. 485.

191 "shocked"; "Outside . . . in the White House": Adams, p. 256.

191 "hurt feelings"; "wrought up . . . events": Adams, p. 260.

191 "irritated . . . affair"; "was in a mood . . . betrayed": Guhin, pp. 291–92.

193 President Eisenhower's harsh handling of England and France following the Suez crisis, and its consequences: See Gerson, pp. 297ff; Guhin, pp. 292ff; Parmet, pp. 485–87.

195 "my concern . . . Teheran": Brzezinski, p. 488.

195 A high-level military review group concluded that flaws could have been prevented: Holloway Review Group Report, cited by Middleton; Ryan; Sick.

198 "the bomb . . . end of the war": Truman (1955), p. 87.

198 "a master card in our hand": Henry L. Stimson quoted by Feis, p. 80.

198 Analysts suggest A-bomb use was expected to help contain the Soviet Union: Daniels, p. 266; Feis, p. 80; Mee, p. 16; Messer; Wyden, p. 131.

198 President Truman and his advisors were not interested in U.S. intelligence reports on Japanese leaders' readiness to surrender without using

A-bombs: Alperovitz, G. Hiroshima remembered: The U. S. was wrong. *New York Times,* August 4, 1985, p. E21; see also Messer.

CHAPTER 9. WHO WILL BE GOOD POLICYMAKERS AND WHO WILL NOT? HYPOTHESES ABOUT PERSONALITY DIFFERENCES DERIVED FROM THE CONSTRAINTS MODEL

PAGE

204 Most of the personality variables are familiar ones discussed in personality textbooks and in reviews of research on emotional disorders and other areas of personality research: See, for example, Bass; Block; Coelho, Hamburg, & Adams; Elms; Greenstein (1975); Greenstein & Lerner; Singer; Smith (1969).

205 "personality differences . . . force": Elms, p. 83, italics added.

211 Whistleblowers are often severely punished: See Peters & Branch; Weisbond & Franck.

215 Factor analysis data on chronic lack of conscientiousness reported by McCrae and Costa (1984, 1986a) could be interpreted as indicating that this attribute, like most other personality predispositions, is in many cases a characterological defect that is present right from the outset of the person's career. Nevertheless, in a substantial number of cases, chronic lack of conscientiousness might develop as a result of long working hours, chronic emotional stress from clashes with clients or with competitive members of the organization, and other detrimental factors in the work environment that can create a chronic condition of "burnout." See Maslach for an account of the "burnout" syndrome that has been observed in many different professional fields.

222 "psychopathic personality": See Hare; Mensh; Masterson.

224 Personality resources that act as a buffer to moderate impact of psychological stress: See Brown; Gentry & Kobasa; Kobasa & Puccetti.

227 A pluralistic methodological approach to personality research and the varieties of measures that can be used: See, for example, Block; Buss & Craik; Cattell; Craik; Greenstein (1975); Mischel; Singer; Snyder & Ickes.

CHAPTER 10. EFFECTIVE LEADERSHIP PRACTICES: ADDITIONAL HYPOTHESES DERIVED FROM THE CONSTRAINTS MODEL

PAGE

243 The tactic of *fractionating* a complex set of problems into smaller subproblems: For a detailed description of this tactic, see Fisher & Ury.

245 The step specified in Hypothesis 24b of calling attention to the full range of powerful groups and constituencies to which the policymaking group is accountable takes into consideration the positive value of making accountability salient: See Tetlock (1985).

251 Announcing that reports on meetings will be circulated to powerholders and constituencies to whom the policymaking group is accountable, as specified in Hypothesis 30b, again takes into consideration the positive value of making accountability salient: See Tetlock (1985). A related consideration is suggested by social psychological research reported by Zimbardo. His findings indicate that group members display more impulse gratification and less socially responsible behavior under conditions where they expect that all of them will remain anonymous or that the responsibility for the group's action will be diffused, which weakens each person's inner controls based on guilt and shame. It seems likely that this tendency will be counteracted by making the participants realize that interested parties to whom the group is accountable will be able to scrutinize reports about the group's deliberations and can find out who said what about a dubious (self-serving) course of action.

253 Defective coping patterns of defensive avoidance and hypervigilance evoked by severe stress during an acute crisis: See pp. 79–80 for a summary based on Janis & Mann.

255 Evidence from social psychological research repeatedly indicates the value of emphasizing reasonable grounds for *expecting each major threat to be manageable,* as specified in Hypothesis 34b: See, for example, Feshbach; Leventhal (1968, 1973); Leventhal, Singer & Jones; Rodin; Rogers & Mewborn.

258 A military mobilization or alert to demonstrate resolve runs the risk of being misperceived as a direct threat requiring military countermoves: See Jervis (1976); White (1984).

259 Historical record of international conflicts indicates that it is easier for leaders of rival nations to agree on a settlement before either side has committed itself to military action: See Gottfried & Blair; Blechman & Kaplan.

259 Motivational factors that make for refusal of national leaders to back down after they have become committed to military action: See Frank (1982, 1986).

259 Experts on command and control emphasize difficulties in controlling implementers in local command posts when military forces are brought to a state of high alert: See Blair; Bracken; Lebow (1987); Steinbruner (1987).

References

Abelson, R. P., & Levi, A. (1985). Decision-making and decision theory. In G. Lindzey & E. Aronson (Eds.), *The handbook of social psychology* (3rd ed., Vol. 1). New York: Random House.

Adams, S. (1961). *Firsthand report: The story of the Eisenhower administration.* New York: Harpers.

Aldrich, H. E. (1979). *Organizations and environments.* Englewood Cliffs, N.J.: Prentice-Hall.

Allison, G. T. (1971). *Essence of decision: Explaining the Cuban missile crisis.* Boston: Little, Brown.

Allison, G. T., & Halperin, M. H. (1972). Bureaucratic politics: A paradigm and some policy implications. *World Politics, 24* (supplement), 40–79.

Amelang, M., & Borkenau, P. (1982). Über die factorielle Struktur und externe Validität einiger Fragebogen-Skalen zur Erfassung von Dimensionen der Extraversion und emotionalen Labilität [On the factor structure and external validity of some questionnaire scales measuring dimensions of extraversion and neuroticism]. *Zeitschrift für Differentielle und Diagnostische Psychologie, 3,* 119–46.

Appley, M., & Trumbull, I. (Eds.). (1967). *Psychological stress: Issues in research.* New York: Appleton-Century-Crofts.

Argyris, C. (1973). Some limits of national man organizational theory. *Public Administration Review, 33,* 253–67.

Argyris, C., & Schön, D. (1974). *Theory in practice.* San Francisco: Jossey-Bass.

Arnold, M. (1960). *Emotions and personality.* New York: Columbia University Press.

Arnold, M. (Ed.). (1970). *The Loyola symposium: Feelings and emotion.* New York: Academic Press.

Aronson, E., Brewer, M., & Carlsmith, J. M. (1985). Experimentation in social psychology. In G. Lindzey & E. Aronson (Eds.), *The handbook of social psychology* (3rd ed., Vol. 1). New York: Random House.

Auletta, K. (1985a). The fall of Lehman Brothers: Part 1. Power, greed, and glory on Wall Street. *The New York Times Magazine,* Feb. 17, 1985, pp. 29–36, 40, 43, 59–61, 92.

Auletta, K. (1985b). The fall of Lehman Brothers: Part 2. The men, the money, the merger. *The New York Times Magazine,* Feb. 24, 1985, pp. 36–42, 48, 54–58, 70–71.

Auletta, K. (1986). *Greed and glory on Wall Street: The fall of the House of Lehman.* New York: Random House.

Axelrod, R. (Ed.). (1976). *Structure of decision: The cognitive maps of political elites.* Princeton: Princeton University Press.

Axelrod, R. (1984). *The evolution of cooperation.* New York: Basic Books.

Bacharach, S. B., & Lawler, E. J. (1980). *Power and politics in organizations: The social psychology of conflict, coalitions, and bargaining.* San Francisco: Jossey-Bass.

Baker, G. W., & Chapman, D. W. (Eds.). (1962). *Man and society in disaster.* New York: Basic Books.

Bandura, A. (1977). Self efficacy: Toward a unified theory of behavior change. *Psychological Review, 84,* 191–215.

Bardach, E. (1977). *The implementation game: What happens after a bill becomes a law.* Cambridge, Mass.: MIT Press.

Baron, J. (1985). *Rationality and intelligence.* New York: Cambridge University Press.

Barrett, D. M. (1988). Political and personal intimates as advisers: The mythology of Lyndon Johnson and the 1965 decision to enter the Vietnam War. Paper presented at the April 1988 meeting of the Midwest Political Science Association.

Barton, A. H. (1963). *Social organization under stress: A sociological review of disaster studies.* Washington, D.C.: Committee on Disaster Studies, National Academy of Sciences–National Research Council.

Barzini, L. (1970). *The Italians.* New York: Atheneum.

Bass, B. M. (1981). *Stogdill's handbook of leadership: A survey of theory and research* (rev. ed). New York: Free Press.

Bauer, R. A., de Sola Pool, I., & Dexter, L. A. (1963). *American business and public policy.* New York: Atherton Press.

Bazerman, M. H. & Lewicki, R. J. (Eds.). (1983). *Negotiating in organizations.* Beverly Hills, Calif.: Sage.

Behn, R. D., & Vaupel, J. W. (1982). *Quick analysis for busy decision makers.* New York: Basic Books.

Betts, R. K. (1978). Analysis, war, and decision: Why intelligence failures are inevitable. *World Politics, 31,* 61–89.

Betts, R. K. (1982). *Surprise attack.* Washington, D.C.: Brookings.

Bevan, W. J. (1982). A sermon of sorts in three plus parts. *American Psychologist, 37,* 1303-22.

Black, M. (1984). Making intelligent choices: How useful is decision theory? *Bulletin of the American Academy of Arts and Sciences, 38,* 30-49.

Blair, B. G. (1987). Alerting in crisis and conventional war. In A. B. Carter, J. D. Steinbruner, & C. A. Zracket (Eds.), *Managing nuclear operations.* Washington, D.C.: Brookings.

Blanchard, W. H. (1978). *Aggression American style.* Santa Monica, Calif.: Goodyear.

Blechman, B. M., & Kaplan, S. S. (1978). *Force without war: U.S. armed forces as a political instrument.* Washington, D.C.: Brookings.

Block, J. (1981). Some enduring and consequential structures of personality. In A. I. Rabin (Ed.), *Further explorations in personality.* New York: Wiley-Interscience.

Bracken, P. (1983). *Command and control of nuclear forces.* New Haven: Yale University Press.

Braithwaite, R. B. (1956). *Scientific explanation.* Cambridge, England: Cambridge University Press.

Brecher, M. (1980). *Decisions in crisis: Israel 1967 and 1973.* Berkeley: University of California Press.

Breznitz, S. (Ed.). (1983). *The denial of stress.* New York: International Universities Press.

Brown, R. (1986). *Social psychology: The second edition.* New York: Free Press.

Brzezinski, Z. (1983). *Power and principle: Memoirs of the national security advisor, 1977-1981.* New York: Farrar, Straus, Giroux.

Burns, J. M. (1978). *Leadership.* New York: Harper & Row.

Burns, J. M. (1984). *The power to lead: The crisis of the American presidency.* New York: Simon & Schuster.

Burns, R. D. (Ed.). (1983). *Guide to American foreign relations since 1700.* Santa Barbara, Calif.: ABC-Clio.

Buss, D. M., & Craik, K. H. (1984). Acts, dispositions, and personality. In B. A. Maher & W. B. Maher (Eds.), *Progress in experimental personality research: Normal personality processes.* New York: Academic Press.

Butterworth, R. (1976). *Managing interstate conflict 1945-1975.* Pittsburgh: University Center for International Studies.

Carpenter, P. B. (1983). The personal insights of a legislator/psychologist. *American Psychologist, 38,* 1216-19.

Cattell, R. B. (1946). *Description and measurement of personality.* New York: World Book Co.

Coelho, G. V., Hamburg, D. A., & Adams, J. E. (Eds.). 1974. *Coping and adaptation.* New York: Basic Books.

Cooper, C. L. (1970). *The lost crusade.* New York: Dodd, Mead.

Costa, P. T., Jr., & McCrae, R. R. (1985). *The NEO Personality Inventory manual.* Odessa, Fla.: Psychological Assessment Resources.

Costa, P. T., Jr., McCrae, R. R., & Holland, J. L. (1984). Personality and vocational interests in an adult sample. *Journal of Applied Psychology, 69,* 390–400.

Craik, K. H. (1986). Personality research methods: An historical perspective. *Journal of Personality, 54,* 18–51.

Crowne, D. P., & Marlowe, D. (1964). *The approval motive.* New York: Wiley.

Daniels, J. (1950). *The man of independence.* New York: Lippincott.

Darley, J. M., & Gilbert, D. T. (1985). Social psychological aspects of environmental psychology. In G. Lindzey & E. Aronson (Eds.), *The handbook of social psychology* (3rd ed., Vol. 2). New York: Random House.

Dean, J. W. (1976). *Blind ambition.* New York: Simon & Schuster.

Deutsch, M. (1983). The prevention of World War III: A psychological perspective. *Political Psychology, 4,* 3–32.

Digman, J. M., & Takemoto-Chock, N. K. (1981). Factors in the natural language of personality: Re-analysis, comparison, and interpretation of six major studies. *Multivariate Behavioral Research, 16,* 149–70.

Donaldson, G., & Lorsch, J. W. (1983). *Decision making at the top: The shaping of strategic direction.* New York: Basic Books.

Donovan, R. J. (1984). Ike: How great a president? (Review of S. E. Ambrose [1984], *Eisenhower. Vol. 2. The President.* New York: Simon & Schuster.) *The New York Times Book Review,* Sept. 9, 1984, p. 1 and pp. 46–47.

Downs, A. (1967). *Inside bureaucracy.* Boston: Little, Brown.

Dowty, A. (1974). *Middle East crisis: U.S. decision making in 1958, 1970, and 1973.* Berkeley: University of California Press.

Draper, T. (1967). *The abuse of power.* New York: Viking Press.

Dreyfus, H. L., & Dreyfus, S. (1986). *Mind over machine: The power of human intuition and expertise in the era of the computer.* New York: Free Press.

Edwards, W. (1954). The theory of decision making. *Psychological Bulletin, 51,* 380–417.

Einhorn, H. J., & Hogarth, R. M. (1981). Behavioral decision theory: Processes of judgment and choice. *Annual Review of Psychology, 32,* 53–88.

Ellsworth, P. C. (1977). From abstract ideas to concrete instances: Some guidelines for choosing natural research settings. *American Psychologist, 32,* 604–15.

Elms, A. C. (1976). *Personality in politics.* New York: Harcourt Brace Jovanovich.

Epstein, S. (1979). The stability of behavior: I. On predicting most of the people much of the time. *Journal of Personality and Social Psychology, 37,* 1097–1126.

Etheredge, L. S. (1978). *A world of men.* Cambridge, Mass.: MIT Press.

Etheredge, L. S. (1985). *Can governments learn?: American foreign policy and Central American revolutions.* New York: Pergamon.

Etzioni, A. (1968). *The active society.* New York: Free Press.

Etzioni, A. (1986). Mixed scanning revisited. *Public Administration Review, 46,* 8–14.

Feis, H. (1960). *Between war and peace: The Potsdam conference.* Princeton: Princeton University Press.

Feshbach, S. (1986). Implications for changing war-related attitudes. In R. K. White (Ed.), *Psychology and the prevention of nuclear war.* New York: New York University Press.

Festinger, L. (Ed.). (1964). *Conflict, decision, and dissonance.* Stanford: Stanford University Press.

Fiedler, F. E. (1970). *Leadership.* Morristown, N.J.: General Learning Press.

Fisher, R., & Ury, W. (1981). *Getting to YES.* Boston: Houghton Mifflin.

Fiske, S. T., & Taylor, S. E. (1984). *Social cognition.* Reading, Mass.: Addison-Wesley.

Frank, J. D. (1982). *Sanity and survival in the nuclear age.* New York: Random House.

Frank, J. D. (1986). The role of pride. In R. K. White (Ed.), *Psychology and the prevention of nuclear war.* New York: New York University Press.

French, J. R. P., Jr., & Raven, B. H. (1959). The bases of social power. In D. Cartwright (Ed.), *Studies in social power.* Ann Arbor: University of Michigan Press.

Fritz, C., & Marks, E. (1954). The NORC studies of human behavior in disaster. *Journal of Social Issues, 10,* 26–41.

Geis, G., & Stotland, E. (Eds.). (1980). *White-collar crime: Theory and research.* Beverly Hills, Calif.: Sage.

Geneen, H. (1985). Viewpoint: How to make winning decisions. *For members only* (American Express), Apr. 1985, pp. 1 and 4.

Gentry, W. D., Chesney, A. P., Gary, H., Hall, R. P., and Harburg, E. (1982). Habitual anger-coping styles: I. Effect on male/female blood pressure and hypertension status. *Psychosomatic Medicine, 44,* 195–202.

Gentry, W. D., & Kobasa, S. C. (1984). Social and psychological resources mediating stress-illness relationships in humans. In W. D. Gentry (Ed.), *Handbook of behavioral medicine.* New York: Guilford Press.

George, A. L. (1973). The case for multiple advocacy in making foreign policy. *American Political Science Review, 66,* 751–85.

George, A. L. (1979). The causal nexus between cognitive beliefs and decision-making behavior: The "operational code" belief system. In L. S. Falkowski (Ed.), *Psychological models in international politics.* Boulder, Colo.: Westview.

George, A. L. (1980). *Presidential decisionmaking in foreign policy: The effective use of information and advice.* Boulder, Colo.: Westview.

George, A. L., and Smoke, R. (1974). *Deterrence in American foreign policy: Theory and practice.* New York: Columbia University Press.

Gerson, L. J. (1967). John Foster Dulles. In R. H. Ferrell (Ed.), *The American Secretaries of State and their diplomacy.* New York: Cooper Square Publishers.

Gill, S. P. (1986). The paradox of prediction. *Daedalus, 115,* 17–47.

Golan, M. (1976). *The secret conversations of Henry Kissinger: Step by step diplomacy in the Middle East.* New York: Bantam.

Goldberg, L. R. (1981). Language and individual differences: The search for universals in personality lexicons. In L. Wheeler (Ed.), *Review of personality and social psychology* (Vol. 2). Beverly Hills, Calif.: Sage.

Goldberg, L. R. (1982). From ace to zombie: Some explorations in the language of personality. In C. D. Spielberger, & J. N. Butcher (Eds.), *Advances in personality assessment* (Vol. 1). Hillsdale, N.J.: Lawrence Erlbaum.

Goldberger, L., & Breznitz, S. (Eds.). (1982). *Handbook of stress.* New York: Free Press.

Golden, A. S. (1982). Groupthink in Japan Inc. *The New York Times Magazine,* Dec. 5, 1982, pp. 132–39.

Gottfried, K., & Blair, B. G. (Eds.). (1988). *Crisis stability and nuclear war.* New York: Oxford University Press.

Green, D., and Conolley, E. (1974). Groupthink and Watergate. Paper presented at the Annual Meeting of the American Psychological Association.

Greenstein, F. I. (1975). *Personality and politics.* New York: Norton.

Greenstein, F. I. (1982). *The hidden-hand presidency: Eisenhower as leader.* New York: Basic Books.

Greenstein, F. I., and Lerner, M. (Eds.). (1971). *A source book for the study of personality and politics.* Chicago: Markham.

Grinyer, P. H., & Norburn, D. (1975). Planning for exiting markets: Perceptions of executives and financial performance. *Journal of the Royal Statistical Society,* Series A *138,* 70–97.

Guhin, M. A. (1972). *John Foster Dulles: A statesman and his times.* New York: Columbia University Press.

Hackman, J. R., Lawler, E. E. III, & Porter, L. W. (Eds.). (1983). *Perspectives on behavior in organizations* (2nd ed.). New York: McGraw-Hill.

Haig, A. M., Jr. (1984). *Caveat: Realism, Reagan, and foreign policy.* New York: Macmillan.

Halberstam, D. (1969). *The best and brightest.* New York: Random House.

Haldeman, H. R. (with Di Mona, J.) (1978). *The ends of power.* New York: Dell.

Hall, D. K. (1978). The Indo-Pakistani war of 1971. In B. M. Blechman, S. S. Kaplan, & associates, *Force without war: U. S. armed forces as a political instrument.* Washington, D.C.: Brookings.

Hall, R. I. (1981). Decisionmaking in a complex organization. In G. W. England, A. R. Negandhi, & B. Wilpert (Eds.), *The functioning of complex organizations.* Cambridge, Mass.: Oelgeschlager, Gunn & Hain.

Halperin, M. H. (1974). *Bureaucratic politics and foreign policy.* Washington, D.C.: Brookings.

Hamilton, V. (1975). Socialization, anxiety and information processing: A capacity model of anxiety-induced performance. In I. G. Sarason & C. D. Spielberger (Eds.), *Stress and anxiety* (Vol. 2). New York: Wiley.

Hammond, K. R. (1972). Inductive knowing. In J. R. Royce & W. W. Rozeboom (Eds.), *The psychology of knowing.* London: Gordon & Breach.

Hammond, K. R., McClelland, G. H., & Mumpower, J. (1980). *Human judgment and decision making: Theories, methods, and procedures.* New York: Praeger.

Hare, R. D. (1970). *Psychopathy: Theory and research.* New York: Wiley.

Hartmann, R. T. (1980). *Palace politics: An inside account of the Ford years.* New York: McGraw-Hill.

Heilbroner, R. L. (1975). *An inquiry into the human prospect.* New York: Norton.

Hensley, T. R., & Griffin, G. W. (1986). Victims of groupthink: The Kent State University Board of Trustees and the 1977 gymnasium controversy. *Journal of Conflict Resolution, 30,* 497–531.

Herek, G., Janis, I. L., & Huth, P. (1987). Decisionmaking during international crises: Is quality of process related to outcome? *Journal of Conflict Resolution, 31,* 203–26.

Hermann, C. F. (1969). *Crises in foreign policy.* New York: Bobbs-Merrill.

Hogarth, R. M. (1980). *Judgment and choice: The psychology of decision.* New York: Wiley.

Hogarth, R. M., Michaud, C., & Mery, J. L. (1980). Decision behavior in urban development: A methodological approach and substantive considerations. *Acta Psychologica, 45,* 95-117.

Hollander, E. P. (1978). *Leadership dynamics: A practical guide to effective relationships.* New York: Free Press.

Hollander, E. P. (1985). Leadership and power. In G. Lindzey & E. Aronson (Eds.), *The handbook of social psychology* (3rd. ed., Vol. 2). New York: Random House.

Holsti, O. R. (1972). *Crisis escalation war.* Montreal: McGill-Queen's University Press.

Holsti, O. R., & George, A. L. (1975). The effects of stress on the performance of foreign policy makers. *Political Science Annual, 6,* 255-319.

Hoopes, T. (1969). *The limits of intervention.* New York: McKay.

Hoopes, T. (1973). *The devil and John Foster Dulles.* Boston: Little, Brown.

Hoopes, T. (1986). Moderate to a fault. (Review of P. Brendon [1986]. *Ike: His life and times.* New York: Harper & Row.) *The New York Times Book Review,* Nov. 30, 1986, pp. 29-30.

Horan, J. J. (1979). *Counseling for effective decision making: A cognitive-behavioral perspective.* North Scituate, Mass.: Duxbury Press.

Horowitz, M. (1976). *Stress response syndromes.* New York: Aronson.

Janis, I. L. (1951). *Air war and emotional stress: Psychological studies of bombing and civilian defense.* New York: McGraw-Hill.

Janis, I. L. (1958). *Psychological Stress: Psychoanalytic and behavioral studies of surgical patients.* New York: Wiley.

Janis, I. L. (1962). Psychological effects of warnings. In G. W. Baker & D. W. Chapman (Eds.), *Man and society in disaster.* New York: Basic Books.

Janis, I. L. (1971). *Stress and frustration.* New York: Harcourt Brace Jovanovich.

Janis, I. L. (1982a). *Groupthink: Psychological studies of policy decisions and fiascoes.* (Revised and enlarged edition of *Victims of groupthink* [1972].) Boston: Houghton Mifflin.

Janis, I. L. (1982b). Counteracting the adverse effects of concurrence-seeking in policy planning groups: Theory and research perspectives. In H. Brandstatter, J. Davis, & G. Stocker-Kreichgauer (Eds.), *Group decision making.* New York: Academic Press.

Janis, I. L. (1982c). Personality differences in responsiveness to counseling procedures. In I. L. Janis (Ed.), *Counseling on personal decisions: Theory and research on short-term helping relationships.* New Haven: Yale University Press.

Janis, I. L. (1982d). *Stress, attitudes, and decisions. Selected papers.* New York: Praeger.

Janis, I. L. (1985). Sources of error in strategic decision making. In J. M. Pennings (Ed.), *Organizational strategy and change.* San Francisco: Jossey-Bass.

Janis, I. L. (1986). Problems of international crisis management in the nuclear age. *Journal of Social Issues, 42,* 201–20.

Janis, I. L., & Mann, L. (1977). *Decision making: A psychological analysis of conflict, choice, and commitment.* New York: Free Press.

Jervis, R. (1976). *Perception and misperception in international politics.* Princeton: Princeton University Press.

Jervis, R. (1982). Perception and misperception in international politics: An updating of the analysis. Paper presented at the Annual Meeting of the International Society of Political Psychology, Washington, D.C., June 24–27, 1982.

Jervis, R., Lebow, R. N., & Stein, J. G. (1985). *Psychology and deterrence.* Baltimore: Johns Hopkins University Press.

Johnson, R. T. (1974). *Managing the White House: An intimate study of the presidency.* New York: Harper & Row.

Jones, E. E. (1985). Major developments in social psychology during the past five decades. In G. Lindzey & E. Aronson (Eds.), *The handbook of social psychology* (3rd ed., Vol. 1). New York: Random House.

Kahneman, D., and Tversky, A. (1979). Prospect theory: An analysis of decisions under risk. *Econometrica, 47,* 263–91.

Kahneman, D., Slovic, P., & Tversky, A. (Eds.). (1982). *Judgment under uncertainty: Heuristics and biases.* New York: Cambridge University Press.

Kalvern, J., & Russell, A. (1985). Reducing the risk of nuclear war: What can scholars do? *Carnegie Quarterly, 30,* 1–7.

Kaplan, A. (1964). *The conduct of inquiry: Methodology for behavioral science.* San Francisco: Chandler.

Katz, D., & Kahn, R. L. (1966). *The social psychology of organizations.* New York: Wiley.

Kelley, H. H. (1972). *Causal schemata and the attribution process.* Morristown, N.J.: General Learning Press.

Kiesler, C. A. (Ed.). (1971). *The psychology of commitment.* New York: Academic Press.

Killian, L. M. (1952). The significance of multiple-group membership in disaster. *American Journal of Sociology, 57,* 309–14.

Kinder, D. R., & Weiss, J. A. (1978). In lieu of rationality: Psychological perspectives on foreign policy decision making. *Journal of Conflict Resolution, 22,* 707-35.

Kissinger, H. (1982). *White House years.* Boston: Little, Brown.

Kobasa, S. C., & Puccetti, M. C. (1983). Personality and social resources in stress resistance. *Journal of Personality and Social Psychology, 45,* 839-50.

Kohut, H. (1977). *The restoration of the self.* New York: International Universities Press.

Kreitler, H., & Kreitler, S. (1976). *Cognitive orientation and behavior.* New York: Springer.

Lamb, R. B. (1987). *Running American business: Top CEOs rethink their major decisions.* New York: Basic Books.

Lambert, P. (1982). Selecting Japanese management practices for import. *Personnel Management, 14,* 3-41.

Langer, E. (1978). Rethinking the role of thought in social interaction. In J. Harvey, W. Ickes, & R. Kidd (Eds.), *New directions in attribution research.* Hillsdale, N.J.: Erlbaum.

Lasswell, H. D. (1960). *Psychopathology and politics.* New York: Viking. (Paperback edition with "Afterthoughts" of first edition. Chicago: University of Chicago Press, 1930.)

Lawrence, P. R. (1985). In defense of planning as a rational approach to change. In J. M. Pennings (Ed.), *Organizational strategy and change.* San Francisco: Jossey-Bass.

Lazarus, R. S. (1966). *Psychological stress and the coping process.* New York: McGraw-Hill.

Lazarus, R. S., & Folkman, S. (1984). *Stress, appraisal, and coping.* New York: Springer.

Lebow, R. N. (1981). *Between peace and war: The nature of international crisis.* Baltimore: Johns Hopkins University Press.

Lebow, R. N. (1987). *Nuclear crisis management: A dangerous illusion.* Ithaca, N.Y.: Cornell University Press.

Lebow, R. N. (1988). Personal communication (based on research in progress on recently declassified documents and interviews concerning the Cuban missile crisis).

Leventhal, H. (1968). Experimental studies of anti-smoking communication. In E. Borgotta & R. Evans (Eds.), *Smoking and health behavior.* Chicago: Aldine.

Leventhal, H. (1973). Changing attitudes and habits to reduce chronic risk factors. *American Journal of Cardiology, 31,* 571-80.

Leventhal, H., Singer, R., & Jones, S. (1965). Effects of fear and specificity of recommendation upon attitudes and behavior. *Journal of Personality and Social Psychology, 2,* 20–29.

Lindblom, C. E. (1980). *The policy-making process* (2nd ed.). Englewood Cliffs, N.J.: Prentice-Hall.

Lindblom, C. E., & Braybrooke, D. (1970). *A strategy of decision.* New York: Free Press.

Lindblom, C. E., & Cohen, D. K. (1979). *Usable knowledge: Social science and social problem solving.* New Haven: Yale University Press.

Lipsky, M. M. (1978). Implementation on its head. In W. D. Burnham & M. W. Weinberg (Eds.), *American politics and public policy.* Cambridge, Mass.: MIT Press.

Luce, R. D., & Raiffa, H. (1957). *Games and decisions.* New York: Wiley.

Maccoby, M. (1976). *The gamesman: The new corporate leaders.* New York: Simon & Schuster.

Maier, N. (1967). Group problem solving. *Psychological Review, 74,* 239–49.

March, J. G. (1981). Decisions in organizations and theories of choice. In A. H. Van de Ven & W. F. Joyce (Eds.), *Perspectives on organization design and behavior.* New York: Wiley.

March, J. G., & Olsen, J. P. (1976). *Ambiguity and choice in organizations.* Bergen, Norway: Universitetsforlaget.

March, J. G., & Simon, H. (1958). *Organizations.* New York: Wiley.

Markus, H., & Zajonc, R. B. (1985). The cognitive perspective in social psychology. In G. Lindzey & E. Aronson (Eds.), *The handbook of social psychology* (3rd ed., Vol. 1). New York: Random House.

Martin, J. B. (1966). *Overtaken by events.* Garden City, N.J.: Doubleday.

Maslach, C. (1982). *Burn-out: The cost of caring.* Englewood Cliffs, N.J.: Prentice-Hall.

Masterson, J. F. (1981). *The narcissistic and borderline disorders.* New York: Brunner/Mazel.

McCarthy, W. (1977). Symptoms of groupthink in the Watergate tapes: Results of a content analysis. Unpublished paper.

McClelland, D. C. (1975). *Power: The inner experience.* New York: Irvington.

McClintock, D. (1984). Life at the top: The power and pleasures of financier Felix Rohatyn. *The New York Times Magazine,* August 5, 1984, pp. 23–26 and 48–65.

McCrae, R. R., & Costa, P. T., Jr. (1984). *Emerging lives, enduring dispositions.* Boston: Little, Brown.

McCrae, R. R., & Costa, P. T., Jr. (1985). Updating Norman's "adequate taxonomy": Intelligence and personality dimensions in natural language and in questionnaires. *Journal of Personality and Social Psychology, 49,* 710–21.

McCrae, R. R., & Costa, P. T., Jr. (1986a). Clinical assessment can benefit from recent advances in personality psychology. *American Psychologist, 41,* 1001–3.

McCrae, R. R., & Costa, P. T., Jr. (1986b). Personality, coping and coping-effectiveness in an adult sample. *Journal of Personality, 54,* 385–405.

McCrae, R. R., & Costa, P. T., Jr. (in press). Validation of the five-factor model of personality across instruments and observers. *Journal of Personality and Social Psychology.*

McCrae, R. R., Costa, P. T., Jr., & Busch, C. M. (1986). Evaluating comprehensiveness in personality systems: The California Q-Set and the five factor model. *Journal of Personality, 54,* 430–46.

McGuire, W. J. (1969). The nature of attitudes and attitude change. In G. Lindzey & E. Aronson (Eds.), *The handbook of social psychology* (2nd ed., Vol. 3). Reading, Mass.: Addison-Wesley.

McGuire, W. J. (1985). Attitudes and attitude change. In G. Lindzey & E. Aronson (Eds.), *The handbook of social psychology* (3rd ed., Vol. 2, pp. 233–46). New York: Random House.

McLaughlin, M. (1976). Implementation as mutual adaptation. In W. Williams & R. Elmore (Eds.), *Social program implementation.* New York: Academic Press.

Mee, C. L., Jr. (1975). *Meeting at Potsdam.* New York: Evans.

Meichenbaum, D. (1985). *Stress inoculation training.* New York: Pergamon Press.

Mensh, I. N. (1965). Psychopathic condition, addictions, and sexual deviations. In B. B. Wolman (Ed.), *Handbook of clinical psychology.* New York: McGraw-Hill.

Merton, R. K. (1976). *Sociological ambivalence and other essays.* New York: Free Press.

Messer, R. L. (1985). New evidence on Truman's decision. *Bulletin of the Atomic Scientists, 41,* 50–56.

Middleton, D. (1981). Going the military route. *The New York Times Magazine,* May 17, 1981.

Miller, D. W., & Starr, M. K. (1967). *The structure of human decisions.* Englewood Cliffs, N.J.: Prentice-Hall.

Mintzberg, H., Raisinghani, D., & Thoret, A. (1976). The structure of unstructured decision. *Administrative Science Quarterly, 21,* 246–75.

Mischel, W. (1968). *Personality and assessment.* New York: Wiley.

Moscovici, S. (1985). Social influence and conformity. In G. Lindzey & E.

Aronson (Eds.), *The handbook of social psychology* (3rd ed., Vol. 2). New York: Random House.

Nakamura, R. T., & Smallwood, F. (1980). *The politics of policy implementation.* New York: St. Martin's.

Neale, M. A., & Bazerman, M. H. (1985). Perspectives for understanding negotiation. *Journal of Conflict Resolution, 29,* 33–55.

Nelson, R. R. (1977). *The moon and the ghetto.* New York: Norton.

Nemeth, C. (1979). The role of an active minority in intergroup relations. In W. Austin & S. Worchel (Eds.), *The social psychology of intergroup relations.* Monterey, Calif.: Brooks/Cole.

Nemeth, C. (1986). Differential contributions of majority and minority influence. *Psychological Review, 93,* 1–10, 23–32.

Neustadt, R. E., & May, E. R. (1986). *Thinking in time: The uses of history for decision makers.* New York: Free Press.

Nierenberg, G. I. (1973). *Fundamentals of negotiating.* New York: Stone-Hawthorne Books.

Nisbett, R., & Ross, L. (1980). *Human inference: Strategies and shortcomings of social judgment.* Englewood Cliffs, N.J.: Prentice-Hall.

Norman, W. T. (1963). Toward an adequate taxonomy of personality attributes: Replicated factor structure in peer nomination personality ratings. *Journal of Abnormal and Social Psychology, 66,* 574–83.

Odiorne, G. S. (1974). *Management and the activity trap.* New York: Harper & Row.

Ouchi, W. G. (1980). Markets, bureaucracies, and clans. *Administrative Science Quarterly, 25,* 129–41.

Ouchi, W. G. (1981). *Theory Z: How American business can meet the Japanese challenge.* Reading, Mass.: Addison-Wesley.

Ouchi, W. G., & Price, R. L. (1983). Hierarchies, clans, and theory Z: A new perspective on organizational development. In J. R. Hackman, E. E. Lawler III, & L. W. Porter (Eds.), *Perspectives on behavior in organizations* (rev. ed.). New York: McGraw-Hill.

Paige, G. D. (1968). *The Korean decision: June 24–30, 1950.* New York: Free Press.

Parmet, H. S. (1972). *Eisenhower and the American crusades.* New York: Macmillan.

Peabody, D., & Goldberg, L. R. (in press). Variation and invariance in personality structures: Determinants of factors derived from trait adjectives.

Pennings, J. M. (Ed.). (1985). *Organizational strategy and change.* San Francisco: Jossey-Bass.

Peters, C., & Branch, T. (1972). *Blowing the whistle*. New York: Praeger.

Pfeffer, J. (1981). *Power in organizations*. Boston: Pitman.

Pfeffer, J. (1985). Organizations and organization theory. In G. Lindzey & E. Aronson (Eds.), *The handbook of social psychology* (3rd ed., Vol. 1). New York: Random House.

Pressman, J. L., & Wildavsky, A. (1973). *Implementation*. Berkeley: University of California Press.

Pruitt, D. G., & Rubin, J. Z. (1986). *Social conflict: Escalation, stalemate, and settlement*. New York: Random House.

Quinn, J. B. (1980). *Strategies for change: Logical incrementalism*. Homewood, Ill.: Irwin.

Radin, B. A. (1977). *Implementation, change, and the federal bureaucracy*. New York: Teachers College Press.

Radloff, R., & Helmreich, R. (1968). *Groups under stress: Psychological research in Sealab II*. New York: Appleton-Century-Crofts.

Raven, B. H. (1974). The Nixon group. *Journal of Social Issues, 30,* 297–320.

Raven, B. H., & Rubin, J. Z. (1977). *Social psychology: People in groups*. New York: Wiley.

Reedy, G. E. (1970). *The twilight of the presidency*. New York: World.

Rein, M., & Rabinovitz, F. F. (1978). Implementation: A theoretical perspective. In W. D. Burham & M. W. Weinberg (Eds.), *American politics and public policy*. Cambridge, Mass.: MIT Press.

Rodin, J. (1985). The application of social psychology. In G. Lindzey & E. Aronson (Eds.), *The handbook of social psychology* (3rd ed., Vol. 2). New York: Random House.

Rogers, R. W., & Mewborn, C. R. (1976). Fear appeals and attitude change: Effects of a threat's noxiousness, probability of occurrence, and the efficacy of coping responses. *Journal of Personality and Social Psychology, 34,* 54–67. (Excerpted in R. White [Ed.], [1986], *Psychology and the prevention of nuclear war*. New York: New York University Press.)

Rotter, J. B., Seeman, M., & Liverant, S. (1962). Internal versus external locus of control reinforcement: A major variable in behavior theory. In N. F. Washburne (Ed.), *Decisions, values and groups*. London: Pergamon.

Rozelle, R. M., & Baxter, J. C. (1981). Infuence of role pressures on the perceiver: Judgments of videotaped interviews varying judge accountability and responsibility. *Journal of Applied Psychology, 66,* 437–41.

Ryan, P. B. (1985). *The Iranian rescue mission*. Annapolis, Md.: Naval Institute Press.

Sanderson, M. (1979). *Successful problem management.* New York: Wiley.

Sarbin, T., & Allen, V. I. (1968). Role theory. In G. Lindzey & E. Aronson (Eds.), *The handbook of social psychology* (2nd ed., Vol. 1) Reading, Mass.: Addison-Wesley.

Schelling, T. (1962). Foreword to R. Wohlstetter, *Pearl Harbor.* Stanford: Stanford University Press.

Schilling, W. R. (1971). The American foreign policy making process. In D. M. Fox (Ed.). *The politics of U. S. foreign policy making: A reader.* Pacific Palisades, Calif.: Goodyear.

Schlesinger, A., Jr. (1965). *A thousand days.* Boston: Houghton-Mifflin.

Schön, D. A. (1983). *The reflective practitioner.* New York: Basic Books.

Scriven, M. (1976). Maximizing the power of causal investigations: The modus operandi method. In G. V. Glass (Ed.), *Evaluation studies review annual* (Vol. 1). Beverly Hills, Calif.: Sage.

Selznick, P. (1957). *Leadership in administration: A sociological interpretation.* New York: Harper & Row.

Sheehan, N., et al. (1971). *The Pentagon Papers as published by The New York Times.* New York: Bantam.

Sick, G. (1985). *All fall down: America's tragic encounter with Iran.* New York: Random House.

Simon, H. A. (1957). *Administrative behavior: A study of decision-making processes in administrative organizations* (2nd ed.). New York: Free Press.

Simon, H. A. (1967). Motivational and emotional controls of cognition. *Psychological Review, 74,* 29–39.

Simon, H. A. (1976). *Administrative behavior: A study of decision-making processes in administrative organizations* (3rd ed.). New York: Free Press.

Simon, H. A. (1985). Human nature in politics: The dialogue of psychology and political science. *American Political Science Review, 79,* 293–305.

Singer, J. L. (1984), *The human personality.* New York: Harcourt Brace Jovanovich.

Slovic, P., & Fischhoff, B. (1983). How safe is safe enough? Determinants of perceived and acceptable risk. In L. C. Gould & C. A. Walker (Eds.), *Too hot to handle: Public policy issues in nuclear waste management* New Haven: Yale University Press.

Slovic, P., Fischhoff, B., & Lichtenstein, S. (1977). Behavior decision theory. *Annual Review of Psychology, 28,* 1–39.

Slovic, P., Fischhoff, B. & Lichtenstein, S. (1985). Characterizing perceived risk. In R. W. Kates, C. Hohenemser, & J. X. Kasperson (Eds.), *Perilous progress: Technology as hazard.* Boulder, Colo.: Westview.

Small, S. A., Zeldin, R. S., & Savin-Williams, R. C. (1983). In search of personality traits: A multimethod analysis of naturally occurring prosocial and dominance behavior. *Journal of Personality, 51,* 1–16.

Smith, M. B. (1969). *Social psychology and human values.* Chicago: Aldine.

Smith, M. B. (1986). Kurt Lewin Memorial Address, 1986: War, peace, and psychology. *Journal of Social Issues, 42,* 23–38.

Snyder, M., & Ickes, W. (1985). Personality and social behavior. In G. Lindzey & E. Aronson (Eds.), *The handbook of social psychology* (3rd ed., Vol. 2). New York: Random House.

Spielberger, C. D., & Sarason, I. G. (Eds.). (1975). *Stress and anxiety* (Vols. 1 & 2). New York: Wiley.

Stagner, R. (1967). *Psychological aspects of international conflict.* Belmont, Calif.: Brooks/Cole.

Starbuck, W. H. (1983). Organizations as action generators. *American Sociological Review, 48,* 91–102.

Starbuck, W. H. (1985). Acting first and thinking later: Theory versus reality in strategic change. In J. M. Pennings (Ed.), *Organizational strategy and change.* San Francisco: Jossey-Bass.

Starbuck, W. H., & Nystrom, P. C. (1981). Why the world needs organizational design. *Journal of General Management, 6,* 3–17.

Stein, J. G., & Tanter, R. (1980). *Rational decision making: Israel's security choices.* Columbus, Ohio: Ohio State University Press.

Steinbruner, J. D. (1974). *A cybernetic theory of decision.* Princeton: Princeton University Press.

Steinbruner, J. D. (1987). Choices and trade-offs. In A. B. Carter, J. D. Steinbruner, & C. A. Zracket (Eds.), *Managing nuclear operations.* Washington, D.C.: Brookings.

Steiner, G. A. (1979). *Strategic planning.* New York: Free Press.

Stotland, E. (1969). *The psychology of hope.* San Francisco: Jossey-Bass.

Stryker, S. & Statham, A. (1985). Symbolic interaction and role theory. In G. Lindzey & E. Aronson (Eds.), *The handbook of social psychology* (3rd ed., Vol. 1). New York: Random House.

Suedfeld, P., & Tetlock, P. E. (1977). Integrative complexity of communications in international crises. *Journal of Conflict Resolution, 21,* 168–78.

Taylor, D. W. (1965). Decision making and problem solving. In J. March (Ed.), *Handbook of organizations.* Chicago: Rand McNally.

Taylor, S. E. (1982). The availability bias in social perception and interaction. In D. Kahneman, P. Slovic, & A. Tversky (Eds.), *Judgment under uncertainty: Heuristics and biases.* New York: Cambridge University Press.

Tetlock, P. E. (1979). Identifying victims of groupthink from public statements of decision-makers. *Journal of Personality and Social Psychology, 49,* 1565–85.

Tetlock, P. E. (1983a). Policy-makers' images of international conflict. *Journal of Social Issues, 39,* 67–86.

Tetlock, P. E. (1983b). Psychological research on foreign policy: A methodological overview. In L. Wheeler (Ed.), *Review of personality and social psychology* (Vol. 4). Beverly Hills, Calif.: Sage.

Tetlock, P. E. (1985). Accountability: The neglected social context of judgment and choice. In B. M. Staw and L. Cummings (Eds.), *Research in organizational behavior* (Vol. 1). Greenwich, Conn.: JAI Press.

Tetlock, P. E. (in press). Methodological themes and variations. In P. E. Tetlock, J. Husband, R. Jervis, P. Stern, & C. Tilly (Eds.), *Behavior, society, and nuclear war* (Vol. 1). New York: Oxford University Press.

Tetlock, P. E., & Kim, J. I. (1987). Accountability and judgment processes in a personality prediction task. *Journal of Personality and Social Psychology, 52,* 700–709.

Tetlock, P. E., & McGuire, C. (1986). Cognitive perspectives on foreign policy. In S. Long (Ed.), *Political behavior annual* (Vol. 1, pp. 255–73). Boulder, Colo.: Westview. (Excerpted in R. White [Ed.], [1986], *Psychology and the prevention of nuclear war.* New York: New York University Press.)

Thomson, J. G., Jr. (1968). How could Viet Nam happen? An autopsy. *The Atlantic Monthly,* April 1968, pp. 47–53.

Truman, H. S. (1955). *Memoirs, Vol. 1. Year of decisions.* Garden City, N.Y.: Doubleday.

Truman, H. S. (1956). *Memoirs, Vol. 2. Years of trial and hope.* Garden City, N.Y.: Doubleday.

Tucker, R. C. (1981). *Politics as leadership.* Columbia, Mo.: University of Missouri Press.

Tupes, E. C., & Christal, R. E. (1961). *Recurrent personality factors based on trait ratings* (USAF ASD Technical Report No. 61-97). Lackland Air Force Base, Texas: U.S. Air Force.

Turk, D. C., & Genest, M. (1979). Regulation of pain: The application of cognitive and behavioral techniques for prevention and remediation. In P. Kendall & S. Hollon (Eds.), *Cognitive-behavioral interventions: Theory, research, and practices.* New York: Academic Press.

Tversky, A. (1972). Elimination by aspects: A theory of choice. *Psychological Review, 79,* 281–99.

Tversky, A., & Kahneman, D. (1973). Availability: A heuristic for judging frequency and probability. *Cognitive Psychology, 5,* 207-32.

Tversky, A., & Kahneman, D. (1974). Judgment under uncertainty: Heuristics and biases. *Science, 185,* 1124-31.

Van De Ven, A., & Joyce, W. (Eds.). (1981). *Perspectives on organization design and behavior.* New York: Wiley.

Van Meter, D. S., & Van Horn, C. E. (1975). The policy implementation process: A conceptual framework. *Administration and Society, 6,* 447.

Vroom, V. H., & Jago, A. G. (1988). *The new leadership: Managing participation in organizations.* Englewood Cliffs, N.J.: Prentice-Hall.

Vroom, V. H., & Yetton, P. W. (1973). *Leadership and decision-making.* Pittsburgh: University of Pittsburgh Press.

Wahlke, J. C., Eulau, H., Buchanan, W., & Ferguson, L. C. (1962). *The legislative system.* New York: Wiley.

Waller, N. G., & Ben-Porath, Y. S. (1987). Is it time for clinical psychology to embrace the five-factor model of personality? *American Psychologist, 42,* 887-89.

Weick, K. E. (1979). *The social psychology of organizing* (2nd ed.). Reading, Mass.: Addison-Wesley.

Weick, K. E. (1984). Small wins: Redefining the scale of social problems. *American Psychologist, 39,* 40-49.

Weick, K. E. (1985). Systematic observational methods. In G. Lindzey & E. Aronson (Eds.), *The handbook of social psychology* (3rd ed., Vol. 1). New York: Random House.

Weisbond, E., & Franck, T. (1975). *Resignation in protest.* New York: Grossman.

West, C. K. (1981). *The social and psychological distortion of information.* Chicago: Nelson-Hall.

Wheeler, C. J. (1986). The magic of metaphor: Polytheism and the inferiority complex of the social sciences. (Working paper.)

Wheeler, C. J. (1987). The magic of metaphor: A perspective on reality construction. *Metaphor and Symbolic Activity, 2,* 223-37.

Wheeler, D., & Janis, I. L. (1980). *A practical guide for making decisions.* New York: Free Press.

White, R. K. (1984). *Fearful warriors: A psychological profile of U.S.-Soviet relations.* New York: Free Press.

White, R. K. (Ed.). (1986). *Psychology and the prevention of nuclear war: A book of readings.* New York: New York University Press.

Wiggins, J. S. (1968). Personality structure. *Annual Review of Psychology, 19,* 293-350.

Wilensky, H. L. (1967). *Organizational intelligence.* New York: Basic Books.

Withey, S. (1962). Reaction to uncertain threat. In G. W. Barker & D. Chapman (Eds.), *Man and society in disaster.* New York: Basic Books.

Wyden, P. (1979). *Bay of Pigs: The untold story.* New York: Simon & Schuster.

Wyden, P. (1984). *Day one: Before Hiroshima and after.* New York: Simon & Schuster.

Yates, D., Jr. (1985). *The politics of management: Exploring the inner workings of public and private organizations.* San Francisco: Jossey-Bass.

Young, S. (1966). *Management: A systems analysis.* Glenview, Ill.: Scott, Foresman.

Zeleny, M. (1981). Descriptive decision making and its applications. *Applications of Management Science, 1,* 327–88.

Zimbardo, P. G. (1970). The human choice: individuation, reason, and order versus deindividuation, impulse, and chaos. In W. J. Arnold & D. Levine (Eds.), *Nebraska Symposium on Motivation, 1969.* Lincoln: University of Nebraska Press.

Author Index

Subject Index

attitudes of, toward their organization, *212-13,* 216-18, 220, 222, 225, 228
conscientiousness of, 208-9, *212-13,* 215, 221
dependency of, on cohesive group, *212-13,* 220
hostility of, *212-13,* 226
leadership practices of, 231-64, 325-41
openness of, 208-9, *212-13,* 215
personality hardiness of, *212-13,* 224-25, 324
power and status needs of, 45, 48, 149t, 150, *212-13,* 219-20, 244
self-confidence (or self-efficacy) of, 147-48, 207, *212-13,* 217
social approval needs of, *212-13,* 219-20
stress coping style of, *212-13,* 215-16, 223-25
stress tolerance of, *212-13,* 215-16, 223-25, 228, 253, 322-24
Policymakers' resistance to criticisms from implementers, 38-40, 337-38
Policymaking, 4, 7, 11-19, 267-70; *see also* Constraints model of policymaking; Groups, policymaking; Vigilant problem solving
errors, 13, 14, 24, 39, 84-85, 130-31, 157, 162-65, 171, 175-77, 190, 308
of commission, 236-37, 238
of omission, 234, 236-37
hidden agendas in, 169, 188, 221
interactive (based on bargaining), 173-83, 187, 245
prescriptions for improving, 11, 19, 22, 23, 90, 92, 120, 133-34, 152, 153, 167-69, 171-72, 173, 175, 200, 203-4, 231-64, 286, 325-41
quality of process related to outcome of, 21-22, 34, 39, 119-35, 140, *154-55,* 171-72, 175-76, 180, 287, 294-99
resources of the organization, *16,* 17, 28, 92, 94, 111, 121, 140-42, 149t, 150, 151, 152, *154-55,* 157, 160, 163-64, 176, 216-18, 241-43
strategy
affected by perceived importance of the problem, 43-44, 113, 140-48, *154-55,* 157-60, 162, *212-13*
affected by perceived manageability of constraints, 140-48, *154-55,* 157-60, 162, 185, 243
variability shown by the same individual in, 113-14

Pollution, problems of, 8-11
Power, 4-5, 180-82, 265-67; *see also* Acceptability of a policy decision; Implementation
feedback model of, 180, 332-34
and leadership, 265-67, 268, 306-8, 312
organizational safeguards against misuse of, 18-19
and status, policymakers' needs for, 45, 48, 149t, 150, *212-13,* 219-20, 244
struggles, 15, 54, 160, 168, 177-78, 180-83, 216, 218
Precipitate vs. gradual threats, 145-46, 153
Preconceptions: *see* Presumptions, policymakers'
Prejudices: *see* Presumptions, policymakers'
Prescriptions for improving policymaking, 11, 19, 22, 23, 90, 92, 104-6, 111, 120, 133-34, 152, 153, 167-73, 175, 200, 203-4, 231-64, 286, 325-41
"Preserve group harmony" decision rule: *see* Groupthink
Presumptions, policymakers', 3, 15, 23, 44, *59,* 95, 98-106, 121, 131, 143, 149t, 158, 164, 169, *192,* 206, 216-17, 220, 222, 260, 290-92
Probability estimates, 96, 287-89, 296-97
Problem, importance of: *see* Importance of the problem
Procrastination, 80, 149t, 152, 224; *see also* Defensive avoidance; Time limitations and deadlines
Procter and Gamble Corporation, 62
Professional policy analysis, critique of, 172-74
Profits of business firms, 294-96
"Prospect" theory, 290
Psychiatric disorders of policymakers, 78, 222, 223, 284
Psychological stress, 15, *16,* 28, 57, *59,* 77-81, *82,* 147-48, 149t, 150, 152-53, 220, 285-87, 303-6
inoculation training, 251-53, 286, 330
leadership practices to counteract unfavorable effects of, 236, 251-62
tolerance, individual differences in, *212-13,* 215-16, 223-25, 228, 253, 322-24

Quality of policymaking, 4, 7, 10, 11, 16-23, 28-35, 44, 56, *59,* 61, 66, 71, 78, 90, 95, 108, 142, 151, 157, 160, 162-64, 183-84

Printed in the United States
By Bookmasters